The
Copyeditor's
Workbook

The Copyeditor's Workbook

Exercises and Tips
for Honing Your Editorial Judgment

ERIKA BŰKY,
MARILYN SCHWARTZ,
AND AMY EINSOHN

UNIVERSITY OF CALIFORNIA PRESS

University of California Press, one of the most distinguished university presses in the United States, enriches lives around the world by advancing scholarship in the humanities, social sciences, and natural sciences. Its activities are supported by the UC Press Foundation and by philanthropic contributions from individuals and institutions. For more information, visit www.ucpress.edu.

University of California Press
Oakland, California

The authors gratefully acknowledge permission to reproduce the following illustrations:

p. 1. Cartoon © 2005 Eve Corbel. True Funnies. "No Pringles" was first published in *Geist*, the magazine that dares to be smart, funny and Canadian. Visit geist.com for more.
p. 7. Cartoon by Jack Ziegler/The New Yorker Collection/The Cartoon Bank.
p. 47. Cartoon by William Haefeli/The New Yorker Collection/The Cartoon Bank.
p. 129. Cartoon by Joe Dator/The New Yorker Collection/The Cartoon Bank.

Library of Congress Cataloging-in-Publication Data

Names: Bűky, Erika, author. | Schwartz, Marilyn, author. | Einsohn, Amy, author. | Complemented by (work): Einsohn, Amy. Copyeditor's handbook 2019
Title: The copyeditor's workbook : exercises and tips for honing your editorial judgment / Erika Bűky, Marilyn Schwartz, and Amy Einsohn.
Description: Oakland, California : University of California Press, [2019] | Includes bibliographical references.
Identifiers: LCCN 2018049374 | ISBN 9780520294356 (pbk. : alk. paper) | ISBN 9780520967519 (pdf)
Subjects: LCSH: Copy editing—Handbooks, manuals, etc.
Classification: LCC PN4784.C75 B78 2019 | DDC 808.02/7—dc23
LC record available at https://lccn.loc.gov/2018049374

Manufactured in the United States of America

27   26   25   24   23   22   21   20   19
10   9   8   7   6   5   4   3   2

Contents

Preface

The idea for this book began in conversations with Amy Einsohn shortly after the publication, in 2000, of *The Copyeditor's Handbook,* her indispensable introduction to professional editing. The fifteen printed exercises included in the original *Handbook* and in two subsequent editions instructed copyediting students to scrawl corrections in the pages of the book, then to check their work against hand-marked answer keys in the back matter. These exercises provided a light warm-up for our students—I was a fellow instructor as well as Amy's acquisitions editor—but left them clamoring for a real workout. *More practice!* they urged. *More feedback!* (Despite our best efforts, we failed to eradicate this voguish use of the word from their vocabulary.) Accordingly, I prompted Amy to develop a separate, expanded workbook, with drills available in both print and digital form. The shift to on-screen copyediting was by then well under way, and we wanted to challenge editors both to build their skills and to use new tools.

Although Amy was not able to complete the project herself, she bequeathed extensive notes for retooling her entire *Handbook* for a fourth edition, a task I undertook at the bidding of the University of California Press and with the generous permission of her husband, Chris Raisner. *The Copyeditor's Workbook,* co-written with Erika Búky, is part of that project, the companion to that substantially revised edition of the *Handbook,* whose organization and content are paralleled in this volume. Besides including the original fifteen exercises, revised and updated following Amy's notes, we have added many new exercises, with answer keys and detailed explanations of our corrections and editorial decisions. Whether the drills are undertaken separately or alongside the new *Handbook,* they provide a thorough workout in the basic knowledge and skills required of contemporary editors.

Each exercise is preceded by a headnote introducing the skills under review, providing instructions, describing the context and target readership of the examples where pertinent, and citing any required source details and permissions notices. The format of the exercises varies according to the skills to be learned. Some drills consist of individual sentences. Others assign on-screen tasks or pose questions to be answered through research. Many consist of passages of text such as might be encountered "in the wild." Drills of increasing difficulty and length, including passages resembling the most ferocious publishers' copyediting tests in the business, allow users to advance in skill. Passages prepared for different purposes and audiences challenge users to deploy research abilities and to demonstrate editorial reasoning.

The answer keys in this workbook illustrate several techniques for marking copy, including marking PDFs and even hand marking hard copy. Although most copyeditors now wield the revision-tracking feature of a word processing application to record changes in a manuscript, they must sometimes use these other methods, however cumbersome or antiquated. The answer keys likewise demonstrate various methods for querying authors—writing bubble queries on hard copy and, in edited files, embedding queries in the text, placing them in footnotes, or using a word processor's commenting feature.

Several early exercises introduce readers to a range of dictionaries, style guides, and other resources consulted by copyeditors, but the answer keys to subsequent exercises on editorial style (chapters 4–13) generally follow the Merriam-Webster dictionaries and *The Chicago Manual of Style,* the authorities favored by most US book publishers. For discretionary edits, however, commentaries accompanying the answer keys often weigh alternative solutions, where they exist, and explain the authority and reasoning behind the corrections. Beyond some basic conventions mastered in early drills, clear-cut "right" and "wrong" editorial decisions rarely exist. Novice editors often want rules and may incline toward rigidity and prescriptiveness; experienced editors know that few rules remain unbroken by good writers and that several defensible solutions to an editorial problem may exist. Best practice requires the use of *editorial judgment,* the development of which is the ultimate objective of the *Workbook.*

Readers may discover that, despite our care, we have erred here or there. Amy used to counsel students with an inclination to editorial hubris that they should never forget Muphry's Law, a corollary of Murphy's Law which holds that if you write anything criticizing editing or proofreading, there will be a fault of some kind in what you have written; moreover, any book devoted to editing or style will be internally inconsistent. That is to say, editing can be a humbling (and sometimes a humiliating) profession. An error spotted in the first edition of *The Copyeditor's Handbook* was a (curiously apt) reference to the Word Wide Web, which had evaded the close scrutiny of the redoubtable author and her spell-checker, two peer reviewers, a production editor, a copyeditor, two proofreaders, and an indexer. Thus we anticipate and welcome readers' corrections and trust they will be offered in Amy's own spirit of tolerance and generosity.

Marilyn Schwartz

DOWNLOADABLE EXERCISES

Although a number of exercises in this workbook can be completed on paper, many are intended to be completed on-screen, using the revision-tracking features of a word processor such as Microsoft Word (the de facto standard for copyediting at the time of writing). The files for the on-screen exercises are available for download from https://www.ucpress.edu/go/copyeditorsworkbook.

ACKNOWLEDGMENTS

We are grateful to all those at the University of California Press who have supported this project, smoothed our prose and our feathers, and brought their expertise to bear on a challenging project: Eric Schmidt, Archna Patel, our longtime colleague and friend Dore Brown, and our courageous, kind, and meticulous copyeditor, Juliana Froggatt. We also thank our book designers, Claudia Smelser and Barbara Haines, and our proofreaders, Anne Canright and Sue Heinemann. All of them patiently grappled with complex typographic and layout issues and the additional difficulty of distinguishing between intentional errors and inadvertent goofs.

Erika Bűky and Marilyn Schwartz
2019

Abbreviations

Full publication details are provided in the Selected Bibliography.

AHD	*American Heritage Dictionary of the English Language,* 5th ed.
AP Stylebook	*The Associated Press Stylebook and Briefing on Media Law 2018*
APA	*Publication Manual of the American Psychological Association,* 6th ed.
Bernstein	Theodore Bernstein, *The Careful Writer: A Modern Guide to English Usage*
Butcher's	Judith Butcher, Caroline Drake, and Maureen Leach, *Butcher's Copy-editing: The Cambridge Handbook for Editors, Copy-editors and Proofreaders,* 4th ed.
Chicago	*The Chicago Manual of Style,* 17th ed.
Copperud	Roy H. Copperud, *American Usage and Style: The Consensus*
CSE	*Scientific Style and Format: The CSE Manual for Authors, Editors, and Publishers,* 8th ed.
DEU	*Merriam-Webster's Dictionary of English Usage*
Ed Can Engl	*Editing Canadian English: A Guide for Editors, Writers, and Everyone Who Works with Words,* 3rd ed.
Fowler's	*Fowler's Dictionary of Modern English Usage,* 4th ed., ed. Jeremy Butterfield
Garner's	Bryan A. Garner, *Garner's Modern English Usage,* 4th ed.
GPO	*GPO Style Manual: An Official Guide to the Form and Style of Federal Government Publishing,* 31st ed.
Gregg	*The Gregg Reference Manual,* 11th ed., ed. William A. Sabin
M-W Collegiate	*Merriam-Webster's Collegiate Dictionary,* 11th ed.
M-W Unabridged	*Merriam-Webster Unabridged* (online)
MAU	Wilson Follett, *Modern American Usage: A Guide,* rev. ed., ed. Erik Wensberg
New Oxford	*New Oxford Style Manual,* 3rd ed.
Partridge	Eric Partridge, *Usage and Abusage: A Guide to Good English,* new ed., ed. Janet Whitcut

Web New World   *Webster's New World College Dictionary,* 5th ed.

Web3   *Webster's Third New International Dictionary of the English Language, Unabridged*

WIT   *Words into Type,* 3rd ed.

Exercises

Lesser-Known Editing
and Proofreading Marks

z-z-z-z   delete—no one cares

    mixed metaphor, eh?

    insert 4-letter word for emphasis

    remove permanently from your lexicon

    too long

    too silly

    you wish

    pls revisit your politics

    pls cut the crap

    pls paraphrase—obviously stolen from Web

    pls don't eat Pringles while you work

© 2005 Eve Corbel True Funnies

A COPYEDITING CHALLENGE: Test Your Skills

This preliminary exercise evaluates your ability to correct basic errors of punctuation, grammar, usage, and sentence structure; apply a consistent style to the treatment of compound forms, capitalization, numbers, and italics; and revise unidiomatic, awkward, prolix, and biased language. Try to solve problems with efficient, limited intervention; avoid wholesale rewriting unless necessary.

1. Sales potential has become a critical component of the decision to publish a book. No longer is it's intellectual impact or quality the sole criteria for investment by a traditional publishing house. But a growing number of independent authors is building their names and making great incomes from bypassing the old system.

2. 20-something male high-school grads used to comprise the most dependable working cohort in America. Today one in five are now essentially idle.

3. As your Assemblymember for six years, the Education, Health and Safety of our children has been my number one legislative priority. I supported Universal Health Care, and championed the *Healthy Families Program* for 740,000 poor children. I voted to keep the state's Redevelopment Agencies to assist citizens with the growing housing affordability crisis and I passed laws to reduce neighborhood crime. As the Chairman of the Assembly Labor and Employment Committee, I fought to protect your pensions and fair wages for working families. I sponsored laws to rescue our children from Human Traffickers, provide services for seniors, the disabled and our youth.

4. We need to take steps to make sure everyone has the support they need to thrive.

5. I could careless whether Kriss Kringle brings me two new Lexis's this year.

6. Made from a premium cotton twill/lycra blend, these chinos feature a durable stain and wrinkle resistant treatment so they come out of the dryer ready-to-wear. Plus, they exceed our rigorous standards for shrink-resistance.

7. The rainbow of intellectual traditions that colored Israeli and particularly Sabra environmental values may have marveled, embraced or attacked the land. But nobody hid from it.

8. Jainism, along with Buddism, is the only surviving example of India's ancient nonvedic religious traditions

9. The Secretary of the Department, Mrs. William Smith, cheerfully patches over all problems and difficulties in cramming the book's revisions into her other duties with one hand while she also scales a separate set of computer/instructional Mt. Everest's with the other.

10. The phenomena of reproduction not only is at the heart, core and 'soul' of social life for many if not most people but also across an array of social differences that is truly quite stunning.

11. For all intensive purposes the Twentieth Century brick and motor store is dead, having been superceded by online shopping malls and flea markets, like amazon.com and Ebay.

12. Among the many new proposals for controlling insects, which attack crops, is the incorporation of bio-rational insecticides into plants which because of genetic adaptation in pests will not provide the hoped for "final solution" to the pest problem.

13. I could of chose to memorize Edgar Allen Poe's "The Raven or Emily Dickenson's "I'm No Body!", but instead I recited "The Pledge of Allegiance."

14. Don't expect an apology from the sheriff leading the response to the protesters, especially for his recent — and, in some circles, controversial — action against demonstrators, who he believes have become increasingly aggressive.

15. The Pirelli calendar has departed from its sexy tradition in this year's edition, with photographer Peter Lindbergh foregoing photoshop and filters to focus his lens on unadorned female celebrities.

PART 1

¶ The ABCs of Copyediting

"I'll have the misspelled 'Ceasar' salad and the improperly
hyphenated veal osso-buco."

CHAPTER 1

¶ What Copyeditors Do

EXERCISE 1-1: Comparing Editorial Styles

The heart of copyediting consists of conforming a manuscript to an editorial style, sometimes called *house style* after the publishing house or other "house of business" that determines the conventions its publications must follow. An editorial style comprises all the choices regarding the following:

- valid alternative spellings and compound forms
- capitalization
- punctuation
- numbers and dates
- quotations
- acronyms and other abbreviations
- italics and bold type
- special elements (headings, lists, tables, charts, graphs, other illustrations)
- documentation (notes and bibliographies)

A house style may stipulate other preferences as well, such as favored (or disfavored) terminology and idioms.

As *The Copyeditor's Handbook* illustrates (chapter 1, under "Principal Tasks"), a house style is often defined by specifying a particular dictionary and style manual. For example, many US book publishers hew to *M-W Collegiate* and *Chicago,* whereas US newspapers and magazines often favor *Web New World* and the *AP Stylebook.* But institutions whose primary mission is not publishing (and even many conventional publishers) may modify or simply cobble together their house style on the basis of their own needs, preferences, and idiosyncrasies. And authors generally do what they like. Thus in any given manuscript a copyeditor may encounter a daft mix of British and US spellings and conventions, alternative capitalization of headings, inconsistent treatment of numbers, and other variations.

The goal of this exercise is simply to help you recognize the choices that typically define and distinguish editorial styles. The following two versions of the same passage illustrate different style choices. Neither follows a specific style manual and neither version of the text is more "correct" than the other. Identify the differences between the versions and itemize them according to the categories above.

VERSION 1

The Bay Of Pigs Invasion, Poison Pills And Exploding Cigars*

In 1959, the Cuban nationalist Fidel Castro entered Havana with his guerilla army, ousting Cuba's anti-Communist President, General Fulgencio Batista, in an historical revolution. Upon being sworn in as Prime Minister, Castro immediately acted to reduce U.S. influence in the island. He nationalised U.S. industries operating in Cuba, initiated land reform and exhorted other Latin American governments to break free of U.S. domination as well.

The establishment of a pro-Communist regime just 100 miles from the United States made U.S. officials nervous. When Castro formalised diplomatic relations with the Soviet Union in 1960, the United States retaliated by declaring an embargo on Cuban sugar, some 80% of which was exported annually to the United States. To prop up the Cuban economy, threatened with collapse by the embargo, the U.S.S.R. arranged to buy the sugar.

The Cuban Sugar Embargo was another episode in the long Cold War between the U.S.S.R. and the United States. Revolutionary Cuba was a proxy foe in the global rivalry between these super-powers, a beachhead of Communism in the Western Hemisphere. U.S. officials resolved that Castro had to be eliminated. During 1959–61, the U.S. State Department and the Central Intelligence Agency (C.I.A.) plotted to remove Cuba's guerilla leader from power by any means necessary.

In April, 1961, John F. Kennedy launched a full scale invasion of Cuba with the co-operation of a brigade of 1400 U.S.-trained Cuban exiles. This covert operation had been planned in the Eisenhower Administration but was executed under Kennedy's order shortly after the 35th President took office. The invasion was a total SNAFU. When Castro quickly foiled a pre-emptive air strike by relocating his tiny airforce before the raid, J.F.K. began to suspect, despite the counsel of his advisers, that the plan might be 'too large to be clandestine and too small to be successful'. The subsequent land invasion at the Bay of Pigs, executed on 17 April 1961, was repelled within 24 hours.

Failure at the Bay of Pigs, however, did not deter Kennedy and subsequent U.S. Presidents from attempting to bring down the Castro Regime through a surreptitious campaign of espionage, sabotage and repeated assassination attempts under the rubric of *Operation Mongoose*. According to some estimates, Castro survived more than 600 such plots, including poison pills and an exploding cigar.

*This summary is based on information from 'Bay of Pigs Invasion' (last modified 2009), History, <http://www.history.com/topics/cold-war/bay-of-pigs-invasion>, accessed 16 March 2017; 'Assassination attempts on Fidel Castro' (last modified 22 January 2017), Wikipedia, <en.wikipedia.org/wiki/Assassination_attempts_on_Fidel_Castro>, accessed 16 March 2017.

VERSION 2

The Bay of Pigs Invasion, Poison Pills, and Exploding Cigars

In 1959 the Cuban nationalist Fidel Castro entered Havana with his guerrilla army, ousting Cuba's anticommunist president, General Fulgencio Batista, in a historic revolution. Upon being sworn in as prime minister, Castro immediately acted to reduce American influence in the island. He nationalized American industries operating in Cuba, initiated land reform, and exhorted other Latin American governments to break free of American domination as well.

The establishment of a procommunist regime just one hundred miles from the United States made US officials nervous. When Castro formalized diplomatic relations with the Soviet Union in 1960, the United States retaliated by declaring an embargo on Cuban sugar, some 80 percent of which was exported annually to the United States. To prop up the Cuban economy, threatened with collapse by the embargo, the USSR arranged to buy the sugar.

The Cuban sugar embargo was another episode in the long cold war between the USSR and the United States. Revolutionary Cuba was a proxy foe in the global rivalry between these superpowers, a beachhead of communism in the western hemisphere. US officials resolved that Castro had to be eliminated. During 1959–1961 the US State Department and the Central Intelligence Agency (CIA) plotted to remove Cuba's guerrilla leader from power by any means necessary.

In April 1961 John F. Kennedy launched a full-scale invasion of Cuba with the cooperation of a brigade of fourteen hundred American-trained Cuban exiles. This covert operation had been planned in the Eisenhower administration but was executed under Kennedy's order shortly after the thirty-fifth president took office. The invasion was a total snafu. When Castro quickly foiled a preemptive air strike by relocating his tiny air force before the raid, JFK began to suspect, despite the counsel of his advisors, that the plan might be "too large to be clandestine and too small to be successful." The subsequent land invasion at the Bay of Pigs, executed on April 17, 1961, was repelled within twenty-four hours.

Failure at the Bay of Pigs, however, did not deter Kennedy and subsequent US presidents from attempting to bring down the Castro regime through a surreptitious campaign of espionage, sabotage, and repeated assassination attempts under the rubric of Operation Mongoose. According to some estimates, Castro survived more than six hundred such plots, including poison pills and an exploding cigar.

Note: This summary is based on information from "Bay of Pigs Invasion," History, http://www.history.com/topics/cold-war/bay-of-pigs-invasion, last modified 2009, accessed March 16, 2017; "Assassination attempts on Fidel Castro," Wikipedia, en.wikipedia.org/wiki/Assassination_attempts_on_Fidel_Castro, last modified January 22, 2017, accessed March 16, 2017.

This exercise introduces you to the preliminary formatting tasks common to many editing assignments. Because authors' computer skills and publishers' procedures vary widely, documents for editing may come to the editor with a jumble of text fonts, sizes, and spacing. Cleaning up file formatting before editing not only enables you to focus your attention on clarity and meaning but also helps eliminate inconsistencies that may result in expensive problems at later stages of production.

Word processing macros that automate repetitive tasks can make file cleanup much more efficient; see chapter 1 and the Selected Bibliography of *The Copyeditor's Handbook* for further information about resources and the use of macros. (At the time of publication, two of the most widely used commercial macro packages are FileCleaner, from the Editorium, and PerfectIt, from Intelligent Editing.) But don't count on such tools to regularize *all* haphazard formatting.

The following passages are excerpts from chapter 10 of Ellen Rosen, *Making Sweatshops: The Globalization of the U.S. Apparel Industry* (Berkeley: University of California Press, 2002), pp. 177–201 (reproduced by permission of University of California Press). The formatting has been altered and wording changes and editorial errors introduced. Abridgments of the original are indicated by ellipsis dots set in square brackets: [. . .].

For any copyediting assignment that requires file cleanup, you should confirm the publisher's or client's requirements before beginning work. For this exercise, use the following guidelines.

- Turn off revision marking for formatting changes.
- Leave the document size, header and footer specifications, and margins as set (US letter-size paper, with one-inch margins on all sides).
- Make only mechanical and formatting changes. Avoid changing punctuation, capitalization, or wording.
- Use a standard, readable font such as Times New Roman 12 for all elements (except footnote signals, for which you may use the default settings of your word processor for the given body text size). Turn off automatic hyphenation.
- Use typesetter's ("curly" or "smart") quotation marks and apostrophes. Use double quotation marks for quoted words and phrases, and single quotation marks for any quoted terms within quotations.
- Replace underlining with italics.
- Use en dashes rather than hyphens in number ranges for dates and pages (but not in URLs): 123–25, not 123-25.
- Use the em dash character (—), closed up to words on either side, rather than double hyphens (--) or spaced en dashes (–).
- Replace multiple wordspaces with single spaces, within and between sentences.
- For ellipsis dots, use three or four spaced periods (. . .) rather than the ellipsis character (…).

- Chapter number, title, and subtitle: Set flush left, each on its own line, double spaced.
- Subheads in text: Set flush left, with an additional linespace above and below. (Assume for this exercise that all subheads are level 1 subheads.)
- Body text: Set flush left, with the first line indented 0.5 inches. Use paragraph formatting options rather than tabs for indentation. Eliminate extra linespaces between paragraphs.
- Block quotations: Set with the whole block indented an additional 0.5 inches on the left and no extra indent for the first line.
- Footnote signals: Use arabic numerals.
- Set URLs in roman type, with no underlining. Remove active hyperlinks.

Before starting on any editing project, make a backup copy of the original files and store it safely. If your word processor has autocorrect or autoformatting features set by default, or if you frequently work in languages other than English, review and turn off any features that may interfere with file cleanup, such as automatic capitalization, use of alternative styles of quotation marks, and automatic formatting of hyperlinks.

During file cleanup, you may notice problems that warrant editorial attention, such as nonstandard spellings or garbled text. Rather than make any substantive changes at this stage, flag these items for later attention: either note the problem and the location in a separate file or use a consistent, distinctive, and easily removed form of annotation, such as highlighting in a specific color. Any such annotations should be removed before returning a manuscript to an author or client.

If editing this file on a computer is impractical, you may choose to review the printed version and note by hand instances of the formatting issues listed above.

Chapter 10 The U.S Retail Industry A Brief History

Only twenty-five years ago 'mom and pop' clothing stores flourished along with large department stores and discount chains. Today, however, highly concentrated, vertically integrated, US retail transnationals, selling vast quantities of apparel items, have put many of the smaller stores and even the larger department stores out of business. The new forms of corporate retailing has played a crucial role in the globalization of the textile / apparel complex. Today transnationals compete for market share and market power, both nationally and internationally.
For the past twenty years retailing has been driving the thrust of US trade policy in textiles and apparel. The needs of these retailers have shaped the restructuring of the textile and apparel producers who supply them with merchandise. [i] Corporate retailers have been able to increase their power over textile and apparel producers because of increasing

---

[i] Frederick H. Abernathy, John T. Dunlop, Janice H. Hammond and David Weil, A Stitch in Time: Lean Retailing and the Transformation of Manufacturing—Lessons from the Apparel and Textile Industries, Oxford University Press, New York and Oxford, 1999. This recent book is among the most scholarly and empirically sound treatments of this position.

opportunities to benefit from the expansion of low wage apparel production in developing countries.

America's apparel retailers have become among the most powerful supporters of trade liberalization for textiles and apparel. Ending quotas and reducing tariffs has not only accelerated the globalization of apparel production, but has led to a new round of vertical integration and concentration in apparel retailing. Competition in this industry is now based on the efforts of retailers to increase their market share in a new and intense context of domestic and global competition. Textile and apparel producers have responded to these conditions by trying to develop more efficient ways to produce apparel. Retailers continue their pressures on government for further trade liberalization, for more access to new low wage production sites and retail outlets.

A Brief History of Apparel Retailing

The history of the US apparel retailing begins with department stores, which first appeared in the early part of the twentieth century. Department stores were initially located in the main shopping district of the downtown area, making it possible for the new urban, middle and upper middle class consumers to enjoy the convenience of one stop shopping, stable prices and the reliability of quality merchandise . Such department stores were owned by individual merchant families. Yet by 1916, Lincoln Filene, the President of Filene's in Boston, recognized the value of

collaboration between retailers in buying merchandise, recruiting executives, training employees, improving advertising, and other associated aspects of the retail business. [ii] He started the Retail Research Association, which two years later was superseded by the Associated Merchandising Corporation (AMC).NEED TO CHECK THIS

Recognizing the need for a more centralized corporate structure for the dispersion of risk, expansion and greater profitability in the industry, Filene began to advocate the formation of a national retail holding company. In 1918 Filene's joined with Abraham and Strauss of Brooklyn, and F & R Lazarus and Company of Columbus, Ohio, to form Federated Department Stores. Holding companies increasingly became the dominant form of retail ownership in this industry. Department stores, selling men's, women's and children's clothing, and other household items, put many smaller, local "mom and pop" specialty stores out of business.   Department stores enjoyed high and stable profits during the affluence of the early postwar boom, allowing retailers to finance expansion from profits. The growth of car ownership and the building of highways led to massive suburbanization. Following their customers to the new bedroom communities, new stores were built - « anchors » of the new suburban shopping malls. A major acceleration of new shopping mall construction took place between 1965 and 1975, [iii] internally financed by the

[ii] Barry Bluestone et. al. The Retail Revolution, 1983, 11.
[iii] See Jack Kaikati, "Don't Discount Off-Price Retailers,' Harvard Business Review, May-June 1985; Samuel Feinberg, The Off Price Explosion, Fairchild Books Special Report, Fairchld Publications, 1984, Bluestone et. al., 1983.

industry in the context of its high profits. By 1977, four major holding companies controlled the majority of America's department store chains--Federated Department Stores, Allied Stores Corp., May Department Stores Company and Dayton Hudson Corp. Together, they included 807 retail outlets and total sales in excess of $11.4 billion—five times the sales of the whole J.C.Penney chain with 1686 stores nationwide. [iv]However, as department stores reached the limits of suburban growth they began to expand their geographic coverage to a national market. In 1986 Neiman Marcus had ... stores in Florida, and Massachusetts. Lord and Taylor, Saks Fifth Avenue, Bloomingdales, have all followed with similar moves. [v]

[. . .]

Restructuring for the New Retail Competition

Needing to reduce operating costs, to increase sales and margins, retailers began to impose new economic pressures on their apparel suppliers. They made three significant changes:
a) in their labor-management relations,
b) in the implementation of "quick response," and
3) the expansion of their "private label" merchandise.

Retailers began to reduce their traditionally large and costly inventories. They also reduced their largely, full time, trained sales staff, made up of career employees. [vi] The new retail competition required fewer managers and minimal sales help; the practice of customer service became economically unsustainable. [vii] Employment in apparel retailing grew 31% between 1973 and 1985, during his period, as stores reduced their full time workers and increased their part-time help. By 1985 the earnings of workers in retail sales had declined dramatically—and were only slightly higher than those of the lowest paid workers employed in eating and drinking places. [viii] What made this possible, were the new microtechnologies, which dramatically increased worker productivity.

[. . .]

The Economics of "Fashion"

A discussion of apparel retailing would not be complete without an analysis of the "fashion" industry. The transformations in apparel retailing in the past two decades occurred in the 1970s in the context of a declining couture industry. Well known "couture" fashion designers had produced individualized couture clothing for wealthy patrons. As this clientele began to shrink many discovered the advantages of higher volume sales in high niche "ready to wear" women's apparel. These designers began to license their names

---

[iv] Bluestone et.al. 1983.
[v] Pais, Sloan School of Management, M.I.T., June 1986, 37.
[vi] Lasker, Cohen and Garter, 1981.
[vii] Klokis, Holly. "Retail Layoffs: Where Will Everyone Go?" Chain Store Age Executive 63(4): 104,106, April 1987.
[viii] Steven E. Haugen, "The Employment Expansion in Retail Trade, 1973-1985," Monthly Labor Review, Aug 1986.

to clothing producers who would hire their own designers to turn out fashions by "Oleg Cassini" or "Gloria Vanderbilt".

As educated women began to enter the US labor force in professional occupations, new demands for women to "dress for success" led American designers like Liz Claiborne to create a new type of clothing for women. By 1974 Liz Claiborne, and others like her, were producing lower cost, high quality "career wear" in Asia. [ix] Retailers, merchandisers and importers could access contractors to produce high quality clothing in Europe (Italy, France, the UK) or Japan, while department store, private label goods were sources in South Korea, Hong Kong, Taiwan and Singapore. Mass merchandisers and lower priced store brands, sourced in a

third tier of medium to low cost, midquality exporters (Brazil, Mexico, low end producers in the NICs, plus the People's Republic of China, and the ASEAN countries of Thailand, Malaysia, the Philippines, and Indonesia). [x]

Large volume discount stores at the lower ends of the market, making large volumes of standardized goods looked to countries like China, Bangladesh, Sri Lanka, and Mauritius. Low end retailers like Walmart and Sears initially sourced apparel in countries in the Caribbean and Central America--Dominican Republic and Guatemala and Jamaica. [xi] A process that has been called "specification contracting" developed:

> ... local firms carry out production according to complete instruc-
> tions issued by the buyers and branded companies that design the
> goods; the output is then distributed and marketed abroad by trad-
> ing companies, brand name merchandisers, large retailers or their
> agents. [This] "buyer driven commodity chain" is common in the
> garment industry. ...foreign capital tends to control the more prof-
> itable export and marketing networks. [xii]

[ix] James Lardner, "The Sweater Trade," in the New Yorker Magazine, 1991. *http://www.newyorker.com /magazine/1988/01/11/i-the-sweater-trade*

[x] Cheng and Gereffi, p. 64-66 in Bonacich et. al.

[xi] Not surprisingly, these corporations were staunch supporters of the Special Access Program of the Caribbean Basin Initiative of 1986.

[xii] The Globalization of Taiwan's Garment Industry, by Gary Gereffi and Mei-Lin Pan. in Bonacich et. al., 1994, 134.

CHAPTER 2

¶ Basic Procedures

EXERCISE 2-1: Hand Marking a Manuscript

Manuscripts are rarely marked by hand these days. Most copyeditors work on-screen using the revision-tracking feature of a word processing application. Yet traditional hand marking of hard copy is sometimes required—for example, when copy has been prepared in a spreadsheet, presentation, or page-design program that doesn't offer revision tracking. In addition, some editors working with PDF files use hand-marking stamps or a stylus to show proposed emendations in the documents on-screen, and authors may use hand-marking symbols when reviewing a printout of their edited files. The goal of this exercise is to acquaint you with traditional hand-marking techniques for such eventualities. *The Copyeditor's Handbook* (chapter 2) describes the conventions. See the appendix in this volume for a list of manual copyediting symbols.

The proprietors of the new restaurant Grodia are ready to send their menu to a web designer, but they would like you to take a look at this printout, just in case there's anything that autocorrect and the spell-checker missed. Mark the basic spelling, capitalization, usage, and grammatical errors, along with internal formatting and spacing inconsistencies. If you catch any errors in specialized foodie terms, that's great, but they're also going to ask the chef to look it over. (Hey, thanks. Here's a Grodia gift card for your hard work.)

GRODIA CON-FUSION Cuisine

Hours: Monday-Thursday 5 P.M.-10 P.M.
Saturday 11 a.m.–11 p.m.
Sun. 11 AM–3 P.M.

Welcome to Grodia? With a cusine that combines the best local ingredients and global food trends, Our Head chef has created a menu that is very unique and tantalising.

Appetizers

Crusty countrystyle baguette with local artisane goat cheese

soup of t he day with House Baked sourgough croutons

Marinated baby Chioggia beats on a bed of mescaline greens

Little Germ lettuce salad with walnuts, pears, and Brie

Devilied duck eggs with chickweed conserva

sustainably farmed Thai king pawns on a bed of shredded kale, season with kumquat and lemon-pepper vinaigrette

###

Entrees

Melee of locally sauced pan-roasted seasonal vegetables

served on a bead of spicy red quinoa

Panfried wild-caught Alaskan samon steak on a mashed
potato cake,topped with citrous sauce roasted asparagus sprinkled
with black volcanic salt from Hawai

Sauted bone-in chicken breast with lemongrass and jasmine
rice, topped with it's own pan juices and accompanied by julian
carrots and candled walnuts

Ham burger grodia: our chfe's special take on this favorite.

Ground buffalo patt in a chia-seed bun, topped with tomato's and a

anchovy & parsley salsa and served with a side of french fries,

Side Orders

French frieds

Steamed seasonal vegetables drizzled with a tomato coolie

Trio of house-made icecreams, gelati, or sorbets, ask your

server for today's flavors—served with Grodia's special cellar-

aged biscotti.

###

DESERTS

Crenelated brûlée delicately flavored with ginger

Pavlova: our chefs Down Under specialty of semicooked meringue smothered with summer berry compost

Sinfull flourless chocolate cake flavored with Maker's Mark (kentucky's finest bourbon), topped with whipped cream, floating in a lake of raspberry coulis

Beverages

Green, white, or black teas—ask your server for our current selection Herbal tisanes—lemon balm or dandylion flower

Expresso coffee, single or double

Macchiato

Latte

our ingredients are obtained from organic and fare trade sources whenever possible

We want you to have a happy dining experience, please check with your Server about special dietary requirements and well do our best to accomodate you!

EXERCISE 2-2: Editing On-Screen

This exercise invites you to apply the on-screen editing techniques described in *The Copyeditor's Handbook,* chapter 2. The following passage (downloadable from https://www.ucpress.edu/go/copyeditorsworkbook) is loosely based on the Wikipedia article "Sans-Serif" (at https://www.wikipedia.org, accessed May 22, 2017), with many changes, abridgments, and additions (including errors).

Copyedit the text and footnotes using revision tracking in a word processor such as Microsoft Word, OpenOffice, Google Docs, or Pages. You need not follow a specific style guide, but you should ensure that the document's capitalization, punctuation, and spelling are internally consistent.

Be sure that your application is set to track all types of changes. If you can adjust the settings for viewing the document and displaying changes, experiment with the options. Depending on the project, you may want to distinguish different kinds of changes, different editors of the document, or other aspects of the editing. A convenient option for changes by a single editor is to use red strikethrough for deleted text and blue underlining (or double underlining, to avoid confusion with hyperlinks) for insertions. For a text with multiple reviewers, and in cleanup editing, it may be preferable to assign a different color to each reviewer's changes (e.g., using the "By author" option in Microsoft Word).

In choosing how to mark up text, note the advice in *The Copyeditor's Handbook,* chapter 2, under "Making Changes On-Screen." Where edited text is to be viewed with all changes inline, as for this exercise, deleting whole words (rather than individual letters within a word) produces more-readable text. If, however, the text is to be viewed with insertions shown inline and deletions in marginal balloons, minimal changes produce less clutter in the margin. (For example, inserting a single letter in a word does not generate a new marginal balloon; retyping the whole word does.)

For queries to the author, use the comment or annotation feature in your application, or insert queries in braces and boldface inline, like this: {**AU: This is a query.**}.

Set your word processor to display nonprinting characters, such as tabs and hard returns. For this exercise, if you're using Word, also set your Track Changes preferences to display all changes inline rather than as marginal balloons.

In the spirit of Wikipedia, edit the prose as lightly or as heavily as you like, but take care to make your markup legible: it may be clearer to strike out several words in a row than to correct one or two letters in each. In the process, you should find and correct at least

- one comma splice
- two instances of inconsistent capitalization
- two instances of inconsistent hyphenation
- two grammatically superfluous commas
- one missing word
- two missing commas
- one misspelling of a place name
- one extraneous tab space
- one instance of duplicated text

A History of Sans-Serif type
by Franklin Baskerville

In typography and lettering, a *sans-serif, gothic,* or simply *sans* letterform is one that does not have extending features called "serifs " at the end of strokes. The term comes from the French word *sans,* meaning "without" and "serif" of uncertain origin, possibly from the Dutch word *schreef* meaning "line" or "pen stroke." Sans-serif fonts are often used for headings rather than for body text. They are also used to convey simplicity and modernity or minimalism.

Letters without serifs have been common in writing across history. Today, sans-serif fonts have become the most prevalent for display of text on computer screens.[1] On lower-resolution digital displays, fine details like seraphs may disappear or too large. **The Origins of Sans Serif letterforms**

Letters without serifs have been common in writing across history. Printing in the Latin alphabet was originally "serif" in style, imitating the forms of manuscript lettering. The earliest printing typefaces which omitted serifs were intended not to render contemporary texts, but to represent inscriptions in Ancient Greek and Etruscan. Thus, Thomas Dempster's De Etruria regali libri VII (1723), used special typefaces intended for the representation of Etruscan epigraphy, and around 1745, Caslon foundry made Etruscan types for pamphlets written by Etruscan scholar John Swinton.[31] Another niche used of a printed sans-serif letterform from in 1786 onward was a rounded sans-serif script font developed by Valentin Haüy for the use of the blind to read with their fingers.

Toward the end of the eighteenth century, neoclassical architects began to incorporate ancient Greek and Roman designs in their designs. The British architect John Soane, for example, commonly used sans-serif letters on his drawings and plans. The lettering style apparently became referred to as "old Roman" or "Egyptian" characters.

In London, 'Egyptian' lettering became popular for advertising, apparently because of its mesmerizing effect on the public. Historian James Mosley, has written that "in 1805 Egyptian letters were happening in the streets of London, being plastered over shops and on walls by signwriters, and they were astonishing the public, who had never seen letters like them and were not sure they wanted to."[2] A depiction of the style was shown in the *European Magazine* of 1805, however the style did not become used in printing for some more years Around 1816, William Caslon IV produced the first sans-serif printing type in England for Latin characters. But no examples of its use have been found. Its popularity flaged until sans-serif typefaces began again to be issued by London type foundries from around 1830 onward. These were quite different in design, arrestingly bold and similar in aesthetic to the slab serif typefaces of the period.

---

1. Many typographers deplore the use of the term *font* to refer to a type design, such as Helvetica or Times Roman. In traditional usage, this is a *typeface*; a *font* is a subset of the typeface in a specific size, style, or weight, such as 14-point Helvetica Italic. In the digital age, however, with millions of users customizing the appearance of their phone and computer applications by way of the Font menu, this distinction has all but vanished.

2. James Mosley, "The Nymph and the Grot: An Update," Type Foundry blog, January 6, 2007, http://type foundry.blogspot.com/2007/01/nymph-and-grot-update.html, accessed May 23, 2017.

Sans-serif lettering and fonts were popular due to their clarity and legibility at distance in advertising and display use, when printed very large or very small. (The same considerations drive their popularity in digital media today.) Because sans-serif type was often used for headings and commercial printing, many early sans-serif designs did not feature lowercase letters. Simple sans-serif capitals, without use of lower-case characters, graced Victorian tombstones. The term *grotesque* became commonly used to describe sans-serifs. The term *grotesque* comes from the Italan word for cave, it was often used to describe Roman decorative styles found by excavation, but had acquired the secondary sense of something malformed or monsterous.

The first use of sans serif as a running text is believed to be the short booklet *Feste des Lebens und der Kunst: **eine Betrachtung des Theaters als höchsten Kultursymbols*** (Celebration of Life and Art: A Consideration of the Theater as the Highest Symbol of a Culture), by Peter Behrens, in 1900.

Throughout the nineteenth and early 20th centuries sans-serif typefacs were viewed with suspicion by many printers, especially those of fine books, as being fit only for advertisements., Indeed, many of the common sans-serif types of the period now seem somewhat lumpy and eccentricly-shaped. In the 1920s, master printer Daniel Berkeley Updike described sans-serif fonts as having "no place in any artistically respectable composing-room," and to this day most printed books use serif fonts for the body text.

Modern Sans-Serif Type

Through the early Twentieth century, an increase in popularity of sans serif fonts took place as more artistic and complex designs were created. Humanist and geometric sans-serif designs shrewdly were marketed in Europea and America as embodying classic proportionswhile presenting a spare, modern image. While he disliked sans-serif fonts in general, the American printer J.L Frazier wrote of Copperplate Gothic in 1925 that "a certain dignity of effect accompanies . . . due to the absence of anything in the way of frills," making it a popular choice for the stationary of professionals such as lawyers and doctors.

In the post-War period, an increase of interest took place in "grotesque" sans-serifs. WLeading type designer Adrian Fruitiger wrote in 1961 on the design of a new face, **Univers,** on the nineteenth century model: "Some of these old sans serifs have had a real reconnaissance within the last twenty years, once the reaction of the 'New Objectivity' had been overcome. A purely geometrical form of type is unsustainable."[3]

By the nineteen-sixties, neo-grotesque typefaces such as Univers and Helvetica had become popular through reviving the nineteenth-century groteques while offering a more unified range of styles than on previous designs, allowing a wider range of text to be set artistically through setting headings and body text in a single font.For example, the Linotype version of the Frutiger type family, named for its designer, includes nineteen different weights and styles for various uses.

---

3. Heidrun Osterer and Philip Stamm, *Adrian Frutiger: The Typefaces; The Complete Works,* ed. Swiss Foundation Type and Typographie (Basel: Birkhaüser, 2014), 88 (e-book).

The relative merits of serif and sans-serif typefaces for various purposes are still hotly debated. Fans of the elegant serif faces used in many twentieth-century printed books lament the tyranny of screen-friendly fonts like Calibri and Arial. Numerous studies have asserted the superior legibility of both styles, though the most significant factor affecting legibility may be the reader's familiarity with the typeface.[4] Wikipedia itself-in a reversal of the tradition of using serif type for body text and a sans-serif typeface for headings—compromised in its 2014 design makeover by using Hoefler Text, a sans-serif face, as the default for its articles but Linux Libertine, a public-domain serif font, for its own logo.

4. See Alex Poole, "Which Are More Legible: serif or sans Serif Typefaces?," Alex Poole blog, http://alexpoole .info/blog/which-are-more-legible-serif-or-sans-serif-typefaces/, Febuary 17, 2008, accessed May 23, 2017.

EXERCISE 2-3: Editorial Markup of PDF Files

Your friend's friend Starshine has hired you to review parts of a draft of a pamphlet she's preparing on the safety of the herbal remedies she sells. She doesn't want to give you an editable word processor file, because she spent a long time formatting her document and she's worried that you might mess it up. She sends you a PDF and asks you to mark that up and email it back to her.

You quickly realize that Starshine has taken most of the material from the website of the US National College of Complementary and Integrative Health (formerly the National College of Complementary and Alternative Medicine, or NCCAM, which is mentioned in the document). Since this material is in the public domain, she is free to reuse it: she will simply need to add a notice crediting the source (details at https://nccih .nih.gov/health/providers/digest/topsupplements-science) and acknowledging that she has made changes to the text.

PDF is a popular and convenient format for sharing, searching, and storing large or complex documents. In publishing, it is valuable for marking up illustrations, such as maps and diagrams, and reviewing proofs. Copyediting text in a PDF document, however, is far more cumbersome than using a word processor. (Some would say it's even more cumbersome than hand marking, and their solution is to print out the document, mark it up by hand, and scan it.) Some editors and publishers use custom "stamps," small graphics that replicate conventional hand marking, which are inserted into the file. It's also possible to mark up a PDF file on a computer or tablet as you would mark up a paper document, using freehand drawing tools. (A stylus makes this task easier.)

For this exercise, use the text markup and drawing tools available in any freely available PDF reader application, such as Adobe Acrobat Reader, to indicate text to be deleted, inserted, or replaced. Use the Comment or Sticky Note feature for editorial queries. If you have access to a set of PDF editing stamps or similar tools, feel free to use those instead. For a list of conventional copyediting symbols, see the appendix.

Editing a PDF file offers excellent reinforcement of the virtues of editorial restraint; correct obvious errors in this file, but don't feel compelled to alter the text to conform to a specific style guide. Fortunately, you'll find that Starshine has made comparatively few transcription errors or additions.

Effectiveness and Safety of Popular Herbal Remedies

1. St. John's Wort

Historically, St. John's wort has been used for centuries to treat mental disorders and nerve pain. Saint John's wort has also been used to tread malaria, as a sedative, and as a balm for wounds, burns, and insect bites. Today, St. John's Wort is used as a folk or traditional remedy for depression, anxiety, and/or sleep disorders.

Strength of Evidence

- St. John's wort has been studied extensively for depressive disorders in both the United States and Europe, and for its interactions with a number of drugs.

Study Results

- A 2009 systematic review of 29 international studies suggested that St. Johnste's wort may be better than a placebo and as effective as standard prescription antidepressants for major depressive of mild to moderate severity.   St. John's wort also appeared to have fewer aide effects than standard antidepressants. The studies conducted in German-speaking countries, where St. John's wort has a long history of use by medical professionals—reported more positive results than those done in other countries, including the United States.
- Two large studies sponsored by NCCAM and the National Institute of Menial Health did not showed no benefit. Neither St. John's wort nor a standard antidepressant medication decreased symptoms of minor depression better than a placebo in a 2011 study. The herb was no more effective than placebo in treating major depression of moderate severity in a 2002 study.
- Basic research studies suggest that St. John's wort may prevent nerve cells in the brain from reabsorbing certain chemical messengers, including dopamine and serotonin. These naturally occurring neurotransmitters are known to be involved in regulating mood, but much remains to be learned about exactly how they work.

Side Effects and Cautions

- Research has shown that St. John's wort interacts with many medications in ways that can interfere with their intended effects. Examples of medications that can be affected include:

     ○ Antidepressants
     ○ Birth control Pills
     ○ Cyclosporine, which prevents the body from rejecting transplanted organs;
     ○ Digoxin, a heart medication
- St. John's wort may cause increased sensitivity to sunlight. Other sideeffects can include anxiety, dry mouth, dizziness gastrointestinal symptoms, fatigue, headache, or sexual dysfunction.
- Taking St. John's wort with certain antidepressants they may lead to increased serotonin-related side effects, which may be potentially serious.
- St. John's wort is not a proven therapy for depression. If depression is not adequately treated, it can become severe. Anyone who may have depression should see a health care provider. There are effective proven therapies available.

3. Aloe Vera

The aloe vera plant has been a source of many folk or traditional remedies and more modern medicinal and cosmetic products. At various times aloe has been used in tropical

treatments to heal wounds, and to treat burns, sunburns, and psoriasis. Today aloe vera gel can be found in hundreds of skin products, including lotions and sun blocks.

Juice from the aloe plant taken orally has been used in folk or traditional remedies for a variety of conditions, including diabetes, asma, epilepsy, and osteoarthritis.

Aloe has also been used orally as a laxative. Aloe latex contains strong laxative compounds. Products made with various components of aloe (aloin, aloe-emodin, and barbaloin) were at one time regulated by the FDA as oral over-the-counter (OTC) laxatives. In 2002, the FDA required that all OTC aloe laxative products be removed from the U.S. market or reformulated because the companies that manufactured them did not provide the necessary safety data.

The Food and Drug Administration (FDA) has approved the aloe vera as a natural food flavoring.

You can grow your own aloe, it is a dessert plant that loves sun and needs very little water. Just break of a stem and spread the gooey gel on burned skin but I wouldn't use it on open wounds or burns

Strength of Evidence

- Only a few small exploratory studies have been conducted on aloe vera gel for wound healing, and for treating burns or abrasions.

Study Results

- The results of these studies suggest that topical aloe gel may help heal burns and abrasions. One study, however, suggested that aloe gel inhibits healing of deep surgical wounds. Aloe gel has not been shown to prevent burns from radiation therapy.
- There is not enough scientific evidence to support aloe vera for any of its many other uses.

Side Effects and Cautions

Topical Aloe Vera

- Use of topical aloe vera is not associated with significant side effects.

Oral Aloe Vera

- A 2-year National Toxicology Program (NTP) study on oral consumption of an extract of aloe vera found clear evidence of carcinogenic activity (colon tumors) in male and female rats. Whether this finding is of relevance to humans has yet to be determined, but it raises concerns about use of oral products containing aloe vera.
- Abdominal cramps and diarrhea have been reported with oral use of aloe vera.
- Diarrhea, caused by the laxative effect of oral aloe aloe vera, can decrease the absorption of many drugs.
- People with diabetes who use glucose-lowering medications should be cautious if also taking aloe by mouth because preliminary studies suggest aloe may lower blood glucose levels.
- There have been a few case reports of acute hepatitis following oral aloe vera use, but a casual relationship has not been established.

EXERCISE 2-4: Querying

As chapter 2 of *The Copyeditor's Handbook* elaborates (under "Querying"), knowing when to query an author and how to query effectively are as important for a copyeditor as a solid grasp of grammar and punctuation. The following examples contain ambiguities, omissions, or infelicities that cannot be addressed simply by rewording: a query to the author is necessary. For each one, compose a query identifying the difficulty and asking the author to resolve it.

1. By weight, cartilage has more water than bone (as much as 70 percent).
2. The bank had branches in New York, Boston, Charleston, and Washington.
3. The guru advocated a low-carbohydrate diet, sexual abstinence, and daily meditation, which was not popular with the community.
4. The war in Iraq waged by President Bush has had far-reaching consequences.
5. Yoga classes are offered on-site Wednesday–Friday.
6. In 2014, according to the UN's FAOSTAT database, the world's top producer of whole dried milk was New Zealand (approximately 1.2 million), distantly followed by Brazil (612,000) and Argentina (230,000).
7. It's been a long wait, but the Proofreaders' Society calendars and diaries for 2018 are nowhere!
8. Stir the toffee mixture constantly over medium-high heat until it reaches a temperature of 300°C (the hard-crack stage).
9. The designs of Augustus Pugin (1812–1852) for the interior of the Palace of Westminster adhered to the principles of the Arts and Crafts movement of the late 1800s and early 1900s.
10. After Sun Yat-sen's death, in June 1925, Wang Jingwei became the head of the Nationalist Party.
11. Women are less successful than men in engineering and laboratory science because they cry when criticized.
12. The high level of the hormones oxytocin and especially vasopressin in male prairie voles motivates them to care for their mate and offspring, since it is highly rewarding.
13. The New Zealand Romney is the country's largest sheep breed.
14. The fractal patterns observed in deep time, and the imagery of descending scales they evoke, suggest that leaps are always built on other leaps in a nested hierarchy that unfolds deep into history's continuum.
15. Bristol Student Accidentally Made Explosive [online news headline].
16. Mechanical keyboards are more expensive to make, so they are usually of higher quality than a standard keyboard.
17. (Bonus) How many copyeditors does it take to screw in a lightbulb?

EXERCISE 2-5: Creating a Style Sheet

For any copyediting project longer than a few pages, you need to prepare a style sheet. It should be comprehensive enough to prevent you from having to search repeatedly through the manuscript to confirm your earlier choices about spelling and usage (particularly for specialized terms), and it should also serve as a clear guide for the author, proofreader, and other reviewers, such as the copyeditor of a companion text.

The style sheet is only a tool, however, not a testament to the copyeditor's diligence: it need not record every common term that an author misspells, nor the names of well-known people or places that the author consistently spells correctly. Guidelines for preparing style sheets are offered in *The Copyeditor's Handbook,* chapter 2 (under "Style Sheets").

Using the categories below, create a style sheet for the text in exercise 2-2. In this example, the alphabetical word list (alpha list) is placed first. This enables the editor to quickly copy and paste terms from the manuscript into the file; the list can then be alphabetized with a sort command. Some editors use macros to expedite these tasks.

Author/Title:

Date:

Dictionary:

Style Manual:

Alphabetical List of Names and Terms

Special Symbols

Dates and Numbers

Miscellaneous Notes

Footnotes

Punctuation

EXERCISE 2-6: Writing a Transmittal Memo

When sending copyedited material to an author for review, the copyeditor should ensure that the author understands both the process and the objective. Unless you can safely assume that this is the case—for instance, if you're working in a newsroom or editing internal business documents—it's appropriate to accompany the edited material with a cover memo to the author or client that gives the rationale for changes, outlines the process for reviewing the editing, and explains what will happen next.

Following the guidelines for transmittal letters in chapter 2 of *The Copyeditor's Handbook* (summarized below), write a brief memo to Dr. Franklin Baskerville, the renowned historian of type who is the imaginary author of exercise 2-2 (intended for publication in *The Editing Geek's Encyclopedia*), explaining your interventions.

GUIDELINES

- Start by saying something nice.
- Outline the conventions used to display changes and queries.
- Explain the basis for your editorial decisions. If you followed a specific style guide and dictionary, name them.
- Mention any pervasive style issues (if applicable).
- Outline larger concerns (if applicable).
- Frame your comments in positive and supportive language: explain changes in terms of addressing the needs of the audience, not the failings of the author.
- Don't be overly familiar or informal.
- Don't be patronizing.
- Don't challenge the author's expertise or competence.
- State the deadline (in this case, give the author a week).
- Explain where and how to return the material and what the next steps will be.
- If applicable, mention arrangements for payment.
- Before transmitting the project, list all the components and double-check that you're including the correct versions of each.

Many editors maintain a lexicon of tactful phrases (often borrowed from mentors and colleagues) for communicating with authors and clients. A form letter that can be adapted for each new project is also handy—but editors need to be especially careful to update all the details of such a letter each time it's used. A communication that addresses the author by the name of a previous client or refers to the author's work as "BOOK_TITLE_HERE" is unlikely to instill confidence in the editor's attention to detail.

CHAPTER 3

¶ Reference Books and Resources

EXERCISE 3-1: Using Dictionaries

Professional editors must possess a current edition of a substantial dictionary—at least one of the college-level, or collegiate, volumes—and must have access to an authoritative unabridged dictionary at a public library, in an office reference collection, or through an online subscription. Editors sometimes consult several dictionaries on gnarly issues because information can vary, owing to differences in global dialects of English and in dictionary publishers' proprietary language corpora. In addition, publishers may require different dictionaries: for example, many US book publishers, following *Chicago* (Chicago style), rely on the current edition of *M-W Collegiate;* many magazine and news publishers, following Associated Press (AP) style, stipulate *Web New World.* Freely accessible (but not always current or authoritative) online dictionary aggregators and crowdsourced lexicons further challenge editors to identify and marshal the most reliable print and internet resources. The relative merits of various dictionaries are described in chapter 3 (under "Four Essential Books") of *The Copyeditor's Handbook.*

Editors use dictionaries not just to determine definitions and spellings but also to learn about irregular and variant forms of words; capitalization and hyphenation; parts of speech; correct usage; initialisms, acronyms, and other abbreviations; symbols; common foreign language words and phrases; and even biographical and geographical information.

Beginning with the most definitive resources listed below and, as needed, consulting aggregated and crowdsourced references (full publication details and URLs are provided in the Selected Bibliography), answer the following questions concerning definitions and origins of obscure words, choices between alternative spellings and forms, and correct use of disputed and emerging new terms.

COLLEGIATE DICTIONARIES

Merriam-Webster's Collegiate Dictionary, 11th ed.: print; free online access
Webster's New World College Dictionary: print; subscription-based online access

UNABRIDGED DICTIONARIES

American Heritage Dictionary of the English Language, 5th ed.: print; free online access
Merriam-Webster Unabridged: subscription-based online successor to *Webster's Third New International* (below)

Webster's Third New International Dictionary of the English Language, Unabridged:
   print, retired in 2011

SPECIALIZED DICTIONARIES

Green's Dictionary of Slang: print, free online access

ONLINE AGGREGATED AND CROWDSOURCED DICTIONARIES

OneLook Dictionary Search: free online access
Urban Dictionary: free online access
Wiktionary: free online access
YourDictionary: free online access

1. Define *mushfaker.* Where did you find this definition?
2. What are the respective plural forms of *alumnus* and *alumna*? Is *alums* an acceptable gender-neutral plural form? If so, in what circumstances? If not, what plural form would you recommend, and why?
3. *Log on, log-on, logon, log in, log-in, login*: How would you distinguish these forms? Which would you use and why?
4. Choose the correct noun form and explain your reasoning: *rock and roll, rock-and-roll,* or *rock 'n' roll.*
5. Which is the correct (or preferred) plural form: *avocados* or *avocadoes? hoofs* or *hooves?*
6. Is it proper to use *Skype* as a verb? If so, should the word be capitalized (to Skype) or lowercased (to skype)?
7. What does *IoT* stand for?
8. Define *nimby.* Where does this word come from? What is the correct plural form?
9. List three plural forms for *octopus.* Which is the preferred form?
10. *Gypsy, Gipsy, gypsy,* or *gipsy*? Or should you use another term altogether?

EXERCISE 3-2: Using Style Manuals

For professional editing you should have at least one general style manual (and preferably several) to guide your choices among the often differing conventions that constitute
particular editorial styles: alternative spellings, hyphenation, punctuation, capitalization, numbers and numerals, quotations, acronyms and other abbreviations, italics and
bold type, and special apparatus (e.g., headings, lists, tables, notes and other documentation of sources). You may also need to supplement a general manual with specialized
guides outlining editorial conventions tailored for writing in particular occupations and
subject areas, such as journalism, business, government, law, the humanities, the social
sciences, or a field of science, technology, engineering, or mathematics. Current editions
of some of the major general and specialized style manuals are listed in this workbook's
Selected Bibliography. Chapter 3 of *The Copyeditor's Handbook* (under "Four Essential
Books") and the annotations in the Selected Bibliography of that volume explore the
matter of style guides in more detail.

Imagine that an author preparing a four-thousand-word general interest article on
the recent history of San Francisco has asked you how to handle certain conventions.
Select *one* style guide from *each* of the three categories below and compare their answers
to your author's queries. (If you don't have copies of these references on your personal
bookshelf, you may be able to consult them in your public library or to access them
online; some are available with a free trial subscription.) Then choose the answers that
seem best suited to your author's project. Be prepared to explain your choices.

This exercise introduces you to different style manuals and challenges you to find,
compare, and evaluate their recommendations.

CATEGORY 1: GENERAL STYLE MANUALS (US)

The Chicago Manual of Style, 17th ed.
The Gregg Reference Manual, 11th ed.

CATEGORY 2: GENERAL STYLE MANUALS
(OTHER ENGLISH-SPEAKING COUNTRIES)

Judith Butcher, Caroline Drake, and Maureen Leach, *Butcher's Copy-editing: The
    Cambridge Handbook for Editors, Copy-editors and Proofreaders,* 4th ed.
*Editing Canadian English: A Guide for Editors, Writers, and Everyone Who Works with
    Words,* 3rd ed.
New Oxford Style Manual, 3rd ed.

CATEGORY 3: SPECIALIZED STYLE MANUALS (US)

Associated Press Stylebook and Briefing on Media Law 2018 (journalism)
*GPO Style Manual: An Official Guide to the Form and Style of Federal Government
    Publishing,* 31st ed. (government agencies and business)

Publication Manual of the American Psychological Association, 6th ed. (social sciences)
Scientific Style and Format: The CSE Manual for Authors, Editors, and Publishers, 8th ed.
    (sciences)

1. How should I treat the name of the geographical region around the San Francisco
    Bay?
    (a) the Bay Area
    (b) the Bay area
    (c) the bay area

2. Which is the correct punctuation of the following?
    (a) "One day", wrote the columnist Herb Caen, "if I go to heaven, I'll look around and
         say, 'It ain't bad, but it ain't San Francisco!'"
    (b) "One day," wrote the columnist Herb Caen, "if I go to heaven, I'll look around and
         say, 'It ain't bad, but it ain't San Francisco!'"
    (c) 'One day', wrote the columnist Herb Caen, 'if I go to heaven, I'll look around and
         say, "It ain't bad, but it ain't San Francisco!"'
    (d) 'One day,' wrote the columnist Herb Caen, 'if I go to heaven, I'll look around and
         say, "It ain't bad, but it ain't San Francisco!"'

3. How should I represent percentages in the text?
    (a) a San Francisco job growth of only seven percent between 1990 and 2000
    (b) a San Francisco job growth of only 7 percent between 1990 and 2000
    (c) a San Francisco job growth of only 7% between 1990 and 2000
    (d) a San Francisco job growth of only 7 per cent between 1990 and 2000

4. What is the correct spelling of a compound term formed with the suffix *wide*?
    (a) a city wide housing shortage
    (b) a city-wide housing shortage
    (c) a citywide housing shortage

5. How should I treat the name of a historic natural disaster?
    (a) the 1989 Loma Prieta Earthquake
    (b) the 1989 *Loma Prieta Earthquake*
    (c) the 1989 Loma Prieta earthquake

6. How should I format a date in a source citation (note or bibliographical listing)?
    (a) October 17, 1989
    (b) Oct. 17, 1989
    (c) 17 October 1989
    (d) 17 Oct. 1989
    (e) 17/10/89
    (f) 17.10.89
    (g) 17. x. 89
    (h) 1989 Oct 17
    (i) 1989-10-17
    (j) 1989, October 17

7. How should I form the possessive of a name that ends with *s*?
    (a) Mayor Art Agnos support of homeless people displaced by the earthquake
    (b) Mayor Art Agnos' support of homeless people displaced by the earthquake
    (c) Mayor Art Agnos's support of homeless people displaced by the earthquake

8. How should I style the name of the local street newspaper in the text?
    (a) *The San Francisco Street Sheet*
    (b) the *San Francisco Street Sheet*
    (c) the *Street Sheet* (San Francisco)
    (d) the Street Sheet

9. How should I treat the abbreviation for the North American Free Trade Agreement
    when it is used as an adjective?
    (a) a NAFTA provision
    (b) an NAFTA provision
    (c) a Nafta provision

FOR FURTHER DISCUSSION

- How did you go about finding answers in each of your three chosen manuals?
- Why does the advice in some of these manuals differ?
- If you cannot find a definitive answer in any of your chosen style manuals, what additional resources might you consult?
- In the end, what considerations influenced your style decisions?

Many decisions that editors face don't involve basic grammar at all, but rather *usage,* that is, conventions governing the use of words and idioms in so-called Standard English, as established by the habits of careful speakers and writers of the language. The intuitions of language-conscious editors are valuable in resolving gnarly usage problems, but the "it sounds funny" ("ISF") instinct, even in those with native English fluency, is not infallible. For informed guidance, editors must often turn to usage guides—not just to the brief usage notes in dictionaries, style manuals, and general books on writing but to resources devoted entirely to the conventions of written English.

But these usage authorities sometimes offer conflicting advice. Divergent opinions may reflect different English dialects (e.g., American or British English); a focus on different registers, or levels of formality (e.g., formal, informal, or intimate); changes in the traditional meanings and uses of words and idioms over time; and, especially, commentators' personal tastes and judgments. Chapter 3 of *The Copyeditor's Handbook* (under "Four Essential Books") illustrates the range of opinion by comparing the advice of the lenient *DEU* with that of the orthodox *Garner's* on two commonly contested usage issues: singular *data* and sentence-modifying *hopefully.*

Editors working on corporate communications, blogs, and other content requiring a stylish, informal tone may prefer a guide such as *DEU,* which simply describes current usage in a nonjudgmental way. Editors working on academic or professional content, in which communication must be precise and usage tends to be conservative, may favor a guide such as *Garner's,* which prescribes suitably circumspect language. Editors handling a variety of material often consult several resources to canvass the range of evidence and opinion before making a decision appropriate for a given situation. To be sure, editors on deadline rarely have the luxury to investigate every linguistic nuance. A mastery of many common usage issues allows them to work quickly, but they also take the time necessary to research difficult topics and, when assignments are completed, to expand and update their basic knowledge. (Fortunately, most professional editors enjoy reading books on grammar and usage!)

The goals of this exercise are to teach you how to evaluate usage with sound research, to distinguish the linguists from the pedants, and to challenge spurious rules you may have been taught to follow. This exercise is intended not to be prescriptive with respect to your own writing but to encourage reflection about the rationale for making changes in someone else's. Here you will investigate a questioned usage, weigh the advice offered by different authorities, and then decide whether to let the usage stand or to revise it. Knowing when to stet is as important as knowing when and how to correct an error. You should be prepared to justify your decision.

Select three of the popular usage guides listed below from your personal bookshelf, an office reference collection, or your public library. Look up the boldface italic phrases in the following sentences, explain the usage issue, and specify whether and how the phrases should be emended.

For further discussion: Which usage guide(s) did you find most useful, and why?

Theodore Bernstein. *The Careful Writer: A Modern Guide to English Usage.* 1965. Reprint, New York: Free Press, 1995.

Roy H. Copperud. *American Usage and Style: The Consensus.* New York: Van Nostrand Reinhold, 1980.

Wilson Follett. *Modern American Usage: A Guide.* Rev. ed. Edited by Erik Wensberg. New York: Hill & Wang, 1998.

Fowler's Dictionary of Modern English Usage. 4th ed. Edited by Jeremy Butterfield. Oxford: Oxford University Press, 2015.

Bryan A. Garner. *Garner's Modern English Usage.* 4th ed. New York: Oxford University Press, 2016.

Merriam-Webster's Dictionary of English Usage. Reprint. Springfield, Mass.: Merriam-Webster, 1994.

Eric Partridge. *Usage and Abusage: A Guide to Good English.* New ed. Edited by Janet Whitcut. New York: W. W. Norton, 1995.

1. A self-driving car will behave **differently** on the German autobahn **to** how it will in the Italian Alps.
2. The continuously variable automatic transmission (CVT) of the Subaru Forester doesn't seem as responsive and refined as a traditional automatic; **on the other hand**, the optional turbocharged engine provides spirited acceleration.
3. **All** cats are **not** alike.
4. In an essay of **five hundred words or less**, explain why Santaclaws deserves a free lifetime supply of Fancy Feast cat food.
5. In 2011 we got two feet of floodwater in our basement **due to** unusually heavy rains.
6. **As far as our insurance coverage**, it's fortunate that our basement didn't flood again.
7. We had **over** four inches of rain yesterday!
8. The last storm completely **decimated** our just-sprouted seedlings.
9. Profound political differences **among** the progressive, centrist, and conservative factions of the Democratic Party will be difficult to reconcile.
10. The television series *Okkupert* (*Occupied*)—a political thriller in which Russia, with support from the European Union, occupies Norway to "help" restore its oil production—**begs the question,** Would the peace-loving people of Norway cooperate with or violently oppose a velvet glove invasion?
11. When a couple are united in an arranged marriage, they have a lifetime to get to know **one another**.
12. The ASPCA is rounding up all cats **which** are not on leashes and placing them in animal shelters.
13. More than 11,900 male drivers died in US traffic accidents in 2009, **while** just under 4,900 women drivers perished that year.
14. Lily, the caretaker's daughter, was **literally** run off her feet.
15. A **verbal** contract isn't worth the paper it's written on.

EXERCISE 3-4: Using the Google Books Ngram Viewer

When editors need information not readily found in standard dictionaries or usage guides, they sometimes resort to linguistic corpora, large computer databases of published texts in English that are used primarily by professional lexicographers and linguists. One widely consulted database for English is accessed through the Google Books Ngram Viewer: 155 billion words based on the vast Google Books program, which comprises the digitized contents of participating publishers' catalogs and the collections of more than twelve major university libraries, representing British and American English from 1800 to 2008. The Google corpus—a stew of fiction and nonfiction including reports, proceedings, and perhaps overmuch scientific literature—is less balanced than the Corpus of Contemporary American English and other language corpora compiled by professional linguists (see chapter 3 of *The Copyeditor's Handbook* and the listings in the Selected Bibliography of that volume). But it is far larger and somewhat easier for nonspecialists to use. The Ngram Viewer offers various search options. Editors can narrow their investigation to a particular time frame or dialect (e.g., British or American English), perform wildcard and case-sensitive searches, and specify grammatical inflections, parts of speech, or collocations (uses in the context of specific neighboring words).

Skillful use of any language database requires some statistical and linguistic savvy. Google's Ngram Viewer is thus best deployed to supplement the careful research reported in dictionaries and usage guides. Even busy working editors, when confronted with a gnarly issue of grammar or usage, sometimes poll colleagues in the office or online; a quick survey with this online tool likewise discloses how a multitude of editors have handled a given problem. (The Ngram Viewer also provides recreation for linguistically curious editors.)

The goals of this exercise are to introduce you to this freely accessible resource, to help cultivate your proficiency in defining searches, and to encourage you to explore your language using some of the big-data tools now available to editors. At https://books .google.com/ngrams, first read "About Ngram Viewer"; then investigate the questions below and report your findings.

1. Ping-Pong? Ping-pong? ping-pong? *M-W Unabridged* lists *Ping-Pong* (noun, trademarked name) and *ping-pong* (noun; verb); the online *AHD* lists only *Ping-Pong* (noun, trademarked name). What is the most common capitalization of this term? How well established is the verb form?

2. chaise lounge? chaise longue? Both *M-W Unabridged* and the online *AHD* list these spellings as equal variants. Which is the more common variant in British English? in American English?

3. Web page? web page? webpage? *AHD* online lists *Web page* and *webpage* as equal variants; *M-W Unabridged* does not list any form of the term, but the generally more current information in the online *M-W Collegiate* records *Web page.* Is the solid compound *webpage* gaining a foothold?

4. pant suit? pants suit? pantsuit? When did the solid compound *pantsuit* emerge in American English?

5. people who are . . . ? people that are . . . ? Using the relative pronoun *that* to refer to people is perfectly acceptable, according to leading usage authorities, despite the strenuous objection of a few editors and language mavens and the lone opposition of *APA* (3.20). How widespread is the practice of writing "people that are" instead of "people who are"?

EXERCISE 3-5: Using Practical Grammar

Editors often rely on the concepts and terminology of traditional grammar—the model with eight principal parts of speech and four basic sentence types that many editors have learned in school—despite more nuanced descriptions of English advanced by modern linguistics. In editing for Standard Written English (and in judging when to depart from it), you must be able to identify and differentiate some basic grammatical elements that affect your decisions. Without a working knowledge of traditional grammar, you may have difficulty distinguishing between, say, a passive voice verb and a merely colorless one, or knowing when a comma must separate parts of a sentence and when a comma is discretionary. Even though editors generally avoid trying the patience of authors by offering pedantic grammatical explanations for changes, you must grasp the principles of grammar to apply rules and conventions with confidence.

If you missed those weeks of school when basic English grammar was covered or if you have long forgotten your lessons, you can brush up by reading the survey of basic English grammar provided in any standard handbook for college writers or in one of several excellent resources, here listed from the most recent to a still-respected old authority (full publication details are provided in the bibliography):

The Chicago Manual of Style, 17th ed., pp. 223–362
Diane Hacker and Nancy Sommers, *A Writer's Reference,* 8th ed., pp. 333–53
Mark Lester and Larry Beason, *The McGraw-Hill Handbook of English Grammar and Usage,* 2nd ed., pp. 1–108
Gordon Loberger and Kate Shoup, *Webster's New World English Grammar Handbook,* 2nd ed., pp. 5–234
Words into Type, 3rd ed., pp. 339–404

And if you're ready for the AP course, try

Bryan A. Garner, *The Chicago Guide to Grammar, Usage, and Punctuation,* pp. 13–180

Ideally, your personal library should contain one or more grammar references. If you're not yet prepared to invest in a grammar book, you can find some of these recommended books at your place of business or in your public library. But beware of online grammar resources that lack an authoritative imprint.

The goal of this exercise is to reinforce your recognition of some basic grammatical structures underlying standard grammar, syntax, punctuation, and usage. In the following passage, identify at least one example of each of the grammatical elements itemized below by citing the sentence in which it occurs (use the superscript letters in the text to specify the sentence) and the applicable words or phrases.

1. active voice verb: a verb whose subject performs the action
2. passive voice verb: a verb whose subject receives the action
3. independent clause: a clause containing a subject and verb, with any modifiers and complements, capable of standing alone as a complete thought and as a sentence
4. dependent clause: a clause containing a subject and verb, with any modifiers and complements, usually beginning with a subordinating conjunction, relative pronoun, or relative adverb and not capable of standing alone as a complete thought; functions as an adjective (restrictive or nonrestrictive), adverb, or noun
5. simple sentence: a sentence containing one independent clause
6. compound sentence: a sentence containing two or more independent clauses
7. compound predicate: two or more verbs governed by a single subject
8. appositive phrase: a phrase describing a noun or pronoun by renaming it; functions as a noun and may be restrictive or nonrestrictive
9. prepositional phrase: a phrase consisting of a preposition and noun or pronoun with any modifiers; functions as an adjective or adverb
10. participial phrase: a phrase consisting of a present or past participle of a verb and any modifiers and complements; functions as an adjective
11. absolute phrase: an idiomatic construction usually consisting of a present or past participle, with any modifiers and complements; functions as a sentence-level modifier
12. gerund phrase: a phrase consisting of the present participle of a verb with complements; functions as a noun
13. infinitive phrase: a phrase consisting of the infinitive form of a verb with complements; functions as a noun, adjective, or adverb

Bonus: Identify a restrictive dependent clause (4); a restrictive appositive (8).

[a]Our repertoire of punctuation marks excludes many quaint symbols that were once proposed for inclusion. [b]Since the printing press was invented, at least nine different writers and type designers have promoted a distinctive character to flag irony or sarcasm. [c]Variously styled, this *point d'ironie, percontation point, tilde, sarcasm point, snark, ironieteken,* or *SarcMark* was intended to aid readers who were unable to detect mockery without a typographic cue. [d](The demand for such a mark has declined with the invention of emoticons and emoji.) [e]A twentieth-century Madison Avenue adman vigorously campaigned for the *interrobang,* a fusion of the question mark and exclamation point conveying a mixture of doubt and surprise. [f]This mark had its day during the 1960s. [g]American Type Founders actually cast it for the newly designed typeface Americana, and the Remington Rand typewriter company offered it as a replaceable key and typehead on the Model 25 electric. [h]But securing a place for this mark in the canon of modern punctuation proved difficult. [i]Ultimately, the decline of hot metal composition, the technical limitations of early photocomposition, and cultural resistance to changing the modern writing system thwarted advocates' efforts. [j]Considering this failure, the enduring popularity of the interrobang seems surprising. [k]It still has a cult following (and a T-shirt) and even occupies a position in Unicode, the standard computer character set, although few Unicode fonts include the character.

The short-lived interrobang.

EXERCISE 3-6: Doing Internet Research

> As Gandhi once said, "Half my quotes on Pinterest are fake."
> —Matt Novak, "7 Gandhi Quotes That Are Totally Fake," *Gizmodo*, July 10, 2015

In the pre-internet era, copyeditors were expected to confirm only information that could be checked in standard desktop reference books, such as the correct spelling of the names of well-known people and places, the dates of major historical events, the wording of familiar quotations, and the accuracy of conversions between metric and imperial measurements. Verification of such fundamentals merely helped avoid authorial pratfalls; editors were not formally responsible for fact-checking an author's work.

Now that the internet places petabytes of information at their fingertips, copyeditors can use their search engines or a handful of authoritative websites they've bookmarked to perform these basic checks. Certain other copyediting tasks, too, such as tracking down a source or confirming bibliographic details, are sometimes more efficiently dispatched by firing up a search engine or making a quick trip to a trusted website than by querying an author. One risk of having such convenient search tools is mission creep: editors must resist the urge to trawl the internet for hours in pursuit of trivial—and not always reliable—details rather than flagging suspect content for the author's attention. Another risk is confrontation: even when the evidence of an error is compelling, editors must craft circumspect queries to avoid directly challenging an author's expertise. Bottom line: Editors must focus on their core responsibilities unless they are formally vested with (and appropriately remunerated for) the additional work of fact-checking.

Still, all copyeditors now need basic internet research skills to do their job. They should learn how to search the internet efficiently; know several major search engines; and identify useful web resources. This exercise encourages you to build your proficiency in internet research. Here you will learn to use some online reference tools—both familiar and offbeat—and begin to develop your own trustworthy sources of information. Choosing from the assorted websites listed below, find answers to the following (admittedly arcane) questions.

Bonus: List additional general and specialized online resources that you believe can be trusted.

Amazon: https://www.amazon.com/. Bibliographic data for books. For some works, includes a "Look Inside" feature with images of the title and copyright pages.
A caveat: Publishing details and even images of front-matter pages may contain errors; they should be confirmed in a second source.

Atlas Obscura: https://www.atlasobscura.com/. A collaborative website of curious hidden spots of the world.

The Chicago Manual of Style Online: http://www.chicagomanualofstyle.org/. Subscription-based digital edition of *Chicago,* with open-access aids, such as *Style Q&A.*

Encyclopedia Britannica: https://www.britannica.com/. Scaled-down free online version of a major encyclopedia.

Google Books: https://books.google.com/. Full text of books and magazines scanned and stored in Google's extensive digital database.

Internet Archive: https://archive.org/. Nonprofit library of free books, movies, software, music, and websites, with image captures of superseded web pages going back to 1996 in its Wayback Machine.

IUCN: International Union for Conservation of Nature: https://www.iucn.org/. Research of an international network of government and civil society environmental organizations.

Library of Congress: https://www.loc.gov/. Portal to the vast Library of Congress Online Catalog, US copyright information, and other resources.

Quote Investigator: http://quoteinvestigator.com/. Garson O'Toole's research to authenticate and source quotations.

TinEye Reverse Image Search: https://www.tineye.com/. Searchable image database.

Trademark Checklist, International Trademark Association: https://www.inta.org /Media/Lists/Trademark%20Checklist/AllItems.aspx. Trademarks owned by INTA members, with guidelines for their treatment.

United States Board on Geographic Names: https://geonames.usgs.gov/. Official spelling and treatment of US place names.

Wikipedia: https://www.wikipedia.org/. Crowdsourced multilingual encyclopedia. A cautionary note: Owing to the site's open, collaborative nature, content may contain errors, and articles on contentious topics may be repeatedly altered by parties to the controversy.

The World Factbook: https://www.cia.gov/library/resources/the-world-factbook/index .html. Detailed information on over 250 world entities, maintained by the Central Intelligence Agency.

World Health Organization: http://www.who.int/en. Research and programs of the United Nations organization dedicated to promoting international health.

WorldCat: http://www.worldcat.org/. Union catalog itemizing the collections of 72,000 libraries in 170 countries and territories that participate in the Online Computer Library Center (OCLC) global cooperative. Warning: Because WorldCat is a compilation of multiple databases, it may yield multiple, differing records for a given work.

1. In 2015 the US Postal Service released a commemorative stamp honoring the author Maya Angelou and featuring the quotation "A bird doesn't sing because it has an answer, it sings because it has a song." Did this quotation originate with Angelou? If not, to whom should these words be attributed?

2. The book *UFO Sightings Desk Reference: United States of America, 2001–2015* by Cheryl Costa and Linda Miller Costa was recently reviewed in the online edition of the *Daily Mail.* Does this book actually exist or is it a hoax?

3. Verify the following quotation by Virginia Woolf and provide a full bibliographic citation for it: "Words do not live in dictionaries; they live in minds."

4. An author writes that the 2016 infant mortality rate in the United States was more than twice that of Iceland. Is this correct?

5. Identify the title of the painting to the right and the name of the artist. Where can you find a copy suitable for use in print or on a website? Is permission required for its use in a publication?

6. Is it true that the middle initial *S* in the name of the thirty-third president of the United States doesn't stand for anything? Should the name be written Harry S Truman or Harry S. Truman? What about e e cummings versus E. E. Cummings? bell hooks versus Bell Hooks? Sean Combs, Puff Daddy, Puffy, P. Diddy, or Diddy? Prince, The Artist Formerly Known as Prince, or ♀ ?

7. Consider the following sentence: "In the loony tunes, heavily photoshopped version of Sarah's life on Facebook, Sarah, sheathed in skin-tight levis and a spandex top, is shown lounging in her jeep while eating a popsicle and sipping a frappuccino." Which words are trademarked? Is any special treatment of these words required?

8. Identify which of the following are the names of real US cities and correct any errors in the authentic place names: Angels Camp, California; Bat Cave, North Carolina; Bug Tussle, Oklahoma; Deadmans Corner, Maine; Gun Barrel City, Texas; Hell, Michigan; Intercourse, Pennsylvania; Looneyville, West Virginia; Monkey's Eyebrow, Kentucky; Mosquitoville, Florida; Mousetown, Maryland; Sandwich, Massachusetts; Whynot, Mississippi; Zigzag, Oregon.

9. Percy was driving 150 km/h when he was pulled over. How far over the posted speed limit of 65 mph was he going? Marcy, who is 1.5 m tall, weighs 13 stone. Is she overweight? Which is more: 2 tonnes or 4,200 pounds?

10. When modern physicians take the Hippocratic oath, do they still swear, "First, do no harm"?

11. Which disease kills more people globally: malaria or tuberculosis?

12. How close to extinction is *Panthera uncia*?

13. What contemporary novel features the Garden of Cosmic Speculation? Is this garden open to the public? Are there photographs of it?

14. What did the first home page for Google look like?

EXERCISE 3-7: Specialized Style Guides

Search online for style guides for organizations or publications in two or three areas that interest you, such as local or regional history, sports, advocacy, food and wine, creative pursuits, or specific academic disciplines. (Look for a title like "Guidelines for Authors" or "Editorial Style Guide.") If your chosen publication follows an existing style guide, which one is it? If it does not, what are its major recommendations regarding general issues such as styling of numbers or use of personal titles? What recommendations does it make for terms and usages specific to the subject area?

If you have trouble locating a style guide, examine a publication in an area of interest to you and determine the general aspects of its style, using the categories in exercise 2-5 as a guide.

Here are a few suggestions to get you started:

Economist
Hesperia (journal of the American School of Classical Studies at Athens)
Journal of Herpetology
Journal of the Oral History Society (UK)
United Nations
University of Michigan School of Education
World of Fine Wine
a nature guide
a photography instruction book

PART 2

Editorial Style

"I have two mommies. I know where the apostrophe goes."

¶ Punctuation

EXERCISE 4-1: Punctuation

This exercise provides practice in applying some basic conventions of punctuation outlined in *The Copyeditor's Handbook,* chapter 4.

Pay special attention to treatment of the following:

- antithetical elements
- compound sentences
- coordinate adjectives
- direct and indirect questions
- dates and places
- quotations
- restrictive and nonrestrictive modifiers
- terminal marks

Watch out for ambiguous sentences. Punctuation often clarifies an author's meaning, but occasionally it contributes to misinterpretation. Some of these sentences require a query to the author before they can be emended; others, though properly punctuated, may need deeper revision.

1. The man wearing the long-sleeved red gingham shirt told amusing tall tales

2. The accountant asked whether the receipts were in order

3. The accountant asked "Are the receipts in order"

4. School curriculums have traditionally been the domain of politicians and

    educators not judges

5. The promoter said that if no more ticket requests came in the concert would

    be canceled

6. Harvard freshmen who have reading scores below the national average performed better than expected on the math aptitude test

7. You can teach yourself basic computer skills using a how-to book but a better choice is to ask a knowledgeable sympathetic friend for tutoring

8. Each hospital has a service office whose staff members will answer your questions about hospital policies

9. From June 1 through June 3 1998 the Chamber of Commerce of Oakland California hosted its third annual conference for small businesses

10. All part-time employees who are not covered by the new contract will be laid off

11. The three-person Board of Appeals today dismissed the case arguing that employees' workplace email communications should constitute a "zone of privacy."

12. According to the *New York Times*, Steve Bannon and Sean Spicer, the White House press secretary, began a campaign this weekend to blame congressional Democrats for the failure of the proposed bill.

13. Even if government officials cared about the poor, mostly black victims of Katrina enough to change their schedules, the administration would probably have bungled the relief effort, because FEMA is now run by political appointees with no experience in disaster relief.

14. What can individuals do to reduce traffic congestion? Dont' drive, telecommute or take public transportation.

EXERCISE 4-2: Restrictive versus Nonrestrictive Modifiers

One of the most challenging decisions in punctuation is whether to use or omit commas with modifying words, phrases, and clauses. In determining the correct treatment of appositives, relative clauses, and other types of modifiers, champion punctuators must often distinguish between *restrictive* ("essential" or "limiting") and *nonrestrictive* ("nonessential," "nonlimiting," or "parenthetical") modifiers. The former omit commas unless they are required by some other syntactical feature of the sentence; the latter use commas to set the modifier off from the surrounding sentence. The subtleties of choosing the right punctuation for the intended meaning are discussed and illustrated at length in *The Copyeditor's Handbook,* chapter 4, under "Function 2: Joining Clauses" and "Function 3: Setting Off Phrases."

In the following sentences, decide whether the modifiers shown in bold italic type are restrictive or nonrestrictive and punctuate them accordingly. If you need to query the author to determine the intended meaning, avoid using the words *restrictive* and *nonrestrictive* (or *essential* and *nonessential*): most authors are unfamiliar with these grammatical terms.

1. Beware of all enterprises ***that require new clothes***.

2. If my relative spent some of his money on a back-pain specialist, ***who could teach him exercises that would prolong his working life by another decade***, shouldn't that be considered an investment?

3. The Pentagon has decided that it will not award the Purple Heart to Desert Storm war veterans, ***who suffer only from post-traumatic stress disorder***.

4. Repairs to windows ***which are judged to be in the worst condition*** will be prioritized.

5. Ms. Chetwin said fresh chicken, ***which is not cooked correctly***, is considered responsible for half of all campylobacter cases.

6. When ***my oldest brother Robert, who was a quiet, studious fellow***, went off to college, he turned into ***Conan the Barbarian***.

7. In Mao Zedong's writings, there is no distinction between Mao, *the theoretician*, and Mao, *the political strategist*.

8. The greatest growth occurred in the northern half of Illinois *where communities were newer and more progressive and where antislavery strength was concentrated*.

9. But none of the Americans viewed the journey in quite the same light as did Baldwin Mollhausen *whose drawings of the trip are a chronicle of German Romanticism*.

10. The trail at the Oakland Zoo allows visitors to observe California wildlife species *like mountain lions and grisly bears which reside in the state today*.

EXERCISE 4-3: Editorial Zealotry: A Light Copyedit

This passage is adapted from Arthur Plotnik, *The Elements of Editing: A Modern Guide for Editors and Journalists* (New York: Macmillan, 1982), pp. 2–4. It is reprinted with the permission of Scribner, a division of Simon & Schuster, Inc. All rights reserved. Much of the language has been changed, and all the errors were introduced for the purpose of this exercise, which not only challenges you to look for punctuation errors but also previews editorial issues covered in chapters 5 through 8 of *The Copyeditor's Handbook*.

Do a light copyedit.

Some overly zealous copyeditors will pour over a manuscript, and change

every "till" to 'until' or vice versa, depending on their training, their

grammatical ear, and their ideas about prose style. Although editors must try

to forestall the deprecation of English into colloquial swill, they should never

adopt a self-styled purism that does not allow for some vareity of expression.

When a tyrranical editorial coordinator waves Fowler, Wilson Follett, and other

venerable guardians, his staff should wave back Theodore Bernstein's *Miss*

Thistlebottom's Hobogoblins, a thoughtfull debunking of scared cows in usage,

or William Morris and Mary Morrris's *Harper Dictionary of Contemporary*

Usage which explores the differences of opinion among the so-called "experts."

A second danger: Some novice copyeditors misinterpret the

recommendations in *The Elements Of Style* as a mandate to change such

sentences as "the outcry was heard round the world" to "every-one in

the world heard the outcry." True, the active voice is more forceful, and a

procession of passive constructions is a sure cure for insomnia. But the

passive voice is preferable when the writer's goal is variety or emphasizing an

important word in a sentence.

Do a medium copyedit of the following paragraphs. You may use the dictionary and style guide of your choice, but note that the answer key follows *Chicago* and *M-W Collegiate*. Although the instructions for the one-page exercise 4-3 do not stipulate the preparation of a style sheet, this multipage document requires you to maintain a scrupulous formal record of your style decisions. *The Copyeditor's Handbook,* chapter 2, under "Style Sheets," counsels copyeditors to prepare a style sheet for any project longer than a few pages, a habit that aids not just copyeditors and authors but also production staff who handle subsequent iterations of a project.

The Liberation of American Humor

Among my favourites in the galaxy of American humorists are the icon-smashing, potty mouth, stand-up comic, who assaults cultural orthodoxies and speaks, no, swears, truth to power. Lenny Bruce, ranked number three (after Richard Pryor and George Carlin) on *Rolling Stone Magazine*'s 2017 list of 50 best standups of all-time improvised comedy routines on politics, religion and sex were so peppered with vulgarities that he along with his night club hosts was repeatedly arrested for obscenity. Bruce's transgressive humor caused England, Australia, as well as several US cities to declare him personal non grata, his unmuzzled performances prompted television executives to ban him. Undercover police began surveilling his comedy club act in New York in 1964, and charged him with obscenity after a particularly blue monologue at the Cafe au Go Go. The widely-publicized 1964 trial that followed was regarded as a landmark case for freedom of speech in the United States. Despite testimony and petitions on his behalf by artists, writers, and educators including Woody

Allen, Bob Dylan, Jules Feiffer, Norman Mailer, Alan Ginsberg, William Styron,

James Baldwin, and sociologist Herbert Gans, Bruce was convicted.

But so-called "dirty words" was not the real issue, censorship of

unpopular opinions, forcefully expressed, was. Bruce prepared the way for

an era of radical social and political opposition to "the Establishment" in the

form of black (and sometimes blue) humor. CBS's *Smothers Brothers Comedy

Hour*—a typical comedy-variety television show launched in 1967, pushed

the boundaries of permissible network satire and hosted countercultural

musical guests such as Buffalo Springfield, The Who, and folksinger/activist

Pete Seeger (blacklisted on commercial TV since 1950, who's controversial

sixth verse of *Waist Deep in the Big Muddy* insinuated criticism of President

Lyndon Johnson's Viet Nam war policy and resulted in a redaction of the entire

performance from the season two premier. Due to persistent conflicts with

network censors over such political and social content, the *Smothers Brothers

Comedy Hour* was abruptly cancelled in 1969 despite its popularity with

younger audiences. [Older viewers preferred NBC's opposite show, the western

saga *Bonanza*.]

George Carlin, a disciple of Lenny Bruce, aired darkly comic remarks

on the English language, psychology, religion, and various "taboo" subjects.

He often satirized contemporary US politics and the excesses of American

culture. A riff on his famous "Seven Words You Can Never Say on Television"

routine of the early 1970s, later formed the basis of the 1978 U.S. Supreme

Court case *F.C.C. v. Pacifica Foundation* which affirmed the government's power to regulate indecent material on the public airways. (Obscene content is not protected under the 1st amendment, some indecent or profane content, which does not meet all three criterions for obscenity, may in some cases be protected but is regulated. This case resulted in the F.C.C. guideline prohibiting such content on the public airways between 6 a.m. and 10 p.m. when children are likely to be in the audience). But Carlin's "dirty words" routine too actually concerned not a list of proscribed words but the issue of censorship itself.

In the same tradition of transgressive humor Bill Maher sparked controversy with his deliberately provocative remarks on *Politically Incorrect.* ABC canceled the show shortly after Maher's "politically incorrect" comments about the 9/11 attackers prompted outraged sponsors to withdrew their support. The program was later revived as *Real Time with Bill Maher* on cable TV's HBO network where its host can take jabs at conventional pieties with greater impunity. John Stewart's *Daily Show,* Steven Colbert's *Colbert Report,* and other edgy comedy acts testing the limits of political and social humor, all have likewise found audiences on cable networks, which as subscription based broadcasters answer primarily to their self-selected customers not to the Federal Communications Commission that regulates the public airways more strictly. Succeeding David Letterman as the host of CBS's *The Tonight Show,* Colbert now evinces or perhaps feigns unease at broadcast TV's constraints on his free-range jokes. Is he poking the CBS censor in the eye or is he really on

a five-second delay. Ultimately the liberation of American humor may depend

on the internet, that wild west of unfettered and sometimes horrifying self

expression.

CHAPTER 5

¶ Spelling and Hyphenation

EXERCISE 5-1: Compound Forms

Choosing correct spellings is usually simple. But determining the treatment of compound forms challenges even experienced editors: *open* (copy editor)? *hyphenated* (copy-editor)? or *solid* (copyeditor)? To verify the spelling of *permanent compounds,* an editor must rely on a trustworthy, up-to-date dictionary—usually the one required by house style—and find the form specified for the applicable part of speech. If that dictionary does not include the term, the editor must next consult an authoritative style manual for guidance on the formation of *temporary compounds.* In styling these, the editor must consider the syntax of the sentence: for example, a compound unit modifier is usually hyphenated if it precedes, but unhyphenated if it follows, the modified word (a thought-provoking discussion *but* a discussion that is thought provoking). Besides consulting a dictionary and a style manual, an editor must sometimes weigh the possibility of misreading, authors' strong preferences, and the conventions familiar to a given readership. Treatment of compound forms is discussed in *The Copyeditor's Handbook,* chapter 5, under "One Word or Two?"

The goal of this exercise is to give you a workout in applying these principles. "Sprinkle" hyphens, close-up marks, and wordspaces in the following sentences. The answer key to this exercise follows *M-W Collegiate* and *Chicago,* but you may follow other authoritative references if you prefer.

1. There was an above average turnout by middle aged working class voters in the south eastern states.

2. He submitted a hastily written report that documented his half baked effort to revise his predecessor's ill conceived cost cutting plan.

3. To replicate this early nineteenth century experiment, the high school students needed two gallon test bottles, a four inch long tube, a six or seven foot plank, and two to three teaspoons of salt.

4. The ideal candidate will have strong skills in problem solving, decision

   making, film making, book keeping, and proof reading.

5. He is self conscious about his 45 percent productivity decline and five fold

   increase in tardiness.

6. As a comparison of the pre and post test scores for the fourth, fifth, and

   sixth grade students showed, highly motivated young students can learn

   the most basic aspects of socio economic theory.

7. He sat cross legged at the cross roads cross questioning the pollster about

   the cross over vote and the cross fire over the nomination.

8. The state of the art amplifier is over there with the other out of order

   equipment that the under appreciated copy editors and their anti

   intellectual co workers left behind.

9. Adult-sponsored and -supervised play, especially in middle- and upper-class

   suburbia, has taken the place of unorganized sport.

10. This letter is addressed to all my Boston Red Sox fan friends.

11. The cat loving but severely-asthmatic copyeditor wrote to the New Zealand

    Siberian cat breeder about obtaining a pedigree hypo-allergenic kitten to

    keep her company in her solitary day-job.

12. She concluded, however, that the eyewatering two thousand dollar price-

    tag for such a kitten was too high.

13. When user defined application specific keyboard shortcuts conflict with

    operating system commands, the application may freeze.

14. Recent discussions of longstanding questions about funding healthcare, child care, and short and long term treatment for mental health disorders have been contentious.

15. This quick on-line quiz will tell you whether your dress and demeanor qualify as authentically-hipster, merely hipster adjacent, or hopelessly main-stream.

EXERCISE 5-2: A Publisher's Catalog: A Light Copyedit

The following capsule reviews will be published in a mail-order catalog. You are being asked to do a light copyedit following *M-W Collegiate* and *Chicago*. Compose queries as needed and keep a style sheet. This exercise is based on blurbs that appeared in the winter 1995 catalog published by Daedalus Books, PO Box 9132, Hyattsville, MD 20181, and is used with permission of the publisher. For the purpose of this exercise, errors were introduced and other changes were made to the published text.

A FROLIC OF HIS OWN. William Gaddis. Poseidon. $25.00

A *Frolic of His Own*, William Gaddiss' long anticipated fourth novel, is a funny, accurate tale of lives caught up in the toils of law. Oscar Crease, middle-aged college instructor, savant, and playwright is suing a Hollywood producer for pirating his play *Once at Antietam*, based on his grandfather's experiences in the Civil War, and turning it in to a gory block-buster called *The Blood in the Red White and Blue*. Oscar's suit, and a host of other lawsuits--which involve a dog trapped in an outdoor sculpture, wrongful death during a river baptism, a church versus a soft drink company, and even Oscar himself after he is run over by his own car--engulf all who surround him, from his free-wheeling girlfriend to his draconian, nonagenarian father, Federal Judge Thomas Creese. Down this tortuous path of depositions and decrees, suits and countersuits, the most lofty ideas of our culture are rung dry in the often surreal logic and language of the law.

THE BIRD ARTIST. Howard Norman, FSG. $20

Howard Norman's spellbinding novel is set in Newfoundland in 1911. The novel not only shares its place, but also its tone and passion, with *The Shipping News*. Fabian Vas's story, told with simplicity and grace, takes place against a spare beautiful landscape. At age 20, Fabian is working at the boatyard, taking a correspondence course in bird painting, and sleeping with Maraget Handle, a woman of great beauty, intelligence, and waywardness. When his father leaves on a long hunting expedition and his mother takes up with the lighthouse keeper, Fabian looses his bearings. The author's intense observation of people and nature make for a remarkably good novel.

A PERSONAL MATTER. Kenzaburo Oë. $7.95

A Personal Matter, here translated by John Nathan, is probably Oë's best known novel. It is the story of a man's relationship with his severely brain-damaged child. As he plots the child's murder, he finally realizes that he must take responsibility for his son. The novel, written out of Oé's profound despair after the birth of his own disabled child (now a 31-year-old successful composer) is original, different, tough in its candor and beautiful in its faithfulness to both intellectual precision and human tenderness.

EXERCISE 5-3: A Health Newsletter: A Medium Copyedit

The following paragraphs are based on information in various health advisories provided by *Berkeley Wellness* (a health newsletter), Kaiser Permanente (a health maintenance organization), and the juggernaut Wikipedia. Several previous exercises invited you to get your feet wet; this one offers a full immersion. Besides reviewing the knowledge and skills covered in *The Copyeditor's Handbook,* chapters 1–5, this exercise gives you a taste of chapters to come by challenging you to wrangle problems of capitalization, numbers treatment, abbreviations, grammar and usage, and literary style.

Assuming this text has been prepared for the general public, do a medium to heavy copyedit. Follow your preferred dictionary and style guide, but note that the answer key is based on the Merriam-Webster dictionaries, with *AHD* as backup, and *Chicago.* Prepare a style sheet.

The Bugs of Summer and Other Seasons

Mosquitos

It's a well known fact that mosquitos transmit Malaria, Yellow Fever, West Nile Virus, the most recent villain—Zika Virus and several less known others. Only female mosquitoes bite. When she does, she injects her saliva into your skin which makes your blood flow. The saliva is what caused the swelling and that itchy sensation.

To avoid being bitten eliminate any standing water in your yard. Wear a loose fitting long sleeve shirt and pants when you go outside. The little blood-suckers can bite through tight fighting clothes. Also apply DEET (best to use 20–30% not higher percentages). For those who prefer a more natural approach be aware that only the synthetic version of lemon eucalyptus (p-methanediol) is effective. All other botanicals are limited in prevention.

If you get bitten apply calamine lotion or a corticosteroid cream. Call

your doctor if you develop aches, fever, headache, joint pain, or a rash—even

weeks later, since mosquito born diseases can take awhile to produce symptoms.

Ticks

Ticks bite and suck blood like tiny vampires. They transmit many serious

diseases, including Lyme Disease. This disease is mostly concentrated in

states of the northeast and midwest, but there are many cases in other states

as well and on every continent except Antartica.

To avoid ticks, clear overgrown brush and piles of leaves from your

property. When out in the woods or tall grass, wear a light colored shirt with

long sleeves and long pants tucked into socks or boots. Use an insect repellent

containing DEET on your skin and permethrin on your clothes.

After being outdoors, check your entire body for ticks with a

magnifying glass (ticks are tiny). Check your children and pets too. If you

discover a tick, don't use a lighted match, vasoline, or gasoline to remove it.

Instead, use tweezers to grasp its body as close to your skin as possible. Pull

gently and steadily upward. Don't twist the tick, since that may break off the

mouth-parts and lead to an infection. Don't crush, puncture, or squeeze the

tick's body. If the mouthparts break off in the skin, use tweezers as if removing

a splinter. Thoroughly clean the area with rubbing alcohol or soap and water.

If a rash or fever or flu-like symptoms develops within a few weeks,

it could indicate Lyme disease. See a doctor if you have these symptoms.

The disease is usually treated in early stages with aural antibiotics. For later

manifestations of Lyme disease, such as neurological, joint, or heart problems,

you may need a longer course of antibiotics administered intervenously.

Although some people eventually recover without treatment,

antibiotics improve recovery time and help avoid complications of the disease.

But taking antibiotics for more than 30 days offer no added benefits and may

be dangerous. A diagnosis of so called "chronic Lyme disease" and the efficacy

of extended and alternative treatments advertised on the Internet are not

supported by reputable scientific studies.

Chiggers

Chiggers are miniscule but their bites cause severe itching and redness. They

attack tight areas, such as the groin, underarms, or waist.

To avoid getting bitten, use a repellent that contains DEET and spray

permethrin on clothes. Wear long pants tucked inside socks and long sleeves.

To treat chigger bites, wash the area with soap and water immediately. Apply

an antiitch cream such as calamine lotion or hydrocortisone. Wash clothes in

hot water.

No See Ums

The tiny insects called no see ums, biting midges, or biting gnats appear in swarms with warm weather but are only active for a few weeks in most places. Still, they can be very annoying. Their bite looks like a small red dot and sometimes develops into an itchy welt the size of a quarter.

To avoid no see ums, apply an insect repellent containing DEET. Wear long sleeves and long pants to minimize exposed skin. Avoid swarms if you can. If you get bitten apply a cold compress and antiitch cream.

Wasps

Wasps often build their nests in trees or under the eves of houses. Don't mess with these nests if you can avoid them.

If you do get stung, wash the area with soap and water and remove the stinger by scraping a fingernail or the edge of a credit card over the area. Don't squeeze the sting or use tweezers. To reduce swelling, wrap ice in a cloth and apply to the sight. Swelling is usually mild and temporary, but if the effected area becomes large and red, you may have an infection and should see a doctor.

If you develop chest pain, shortness of breath, or intense sweating shortly after being stung, seek medical help immediately. These symptoms may indicate a severe allergic reaction.

¶ Capitalization and the Treatment of Names

EXERCISE 6-1: Capitalization

Proper nouns—names for individual persons, places, and organizations—are traditionally capitalized in English. For the treatment of other terms, editors usually follow one of two conventions: *down style,* a restrained use of capitalization described in *Chicago* and favored in most book publishing, or *up style,* a more liberal use of capitalization illustrated in some newspapers and magazines. These conventions, along with many variations, exceptions, and special cases, are described in *The Copyeditor's Handbook,* chapter 6.

The first three capsule biographies and reports below are based on Samuel Kernell and Samuel Popkin, eds., *Chief of Staff: Twenty-Five Years of Managing the Presidency* (Berkeley: University of California Press, 1986), and are used with permission of the publisher. For the purpose of this exercise, errors were introduced and other changes were made to the published text. The remaining examples were created specifically for this exercise. Edit them all for down style capitalization.

1. After serving for five years as President Eisenhower's Staff Secretary, General Andrew J. Goodpaster assumed many of the duties of Chief of Staff in 1958. During Eisenhower's administration, General Goodpaster supervised the National Security Council Staff, briefed the President on intelligence matters, and was White House Liaison for defense and national security.

2. Before being appointed special assistant and counsel to President Johnson in 1965, Harry McPherson had served as counsel to the Democratic policy committee in the Senate, Deputy Undersecretary of the Army, and

assistant Secretary of State. He is now an attorney in Washington, DC, and

vice-chairman of and general counsel to the John F. Kennedy Center for

the performing arts.

3. General Alexander Haig was deputy to national security adviser Henry

Kissinger during the early days of President Nixon's administration. He

became Nixon's chief of staff in 1973. In 1974 he was named Supreme

Commander of NATO, a post he held until 1979 when he retired to enter

private industry. He returned to Government service as Secretary of State

during the first eighteen months of President Reagan's first term.

4. Christine Lagarde became Managing Director of the International Monetary

fund in July, 2011. Born in Paris and raised in Le Havre, as a teenager she

was a member of the French National Synchronized Swimming Team. She

was educated at the université Paris Nanterre and the Institut d'études

politiques d'Aix-en-provence (Sciences Po Aix). Specializing in labor

and antitrust law, she went on to become the first woman to head the

international law firm Baker & McKenzie (now Baker McKenzie). From

2005, she held several French ministerial posts, including trade minister,

Minister of Agriculture, and Minister for Economic Affaires, finance, and

Employment.

5. At the international Meeting on Renewable Energy and Sustainable

Technologies held in 2015, the keynote speech was given by Prof. Sunil

Substrate of the Department of applied Physics and materials Science,

The Ancient Ivy University, Bobonia. Members of the afternoon Panel on Sustainable Computing technologies included Professor Nina Nanochip, holder of the Ada Lovelace chair in electrical engineering at the Technical University of Bobonia, and Dr. Felix Fotovoltaio, Research and Development Director of Bobonia Sunshine Industries SA.

6. In early 2018, an article in *Nature Scientific Reports* reported that the chameleon's beauty goes more than skin-deep: some chameleons (family Chamaeleonidae) found in Africa and on the Island of Madagascar have bony formations in the skull and sometimes other parts of the skeleton that glow (flouresce) under Uv light. The study focused on the genus Calumma, which includes the species *C. globifer, C. Tsaratananaense,* and *C. guibei.* A striking photograph of the fluorescence phenomenon was posted on the Newsweek website.

EXERCISE 6-2: Finding Work: A Light Copyedit

This exercise is the text of a short handout by the veteran editor Edna Editrix addressed to people seeking entry-level editorial jobs. It draws on all the material covered in *The Copyeditor's Handbook,* chapters 4–6. Do a light copyedit: emend basic errors and enforce conventions of editorial style but restrain the temptation to rewrite sentences, however inelegant, that are correct and clear. Follow your chosen dictionary and style manual and prepare a style sheet. If you have queries, use the comments or notes feature of your editing software or insert boldfaced queries within curly braces.

Finding Work

Back in the day, editors aspiring to break into U.S. publishing were often advised to move to New York city. This advice sometimes rankled with professionals elsewhere; so much so that one San Francisco Bay area editor's group produced a t-shirt printed with the slogan "We Don't Care How They Do It In New York." Today, beginning editors are far less likely to be gofer-ing in a smoke-begrimed, book-lined office in Manhattan than sitting at home in front of a computer, working for employers and clients who may be thousands of miles away. Some may work night shifts to liase with Corporate offices in EUrope or Asia.

These days too, social media platforms like Linkedin make it easy for editors to advertise their skills and services, network with professionals in related fields, and pursue opportunities advertised online. Organizations such as ACES and *Copyediting Magazine* (and Editors Canada for those north of the border) maintain job boards accessible to their members and subscribers.

Remember, when using online platforms to find work, that prospective

employers may search the Internet for more information about you. Check the

Privacy Settings on your social media accounts, and keep your public presence

dignified (and free of missspellings). If you don't want to use your real

name as part of your e-mail address or login name, choose an appropriately

professional alternative moniker.

Despite advances in technology, some of the traditional advice for

seeking publishing work still holds. Go to the Public Library and look at the

most recent edition of *Literary Marketplace* (*LMP*, published by Information

Today, Inc.)—or, when you have a block of time available do some research,

purchase a week's subscription to the online edition at ww.literarymarketplace

.com. Turn to the subject index and notice how many different kinds of book

publishers there are, not just fiction and nonfiction but el-hi (elementary and

high school) and college textbook publishers, legal and medical publishers,

science and math publishers, foreign language publishers, and publishers

of children's books, art books, scholarly books, wilderness books, computer

books, gardening books, cook books, and every stripe of how-to-books. Even as

brick-and mortar bookstores are reportedly vanishing from the landscape, book

sales are thriving.

Turn to the full entries for each publisher that catches your eye and

take note of how many titles the company publishes. A company that produces fewer than eight or ten titles a year is most likely a two-or-three-person operation, staffed by it's owners. But the names of any larger publishers should go on your job hunting list.

While you're at the library, you might also also look at the current edition of *Writer's Market* (Writers Digest Books). You'll be surprised to see how large the universe of magazine publishers is. There are hundreds of small trade magazines, and hundreds of local and regional magazines. Aspirating scholarly editors might check out the annual *Association of Univeristy Presses directory*.

As you're compiling your list, don't forget the corporate sector. The obvious employers in the corporate sector are retail companies that produce print and online catalogues and other promotional materials, but many firms whose primary business lie elsewhere do an enormous amount of publishing: banks, law firms, phone companies, hospitals, universities, museums, manufactures of high tech equipment, and consulting firms in all fields. Any business that provides client manuals, documents, or reports, or that produces a newsletter for employees or for clients needs editors. Many companies do not advertise, but list their openings on their Web sites.

Finally, there's the government sector. Hordes of editors are employed in almost every department of municipal, county, state, and federal goverments. Some of these positions require subject-matter expertise, but others do not. Check with nearby government offices to find out whether you need to take a Civil Service Exam and how openings are posted.

In all four sectors, there is stiff competition for entry-level jobs. To improve your chances of landing a job, whether shortterm or permanent:

1. Follow the employer's directions for submitting an application. Candidates who fail to do so are often wedded out immediately: Don't be one of them! If the application process requires a résumé and cover letter, make sure these are easy to read, error free, and have a consistent editorial style (punctuation, treatment of dates, use of abbreviations, etc). Tailor these documents to the job at hand incorporating key terms from the job description and stated requirements. Don't just list your previous job titles— take a sentence or two to describe what you did in those positions. Be sure to include any relevant subject-matter expertise and auxiliary skills (such as graphic design, or ebook production).

2. Don't dwell on your writing skills (unless the job callls for writing— most managing editors believe there is little or no correlation between writing skills and editing skills. And don't dwell on your academic credentials unless you're applying to a scholarly press or journal.

3. If you have work samples, prepare a portfolio, which may include published books or articles and screen shots of online material. (Be sure that none of these samples violate Non-Disclosure Agreements signed with previous employers or clients.) Include a description of the work you did on each project.

4. Be prepared to take proofeading, copyediting, and other proficiency tests. If you are invited for an interview, present yourself professionally. If it's a skype interview, remove any distracting items including kittens, from the background.

¶ Numbers and Numerals

EXERCISE 7-1: Numbers and Numerals in Nontechnical Text

Copyedit these sentences following the conventions that apply to nontechnical text, as described in *The Copyeditor's Handbook,* chapter 7.

1. The mortgage loans in default range from $35 to $500,000.

2. For more information, see Degas's article in volume xlii of the *Journal of Higher Studies.*

3. From 1991–1994, the town's population increased by ten percent.

4. The new fighter planes cost $.25 billion each.

5. The insurance surcharge is $.75 for twenty-five-dollars' coverage, $1.40 for $25–50, and $1.80 for $50–100.

6. The atmosphere weighs 5,700,000,000,000,000 tons.

7. The sales data for the 3d quarter of '94 are presented on pages 113–5, 300–8, and 201–09.

8. Amendments 1 through 10 of the Constitution are known as the Bill of Rights.

9. The vote in the Electoral College was 185 to 184 in 1876.

10. 2008 is a year most investors would like to forget.

11. Using Carbon-14 dating, scientists have determined that the Hopewell earthworks first appeared in Southern Ohio in about 100 B.C, and that the last elaborate valley earthwork was constructed in about 550 AD.

12. The burial mounds on the Hopewell farm range from 160 to 470 feet (48 to 141 km.) in length and from 20 to 32 feet (6 to 10 m) in height.

13. Alexander the Third of Macedon Alexander the Great was born in 356 B.C.E. and ruled 336–24 BP.

15. With a number of camera phones now boasting resolutions in the range of 16-20 megapixies (MP), it's hard to recall the days, only 10 years ago, when the technology writer for the *New York Times* assured readers that a resolution of 5 or 6MP was more than enough. But he had a point: larger images require more storage space, and many phone users find that 64-Gb SSD's soon fill up with selfies.

16. Between 25%–30% of students complained that the 2nd-year chemistry course was too hard.

17. Google's name is reportedly derived from mistyping *googol,* which is the number 10^{100} (the numeral 1 followed by 100 0s).

18. The small New Zealand town of Kaitangata, located at 46°16' S 169°51' East, became famous in July of 2016 when international media outlets incorrectly reported that it was offering free housing worth up to NZD230K (then worth approximately U.S. $160K or £130) to new immigrants.

19. To calculate the shrinkage rate of your fabric, measure before and after washing, subtract the finished dimensions from the original dimensions, and divide the results by the original dimensions. If your sample measured 10 × 10 inches before washing and 9 × 8 inches afterward, the shrinkage in width is 10 percent (10 − 9 = 1, and 1 ÷ 10 = 0.1, or 10 percent), and the shrinkage in length is 8 percent.

20. In a questionnaire on the probability of a bioterrorist attack, 29 respondents suggested at least a 75% likelihood, on a scale from 0 to 100 percent, that there would be an attack causing at least one hundred people to fall ill.

EXERCISE 7-2: Numbers and Numerals in Technical Text

The following economic summary will appear in an informal in-house report distributed to the seven people who work at the international trading desk. Copyedit these sentences following the conventions that apply to technical text as described in *The Copyeditor's Handbook*, chapter 7.

Bobonia's economy contracted sharply in the 2d quarter. Exports declined

by 14.5%, the worst monthly performance in 12 and a half years. Electronic

manufacturers were particularly hard hit. Imports, however, continued to rise,

which plunged the trade deficit to $1.25 billion. This deficit is likely to worsen

before it improves and the revised government forecast calls for it to reach

$1.75 billion by late Fall.

Domestically, inflation remains almost nonexistent, at an annual rate

of only 1%. Unemployment rates--6.5% in June, compared to 6.8% in March--

also continued to move lower. On the good news, consumer confidence

measured by the Univeristy of Bobonia National Feelgood Scale rose from

105.5 in March to 109 in June.

Short-term interest rates were unchanged: the overnight rate is 5.25%,

and the average yield on 30-year government notes is 5.35%.

The currency has strengthened since mid-March when the Bobonian

Bobble traded at 5.4550 to the U.S. dollar. On June 30, the Bobble closed at

5.580 to the dollar on the London Worthless Currency exchange.

EXERCISE 7-3: Editing a Recipe

Cookbooks make up a prominent segment of the print publishing market, and foodie websites and blogs offer a vast selection of free recipes. Copyeditors may also encounter recipes in corporate and community newsletters, health publications, memoirs, and even works of fiction.

Today, most professionally published recipes conform to a fairly standard format, consisting of a list of ingredients followed by instructions. Beyond that, style preferences vary by author, publisher, and region: hence a recipe for a Mexican-style stew may call for chile, chili, or chilli peppers, and quantities may be expressed in units of volume, weight, or a combination of the two. Some recipe instructions are chatty, some terse.

Regardless of these differences, every recipe should include a complete list of ingredients, and the instructions should clearly describe the preparation and use of every ingredient listed and all the steps in preparing the recipe.

The following holiday cookie recipe has been transcribed from a handwritten family collection (see photo). Convert this sometimes telegraphic recipe into a more modern, user-friendly style, first listing ingredients in the order they are used and then providing instructions. Follow the guidelines in *The Copyeditor's Handbook,* chapter 7, for styling numbers in technical documents. (You may also find it helpful to consult the discussion of abbreviations in chapter 9.) Since Aunt May is not in a position to respond to questions about her recipe, don't query; use your judgment.

For additional guidance, consult any popular cooking reference, such as a classic cookbook like *Joy of Cooking,* the Epicurious website, or the cooking section of a major news outlet. Aspiring food editors might also peruse *The Recipe Writer's Handbook,* by Barbara Gibbs Ostmann and Jane L. Baker, or *Will Write for Food,* by Dianne Jacob.

Metric conversions and some ingredient substitutions have been supplied; style them consistently. Teaspoons and tablespoons do not need to be converted to metric units. (For the record, a teaspoon is equivalent to approximately 5 milliliters and a tablespoon to 15 milliliters.)

Modern recipes generally specify the quantity or number of portions a recipe yields; this one does not (because the recipe tester had eaten a number of the cookies before remembering to count). Feel free to test the recipe and add this information.

A family recipe.

Frosted Chocolate Logs

(This recipe comes from my mother's older sister, my aunt May), who was a

great cook)

Cream:

1 c. margarine (about 220 grams), or you can use butter

2 square (2 oz., 55g) melted unsweetened baking chocolate or extra-dark

bittersweet chocolate

3/4 c. (150 gm) sugar

1 egg

1 Tbsp vanilla

Sift together & add:

3 c. flour (350 grams)

1 teaspoon salt

1 tsp baking soda

Try to handle as little as possible, if too sticky chill 1/2 hour if too dry add

1/2T to 1T more vanilla. Roll into 1/2" (1 1/4 cm) thick rolls and cut into 2" (5

cm) lengths to form logs.

Bake on greased sheets at 350°F (180C) 10 min. Cool and frost.

Frosting:

To 1 cup (110g) powdered sugar very slowly add milk, stirring until the mixture

is thick but spreadable. Cover top of each log with frosting. Dip frosted surface

into 1 c. finely chopped or grated nuts or coconut.

❡ Quotations

EXERCISE 8-1: Quotations

Copyedit the following passages for punctuation and syntactic fit, discussed under "Punctuation of Quotations" and "Syntactical Fit" in *The Copyeditor's Handbook,* chapter 8. Query as necessary about accuracy and appropriate attribution.

1. Einstein said, God doesn't play dice with the world.

2. Einstein also said to "Never wear a plait shirt with striped pants."

3. In her entertaining account of working as an editor at the *New Yorker*, Mary Norris describes learning to exercise restraint when reviewing the prose of some of the magazine's most famous contributors: "When Pauline Kael typed 'prevert' instead of 'pervert,' she meant "prevert" (unless she was reviewing something by Jacques Prévert)" ("Holy Writ: Learning to Love the House Style",*New Yorker*, Feb 23 and March 2, 2015).

4. In another *New Yorker* piece, an unflattering review of Lynne Truss' *Eats, Shoots and Leaves,* Louis Menand comments on the common punctuation errors that Truss finds maddening: "When deli owners put up signs that read " 'Iced' Tea," the single quotation marks are intended to add extraliterary significance to the message, as if they were the grammatical equivalent of red ink". "Bad Comma," *New Yorker*, June 28, 2004.

5. Will the Middle French motto "Honi soit qui mal y pense" (roughly translated as, "Shame on anyone who thinks evil of it") be removed from British passports after 'Brexit'?

6. As Michael Ignatieff has observed, "Samuel Beckett's 'Fail again. Fail better' captures the inner obstinacy necessary to the political art" ("Getting Iraq Wrong," *New York Times*, August 5, 2007).

You are being asked to do a light copyedit on the following short piece, which is to appear in a consumer newsletter. Prepare a style sheet.

Every month the It's Our Money Institute in New York city publishes a list of particularly outrageous, ironic or ridiculous wastes of tax-payers taxes. Here are some of last years winners:

The Economic Developement gave Bedord, Indiana $.7 million dollars to build a model of the pyramid of Cheops and a 800-feet replica of The Great Wall of China to "attract tourists and "demonstrate the value of limestone in the building industry".

The National Science Foundation spends $14,4012 to test the affects of inflation on the behavior of rats and pigeons. The studies' conclusions: when given a choice animal "consumers" opt for cheaper goods, just as people do.

The Federal Highway Administration broke the record for cost over-runs on a civilian project. The Intestate Highway System now cost $ 100,300 million or 267% of what congress originally approved, due to inflation, delay, and mismanagment.

The Department of Agriculture spent fourty-thousand dollars on a year-long study of food preferences and popular stereotypes. Results ? The public sees fast-food-addicts as patriotic, conservative, and hard workers. Vegetarians are intellectual and creative, gourmets like small families, mixed doubles in tennis, and "live in the fast lane" The

National Endowment For the Arts granted $7,000 for a sound and light show to make Wisconsins' state capital building in Milwaukee "send forth human and planetary energies in a massage of world peace.' The one performance was marred when half the lights failed to work and the recorded broadcast from the dome was illegible.

The U. S. Army's Materiel Development and Readyness Command (DARCON) spent $38 million and 13 years to develop a new gas mask, the XM30, that usually malfunctions within 48 hours. The Army's training and Doctrine Command found the XM-30s generally inferior to the 17-year old M17AL mask it was designed to replace.

The Defense Department paid #13,000 to test the possible side-effects of extremely-low-frequency radio waves on a hereford bull named Sylvester. After 6 years, Sylvestre was autopsied and judged "essentially a normal bull though somewhat obese." A Navy Vice Admiral admitted that the experiment has no value due "to the limited size of the sample data base."

CHAPTER 9

¶ Abbreviations and Symbols

EXERCISE 9-1: Medical Language: Abbreviations and Symbols

This manuscript is the opening section of a magazine article prepared by an experienced writer. It is based on an excerpt from Diane Johnson, "Doctor Talk," in *The State of the Language,* edited by Leonard Michaels and Christopher Ricks (Berkeley: University of California Press, 1980), pp. 396–98, and is used with permission of the publisher. For purposes of the exercise, errors were introduced and other changes were made to the published text.

Read about the treatment of abbreviations and symbols in *The Copyeditor's Handbook,* chapter 9. Then do a light copyedit, one that respects the author's distinctive style, and prepare a style sheet.

Until recent times, doctors spoke a magic language, usually Latin, and mystery

was part of your cure. But ~~modren~~ *modern* doctors are rather in the situation of

modern priests; having lost their magic language, they run the risk of losing

the magic powers too.

    For us, this means that the doctor may lose his ability to heal us by

our faith; and doctors, sensing powerlessness, have been casting about for new

languages in which to conceal the nature of our afflictions and the ingredients

of their cures. They have devised two dialects, but neither seems ~~quiet~~ *quite* to

serve for every purpose. For this is a time of transtion and trial for them,

marked by various strategies, of which the well known illegible handwriting on

your prescription is but one. For doctors themselves seem to have lost faith too, in themsevles and in the old mysteries and arts. They have been taught

to think of themselves as scientists, and so it is first of all to the language of

science they they turn, to control, and confuse us.

Most of the time scientific language can do this perfectly. We are

terrified, of course, to learn that we have "prolapse of the mitral valve", we

promise to take our medicine and stay on our diet, even though these words

describe a usually innocous finding in the investigation of an innocent heart

murmur. Or we can be lulled into a false sense of security when the doctor

avoids a scientific term: "You have a little spot on your lung", even when what

he puts on the chart is "probable bronchogenic carcinoma."

With patients, doctors can use either scientific or vernacular speech,

but with each other they speak science, a strange argot of Latin terms, new

words, and acronyms, that yearly becomes farther removed from everyday

speech and is sometimes comprised almost entirely of numbers and letter:

"His pO_2 is 45; pCO_2, 40; and pH 7.4.' Sometimes it is made up of peculiar

verbs originating from the apparatus with which they treat people: "well,

we've bronched him, tubed him, bagged him, cathed him, and PEEPed him"

the intern tells the attending physician. ("We've explored his airways with

a bronchoscope, inserted an endotrachial tube, positioned a cathater in his

bladder to monitor his urinary output, provided assisted ventilation with

a resuscitation bag, and used positive end-expiratory pressure to improve

oxygenation.") Even when discussing things that can be expressed in ordinary words, doctors will prefer to say "he had a pneumonectomy," to saying "he had

a lung removed."

One physician remembers being systematically instructed,

during the fifties, in scientific-sounding euphemisms to be used in the

presence of patients. If a party of interns were examining an alcoholic

patient, the wondering victim might hear them say he was "suffering from

hyperingestation of ethanol." In front of a cancer patient they would discuss

his "mitosis." But in recent years such discussions are not conducted in

front of the patient at all, because, since Sputnik, laymen's understanding

of scientific language has increased so greatly, that widespread ignorance

cannot be assumed.

Space exploration has had its influence, especially on the *sound* of

medical language. A CAT-scanner (computerized automated tomography),

de rigueur in an up-to-date diagnostic unit, might be something to look at

the surface of Mars with. The resonance of physical rather than biological

science has doubtless been fostered by doctors themselves, who, mindful of

the extent to which their science is really luck and art, would like to sound

microscopically precise, calculable and exact, even if they cannot. Acronyms

and abbreviations play the same part in medical language that they do in other

walks of modern life. We might be irritated to read on our chart "that this SOB

patient complained of DOE five days PTA." (It means: "this Short Of Breath

patient complained of Dyspnea on Exertion five days Prior To Admisssion.") To

translate certain syllables, the doctor must have yet more esoteric information.
Doctor A, reading Doctor B.'s note that a patient has TTP, must know whether
Dr. B is a hematologist or a chest specialist in order to know whether the
patient has thrombotic thrombocytopenic purpura, or traumatic tension
pnuemothorax. That pert little ID means identification to us, but Intradermal
to the dermatologist, Inside Diameter to the physiologist, and Infective Dose to
the bacteriologist.

But sometimes doctors must speak vernacular English, but this
is apparently difficult for them. People are always being told to discuss
their problem with their doctor, which, considering the general inability of
doctors to reply except in a given number of reliable phrases, must be some
of the worse advice ever given. Most people, trying to talk to the doctor--
trying to pry or to wrest meaning from his evasive remarks ("I'd say you're
coming along just fine.")--have been maddened by the vague and slightly
inconsequential nature of statements which, meaning everything to you,
ought in themselves to have meaning but do not, are noncommittal, or
unengaged, have a slightly rote or rehearsed quality, sometimes a slight
inappropriateness in the context ("it's nothing to worry about really").
This is the doctor's alternative dialect, phrases so general and bland as to
communicate virtually nothing.

This dialect originates from the emotional situation of the doctor.
In the way passers-by avert their eyes from the drunk in the gutter or the

village idiot, so the doctor must avoid the personality, the individuality, any involvement with the destiny, of his patients. He must not let himself think and feel with them. In order to retain objective professional judgment, the doctor has long since learned to withdraw his emotions from the plight of the patient.

EXERCISE 9-2: A Travel Guide: More Abbreviations and Symbols

Edit the following excerpt from a travel guide produced by Bobonia Tours, with partic-ular attention to clear and consistent treatment of abbreviations and symbols. You may wish to follow a standard style manual, model your style on that of a published travel guide, or set your own style. (Note that the popular travel publishers Lonely Planet and Rough Guides are based in Australia and the United Kingdom, respectively.) Record your decisions on a style sheet.

Outdoor Activities in Bobonia

Although tiny, remote, and seemingly preoccupied with financial affairs,

outdoor opportunities in Bobonia are surprisingly rich. Bobonians are a happy,

outgoing people, happy to share their knowledge of mountain trails, fishing

spots, and safe swimming beaches. Many of these lie only a short drive or bus

ride from the center of Bobonia City. Here are a few things to know before you

head out.

Weather

Because of its temperate latitude (42–44 deg N) and maritime climate,

Bobonia enjoys mild weather most of the year. Summer high temperatures

rarely exceed 30°C (86°F), and winter temperatures rarely drop below freezing,

except in the highest peaks of the Caringian Mountains. Even so, conditions

can change rapidly: hikers and boatmen should be prepared for high winds

(gales exceeding 50 mph are not unusual) and heavy rain, especially above altitudes of 1000 m (3,300 ft/). Weather forecasts are provided hourly on

Radio Bobonia FM (99.5 Mhz) and online at www.bobweather.bo.

Transportation

and so on,

Car rental agencies like Hertz, Avis, ~~etc.~~, have branches at Casimir Bobon

Airport, however taking the bus may be a safer and more relaxing option

for visitors unfamiliar with Bobonian road conditions. Drivers should keep

in mind that Bobonia City imposes heavy congestion charges at peak traffic

pm

times (7:30–9:30 am and 4–6:00 ~~p.m.~~), collected by means of an electronic

#

transponder (ETP).Within the city, a single-ride bus ticket costs 10 bobbles

(BB); children under five ride free. A 10-ride pass is available for BB80. For

destinations outside the city, fares range 15–65 BB, depending on distance.

Bus schedules are available on the Bobonian Transportation Dept website

(www.bobtrans.bo//bus).

such as Uber

Ride services, ~~e.g., Uber~~ and Lyft, are banned in Bobonia, but

hitchhiking is common. Riders are expected to contribute a couple of BB

toward the cost of a long trip. (N.B. Hitch at your own risk. This guide does not

recommend hitchhiking).

Cycling is a popular way of getting around in Bobonia. You can rent a

mountain bike at City Sports (34 Casimir Ave, ph. 32345) for BB150/day.

Visiting Caringia National Park

Only 45 *a* min) drive *#* from central Bobonia City, this jewel of a park is well worth

a visit. Trek up the steep slopes of 2100-m Mt Casimir (6,900 ft)) and view the

turquoise waters of Caldera Lake, or follow the forested Casimir Circle trail

around the lower slopes of the volcano and catch a glimpse of the brilliantly

colored Vermilion-Winged Caringian Parrot. A full circuit takes 10 to 14 hours

(most hikers spend a night at the hut on the NE side of the mountain) and

requires crossing the sometimes-turbulent Caringia river, but many shorter

hikes are possible. See the excellent park map issued by the Bobonian

Department of Conservation (BobDoc). A wheelchair and stroller-accessible

trail starts from the visitor's center at the main park entrance and winds along

the creek for about a mi.) and a Bobdoc ranger leads interpretive walks along

this trail at 11:30 *am* and 2:30 *PM* daily.

   To get to the park from Central Square, follow the red signs for

highway 2 *N* ~~north~~ or take bus #3 which runs every hour from the stop outside

the Bobonia Global Bank.

CHAPTER 10

¶ Tables, Graphs, and Art

EXERCISE 10-1: Editing Tables

A table provides information—often numerical information—in a form that is more efficient than a prose description. A relatively simple table can usually be edited by following the guidelines in *The Copyeditor's Handbook,* chapter 10, or *Chicago:* checking the numbering and location of the table in the manuscript; imposing mechanical consistency; verifying that any required source attributions are provided; and flagging an unusually small or large table for restructuring.

In addition, an editor should scan the table for internal inconsistencies. In the following table, you should spot six items to query or correct even if you have no idea what "present value" means.

TABLE 20. Present Value of One Dollar			
Year	5%	6%	8%	9
1	0.952	0.943	.0926	0.917
2	0.907	0.890	0.857	0.842
3	0.864	0.840	0.794	0.772
3	0.823	0.592	0.735	0.708
5	0.784	0.747	0.681	0.65

EXERCISE 10-2: Restructuring Tables

Sometimes authors have difficulty constructing tables that tell their story effectively. A table may present information that can be conveyed more directly in a brief prose statement or a simple multicolumn list. Conversely, a table may present altogether too much information or may not format data clearly. An odd-size table—one that is exceptionally long or wide or includes odd-size columns—may not fit on a printed page or in a designated digital environment or may be difficult to read.

The following three tables present data about various degree recipients at Utopia University. How is a reader to compare the numbers for the different degree-granting departments without getting whiplash? Suggest a way to combine tables 21, 22, and 23 into one table (to be labeled table A).

TABLE 21. Department of History, Degree Recipients, 1993–1995

	Bachelor's Degree	Master's Degree	Doctoral Degree
1993	456	87	5
1994	778	95	8
1995	892	106	12

Source: Office of the President, Utopia University Data Profile, 1995, p. 13.

TABLE 22. Department of English, Degree Recipients,
1993–1995

	Bachelor's Degree*	Master's Degree	Doctoral Degree
1993	745	47	9
1994	798	52	11
1995	695	65	9

Source: Office of the President, *Utopia University Data Profile,* 1995, p. 15.

*Does not include students in the dual-major program.

TABLE 23. Department of Psychology, Degree Recipients,
1993–1995

	Bachelor's Degree	Master's Degree	Doctoral Degree
1993	275	32	4
1994	298	29	7
1995	302	30	9

Source: Office of the President, *Utopia University Data Profile,* 1995, p. 18.

EXERCISE 10-3:   Editing More Complex Tables

The following table, reporting fatal automobile crashes resulting from distracted driving, is adapted from a report by the US National Highway Traffic Safety Administration. For the purposes of this exercise, errors have been introduced. The table includes multiple levels of column headings (spanner heads) and notes. Copyedit the table for consistent treatment of headings and numbers. Query any missing or odd-looking information.

Adding queries and tracked changes to a table may lead to untidy-looking line breaks and asymmetries in the table cells. You may want to reassure the author that these are temporary or to provide a copy of the edited table with changes accepted, to approximate the final appearance. In addition, if the table will be professionally typeset, you may want to remind the author that final choices about its design—including orientation, type size, placement and weight of grid lines and shading, and choice of fonts—will be made during page layout.

TABLE 2.

Drivers Involved in Fatal Crashes by Age, Distraction, and Cell Phone Use

Age group	Total Drivers		Distracted drivers			Drivers Using Cell Phones		
	Number	% of Total Drivers	Number	% of Total Drivers	% of distracted drivers	Number	% of distracted drivers	% of Cell Phone Drivers
15-19	3, 181	7	290	9%	9%	64	22%	14%
20-30	11428	24	891	8%	27%	151	17%	33%
30-39	8,479	17	612	7&	19%	101	17%	2%
50-59	7,785	16	376	5%	12%	50	13%	11%
60-69	5,012	10	275	5%	8%	15	5%	3%
70+	4,255	9	287	7%	9%	12	4%	3%
Total	48613	100	3,263	7%	100%	456	14%	100%[a]

Source: National Center for Statistics and Analysis, *Distracted Driving 2015*, Traffic Safety Facts Research Note, Report No. DOT HS 812 381 (Washington, DC: National Highway Traffic Safety Administration, March 2017), available online at http://www.nhtsa.gov/sites/nhtsa.dot.gov/files/documents/812_381_distracteddriving2015.pdf.

[a]The total includes sixty drivers 14 and younger, 6 of whom were noted as distracted. The total also includes 973 drivers of unknown age, 44 of these were noted as distracted.

EXERCISE 10-4:   Editing Graphs

The following column graph is based on the same data as the table in exercise 10-3. Addressing queries and instructions to a hypothetical author who will provide the final version of the graph, copyedit the caption, legend, and axis labels for correctness and consistency. Because the graph is a JPEG image, text within the image frame cannot be edited directly. Either print out a copy to mark up by hand, or list changes and queries in a logical fashion below the graph.

Figure 1. Percentage Distribution Of Drivers Involved In Fatal Crashes by age, distraction, and cell-phone use, 2015.

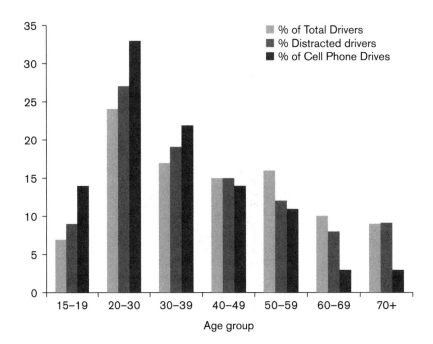

Source: Adapted from National Center for Statistics and Analysis, *Distracted Driving 2015,* Traffic Safety Facts Research Note, Report No. DOT HS 812 381 (Washington: National Highway Traffic Safety Administration, 3/17), available online at http://www.nhtsa.gov/sites/nhtsa.dot.gov/files/documents/812_381_ distracteddriving2015.pdf.

¶ References

EXERCISE 11-1: Editing Author-Date References

Using these sample formats, copyedit the following portion of an author-date reference list as described in *The Copyeditor's Handbook,* chapter 11:

Book:

Surname, First name. Year. *Book Title: Book Subtitle.* City: Publisher. [Use traditional state abbreviations rather than postal abbreviations.]

Journal article:

Surname, First name. Year. "Article Title." *Journal Title* 1:123–35.

Multiple authors:

Surname, First, and First Surname. Year. . . .

Abben, Pilar. 1985. "A Modern Approach to Algebra," *Mathematical Monthly* 17: 55–68.

Adder, William and Mary. 1980. *Statistics in the Social Sciences.* Evanston Illinois: Schoolbooks Press, 1980.

Adder, William and Mary. *1982. How To Write Social Science Papers.* New York: Wise Owl.

Akmore, G. 1983, "A Study of the Affects of Peer Teaching in College Remedial Mathematic Courses." *American Mathematical Monthly* 18: 149–67.

Aiken, Lydia, ed., *Probelms in English Grammar.* Boston, Tiara Books.

Allen, Pattrick. 1993. *Composition for Beginnning ESL Students.* New York:

Language Laboratory

Allen, P. and Anita Zamorra, 1994. "Error Analysis in Quasi-Experimental

Designs." *Analytic Quarterly* 9:63–53.

Ammonds, Carolyn. 1794. *A Short Course in Speedwriting.* Santa Barbara,

Santa Luisa Community College.

Anderson, Vito. 1991. "A Response to President Clinton's Proposal for Head

Start." *Preschool Reporter* 15:1.

EXERCISE 11-2: Taming Citation Managers

Many writers use citation management applications, such as EndNote and Zotero, to keep track of their sources and to prepare notes, bibliographies, and reference lists. In addition, many online library catalogs (including WorldCat, a combined catalog of the holdings of thousands of libraries around the world) and other digital repositories provide ways for users to copy or export citations for inclusion in their own databases or documents. All these tools generally purport to be able to format the source information according to a range of accepted styles, but the results (so far) are often flawed, whether because the source information is not entered correctly, because the tools fail to parse the information correctly, or because the formatting they offer doesn't actually conform to the specified style. For the copyeditor, the results may mean a headache (or, more optimistically viewed, security of employment).

Applications and macro packages for tidying up citations are available, and a word processor's wildcard find-and-replace operations can speed up mechanical corrections considerably, but these tools cannot rectify missing or incorrect information, and, like citation management software, they require care in their use to ensure that no information is scrambled or deleted.

This exercise presents two short reference lists that have been exported from various applications and databases that offer APA and Chicago style as formatting options. Copyedit each one for full conformity with the desired style. (This is the real deal: no additional errors have been introduced into the individual citations for the purposes of this exercise.) Query any missing or potentially inaccurate information—or, if you wish, use the URLs supplied to verify information.

Even if you don't own *APA* or *Chicago,* you can find brief guides to their respective citation styles online. The freely accessible "Chicago-Style Citation Quick Guide" can be found at http://www.chicagomanualofstyle.org/. There is no APA equivalent, but several university websites offer simplified APA style guidelines. The Purdue Online Writing Lab's APA style page considerately provides a correctly formatted citation for itself: Paiz, J., Angeli, E., Wagner, J., Lawrick, E., Moore, K., Anderson, M., . . . Keck, R. (2010, May 5). *General format.* Retrieved from http://owl.english.purdue.edu/owl/resource/560/01/.

1. Copyedit the following reference list, for an article about chronic fatigue syndrome, for full conformity with APA style.

    Blood simple? (2016, September 1). *The Economist.* Retrieved

    from https://www.economist.com/news/science-and-

    technology/21706241-new-test-may-diagnose-mysterious-illness-

    and-also-help-explain-it-blood

Blood simple? - Chronic-fatigue syndrome. (n.d.). Retrieved

   February 14, 2018, from https://www.economist.com/news/

   science-and-technology/21706241-new-test-may-diagnose-

   mysterious-illness-and-also-help-explain-it-blood

Basu, N., Kaplan, C. M., Ichesco, E., Larkin, T., Harris, R. E.,

   Murray, A., . . . Clauw, D. J. (n.d.). Neurobiological features

   of fibromyalgia are also present among rheumatoid arthritis

   patients. *Arthritis & Rheumatology*, n/a-n/a. https://doi.

   org/10.1002/art.40451

In Engdahl, S. (2012). *Chronic fatigue syndrome.* Detroit:

   Greenhaven Press.

Ostrom, Neenyah. 50 things you should know about the chronic

   fatigue syndrome epidemic / Neenyah Ostrom. TNM ed. New

   York, N.Y. : St. Martin's Press, c1993.

Janse, A., Worm-Smeitink, M., Bleijenberg, G., Donders, R., &

   Knoop, H. (2018). Efficacy of web-based cognitive–behavioural

   therapy for chronic fatigue syndrome: randomised controlled

   trial. *The British Journal of Psychiatry*, 212(2), 112–118. https://

   doi.org/10.1192/bjp.2017.22

Wang, Y.-Y., Li, X.-X., Liu, J.-P., Luo, H., Ma, L.-X., & Alraek, T.

   (2014). Traditional Chinese medicine for chronic fatigue

   syndrome: A systematic review of randomized clinical trials.

Complementary Therapies in Medicine, 22(4), 826–833. https://

doi.org/10.1016/j.ctim.2014.06.004

2. Copyedit the following exported bibliography entries, for an essay about the novelist Teju Cole, for true conformity with basic Chicago style, as described in chapter 14 of *Chicago* (not the author-date style described in chapter 15).

Cole, Teju. 2012. *Open city: a novel.*

Cole, Teju. 2015. *Every day is for the thief.*

"Teju Cole on A House for Mr Biswas by VS Naipaul – a

Novel of Full-Bore Trinidadian Savvy | Books | The

Guardian." Accessed February 14, 2018. https://

www.theguardian.com/books/2016/feb/12/

teju-cole-vs-naipaul-a-house-for-mr-biswas-trinidad-novel.

Kakutani, Michiko. "'Open City' by Teju Cole - Review." The New

York Times, May 18, 2011, sec. Books. https://www.nytimes.

com/2011/05/19/books/open-city-by-teju-cole-book-review.

html.

EXERCISE 11-3: Editing Reference Notes

In the reference note system, typically used in humanities research, sources are identified in notes keyed to the running text by symbols or superscript numerals. The notes may be placed at the foot of the page (footnotes) or gathered at the end of the article, document, book chapter, or book (endnotes). If a manuscript includes a bibliography listing all the works cited in the notes, complete publication details are sometimes omitted in the notes in favor of shortened forms (author's surname, abridged title, and relevant page numbers), although some publishers and authors prefer that full details be supplied in the first note that mentions a source. A full bibliography, usually titled "Bibliography," may include additional works that the author has consulted but not cited in the notes; conversely, a carefully pruned "Selected Bibliography" may omit some sources cited in passing, provided full publication details are given in the notes.

The basic forms for reference notes and bibliographies in the humanities vary somewhat in different style manuals. Always ask your editorial coordinator or client author to specify a preferred style guide and the degree of tolerance for systematic departures from it in hybrid citation forms used in a given manuscript. Also ask whether you are required to verify or spot-check the accuracy of citations or to validate URLs: these responsibilities are not customary in traditional publishing but may be expected in nontraditional settings.

The following text is excerpted from Harvey Schwartz, "A Legacy of Activism: Dockworker Unionism in the San Francisco Bay Area" (unpublished manuscript), and is used by permission of the author. For the purposes of this exercise, changes and errors have been introduced. Do not edit the text; just peruse it for the provision of source attributions. Edit the notes and bibliography to conform to the applicable style outlined in *Chicago*. (If you don't have a copy of this manual or a subscription to the online edition, you can use the condensed guidelines in Kate L. Turabian, *A Manual for Writers of Research Papers, Theses, and Dissertations,* or consult the freely accessible "Chicago-Style Citation Quick Guide" at http://www.chicagomanualofstyle.org/.) For this assignment, provide full publication details in the first citation of each source in the notes. Follow the copyediting procedures described in *The Copyeditor's Handbook,* chapter 11, under "Reference Note System."

Founded in 1853, when the state of California was only three years old, the

Riggers and Stevedores Union Association was the first major representative

body for waterfront employees in the San Francisco Bay Area. In the era

of sailing vessels this union consisted of skilled ship riggers and seasoned

cargo handlers. Stevedore foremen often hired less experienced "men along the shore," or *longshoremen*, to physically work cargo. Between 1890 and

1910, as bigger steel ships replaced wooden vessels, cargo handling became

casual work. Eventually, the label *stevedore* came to refer to a cargo-moving

contractor or company; the label *longshoreman* (or *docker*) came to refer

to a hold worker or a dockworker. In those years of change, the Riggers and

Stevedores opened its membership, expelled contracting stevedores, and

became a more broadly based union.[1]

In 1901 the San Francisco longshoremen joined a major strike by the

City Front Federation, a coalition of wagon drivers, sailors, ship fitters, and

other waterfront workers. The strike began with a lockout of city teamsters

who were demanding union recognition and improved working conditions. The

strike had only limited success. But the violence against strikers that erupted

during the confrontation led directly to the creation of a Union Labor Party in

San Francisco. This independent third party successfully elected its candidate

to the office of mayor in late 1901 and reelected him in 1903 and 1905. The

Union Labor Party played a dominant role in San Francisco politics over the

next decade.[2]

1. Robert W. Cherny, "Longshorement of San Francisco Bay, 1849-1960," in *Dock Workers: International Exploration in Comparative Labour History, 1790-1970*, edited by Sam Davies et. al., Vol. I (Aldershot, England: Ashgate Publishers, 2000), 102-103, 120.

2. Robert Edward Lee Knight, *Industrial Relations in the San Francisco Bay Area, 1900-1918* (Berkeley and Los Angeles: University of California Press, 1960), pp. 72-93; Cherny, "Longshoremen," 120-121. See also Walton Bean, *Boss Ruef's San Francisco: The Story of the Union Labor Party, Big Business, and the Graft Prosecution* (Berkeley: University of California Press, 1968).

Elsewhere along the Pacific Coast, local groups of longshore workers forged a regional alliance during the early years of the twentieth century. By 1916 the dockworkers in all the major West Coast ports were affiliated nationally with the American Federation of Labor's International Longshoremen's Association (ILA) as an autonomous unit called the Pacific Coast District No. 38, ILA.[3] San Francisco's Riggers and Stevedore's Union had joined the ILA around 1900; it later left that organization but rejoined shortly before 1916. At the time, San Francisco was the biggest port along the West Coast, so San Francisco's membership was crucial to the unity of ILA District 38. The necessity of coastwide unity became clear in 1916, when, in the first major coastwide strike of Pacific Coast dockworkers, the 10,000 to 12,500 members of District 38 shut down all the West Coast's key ports from Bellingham, Washington, to San Diego, California. The district's main demands were for standard coastwide wages and working conditions and a closed shop, which would have required all employees to be ILA members.[4]

The 1916 strike was bitter and violent. On June 16, when the strike was just over two weeks old, Lewis A. Morey, an ILA member from Oakland, California, was shot and killed by an armed guard who was protecting

3. *The ILWU Story: Six Decades of Militant Unionism*, 2nd ed., text and research by Eugene Dennis Vrana, additional research by Harvey Schwartz, edited by Steve Stallone and Marcy Rein (San Francisco: ILWU, 2004), 3; Cherny, "Longshoremen," 122; Ronald Magden, *The Working Waterfront: The Story of Tacoma's Ships and Men* (Tacoma, Wash.: ILWU Local 23, 1982), 31.

4. Cherny, "Longshoremen," 120-123; Magden, *The Working Waterfront*, 31-33; Knight, *Industrial Relations*, 302.

strikebreakers. Two days later, Thomas Olsen, another ILA man, was shot

in the back on a San Francisco dock. He died immediately. Nearly a month

later, a strike committee member from Tacoma, Washington, was knifed when

he confronted two strikebreakers. Another Tacoma striker was killed when a

company guard fired his weapon into a crowd of longshoremen.[5]

In response to the strike, the San Francisco Chamber of Commerce

organized a Law and Order Committee to inflame anti-union sentiment among

business leaders and the general public. On July 17, San Francisco's more than

4,000 members negotiated a separate peace with employers because they

were worried about the possibility of an open shop campaign. (This campaign

materialized during the 1920s despite the San Francisco longshoremen's

efforts to prevent it.) They retained their union conditions, but they did not

win a closed shop or standard coastwide wages and conditions. With the San

Francisco longshoremen under contract, the shipowners were able to bleed

the rest of the coast workers into submission. The employers started by hiring

nonunion men. Soon it was obvious that the strike was lost. The ill feeling

aroused between groups of longshoremen following the experience of 1916

led to a split in the Pacific Coast longshoremen's ranks. After the strike, the

San Francisco longshoremen seceded from the ILA and assumed independent

status. Coastwide, all the ILA locals lost control of jobs on the docks except for

the longshoremen of the Port of Tacoma, who soon regained the union hiring

5. Magden, *The Working Waterfront*, 33-35; Knight, *Industrial Relations*, 303.

hall they had initially lost and who maintained it into the "nonunion" 1920s
and early 1930s.[6]

The independent San Francisco Riggers and Stevedores Union did
not last long. Reacting to heavier sling loads and a speeded-up work pace,
the union struck in 1919. This strike was doomed from the start. It coincided
with the emergence of a decade-long conservative open shop drive across the
entire United States. Anti-union organization and sentiment among employers
was intense. A minor faction of the San Francisco union's membership, which
was influenced by the radical Industrial Workers of the World (the IWW, or
"Wobblies"), persuaded the union to pass a resolution instructing R and S
negotiators to demand stock ownership in steamship companies and seats
on the shipowners' boards of directors. The R and S negotiators did not push
these radical demands, but the employers used them against the union.
Instead of gaining their goals, the San Francisco longshoremen, alone and
without coastwide waterfront allies, were utterly defeated. One union man was
killed during this showdown. The union was destroyed when the employers
replaced it with another, ostensibly independent, organization that in reality
functioned like a "company union."[7]

6. Magden, *The Working Waterfront*, 35-37; Knight, *Industrial Relations*, 304-305; Cherny,
"Longshoremen," 123, 133; Harvey Schwartz, *Solidarity Stories: An Oral History of the ILWU*
(Seattle, WA: University of Washington Press, 2009), 127-128.

7. Cherny, "Longshoremen," 124-127. See also Mary Joy Renfro, "The Decline and Fall of the
San Francisco Riggers and Stevedores Union: A History of the Years 1916 to 1919," senior thesis,
San Francisco State University, 1995, in Labor Archives and Research Center, San Francisco State
University.

This new employer-backed group was officially called the
Longshoremen's Association of San Francisco and the Bay District. Its chief
officer, Jack Bryan, had longshoring experience, but his organization existed to
thwart worker-controlled unionism. The new Association issued a membership
book with a blue cover to distinguish it from the red membership book of the
old Riggers and Stevedores Union. During the company union's heyday, 1919
through 1933, the organization was known on the waterfront simply as "the
Blue Book." Workers had to pay dues and maintain Blue Book membership just
to qualify for waterfront jobs. But membership conferred no real benefits, such
as union representation.[8]

Corrupt hiring practices and inhumane working conditions prevailed
in the Blue Book era. In San Francisco, workers were forced to stand in a
"shape-up" on the waterfront early each morning in order to get employment,
even if they belonged to a regular work gang. Harry Renton Bridges, the future
union leader, stood among them. The San Francisco longshoreman vividly
recalled this shape-up: "We were hired off the street like a bunch of sheep
standing there from six o'clock in the morning in all kinds of weather." To get a
job, workers often had to bribe the hiring bosses with money, alcohol, or other
favors. Henry Gaitan, a longshoreman in the equally corrupt hiring system at

8. David Selvin, *A Terrible Anger: The 1934 Waterfront and General Strikes in San Francisco*
(Detroit: Wayne State University Press, 1996), 44-45; Bruce Nelson, *Workers on the Waterfront:*
Seamen, Longshoremen, and Unionism in the 1930s (Urbana: University of Illinois Press, 1988), 53;
Schwartz, *Solidarity Stories*, 11; Cherny, "Longshoremen," 126-127.

the Port of Los Angeles, later attested that "if you had a nice-looking sister, and liquor, and a wife that would put out, you'd have a job. I seen it here on these docks before we had the [real] union."[9,10]

Those fortunate enough to be hired found that the work was fast-paced and dangerous. The Port of San Francisco was known for its high productivity—but also for an extremely high rate of injury.[11] Bosses raced gangs of longshoremen against each other in an effort to increase the speed of work, at times using ethnic rivalries to provoke such competitions: a predominantly German work gang, for example, would be set against a gang of longshoremen of Portuguese or Italian background. Harry Bridges himself was injured on the job in 1929. In those days, he remembered, injured longshoremen rarely applied for workmen's compensation because they feared being blacklisted by the employers, who were charged by the state for accident claims. Fatigue from long hours of heavy labor with few or no work breaks also contributed to the high injury rate during the nonunion years. Work shifts of twelve, sixteen, and more hours were well known on the San Francisco waterfront.[12]

9. Bridges quoted in Charles P. Larrowe, *Harry Bridges: The Rise and Fall of Radical Labor in the United States*, 2d ed. rev. (Westport, CT: Lawrence Hill, 1977), 8. See also Cherny, "Longshoremen," 103-104, 133.

10. Unpublished Gaitan interview with Daniel S. Beagle and David Wellman, 14 May, 1983, in the ILWU Oral History Collection, Anne Rand Research Library, International Longshore and Warehouse Union, San Francisco.

11. Harvey Schwartz, *Building the Golden Gate Bridge: A Workers' Oral History* (Seattle: University of Washington Press, 2015).

12. Schwartz, *Solidarity Stories*, 12-13; Cherny, "Longshoremen," 106, 111, 133; *The ILWU Story*, 3.

BIBLIOGRAPHY

Afrasiabi, Peter. *Burning Bridges: America's 20-Year Crusade to Deport Labor Leader Harry Bridges.* Brooklyn, NY: Thirlmere Books, 2016.

Cherny, Robert W. "Longshoremen of San Francisco Bay, 1849-1960." In *Dock Workers: International Exploration in Comparative Labour History, 1790-1970,* vol. 1, edited by Sam Davies et al., 102-140. Aldershot, England: Ashgate Publishing, 2000.

Cole, Peter. *Dockworker Power: Race, Technology, and Unionism in Durban and the San Francisco Bay Area.* Champaign: University of Illinois Press, forthcoming in 2018.

Davies, Sam, et al., ed. *Dock Workers: International Exploration in Comparative Labour History, 1790-1970.* Vol. 1. Aldershot, England: Ashgate Publishing, 2000.

Kimeldorf, Howard. *Reds or Rackets? The Making of Radical and Conservative Unions on the Waterfront.* Berkeley: University of California Press, 1988.

The ILWU Story: Six Decades of Militant Unionism. 2nd ed. Text and research by Eugene Dennis Vrana. Additional research by Harvey Schwartz. Edited by Steve Stallone and Marcy Rein. San Francisco: ILWU, 2004.

Larrowe, Charles P. *Harry Bridges: The Rise and Fall of Radical Labor in the United States.* 2nd ed. rev. Westport, CT: Lawrence Hill, 1977.

Levinson, Marc. *The Box: How the Shipping Container Made the World Smaller and the World Economy Bigger*. Princeton, NJ: Princeton University Press, 2006.

Magden, Ronald. *The Working Waterfront: The Story of Tacoma's Ships and Men*. Tacoma, WA: ILWU Local 23, 1982.

Nelson, Bruce. *Workers on the Waterfront: Seamen, Longshoremen, and Unionism in the 1930s*. Urbana: University of Illinois Press, 1988.

Quin, Mike. *The Big Strike*. Olema, CA: Olema Publishing, 1949.

Schwartz, Harvey. "Harry Bridges and the Scholars: Looking at History's Verdict." *California History: The Magazine of the California Historical Society* 59, no. 1 (Spring 1980): 66-79.

_____. *The March Inland: Origins of the ILWU Warehouse Division, 1934-1938*. Los Angeles: Institute of Industrial Relations, University of California, 1978. Reprint, San Francisco: ILWU, 2000.

_____. *Solidarity Stories: An Oral History of the ILWU*. Seattle, WA: University of Washington Press, 2009.

Selvin, David. *A Terrible Anger: The 1934 Waterfront and General Strikes in San Francisco*. Detroit: Wayne State University Press, 1996.

Wellman, David. *The Union Makes Us Strong: Radical Unionism on the San Francisco Waterfront*. Cambridge: Cambridge University Press, 1995.

EXERCISE 11-4: Creating Author-Date Citations

Wouldn't you know it! The publisher has asked you to convert the reference system for exercise 11-3 to author-date format, which is typically used in the social and natural sciences. In the author-date system, sources are cited in the running text, usually in parentheses, with the author's surname, publication year, and applicable page numbers. Semicolons separate multiple sources cited together. (Discursive remarks that are sometimes appended to notes in a reference note system are not accommodated in the author-date system unless separate footnotes or endnotes are added solely for such commentary.) At the end of the document, an alphabetized reference list, usually titled "References" or "Works Cited," supplies complete publication details for the parenthetical references. Unlike a full bibliography in the humanities-style reference system, an author-date reference list omits works consulted but not cited.

Chicago, APA, and *CSE* all offer extensive guidance for in-text citations and reference lists, but these manuals differ somewhat in styling details. For this exercise, follow the models in *Chicago,* Kate L. Turabian's condensed *Chicago* guidelines in *A Manual for Writers of Research Papers, Theses, and Dissertations,* or the freely accessible "Chicago-Style Citation Quick Guide" at http://www.chicagomanualofstyle.org/. Refer to the copyediting procedures described in *The Copyeditor's Handbook,* chapter 11, under "Author-Date System."

CHAPTER 12

¶ Front and Back Matter

EXERCISE 12-1: Editing a Table of Contents

This exercise reviews the order of front and back matter and other elements of complex publications. Copyedit this table of contents for a collection of essays on the history of Western cartoon drawing. Place elements in a conventional order (see *The Copyeditor's Handbook*, chapter 12, or *Chicago*, chapter 1). Ensure that all comparable elements are styled consistently: where variations exist, select whichever you prefer. Correct or query any apparent errors.

Table of Contents: A history of Western Cartooning

Dedication   000

List of illlustrations   000

Contributors   000

Forward, *by Dorothy Dessin*   000

Preface 000

Acknowledgements   000

Introduction   000

Part I • The Early History of Cartoons   000

Chapter 1. The drawings of Lascaux: sacred representations or man-cave

comics?, *by Charlene Chauvet*

2. The Art of Iconic Caricature in European Incunabula, by *Sir Nicholas*

Nozalot   000

Part 2 • Cartoons and Mass Culture   000

Chapter 3. Political Cartoons in England in the Eighteenth Century, *by Barry*

Boswell   000

Chapter 4. Monikers of Midcentury Superheroes, *by Diana Kent*

Part 3 • Animation   000

Chapter 6: Mickey through the Decades: From Ratlike Rodent to Mellow Mouse,

by Donald D. Mintz

Chapter 5: Fred, Barney, and Bam-Bam: Representations of Masculinity in

Prehistoric Bedrock, by Wilma Wilkinson

Part 4: Serials   000

Chapter 7: *Dilbert* and Late-20th-century Workplace Culture, *by Adam Scott*

Chapter 8: Mouseover Messages: Tooltips and Subversion in *Xkcd, by Jane*

Curzon

Appendix A. Time Line of US Newspaper Cartoons

Footnotes

Index

Color plates follow pages 000 and 000

EXERCISE 12-2: Editing a Glossary

Edit the following portion of a glossary that will appear in a book for novice computer users:

- Check for correct alphabetization.
- Peruse entries for consistency of format and length.
- Style entries for capitalization, punctuation, typographic treatment of elements, and handling of multiple definitions and cross-references.
- Query the author if a definition requires rewriting.

See "Back Matter" in *The Copyeditor's Handbook,* chapter 12, for more information about editing and styling glossaries.

alphanumeric sorting. Sorting that treats numbers like letters so that words

with numbers and numbers of equal length can be sorted.

ASCII. Acronym for American Standard Code for Information Interchange,

one of the standard forms for representing characters so that files can be

shared between programs. A DOS Text File is in ASCII format.

backspace. A key on your keyboard which deletes the character to the left of

the cursor.

backup. To copy files for safe keeping.

bandwith. How fast of a computer network or connection can transfer data,

usually measured in bits per second, or bps.

bit. A *binary digit;* the smallest storage unit for data in a computer.

boot. To start a computer by loading the operating system into the computer's

memory.

byte. The amount of space needed to store a single character (number, letter

or code). 1024 bytes equals one kilobyte (Kb or K).

buffer. A temporary data storage area used by computers and some printers.

CHAPTER 13

¶ Markup

EXERCISE 13-1: Markup of Greeked Text

Markup—also sometimes referred to as typecoding, tagging, or styling—involves identifying structural elements of a manuscript that require distinguishing typographic treatment. When you are working on a real document, the content will affect your decisions about markup, especially decisions about the levels of heads. But as this exercise shows, markup is primarily a matter of recognizing and labeling visually distinctive elements.

Designers, typesetters, and printers use the term *Latin* for Latin-like nonsense serving as dummy text in design layouts and sample pages. This pseudo-Latin is sometimes referred to as *greeked text,* a term that makes no sense at all unless you can read Latin: the passage "might as well be Greek" to a Latinist because it is unintelligible. The use of a placeholder passage beginning with the words *lorem ipsum* traces back to the 1500s, when an unknown printer scrambled a Latin passage from Cicero to create a type specimen book. Variations of this muddled *lorem ipsum* text have been common in typesetting since the 1960s; it was popularized in the 1970s by advertisements for Letraset dry-transfer sheets and later used in demonstrations of Aldus Corporation's desktop publishing program PageMaker. Today many applications use pseudo-Latin in samples, and some can generate randomized *lorem ipsum* text—for example, Apple's Pages and Keynote, Google Docs, WordPress, and Microsoft Word.

Referring to the following set of codes, provide markup for this pseudo-Latin passage either by hand-marking a hard copy or by inserting typecodes, including end codes, in the digital document; regular text is the default in this exercise and does not have to be coded. If you are ready for a bigger challenge, use your word processor to define and apply styles. See *The Copyeditor's Handbook,* chapter 13, especially figures 14, 16, and 17, for a detailed discussion of typecodes, end codes, and styling, with examples of markup.

<CN>	chapter number	<NL>	numbered list
<CT>	chapter title	<BL>	bulleted list
<CST>	chapter subtitle	<MCL>	multicolumn list
<A>	A-level head	<EX>	extract
<B>	B-level head	<PX>	poetry extract
<UNL>	unnumbered list	<EQ>	equation

3   Quick Guide to Typecoding: It's All Greek to Me

Lorem ipsum dolor sit amet, con sectetuer adipiscing elit, sed dis nonummy

nibh euismod tincidunt ut laoreet dolore magna allquam:

- •   Lorem ipsum dolor sit amet.

- •   Con sectetuer adipiscing elit.

- •   Sed dis nonummy nibh euismod.

Aliquam erat voluptat. Ut wisi enim ad minim veniam, quis nostrud exerci

tation ullamcorper suscipit lobortis nisl ut aliquip ea commodo consequat:

Lorem ipsum dolor	Dolore magna ut
sit amet, con sect	aliquam erat ut
etuer adipiscing	voluptat ut wisi
elit, sed dis	enim ad minim ad
nonummy nibh.	veniam.

Lorem ipsum dolor sit amet, con sectetuer adipiscing elit.

Sed dis nonummy nibh euismod tincidunt ut laoreet dolore magna aliquam

erat voluptat. Ut wisi enim ad minim veniam, quis nostrud:

$\sum fx$ ffl $4y \geq 6$

Lorem ipsum dolor sit amet, con sectetuer adipiscing elit.

Sed dis nonummy nibh euismod tincidunt ut laoreet dolore magna aliquam erat voluptat:

> Lorem ipsum "dolor sit amet," con sectetuer adipiscing elit, sed dis nonummy nibh euismod tincidunt ut laoreet dolore magna aliquam erat voluptat.

Lorem ipsum dolor sit amet, con sectetuer adipiscing elit, sed dis nonummy nibh euismod:

1. Voluptat suscipit lobortis nisl.
2. Wisi enim dolore magna aliquam erat.
3. Ad minim veniam dis nonummy nibh.

Quis Nostrud Exerci

Tation ullamcorper suscipit lobortis nisi ut aliquip ea commodo consequat.

Lorem ipsum dolor sit amet, con sectetuer adipiscing.

EXERCISE 13-2: Markup of Instructional Text: A First-Aid Guide

The following exercise asks you to apply typecodes (or tags) to a set of instructions for performing cardiopulmonary resuscitation (CPR) and to edit the instructions for clarity, conciseness, logical flow, and consistency. Query any missing or apparently incorrect information. It's best to typecode and copyedit in separate passes through the text.

The instructions are intended as a quick reference guide for people without CPR training, to be disseminated both in print and online. (Note: the basic instructions given here for CPR compressions and rescue breathing are correct and consistent with international guidelines as of early 2018. Note too that the steps of assessing hazards, checking responsiveness, and seeking help are integral parts of emergency protocols. However, details of CPR protocols vary by location and issuing organization. This exercise draws on multiple protocols and is not intended as an actual guide for teaching or doing CPR.)

Typecode each element of this document by selecting from the following list of codes and placing an appropriate code at the beginning of each element. (No end codes are required.) Not all the codes listed may be needed. Don't worry about applying manual formatting, such as paragraph indentation, linespacing, or boldface; part of the point of typecodes is that they allow the designer or typesetter to make those choices and apply them consistently to the various elements. Do, however, ensure that all instances of each element are capitalized and punctuated consistently. Style subheads with headline-style capitalization. For numbers, follow the technical style discussed in chapter 7 of *The Copyeditor's Handbook*: use numerals for all two-digit numbers and for all units of measure.

For a greater challenge, if you're already familiar with the principles of markup or HTML tagging, try creating a set of codes for parts of this workbook or *The Copyeditor's Handbook*.

<TI>	document title
<H1>	level 1 subhead
<H2>	level 2 subhead
<H3>	level 3 subhead
<BL>	bulleted list item (tag each item in the list with the same code)
<NL>	numbered list item (tag each item in the list with the same code)
<SBTXT>	sidebar text
<FCAP>	figure caption
<TXT>	general text (for consecutive general text paragraphs, tag only the first paragraph; all text will be set flush left, with no paragraph indent)

How to do CPR

If you witness a cardiac arrest, it's crucial to call 999 and start CPR

immediately. Read this page to learn how to do CPR and watch our CPR

training video for a step-by-step demonstration. It is easy to learn and saves

lives.

To learn how to perform CPR, follow these simple six steps:

1. Assess dangers

2. Check responsiveness

2. Send for help

3. Check for normal breathing

4. Give 30 chest compressions

5. Give two rescue breaths

6. Repeat until an ambulance arrives

Remember-even if you haven't been trained in CPR with rescue

breathing, you can still use compression-only CPR.

CPR steps

To learn more about performing CPR in an emergency, read the rest of this

page and watch our CPR training video.

If you come across someone who is unconscious, always check for

danger and look for risks before you start helping. Especially traffic, fire, or

electrical hazards.

Step 1. Check Responsiveness

Check for a response. Gently shake the person's shoulders and ask loudly 'are you alright?' or "can you hear me?" Someone who is responsive but cannot speak might be able to open their eyes or squeeze your hand.

Step 2. Send for Help

If the person is unresponsive:

*   stay with the person

*   ask a bystander to call 911 immediately

*   ask a bystander to fetch an automatic electrical defibrillator (AED).

*   If you can't find anyone to help, call 911 before you start CPR.

Step 3. Check for Normal Breathing

In an unconscious person, the muscles of the tongue relax so that the tongue can block the airway, obstructing breathing. Open the person's airway by gently tilting the head back and lifting the chin—when you do this you open their airway.

If there seems to be something in the person's mouth, remove it by sweeping it away with two fingers.

A person in cardiac arrest won't be breathing, or won't be breathing normally. They also won't be conscious.

Check for normal breathing by looking for:

- regular chest movements

- listening for breathing

- feeling for breath on your cheek.

Look, listen, and feel for no more than 10 seconds. Occasional gasps don't count as normal breathing. If you're not sure their breathing is normal, act as if it's not normal.

If you're sure the person is breathing normally, then put them in the recovery position, and call 911. Keep monitoring the person's breathing.

If breathing isn't normal, open their airway. Place one hand on the person's forehead, gently tilt their head back, then lift their chin using two fingers of your other hand under their chin.

Step 4. Give 30 Chest Compressions

Place the person on their back.

Kneeling next to the person's chest.

Place the heel of one hand in the center of the chest. Place your other hand on top of the first. Interlock your fingers.

With straight arms, use the heel of your hand to push the chest down firmly and smoothly, so that the chest is pressed down about 2 inches (5–6 centimeters), and release. Use your body weight to help you push.

Push hard and fast, at a rate of 100 to 120 chest compressions per minute—that's around 2 per second, or similar to the beat of the song "Stayin' Alive." Don't worry about pushing too hard.

Give 30 chest compressions. Count them out loud.

Step 5. Give Two Rescue Breaths

Open the airway again by tilting the head back and lifting the chin.

You need to pinch the soft part of the person's nose closed.

Take a normal breath, place your mouth around the other person's mouth to make a seal, and breathe out steadily.

The chest should rise and fall. Keeping the person's head back and the chin lifted, take your mouth away, take another normal breath, and give a second rescue breath.

Step 6: Continue CPR

Keep performing cycles of 30 compressions and two rescue breaths.

If you can't or would rather not give rescue breaths, then call 911 and deliver compression-only CPR (perform compressions constantly at a rate of 100–120 per minute, with no breaths).

Keep going until trained emergency responders arrive and take over, an AED becomes available, or the victim starts to show signs of regaining consciousness, such as opening their eyes, breathing normally, coughing, vomiting, or speaking.

If an AED becomes available, turn it on immediately and follow the voice prompts.

Discontinue CPR if the situation becomes unsafe or you become too exhausted to continue.

PART 3

Language Editing

"Hire the one that said, 'Whom.'"

JOEDATOR

CHAPTER 14

¶ Grammar and Usage: Principles and Pitfalls

EXERCISE 14-1: Found in the Wild

The following sentences—many from respected, well-edited publications—have been culled from celebrity and science magazines, local and national news reports, book reviews, encyclopedia articles, curated blogs, health advisories, and the like.* These sentences were "found in the wild" and have not been altered for the purposes of this exercise. Like the authentic bloopers posted online in "Copy Edit This!," the irregularly issued *New York Times* quizzes, many of these sentences illustrate just one central problem. Can you identify it?

The intention here is not to embarrass authors or their publishers, nor to encourage a "gotcha" approach to editing: everyone makes mistakes—including, no doubt, the authors of this workbook. The goal of this exercise is to hone your attention to the many subtle errors you may encounter (and sometimes overlook) in your editorial work and to

---

Sources: (1) Kendall Fisher, "Like Mother like Daughter: Jessica Simpson Shares Maxwell's Blonde Moment," Celebuzz, https://www.celebuzz.com/, April 8, 2014. (2) Photo caption, *San Francisco Chronicle,* September 27, 2016, quoted in John Maybury, "Six Years Too Light for Reepen," *Pacifica Tribune,* http://www.pacificatribune.com/, October 7, 2016. (3) Will Kelley, "Great Update to a Technical Publications Standard" (review of *Microsoft Manual of Style,* 4th ed.), Amazon, https://www.amazon.com/, accessed January 16, 2018. (4) "*Ghost World*" (the graphic novel), Wikipedia, https://en.wikipedia.org/, accessed January 16, 2018. (5) John Cassady, "Rational Irrationality" (blog), *New Yorker,* https://www .newyorker.com/, January 7, 2017. (6) Lauren Cared, "Doctors Buck the Insurance System," *East Bay Express,* June 28–July 4, 2006, p. 7. (7) "Kaiser Permanente Thrive Together" (online health newsletter), https://thrive.kaiserpermanente.org/, August 17, 2017. (8) Weston Williams, "Ancient Skulls Unearthed in China Could Belong to Little-Known Extinct Human Species," *Christian Science Monitor,* https://www.csmonitor.com/, March 5, 2017. (9) Michael Nedelman, "Hack Your Brain to Remember Almost Anything," CNN, http://www.cnn.com/, March 9, 2017. (10) M. J. Lee, Lauren Fox, and Deirdre Walsh, "Trump Adds to Chaos of Health Care Deliberations," CNN, http://www.cnn.com/, March 10, 2017. (11) Margaret Beaton, "A Small Act of Scientific Civil Disobedience," *Yes! Magazine,* http://www.yesmagazine.org/, March 13, 2017. (12) Dan Mitchell, "Apple's Got a Secret," *New York Times,* http://www.nytimes.com/, July 1, 2006. (13) "*Helicobacter pylori* Bacteria Cause Ulcers, Not Spicy Foods or Stress," HomemadeHints.com, http://www.homemadehints.com/, accessed January 17, 2018. (14) Verlyn Klinkenborg, "Letter from California: A Hidden Populace in a Vacant Lot," *New York Times,* http://www.nytimes.com/, March 23, 2007. (15) "Doubt Cast on Hormone Replacement," *Baltimore Sun,* http://articles.baltimoresun.com/, April 18, 2002. (16) Charles B. Brenner and Jeffrey M. Zacks, "Why Walking through a Doorway Makes You Forget," *Scientific American,* https://www.scienti ficamerican.com/, December 13, 2011. (17) Josh Butler, "How Donald Trump Destabilised Australia's Prime Minister with One Phone Call," *Huffington Post Australia,* http://www.huffingtonpost.com.au/, February 2, 2017. (18) "Eat Healthy—It Can Pay Off," *Inside Dentistry* (office newsletter), 2nd Quarter, 2017, p. 3. (19) Lee Rainie and Janna Anderson, "Co-dependent: Pros and Cons of the Algorithm Age," Pew Research Center, http://www.pewresearch.org/, February 8, 2017. (20) "Reefer" headline, *Financial Times,* October 9, 2017.

provide an opportunity to apply what you have learned about grammar and usage in *The Copyeditor's Handbook*, chapter 14, as well as to reinforce lessons from previous chapters.

Correct errors and indiscretions, if any, but use a light touch in your editing. Identify the problem(s) in each example or explain your rationale for stetting. Pay attention to the sources of the quotations (see the footnote on p. 131), which determine the editorial style of the originals and may affect your decisions.

1. Jessica took to Instagram to share a hilarious and absolutely adorable photo of her toe-headed daughter with a rose petal on her tongue.

2. Jennifer Molleda looks at the blood-specked face of her husband, Alan Wakim, who had two bullets whiz by his head after going through his windshield on the way to work.

3. As a technical writer, the *Microsoft Manual of Style* is the first style guide I reach for when I am a working on documentation project when the organization doesn't have a corporate style guide.

4. Enid takes an interest in playing pranks on other people, purely for her own benefit, especially a classmate named Josh who she attempts to seduce.

5. Over the past five years, hundreds of millions of dollars of debt attached to Trump's properties has been securitized and sold to mutual funds and other investment institutions.

6. In some cases, United will now reimburse providers more than 40 percent less than it paid out previously.

7. Margarine, however, contains trans fatty acid, which is as harmful, if not more, than saturated fat.

8. But when the team analyzed the skull fragments, they realized that the skulls neither fit the bill for *Homo sapiens* nor Neanderthals but that they shared characteristics of both human species.

9. His hypothesis was based on studies of London taxi drivers, who must memorize thousands of streets and landmarks for a notoriously difficult test called "The Knowledge." Their brains were previously found to have larger hippocampi.

10. Still fewer than five days old, the House Republican bill to repeal Obamacare has an uncertain legislative path ahead.

11. Criminality aside, the fact that so many scientists turn to these informal networks [for distributing scientific literature] begs the question of why barriers to access exist in the first place.

12. Geographic disclosure [of profits instead of profitability by product line] was adequate when pretty much all Apple sold were computers.

13. Helicobacter pylori bacteria cause ulcers, not spicy foods or stress.

14. You don't have to read very much about Spermophilus beecheyi . . . to realize that California ground squirrels are nearly human in their adaptability. And like all creatures that are nearly human in their adaptability, humans consider them pests.

15. About 20 percent of women who reach menopause naturally use hormone replacement at least temporarily.

16. Sometimes, to get to the next object the participant simply walked across the room. Other times, they had to walk the same distance, but through a door into a new room. From time to time, the researchers gave them a pop quiz, asking which object was currently in their backpack. The quiz was timed so that when they walked through a doorway, they were tested right afterwards. As the title said, walking through doorways caused forgetting: Their responses were both slower and less accurate when they'd walked through a doorway into a new room than when they'd walked the same distance within the same room.

17. For non-Australian readers, it cannot be understated how politically damaging the refugee and detention situation has become for Turnbull and his government, with shocking stories of injury, sickness and scandal coming to light seemingly every week.

18. Increase raw and slightly cooked fruits and vegetables, low-diary fat, whole grains, fish, poultry, beans, seeds and nuts.

19. Algorithms have the capability to shape individuals' decisions without them even knowing it, giving those who have control of the algorithms an unfair position of power.

20. Trump demands dog 'Deamers' deal

EXERCISE 14-2: The Truth Is Out There

The following passage has been excerpted from a lengthy report; errors and other modifications have been introduced for the purposes of this exercise.* Besides reading for grammatical lapses, pay attention to the many issues of editorial style covered in part 2 of *The Copyeditor's Handbook:* punctuation; spelling and hyphenation; capitalization and the treatment of names; numbers and numerals; quotations; abbreviations and symbols; and references.

Edit this passage at the medium level, aiming for a general interest readership. Follow *Chicago*'s style guidelines. Prepare a style sheet; be sure to note any discretionary departures from this style that seem warranted by the content and an avid general readership.

CIA's Role in the Study of UFO's 1947–90

95 % of all Americans at least have heard or read something about

Unidentified Flying Objects and 57 % believe they are real. Former U.S.

Presidents Carter and Reagan claim to have seen one. UFOlogists and private

UFO organizations are found throughout the United States. Many are convinced

that the U.S. Government—and particularly CIA—are engaged in a massive

conspiracy and coverup of the issue. The idea that CIA has secretly concealed

its research into UFO's has been a major theme of UFO buffs since the modern

UFO phenomena emerged in the late 1940's.

In late 1993, after being pressurized by UFOlogists for the release

of CIA information on UFO's, DCI R. James Woolsey ordered a review of all

Agency files on UFO's. Using CIA records compiled from that review, this study

*Adapted from Gerald K. Haines, "The CIA's Role in the Study of UFO's, 1947–90," *Studies in Intelligence* (Semiannual ed. 1, 1997): 67–84; reprinted as "A Die-Hard Issue: CIA's Role in the Study of UFO's, 1947–90," *Intelligence and National Security* 14, no. 2 (Summer 1999): 26–49; posted as a public domain PDF document in the Central Intelligence Agency Freedom of Information Act Electronic Reading Room (https://www.cia.gov/library/readingroom), accessed April 2, 2017, at https://www.cia .gov/library/readingroom/docs/DOC_0005517742.pdf.

traces CIA interest and involvement in the UFO controversy from the late 1940s

to 1990. It chronologically examines the Agency's efforts to solve the mystery

of UFO's, its programs that had an impact on UFO sightings, and its attempts

to conceal CIA involvement in the entire UFO issue. What emerges from this

examination is that, while Agency concern over UFO's was substantial until the

early 1950s, CIA has since only paid limited and peripheral attention to the

phenomena.

Due to the tense Cold War situation and increased Soviet capabilities,

a CIA Study Group in the early 1950s saw serious national security concerns

in the flying saucer situation. The group believed that the Soviets could use

UFO reports to touch off mass hysteria and panic in the United States. The

group also believed that the Soviets might use UFO sightings to overload

the U.S. air warning system so that it could not distinguish real targets from

phantom UFO's. H. Marshal Chadwell, Assistant Director of OSI, added that

he considered the problem of such importance "that it should be brought to

the attention of the National Security Council, in order that a communitywide

coordinated effort towards it solution may be initiated."

Chadwell briefed DCI Smith on the subject of UFO's in December,

1952. He urged action because he was convinced that "something was going

on that must have immediate attention" and that "sightings of unexplained

objects at great altitudes and traveling at high speeds in the vicinity of major

U.S. defense installations are of such nature that they are not attributable to natural phenomena or known types of aerial vehicles." He drafted a

memoranda from the DCI to the National Security Council (NSC) and a

proposed NSC Directive establishing the investigation of UFO's as a priority

project throughout the intelligence and the defense research and development

community. Chadwell also urged Smith to establish an external research

project of top level scientists to study the problem of UFO's.

In January, 1953, Chadwell and H.P. Robertson, a noted physicist

from the California Institute of Technology, put together a distinguished

panel of nonmilitary scientists to study the UFO issue. The panel concluded

unanimously that there was no evidence of a direct threat to national security

in the UFO sightings. Nor could the panel find any evidence that the objects

sighted might be extraterrestrials. It did find that continued emphasis on

UFO reporting might threaten "the orderly functioning" of the government

by clogging the channels of communication with irrelevant reports and by

inducing "hysterical mass behavior" harmful to constituted authority. The

panel also worried that potential enemies contemplating an attack on the

United States might exploit the UFO phenomena and use them to disrupt U.S.

air defenses.

To meet these problems, the panel recommended that the National

Security Council debunk UFO reports and institute a policy of public education

to reassure the public of the lack of evidence behind UFO's. It suggested

using the mass media, advertising, business clubs, schools, and even the

Disney corporation to get the message across. Reporting at the height of

McCarthyism, the panel also recommended that such private UFO groups

as the Civilian Flying Saucer Investigators in Los Angeles and the Aerial

Phenomena Research Organization in Wisconsin be monitored for subversive

activities.

¶ Beyond Grammar

EXERCISE 15-1: Editing for Bias-Free Writing

One of the most challenging decisions for an editor is whether (and how) to intervene if the wording in a manuscript invokes stereotypes (based on gender, ethnicity, religion, age, or other group identity), excludes groups in generalizations, or exhibits insensitivity to cultural or other differences. Chapter 15 of *The Copyeditor's Handbook* emphasizes (under "Bias-Free Language") that copyeditors are not censors: authors are free to express their views, however "politically incorrect," and publishers to publish them. But many publishers explicitly vest editors with responsibility for ensuring that authors' manuscripts are free of biased, exclusionary, and inconsiderate language. Businesses seeking global markets want to avoid cultural gaffes. Textbook publishers aiming for widespread text adoptions in the US want to eliminate divisiveness. Government, health, and public service organizations want to speak to everyone under their jurisdiction or care. And authors usually want to avoid inadvertently offending, marginalizing, or snubbing individuals and groups.

Decisions to intervene require editorial judgment: consideration of the publisher's instructions, the author's intention and meaning, the targeted readership, and—because bias-free writing is never just a matter of using or avoiding specific words and phrases—the context in which the language is used. Assuming that you have been instructed to revise or query any dubious phrasings without trampling on the author's prerogatives, imagine that you encounter the following passages in the (invented) contexts specified. Explain each issue and how you would handle it. The goal of this exercise is to heighten your awareness of potentially biased language and to practice appropriate responses.

1. [From a health pamphlet addressed to first-time parents:]

   A new mother can begin bonding by cradling her baby and gently stroking him or her in different patterns. She can also take the opportunity to be "skin-to-skin," holding her newborn against her own skin while feeding or cradling.

2. [From a Wikipedia article about a medical breakthrough:]

Surgery to separate Siamese twins may be easy or difficult. The surgery

can result in the death of one or both twins, especially if they are joined

at the head or share vital organs. In 1955 the neurosurgeon Harold Voris

and his team at Mercy Hospital in Chicago performed the first successful

operation to separate Siamese twins joined at the head.

3. [From a review of a television program:]

Carrie Mathison (Claire Danes), the protagonist of the series *Homeland*,

suffers from manic depression, which makes her volatile and

unpredictable.

4. [From a history of the US moonwalk in 1969:]

Mission commander Neil Armstrong was the first man to set foot on the

lunar surface. His description of the event—"one small step for man, one

giant leap for mankind"—was broadcast on live television worldwide.

5. [From a financial adviser's letter to clients:]

In the stock market crash of September 29, 2008, the Dow Jones Industrial

Average fell 777.68 points in intraday trading. The largest point drop in

history until 2018, it was a literal holocaust for individual retirement

accounts, which lost 40 percent of their value overnight.

6. [From the website for an art gallery expanding its US-based business to Canada:]

   We source the best objects of Eskimo and Indian art for serious collectors, offer a fine selection of ethnic jewelry for our discriminating customers, and restore Oriental rugs.

7. [From an academic study of Christianity:]

   According to the belief system of the followers of this Christian sect, God does not need to be reconciled to man, for His divine love is unchanging. Rather, it is man who must be reconciled with his Maker.

8. [From parking instructions for a public building:]

   Handicapped parking spots are reserved for the disabled. Be considerate! People confined to wheelchairs need ramp access to the entrance.

9. [From a sociological analysis of gender relations in the workplace:]

   Why do we resent a woman who interrupts a male speaker? The answer may be that we fear female aggression and expect deference to male authority. Why do we fail to take women's opinions seriously when their sentences end with that characteristic rising intonation? Because we hear "uptalk" as diffidence.

10. [From the introduction to a book on the "exceptionalism" of US art:]

The element of frontiering individualism that is so historically distinctive in the American condition has endowed our artists and thinkers with an appetite for risk and exploration that sets them off from the European backdrop of our settlement and ancestry.

11. [From the preface to a lower division college textbook:]

The composition of the undergraduate student body at American colleges and universities has significantly changed in recent decades. It now includes a far more diverse group of people in terms of backgrounds and ages. While encouraging the enrollment of these new students, colleges and their faculties have not always adapted their curriculum, learning-skills programs, and teaching styles to fit these new students' needs and concerns. The result is that today students and faculty often come into classrooms not sharing important understandings regarding what needs to be learned and how to learn it. What students often require is a short guide to the "secrets" of learning —how-to lessons of ways to navigate a challenging book, for example, without getting lost in a sea of details. Someone should have shown you this in high school. Unless you went to an elite private or public school, however, it is likely that they did not. Do not fear, it is easy to learn.

EXERCISE 15-2: Editing for Plain Language

The US Plain Writing Act of 2010 requires "clear Government communication that the public can understand and use." Executive Order 13563, "Improving Regulation and Regulatory Review" (2011), further states that the US regulatory system "must ensure that regulations are accessible, consistent, written in plain language, and easy to understand."

The core principles of plain writing for federal communications closely resemble those of William Strunk and E. B. White, whose perennially popular *Elements of Style* has guided (and sometimes misguided) students for about sixty years. For example, government writers should use active voice verbs and simple, concrete language; craft short, declarative sentences; omit needless words; and unify paragraphs with topic sentences and transition words. Updates to this timeless advice encourage government writers to address citizen readers directly (*you*); to adopt a colloquial tone, using contractions and other informal language, when appropriate; to employ examples and lists as aids to clarity; and to modify communication strategies for the web. For further discussion of plain language guidelines, see *The Copyeditor's Handbook,* chapter 15, under "Plain Language Compliance."

The passage below is excerpted from *Federal Plain Language Guidelines* (March 2011; revision 1, May 2011, posted at https://www.plainlanguage.gov/; the entire 118-page document is in the public domain). It is addressed primarily to federal employees who must prepare written content for the public—explanations of laws, instructions for regulatory compliance, health advisories, information about federal programs, and the like. Many state governments and private institutions now also use these guidelines. Virtually all English-speaking countries have similar plain language initiatives.

The excerpts below have been changed (but not much) for the purposes of this exercise; three bullet points in square brackets denote omitted portions of text. Follow the style outlined in *GPO,* which can be freely accessed online at https://www.govinfo .gov/content/pkg/GPO-STYLEMANUAL-2016/pdf/GPO-STYLEMANUAL-2016.pdf. Use *Chicago* as a supplementary reference and *M-W Collegiate* as your dictionary.

Use the codes listed below to supply markup for the elements in the text, as illustrated in *The Copyeditor's Handbook,* chapter 13:

<GT-ni>	general text—no indent (following headings)
<GT>	general text—standard paragraph indent
<BL-f>	bulleted list—first item
<BL-m>	bulleted list—middle item
<BL-l>	bulleted list—last item
<UL1-f>	unnumbered sublist—first item
<UL1-m>	unnumbered sublist—middle item
<UL1-l>	unnumbered sublist—last item

```
<H1>       level 1 subhead
<H2>       level 2 subhead
<H3>       level 3 subhead
```

Then do a medium copyedit of these paragraphs and draft a style sheet.

The Plain Language Action And Information Network (PLAIN) is a community of Federal employees dedicated to the idea that citizens deserve clear communications from Government. We first developed this document in the mid-90s. We continue to revise it every few years to provide updated advice on clear communication. We hope you find this document useful, and that it helps you improve your writing — and your agency's writing — so your users can:

- find what they need,

- understand what they find; and

- use what they find to meet their needs.

We've divided the document into five major topics, although many of the subtopics fit within more than one topic. We start with a discussion of your audience because you should think about them before you start to write your document or your web content. In fact, you should start to think about them before you start to plan. From there we move to organization, because developing a good organization is important during your planning stage. Next, we discuss writing principles, starting at the word level and moving up through paragraphs and sections. This is the most extensive topic. We follow principles of writing documents with principles of writing for the web. We conclude with a short discussion of testing techniques.

When we first wrote this document, we were primarily interested in regulations. We've broadened our coverage, but the document still bears the stamp of its origin. If you have a suggestion about something we should add to address other types of writing, or have a comment on this edition, contact us at www.plainlanguage.gov/contactus.cfm.

[• • •]

I. Think about your audience

One of the most popular plain language myths is that you have to "dumb down" your content so that everyone everywhere can read it. That's not true. The first rule of plain language is: *write for your audience.* Use language your audience knows and feels comfortable with. Take your audience's current level of knowledge into account. Don't write for an 8th grade glass if your audience is composed of PhD candidates, small business owners, working parents, or immigrants. Only write for 8th graders if your audience is, in fact, an 8th grade class.

Make sure you know who your audience us—don't guess or assume.

[• • •]

IV, Write for the web

This section refers to the audience as users since that is a more common term in the web community. To effectively communicate with your web users, you must use plain-language techniques to write web content. This section will explain the differences between print and web writing and how to create sites that work for your users.

a. How do people use the web?

People use the internet to easily find, understand, and use information to complete a task. Unlike print media, people do not read entire web pages. They scan instead. Nielsen and Morkes, in a famous 1997 study, found that 79 percent of their test users always scanned any new page they came across; only 16 percent read word-by-word.

Even with more people using the web, the percent of content that is read on a website has not increased by much. Here are some facts to consider when writing web content:

- In a 2008 study, based on analysis of 45,237 page views, Nielsen found that web users only read about 18% of what's one page.
- As the number of words on a page goes up, the percentage read goes down.

- To get people to read half your words, you must limit your

  page to 110 words or fewer.

What do web users look at?

Since we know web users scan web pages, we need to learn what they

look at. Users often scan pages in an F pattern focusing on the top left side

of the page, headings, and the first few words of a sentence or bulleted list.

On average, users only read the first two words on each line. Also, users can

decide in as little as five seconds whether your site is useful to them.

b. Write for your users

Think about how well your website allows customers to get something done.

- Customers come to your site to perform a task.

- They come because they expect to get self-service.

People come to your website with a specific task in mind. If your

website doesn't help them complete that task, they'll leave.

You need to identify the mission — the purpose — of your website, to

help you clarify the top task your website should help people accomplish.

c. Identify your users and their top tasks

In order to write for your users, you need to know who they are! Here are some general tips to help you identify your users:

- Listen to user questions — what do your visitors ask when they send you an email or call your office?
- Talk to users and ask them what they want.
- Analyze your web metrics to figure out what people are looking for on your website:

What are your most-visited pages and where do people spend the most time?

What top search phrases do people use?

There are many techniques to help you learn about your users. For details and best practices visit www.usability.gov.

d. Write web content

After identifying your users and their top tasks, it is time to actually write web content. If you think it would be easy to just duplicate information you've written for print documents, you are wrong. While the information is helpful, it's not in the right format for the web. Remember, people scan web pages and only read about 18 percent of what's on the page! This means you need to cut whatever you have in print form by 50 percent! Good web content uses:

- The inverted pyramid style. Begin with the shortest and clearest statement you can make about your topic. Put the most important information at the top and the background at the bottom.

- Chunked content. Don't try to pack everything into long paragraphs. Split topics up into logical sections separated by informative headings.

- Only necessary information: Use only the information your users need to achieve their tops tasks. Omit unnecessary information.

Remember:

Your content is NOT clear unless your users can:

- Find what they need

- Understand what they find

- Use what they find to meet their needs

e. Repurpose print material for the web

Don't cut and paste the text of print documents to create web content. People are more likely to leave your webpage, potentially costing you time and money, because they will not take the time to find what they are looking for.

Print writing is different from web writing. Print is very linear and narrative driven. In print, you can go into great detail about mundane things like eating breakfast. If you are a great writer, that can be an interesting story. But, those interesting stories don't work on the web. Instead they slow down web users who are trying to accomplish a task.

Jakob Nielsen (useit.com) explains that "Web users want *actionable* content; they don't want to fritter away their time on (otherwise enjoyable) stories that are tangential to their current goals."

Because the web is "action-oriented," you need to repurpose your print document. Pick out necessary information in your print document that will help your web users and create a new web page.

- Keep the most important and clear message at the top of the web page
- Chunk your content into logical sections
- Use headings to help users navigate the content
- Highlight key facts in a bulleted list
- Explain complex instructions in a visually appealing If/Then table.

EXERCISE 15-3: Counting Heads: Beyond Copyediting

The following entertainment has been prepared for a newsletter addressed to writers and copyeditors. The author, who says "it needs work" and "must be cut by about 100 words," has given you this first draft for "help," that is, for medium to heavy copyediting. Your challenge is to perform some editorial magic: while exercising as much editorial restraint as possible in these circumstances, to make this piece presentable for submission to the newsletter, with attention to overall organization and expository style (discussed in *The Copyeditor's Handbook,* chapter 15), error-free grammar and usage (chapter 14), and consistent editorial style (chapters 4–11). The targeted publication, which is issued in print form and also posted online as a PDF, limits features to about one thousand words and follows *Chicago* and *M-W Unabridged.*

  Prepare a cover letter and style sheet to accompany the edited manuscript when you return it to the author for review.

Headlines, Counting Heads, Crash Blossoms, Eisenhower, and Click-Bait

Australian American newsman and Professor of Journalism at the University

of Kentucky John B. Bremner, who was born in 1920 and died of cancer

in 1987, taught his students that "If you had to reduce all the rules and

recommendations of headline writing to two, they would be: the head must

fit and it must tell the story." In the era of print news, language and esthetics

intersected in the creation of a newspaper headline. They consisted of words

but also broke up text heavy pages of news, directed the eye's attention, and

sometimes startled readers with unusual typography and shapes. Copy boys

used to call it a *head,* but when they wrote an instruction on the layout for

a news page they would spell the word *hed.* This misspelling was deliberate.

Before the introduction of computers into newspaper production, Linotype

operators had to retype every story and headline on the layout sheet or dummy, and copy editors wanted to make sure their instructions were not accidentally typeset and printed along with the news copy. Sometimes they used the abbreviation HTK for "hed to kum," which became the title of Bremner's brief book on headline-writing.

In a printed newspaper, headlines may run a single line or two or three lines deep, depending on the number of columns given to a story. A single line may suffice for the head of a story that occupies half the width of the news page, but the head for a single column story may require several lines and cannot exceed the width of the column. That's where "counting heads" came in before computer technology supplanted traditional printing skills. Al JaCoby, a long-time reporter for *The San Diego Union*, plied his trade back in the 'fifties, 'sixties, and 'seventies. JaCoby, who died in 2008, could remember when an experienced copy boy could exactly fit headlines to the width of a newspaper column by 'counting heads'. Typically, he would calculate a half point for lower-case Fs, Ls, Is, Ts, and Js and for punctuation and wordspaces, a full count for other lower-cased letters except Ms and Ws, which got 1½, as did all capitols and numerals but cap I and number 1 (1), and Ms and Ws (2). All numerals counted as 1½ except 1, which counted 1. "Ike" counted three, "JFK" and "LBJ" each was allotted 4.5, and "Nixon," the subject of many headlines, counted five. "I knew guys who used their knuckles to count out heads. Others would tap out the count with their fingers. The late Tom Keevil, who was one of the best and most competitive smaller-city editor around in the 50s and 60s . . . had a set set of headlines in his mind as models. Thus, the 142 Erbar condensed model line was something like "Mayor Says." Keevil could write a headline in his mind and compare it to the model line and know if it would fit."

If a head was too long, an editor would eliminate or substitute words until it fit the allotted measure. But attempts to abridge headlines sometimes went awry. Fitting headlines into the Procrustrean bed of column width drove some callow copy boys to extremes. JaCoby recalled the practice of the now-defunct *San Antonio Light* of using "ack-ack" (6.5) for "machine gun" (10.5) and "hijack" (5) for "holdup" (5.5), possibly misleading readers into thinking that an anti-aircraft gun had been used in a gang dustup or that a bodega had not just been robbed but hauled away on a flat-bed truck. The anals of journalism (and the internet) are full of examples of misreadings that owe to the overly telegraphic wording of headlines:

Eye Drops off Shelf

Kids Make Nutritious Snacks

Stolen Painting Found by Tree

Violinist Linked to JAL Crash Blossoms

This last example—about a violinist whose career blossomed after his father was killed in the crash of a Japan Airlines flight—has given these misleading headlines a name: crash blossoms.

In the days of hot metal typesetting, even the skillful pruning and swapping of words in heads didn't always work. JaCoby recounted the story of the *New York Times*' "Eisenhower Skinny S". The tradition-bound *Times* would never stoop to using 'Ike' in an all-caps headline. But 'EISENHOWER SAYS' was a half-count too long for a single column article in the *Times*, so in 1952 the *Times*'s editors sent off to Linotype's foundry to have a custom brass matrix made for the President's name, half a count shorter, to use whenever 'EISENHOWER SAYS' was needed. According to a 1952 account, the typecasters redrew the letters of Eisenhower's name (not just the S) and reduced the spaces between them, creating a logotype, a single piece of type that prints a cluster of letters—so EISENHOWER SAYS would fit over a single column news report.

Wordplay may be acceptable in headlines, particularly in features and humorous pieces, although some newspapers explicitly prohibit humor and punning, at least in serious news pieces. Attention-grabbing headlines often play opposites against each other, use a word with a double meaning, invert an idiomatic expression, alter the spelling or pronunciation of a common expression, build a series, surprise with an unusual combination, or use alliteration or rhyme. One of the most famous headlines of the twentieth century (if you discount "Dewey Defeats Truman") is:

Headless Body in Topless Bar

It was printed in the *New York Post* in 1983 and made creator Vincent A. Musetto so famous that it was featured in his 2015 obituary. Today, if you encountered such a headline in your social media newsfeed, you might dismiss it as click-bait. True, the internet didn't create sensational headlines: Wordplay and provocative content have always characterized journalists' efforts to attract readers. The difference is that, whereas traditional news aims to capture the essence of a news report in a pithy, attention-grabbing headline, click-bait overpromises and often misrepresents content to lure readers to another Web site and thus to generate advertising income based on page views. No copyfitting skill and scant linguistic ingenuity is required to create these nearly irresistible headlines, which depend on formulas such as so-called "listicles" ("7 Reasons You Can't Resist This Headline") and emotional appeals to curiosity and outrage ("You Won't Believe" or "What Happened Next Will Shock You").

Sources: Jane T. Harrigan and Karen Brown Dunlap, *The Editorial Eye*, 2nd ed. (Boston: Bedford/St. Martin's, 2004). "John B. Bremner," *Wikipedia*, https://en.wikipedia.org/, accessed February 15, 2018. Adrienne LaFrance, "The Legend of Eisenhower's Skinny 'S,'" *The Atlantic*, June 14, 2016, https://www.theatlantic.com/. Blanca Gonzalez, "Obituary: Alfred JaCoby," *San Diego Union-Tribune*, June 4, 2008, http://legacy.sandiegouniontribune.com/. Ben Zimmer, "Crash Blossoms," *New York Times Magazine*, January 27, 2010, http://www.nytimes.com/. Margalit Fox, "Vincent Musetto, 74, Dies; Wrote

'Headless' Headline of Ageless Fame," *New York Times*, June 9, 2015, https://www.nytimes.com/. Jeffrey Dvorkin, "Why Click-Bait Will Be the Death of Journalism," PBS NewsHour (website), April 27, 2016, https://www.pbs.org/. Bryan Gardiner, "You'll Be Outraged at How Easy It Was to Get You to Click on This Headline," *Wired*, December 18, 2015, https://wired.com/.

Answer Keys

ALL'S WELL THAT
ENDS WELL

Charles Dickens

The following corrections and comments are based on *The Chicago Manual of Style, Merriam-Webster's Collegiate Dictionary, Merriam-Webster's Dictionary of English Usage,* and *Garner's Modern English Usage.* Where applicable, explanations include cross-references to the relevant chapters in *The Copyeditor's Handbook.* These resources are identified by the abbreviations listed in the front matter of this book.

1. Sales potential has become a critical component of the decision to publish a book. No longer is ~~it's~~ its intellectual impact or quality the sole ~~criteria~~ criterion for investment by a traditional publishing house. But a growing number of independent authors ~~is~~ are building their ~~names~~ reputations and making ~~great incomes~~ good money ~~from bypassing~~ by circumventing the old publishing system.

Comment: Watch out for the common—and often overlooked—confusion between *its* (third-person singular possessive pronoun) and *it's* (contraction of *it is*). *Criterion* is the correct singular form of *criteria;* although *criteria* as a singular noun is increasingly common in speech and unedited prose, most usage authorities still consider this use an abomination. (For these two points, see *The Copyeditor's Handbook,* chapter 5, under "Homophones" and "Plurals," respectively.) Despite the dictates of formal grammar, long-standing English idiom allows the phrase "a number of *x*" to take a plural verb when the members of the group are regarded as acting individually, and "the number of *x*" to take a singular verb when the members are acting as a group (*The Copyeditor's Handbook,* chapter 14, under "Subject-Verb Agreement"). The discretionary edits in the remainder of this sentence can be explained thus:

- "reputations" (alternatively, "name recognition") substituted for "names" to clarify the meaning
- "good money" substituted for "great incomes," which mixes registers—the colloquial ("great") and the formal ("incomes")—to jarring effect; the informal "good money" seems consonant with the author's tone
- the idiomatic preposition following the construction "are [achieving something]" is *by,* not *from,* but "by bypassing" is hardly mellifluous; one solution to this unpleasant word echo is to substitute a synonym, "circumventing" (alternatively, "skirting")
- "publishing" added as a modifier to clarify which "system" is being referred to

2. ~~20-something~~ Twentysomething male ~~high-school grads~~ high school graduates used to ~~comprise~~ compose the most dependable working cohort in America. Today one in five ~~are~~ is ~~now~~ essentially idle.

Comment: Most style manuals advise against beginning a sentence with arabic numerals, even if the specified style (e.g., Associated Press style) stipulates the use of numerals for the value; moreover, the adjective "twentysomething," dating from the 1990s, has already made it into *M-W Collegiate* as a closed compound form. The adjectival form of "high school" is not listed in *M-W Collegiate* but is given as an example of an open compound in *Chicago*. (However, the adjective is hyphenated in *AHD*, and an editor would retain the hyphenation if following that dictionary rather than *M-W Collegiate* and *Chicago*.) The clipped form "grad" (for "graduate"), labeled as slang in *M-W Collegiate*, is unsuitable in this context. The revision of "comprise" to "compose" (*or* "constitute" or "make up") here is discretionary: strict usage authorities caution against the use of *comprise* to mean "compose, make up," citing the mnemonic rule "The whole comprises the parts; the parts compose the whole" (see *Garner's*, under "comprise"); more liberal advisers (e.g., *DEU*, under "comprise") accept this usage as firmly established in English prose, even while cautioning that some readers will forever regard it as an error. Likewise, formalists regard the construction "one in *x*" as invariably singular, requiring a singular verb, whereas more liberal commentators aver that the construction is sometimes "notionally" plural and may take a plural verb (see *The Copyeditor's Handbook*, chapter 14, under "Subject-Verb Agreement"). "Today . . . now" is redundant.

3. My number one legislative priority ~~As~~ as your Assembly member for six years, has been the ~~Education, Health and Safety~~ education, health, and safety of our children. ~~has been my number one legislative priority.~~ I supported ~~Universal Health Care,~~ universal health care and championed the ~~*Healthy Families Program*~~ Healthy Families Program for 740,000 poor children. During the growing crisis in affordable housing, I voted to continue ~~keep the state's Redevelopment Agencies to~~ assisting citizens ~~with the growing housing~~ through the state's redevelopment agencies. ~~affordability crisis and~~ I passed laws to reduce neighborhood crime. As the ~~Chairman~~ chair of the Assembly Labor and Employment Committee, I fought to protect your pensions and to secure fair wages for working families. I sponsored laws to rescue our children from ~~Human Traffickers~~ human traffickers, and to provide services for seniors, ~~the disabled~~ people with disabilities, and ~~our~~ youth.

Comment: Where to begin? The first sentence has been reordered to avoid the dangling modifier "As your Assemblymember for six years," with "Assemblymember" revised as an open compound. Although "Assembly" remains capitalized, following the conventional treatment of state legislative bodies, other incorrectly capitalized words and phrases have been lowercased throughout this passage; like institutions and companies, an official program, such as California's Healthy Families Program, retains the capitalization but not the italics for its name (*The Copyeditor's Handbook*, chapter 6, under "Names of Institutions and Companies, Trademarks, and Brand Names"). Two discretionary interventions: the cumbersome and ambiguous "to assist citizens with the growing housing affordability crisis" has been recast; the seemingly unrelated statement about neighborhood crime that follows the coordinate conjunction "and" has been given its own sentence. For the sake of inclusiveness and inoffensiveness—which a political candidate's statement should surely strive for—the gender-neutral "chair" and the person-first formulation "people with disabilities" have been substituted for "Chairman" and "the disabled" (*The Copyeditor's Handbook,* chapter 15, under "Bias-Free Language"). The misleading and awkward constructions "to protect your pensions and fair wages" and "to rescue our children . . . , provide services for seniors, the disabled and our youth" have been emended for clarification, a series comma has been added to the second list (as well as to "education, health, and safety" above), and the repetition of "our" has been excised.

4. We ~~need to~~ must ~~take steps to~~ make sure everyone has the support ~~they~~ needed to
    thrive.

Comment: The needlessly prolix "to take steps to make sure" has been pruned and the word repetition ("We need . . . need to thrive") eliminated. But the chief issue here is one of pronoun agreement: may "they" refer back to the indefinite singular pronoun "everyone"? Some authorities deplore this usage and recommend the singular *he*—or, in the interest of gender inclusiveness, the cumbersome *he or she.* Challenging this stiff opposition to "singular *they*," others argue that the usage is idiomatic, as shown by the ample evidence in literary English (William Shakespeare, the King James Bible, Jane Austen, George Orwell, and other respected writers), and is therefore acceptable in all but the most formal writing. The official style guide for the *Washington Post* removed its objection to the usage in 2015, but many manuals continue to proscribe it. The judicious course for a copyeditor threading a path between these opposing views is to avoid the issue whenever possible, as shown by the simple change here. (See further discussion of this issue in *The Copyeditor's Handbook,* chapter 14, under "Pronoun-Antecedent Agreement.")

5. I ~~could careless~~ couldn't care less whether Kriss Kringle brings me two new ~~Lexis's~~
    Lexuses this year.

Comment: Although the expression "could care less" is common in speech and increasingly tolerated in writing, the correct original phrase is "couldn't care less" (and *not* "careless"!). Despite the objection of Microsoft Word's spell-checker, "Kriss Kringle" (a German name for Santa Claus) is a standard spelling; *M-W Collegiate* recognizes "Kris Kringle" as a variant. The misspelling of "Lexus" is a reminder to verify product names; the plural of such proper names is usually formed by adding *s* or *es* without an apostrophe (*The Copyeditor's Handbook,* chapter 5, under "Plurals").

6. Made from a blend of premium cotton twill ~~/lycra blend~~ and Lycra, these chinos
    feature a durable ~~stain~~ stain- and ~~wrinkle~~ wrinkle-resistant treatment, so they come
    out of the dryer ~~ready-to-wear~~ ready to wear. Plus, they exceed our rigorous standards
    for ~~shrink~~ shrink resistance.

Comment: The opening phrase "a premium cotton twill/lycra blend" is expanded to clarify what the components of the blend are and to avoid using the slash; the trademarked name "Lycra" is capitalized (*The Copyeditor's Handbook,* chapter 6, under "Names of Institutions and Companies, Trademarks, and Brand Names"). The compound adjectives "stain- and wrinkle-resistant" require hyphens, the former as a suspended compound term, but the expressions "ready to wear" and "shrink resistance" are unhyphenated (*The Copyeditor's Handbook,* chapter 5, under "One Word or Two?"). Many editors will quibble over the use of "plus" as a transitional expression (the equivalent of the more formal "in addition"), but it is sometimes accepted in the most colloquial contexts (*DEU*), such as this advertising copy from a mail-order catalog, in which the copywriter is presumably striving for a breezy tone.

7. The ~~rainbow of~~ many intellectual traditions that colored Israeli, and particularly Sabra, environmental values ~~may have~~ prompted different inhabitants to ~~marveled~~ marvel at, ~~embraced~~ cherish, or ~~attacked~~ exploit the land. But ~~nobody hid from~~ no tradition could ignore its presence. **{AU: Is this your meaning?}**

Comment: These two sentences, written by a hypothetical nonnative English speaker, are real head-scratchers! Once the distracting metaphor of a "rainbow" of traditions "coloring" values is somewhat tamed and the predication error identified (a rainbow can't marvel, embrace, or attack), the editor can begin to extrapolate the author's meaning—that a multitude of traditions produced different attitudes and behaviors toward Israel's environment but that no tradition ignored ("hid from") the land. The interpolated phrase "and particularly Sabra" is set off with commas. In a description of actions on the environment, the verbs "embraced" and "attacked" seem unidiomatic; "cherished" and "exploited" work better in this context. These discretionary changes render the sentences somewhat more intelligible to native English speakers.

8. Jainism~~, along with~~ and Buddhism~~, is~~ are the only surviving examples of India's ancient ~~nonvedic~~ non-Vedic religious traditions.

Comment: Recasting the statement in the plural corrects the illogical assertion that *two* religions, Jainism and Buddhism, are "the only surviving example" of an ancient tradition. The term "Vedic" is capitalized, and the prefix "non" must therefore use a hyphen (see the discussion of prefixes and suffixes in *The Copyeditor's Handbook,* chapter 5, under "One Word or Two?"). Don't overlook the missing terminal period.

9. The ~~Secretary of the Department~~ department secretary, ~~Mrs. William~~ **{AU: Pls supply Smith's first name}** Smith, cheerfully ~~patches over~~ resolves all problems and difficulties, ~~in~~ cramming the book's revisions into her other duties ~~with one hand while she also scales a separate set of~~ while mastering complicated computer ~~instructional Mt. Everest's with the other~~ formatting instructions for manuscript preparation **{AU: Is this your meaning?}**.

Comment: The descriptive title "secretary of the department" does not require capital letters (*The Copyeditor's Handbook,* chapter 6, under "Personal Names and Titles"), but this long-suffering department secretary surely merits her own given name, not merely that of her husband and the courtesy title "Mrs." (*The Copyeditor's Handbook,* chapter

15, under "Bias-Free Language"). The metaphor of scaling "a separate set of computer/ instructional Mt. Everest's" (should be "Everests") is as risible as it is baffling; revision with a query to the author seems essential.

10. The ~~phenomena~~ imperative of reproduction not only ~~is at the heart, core and 'soul' of~~ informs social life for many ~~if not most~~ people but also ~~across~~ spans a̲ an stunning array of social differences ~~that is truly quite stunning~~.

Comment: The singular of *phenomena* is *phenomenon* (*The Copyeditor's Handbook,* chapter 5, under "Plurals"). Be that as it may, the statement that the *phenomenon* of reproduction underlies most social life seems so self-evident as to be ludicrous. Revision to "The imperative of reproduction" or "The reproductive drive" clarifies the point. The parallel structure required by the use of the correlative conjunctions "not only . . . but also" must be enforced, preferably using balanced verbs, such as "informs" and "spans" (*The Copyeditor's Handbook,* chapter 14, under "Parallel Form"). The repetitive "heart, core and 'soul'" can be trimmed (and the distracting scare quotes around "soul" eliminated), as can the remaining phrases of the sentence. A radical, if facetious, alternative revision: "Amazing, isn't it? Everyone is interested in sex!"

11. For all ~~intensive~~ intents and purposes, the ~~Twentieth Century~~ twentieth-century ~~brick and motor~~ brick-and-mortar store is dead, having been ~~superceded~~ superseded by online shopping malls and flea markets, ~~like amazon.com~~ such as Amazon and ~~Ebay~~ eBay.

Comment: "For all intensive purposes" is an example of an eggcorn, a set phrase so frequently misheard and misinterpreted that the incorrect variant assumes an air of legitimacy. (The term *eggcorn* derives from the humorously mangled saying "Mighty oaks from little eggcorns grow.") *Chicago* advises lowercasing designations for centuries; the compound adjectives "twentieth-century" and "brick-and-mortar" (*not* "motor"!) require hyphens. "Superseded" is frequently misspelled. The company names should be capitalized, with the unusual treatment of "eBay" preserved (see *The Copyeditor's Handbook,* chapter 6, under "Names of Institutions and Companies, Trademarks, and Brand Names"). The revision of "like" to "such as" reinforces the sense that Amazon and eBay are *examples* of, rather than merely *similar* to, the online retailers replacing brick-and-mortar stores; many usage guides accept these expressions as interchangeable, but here the nuance aids comprehension.

12. Among the many new proposals for controlling insects~~, which~~ that attack crops~~,~~ is the incorporation of ~~bio-~~ biorational insecticides into plants,̲ ~~which~~ but because of genetic adaptation in pests,̲ this approach̲ will not provide ~~the hoped for~~ "final solution" to̲ a̲ panacea for̲ the pest problem.

Comment: The phrase "which attack crops" is revised to function as a restrictive (essential) modifier, with the enclosing commas removed and (as a discretionary change often favored in American English) "which" replaced by "that": the topic of the sentence is the subset of insects that attack crops, not *all* insects (*The Copyeditor's Handbook,* chapter 4, under "Function 2: Joining Clauses" and "Function 3: Setting Off Phrases"). The compound form "biorational" is closed according to *M-W Collegiate* (under ²*bi-* [or *bio-*]) and *Chicago's* hyphenation guide (7.89). The second half of the sentence is revised to clarify its grammatical and logical relationship to the first half. The historically resonant phrase "final solution," which evokes the Nazi Holocaust, is especially offensive in this context; the trivializing scare quotes, signifying *so-called,* do not justify the application of the expression to the total eradication of "pests" that attack crops. Note: Copyeditors' queries explaining the rationale for eliminating scare quotes sometimes avoid using the term *scare quotes,* unfamiliar to many authors, in favor of less alarming alternatives, such as "quotes denoting *so-called.*"

13. I could ~~of chose~~ have chosen to memorize Edgar ~~Allen~~ Allan Poe's "The Raven" or Emily ~~Dickenson's~~ Dickinson's "I'm ~~No Body~~ Nobody!"~~,~~ but instead I recited "~~The~~ the Pledge of Allegiance."

Comment: Although English speakers sometimes mishear the contraction *could've* as *could of,* the correct verb form here is "could have," which requires the past participle "chosen." Poe's middle name and Dickinson's surname are frequently misspelled: the corrections of these names illustrate the need to verify the spelling of proper names for well-known individuals (as well as the titles of famous literary works), which can usually be done quickly online. (The limitations on a copyeditor's responsibility for fact-checking, along with some caveats about deep diving into online research, are discussed throughout *The Copyeditor's Handbook,* chapters 1–3.) Unpaired quotation marks are often overlooked. An embedded quotation ending with a "strong" punctuation mark (a question mark or an exclamation point) does not require a following comma unless essential to prevent misreading (*The Copyeditor's Handbook,* chapter 4, under "Multiple Punctuation"). The names of pledges and oaths do not require quotation marks and normally are not capitalized; the Pledge of Allegiance, capitalized, is explicitly cited as an exception in *Chicago.*

14. Don't expect an apology from the sheriff leading the response to the protesters, especially for his recent — and, in some circles, controversial — action against demonstrators, who he believes have become increasingly aggressive.

Comment: Surprise! There's nothing wrong with this sentence unless you determine that the contraction "don't" should be spelled out—a matter of register, not a point of grammar, since contractions are often tolerated in all but the most formal or professional prose. You might be tempted to change "who" to "whom" in the deceptively constructed relative clause, but that would be wrong: here "who" is the subject of the verb "have become," not the object of the parenthetical interpolation "he believes" (see *The Copyeditor's Handbook,* chapter 14, under "Case of Nouns and Pronouns"). An editor would ordinarily close up the spaces before and after the em dashes, or rules, setting off the interrupting phrase "and, in some circles, controversial," but this emendation depends on house style: many UK publishers set interrupting rules as spaced en (*not* em) dashes, whereas most US publishers set them as closed-up em dashes (and a few retain the spaces fore and aft).

15.   The Pirelli calendar has departed from its ~~sexy~~ tradition <u>of titillation</u> in this year's edition, with <u>the</u> photographer Peter Lindbergh ~~foregoing~~ <u>forgoing</u> ~~photoshop~~ <u>Photoshop</u> and filters to ~~focus~~ <u>train</u> his lens on unadorned ~~female~~ <u>women</u> celebrities.

Comment: The nondiscretionary corrections in this sentence are the capitalization of "Photoshop" (a trademarked name) and the correction of the all-too-common misspelling of "forgoing" (meaning "to give up") as "foregoing" (meaning "to precede"). Although omission of *the* with restrictive appositives is common in journalism ("The camera loves model Gisele Bündchen" instead of "The camera loves the model Gisele Bündchen"), formal prose uses the definite article in such constructions. The replacements of the adjectives "sexy" and "female" are discretionary: "sexy" implies an inherent characteristic of a tradition rather than a tradition whose aim is to titillate; "female" connotes biological sex rather than social gender and thus, some would argue, might seem derogatory in this context (Chicago's online *Style Q&A* accepts the attributive use of *woman* and *women*). The change from "focus" to "train," another judgment call here, reduces the number of *f* sounds ("forgoing Photoshop and filters to focus on . . . ~~female~~ women"); granted, the alliteration may be a deliberate affectation on the part of the writer, but it could grate on readers' ears.

––––––––––

If you missed a great many errors in these sentences, don't be discouraged! This workbook will prepare you to recognize them and other editorial challenges as well. By the time you've completed the exercises, you will have earned your red pencil.

EXERCISE 1-1: Key

Version 1	*Version 2*

Spellings and Compound Forms

guerilla	guerrilla
anti-Communist	anticommunist
historical	historic
nationalised	nationalized
pro-Communist	procommunist
formalised	formalized
super-powers	superpowers
full scale	full-scale
co-operation	cooperation
pre-emptive	preemptive
airforce	air force
advisers	advisors

Capitalization

Communist, Communism	communist, communism
President	president
Prime Minister	prime minister
Sugar Embargo	sugar embargo
Cold War	cold war
Western Hemisphere	western hemisphere
[presidential] Administration	[presidential] administration
[Castro] Regime	[Castro] regime

Punctuation

no serial comma:

   Invasion, Poison Pills And Exploding
     Cigars

   He nationalised . . . , initiated . . .
     and exhorted

   espionage, sabotage and repeated
     assassination attempts

In 1959, . . .
During 1959–61, . . .
April, 1961 . . .

serial comma:

   Invasion, Poison Pills, and Exploding
     Cigars

   He nationalized . . . , initiated . . . ,
     and exhorted

   espionage, sabotage, and repeated
     assassination attempts

In 1959 . . .
During 1959–1961 . . .
April 1961 . . .

Version 1	*Version 2*
Numbers and Dates	
100, 1400, 35th, 24, 600	one hundred, fourteen hundred, thirty-fifth, twenty-four, six hundred
80%	80 percent
1959–61	1959–1961
17 April 1961	April 17, 1961
Quotations	
single quotation marks, terminal punctuation outside quotation marks: 'too large . . . to be successful'.	double quotation marks, terminal punctuation inside quotation marks: "too large . . . to be successful."
Acronyms and Other Abbreviations	
U.S.	US
U.S.S.R.	USSR
C.I.A.	CIA
SNAFU	snafu
J.F.K.	JFK
Italics and Bold Type	
Operation Mongoose	Operation Mongoose
Special Elements (Headings)	
conjunctions and prepositions capitalized: The Bay Of Pigs Invasion, Poison Pills And Exploding Cigars	conjunctions and prepositions set lowercase: The Bay of Pigs Invasion, Poison Pills, and Exploding Cigars
Documentation	
modification dates in parentheses and after titles, URLs in angle brackets: 'Assassination attempts on Fidel Castro' (last modified 22 January 2017), Wikipedia, <en.wikipedia.org/wiki/ Assassination_attempts_on_Fidel_ Castro>, accessed 16 March 2017.	no parentheses for dates, all dates after URLs, no angle brackets for URLs: "Assassination attempts on Fidel Castro," Wikipedia, en.wikipedia.org/wiki/ Assassination_attempts_on_Fidel_ Castro, last modified January 22, 2017, accessed March 16, 2017.
footnote signaled by asterisk in title	no footnote signal
Other	
U.S. (adjective)	American (adjective)
an historic(al)	a historic

EXERCISE 1-2: Key

In this version of the text, superscript numbers are used to indicate footnotes that are part of the original text; superscript letters are used to indicate comments on the exercise, which appear below the original text and footnotes. Highlighting identifies items that may be hard to see otherwise or that will require later attention in copyediting.

Chapter 10
The U.S Retail Industry
A Brief History [A]

[B]Only twenty-five years ago "mom and pop" [C] clothing stores flourished along with large department stores and discount chains. Today,[D] however, highly concentrated, vertically integrated, US [E] retail transnationals, selling vast quantities of apparel items, have put many of the smaller stores and even the larger department stores out of business. The new forms of corporate retailing has [F] played a crucial role in the globalization of the textile/apparel [G] complex. Today transnationals compete for market share and market power, both nationally and internationally.

For the past twenty years retailing has been driving the thrust of US trade policy in textiles and apparel. The needs of these retailers have shaped the restructuring of the textile and apparel producers who supply them with merchandise.[1] [H] Corporate retailers have been able to increase their power over textile and apparel producers because of increasing opportunities to benefit from the expansion of low wage apparel production in developing countries.

America's[I] apparel retailers have become among the most powerful supporters of trade liberalization for textiles and apparel. Ending quotas and reducing tariffs has not only accelerated the globalization of apparel production, but has led to a new round of *vertical integration* and *concentration* [J] in apparel retailing. Competition in this industry is now based on the efforts of retailers to increase their market share in a new and intense context of domestic and global competition. Textile and apparel producers have responded to these conditions by trying to develop more efficient ways to produce apparel. Retailers continue their pressures on government for further trade liberalization, for more access to new low wage production sites and retail outlets.

1. Frederick H. Abernathy, John T. Dunlop, Janice H. Hammond and David Weil, *A Stitch in Time: Lean Retailing and the Transformation of Manufacturing—Lessons from the Apparel and Textile Industries,* Oxford University Press, New York and Oxford, 1999. This recent book is among the most scholarly and empirically sound treatments of this position.

A Brief History of Apparel Retailing **K**

The history of the US apparel retailing begins with department stores, which first appeared in the early part of the twentieth century. Department stores were initially located in the main shopping district of the downtown area, making it possible for the new urban, middle and upper middle class consumers to enjoy the convenience of one stop shopping, stable prices and the reliability of quality merchandise . Such department stores were owned by individual merchant families. Yet by 1916, Lincoln Filene, the President of Filene's in Boston, recognized the value of collaboration **L** between retailers in buying merchandise, recruiting executives, training employees, improving advertising, and other associated aspects of the retail business.[2] He started the Retail Research Association, which two years later was superseded by the Associated Merchandising Corporation (AMC).NEED TO CHECK THIS **M**

Recognizing **N** the need for a more centralized corporate structure for the dispersion of risk, expansion and greater profitability in the industry, Filene began to advocate the formation of a national retail holding company. In 1918 Filene's joined with Abraham and Strauss of Brooklyn, and F & R Lazarus and Company of Columbus, Ohio, to form Federated Department Stores. Holding companies increasingly became the dominant form of retail ownership in this industry. Department stores, selling men's, women's and children's clothing, and other household items, put many smaller, local "mom and pop" specialty stores out of business.   Department **O** stores enjoyed high and stable profits during the affluence of the early postwar boom, allowing retailers to finance expansion from profits. The growth of car ownership and the building of highways led to massive suburbanization. Following their customers to the new bedroom communities, new stores were built—**P**"anchors"**Q** of the new suburban shopping malls. A major acceleration of new shopping mall construction took place between 1965 and 1975,[3] internally financed by the industry in the context of its high profits. By 1977, four major holding companies controlled the majority of America's department store chains—**R**Federated Department Stores, Allied Stores Corp., May Department Stores Company and Dayton Hudson Corp.**S** Together, they included 807 retail outlets and total sales in excess of $11.4 billion—five times the sales of the whole J. C. Penney **T** chain with 1686 stores nationwide.[4] However, as department stores reached the limits of suburban growth they began to expand their geographic coverage to a national market. In 1986 Neiman Marcus had . . . **U**stores in

2. Barry Bluestone et. al. *The Retail Revolution,* 1983, 11.
3. See Jack Kaikati, "Don't Discount Off-Price Retailers," *Harvard Business Review,* May-June 1985; Samuel Feinberg, The Off Price Explosion, *Fairchild Books Special Report,* Fairchld Publications, 1984, Bluestone et. al., 1983.
4. Bluestone et.al. 1983.

Florida, and Massachusetts. Lord and Taylor, Saks Fifth Avenue, Bloomingdales, have all followed with similar moves.[5]

[. . .]

Restructuring for the New Retail Competition **V**

Needing to reduce operating costs, to increase sales and margins, retailers began to impose new economic pressures on their apparel suppliers. They made three significant changes:

a) in their labor-management relations,

b) in the implementation of "quick response," and

3) the expansion of their "private label" merchandise. **W**

XRetailers began to reduce their traditionally large and costly inventories. They also reduced their largely, full time, trained sales staff, made up of career employees.[6] The new retail competition required fewer managers and minimal sales help; the practice of customer service became economically unsustainable.[7] Employment in apparel retailing grew 31% between 1973 and 1985, during his **Y** period, as stores reduced their full time workers and increased their part-time help. By 1985 the earnings of workers in retail sales had declined dramatically—and were only slightly higher than those of the lowest paid workers employed in eating and drinking places.[8] What made this possible, **Z** were the new microtechnologies, which dramatically increased worker productivity.

[. . .]

The Economics of "Fashion"

A discussion of apparel retailing would not be complete without an analysis of the "fashion" industry. The transformations in apparel retailing in the past two decades occurred in the 1970s in the context of a declining couture industry. Well known "couture" fashion designers had produced individualized couture clothing for wealthy patrons. As this clientele began to shrink many discovered the advantages of higher volume sales in high niche "ready to wear" women's apparel. These designers began to license their names to clothing producers who would hire their own designers to turn out fashions by "Oleg Cassini" or "Gloria Vanderbilt." **AA**

5. Pais, Sloan School of Management, M.I.T., June 1986, 37
6. Lasker, Cohen and Garter, 1981.
7. Klokis, Holly. "Retail Layoffs: Where Will Everyone Go?" *Chain Store Age Executive* 63(4): 104, 106, April 1987.
8. Steven E. Haugen, "The Employment Expansion in Retail Trade, 1973–1985," *Monthly Labor Review,* Aug 1986.

As educated women began to enter the US labor force in professional occupations, new demands for women to "dress for success" led American designers like Liz Claiborne to create a new type of clothing for women. By 1974 Liz Claiborne, and others like her, were producing lower cost, high quality "career wear" in Asia.[9] Retailers, merchandisers and importers could access contractors to produce high quality clothing in Europe (Italy, France, the UK) or Japan, while department store, private label goods were sources in South Korea, Hong Kong, Taiwan and Singapore. Mass merchandisers and lower priced store brands, sourced in a third tier **BB** of medium to low cost, midquality exporters (Brazil, Mexico, low end producers in the NICs, plus the People's Republic of China, and the ASEAN countries of Thailand, Malaysia, the Philippines, and Indonesia).[10]

Large volume discount stores at the lower ends of the market, making large volumes of standardized goods looked to countries like China, Bangladesh, Sri Lanka, and Mauritius. Low end retailers like Walmart and Sears initially sourced apparel in countries in the Caribbean and Central America—**CC**Dominican Republic and Guatemala and Jamaica.[11] A process that has been called "specification contracting" developed:

> . . . local firms carry out production according to complete instructions issued by the buyers and branded companies that design the goods; the output is then distributed and marketed abroad by trading companies, brand name merchandisers, large retailers or their agents. [This] "buyer driven commodity chain" is common in the garment industry. . . . foreign capital tends to control the more profitable export and marketing networks.[12] **DD**

EE

9. James Lardner, "The Sweater Trade," in the *New Yorker Magazine,* 1991. http://www.newyorker.com/magazine/1988/01/11/i-the-sweater-trade
10. Cheng and Gereffi, p. 64–66 in Bonacich et. al.
11. Not surprisingly, these corporations were staunch supporters of the Special Access Program of the Caribbean Basin Initiative of 1986.
12. The Globalization of Taiwan's Garment Industry, by Gary Gereffi and Mei-Lin Pan. in Bonacich et. al., 1994, 134.

COMMENTS

A Chapter number, title, and subtitle are set on separate lines. Typecoding may also be applied during file cleanup in conformity with the guidelines provided by the client or publisher. For more information about typecoding, or markup, see chapter 13 of both this workbook and *The Copyeditor's Handbook.*

B Font size, linespacing, and alignment (flush left, not justified, with first line of paragraph indented) should be changed globally. Extra linespaces between paragraphs should be removed.

C Single straight quotation marks should be changed to double typesetter's (curly) quotation marks (but be wary of making a global change that would also affect apostrophes and other marks; see note **I** below).

D Spacing between sentences should be changed to a single wordspace.

E U.S., US, or United States? Correct styling may depend on context; wait until the editing stage to make changes of this sort.

F Correction of this error of subject-verb agreement is a nondiscretionary change, but don't change any wording during file cleanup.

G Spaces around the virgule (slash) should be removed. During copyediting, you may want to eliminate the virgule by rephrasing, but not now.

H Footnote signals should be changed to arabic numerals and closed up to the preceding word or punctuation mark. (Search for a wordspace followed by a footnote signal and remove the wordspace.) Avoid making any substantive or stylistic changes to the notes (such as altering the citation style) until the editing stage.

I Apostrophes and single quotation marks (where needed) should be changed to typesetter's single quotation marks. Watch out, however, for numerical symbols that should not be converted, such as foot and inch symbols, and for reversed apostrophes in terms such as *'cause.*

J Underlining should be replaced with italics. (Note that "and" was not underlined and so should not be italicized.)

K Subheads should be set flush left, with an extra linespace above and below. The boldface applied to this subhead should be removed.

L The manually inserted page break in running text should be removed.

M Residual comments and stray text in a manuscript should not be removed without consulting the author; flag this instance for later querying.

N The tab at the start of the paragraph should be removed. Although some publishers use tabs for paragraph indentation, most prefer that indentation be set as part of the style specifications for text paragraphs.

O This tab, however, should not be removed without querying the author as to whether a paragraph break is intended.

P The hyphen and spaces here should be replaced by a closed-up em dash.

Q Bonus: the guillemets (« »), used in French-language publications to indicate quoted speech, should be replaced with double quotation marks.

R Two hyphens should be replaced by an em dash. (Some publishers prefer an en dash with wordspaces on either side, or a similarly spaced em dash.)

S The form of these business names should be verified by the author and abbreviations consistently styled—but not until the copyediting stage.

T   A single wordspace should be added between initials in a personal or business name and between an initial and a surname. (Some publishers prefer a nonbreaking, fixed-width space.) But because not all initials are part of personal names, it may be preferable to make such corrections as you encounter them during copyediting rather than with automated find-and-replace operations during file cleanup.

U   The ellipsis character should be replaced with spaced dots. Publishers' preferences on this point may vary. But why is the ellipsis there? Query the author in copyediting.

V   Again, the subhead should be set roman, flush left, with spaces above and below.

W   In-text lists may be treated in various ways, depending on the content, the context, and the design specifications for the project. This one should be flagged for attention in copyediting; the items should, at least, be consistently lettered or numbered.

X   Is the text below the list a new paragraph or a continuation of the previous paragraph? Query the author in editing.

Y   Flag the typo for correction in copyediting: "his" should read "this."

Z   Flag the grammatically incorrect comma for removal in copyediting.

AA   The period should be placed inside the quotation marks. The profusion of scare quotes (quotation marks used to call attention to a nonstandard or ironic use of a term) in this passage may merit later consideration in copyediting.

BB   The paragraph break interrupting this sentence should be removed.

CC   The double hyphen should be replaced with an em dash.

DD   The block quotation should be set in roman type and with an additional 0.5-inch left indent. Its punctuation and awkward integration with the text should be addressed in copyediting.

EE   Notes: Check that all global formatting changes have been correctly implemented in the notes as well as in the main text. Underlining in book and journal titles should be replaced with italics.

Note 3: Flag the probable typo "Fairchld" for correction in editing.

Notes 8 and 10: Hyphens in date and page-number ranges should be replaced with en dashes.

Note 9: The URL should be rendered in roman type with no underlining. It contains an active hyperlink. Some publishers may ask you to remove links; others prefer to retain them if the work is to be published online or as an e-book.

Some nondiscretionary note cleanup may be automated by find-and-replace operations: for example, placing commas and periods inside quotation marks for article titles, removing the incorrect first period in "et. al.," and standardizing abbreviations of names of months (such as "Aug" in note 8). But an editor should think carefully before making global changes, as they may produce unintended results that can be tedious to undo.

EXERCISE 2-1: Key

GRODIA CON-FUSION Cuisine

Hours: Monday–Thursday 5 P.M.–10 P.M.
Saturday 11 a.m.–11 p.m.
Sun. 11 AM–3 P.M.

Welcome to Grodia! With a cuisine that combines the best

local ingredients and global food trends, our Head chef has created

a menu that is very unique and tantalizing.

Appetizers

Crusty country-style baguette with local artisan goat cheese

soup of the day with House Baked sourdough croutons

Marinated baby Chioggia beets on a bed of mesclun

greens

Little Gem lettuce salad with walnuts, pears, and Brie

Deviled duck eggs with chickweed conserva

sustainably farmed Thai king prawns on a bed of shredded

kale, seasoned with kumquat and lemon-pepper vinaigrette

###

Entrees ( ) close up

changes ok?

Mélange   sourced
~~Melee~~ of locally ~~sauced~~ pan-roasted seasonal vegetables

served on a bead of spicy red quinoa

Panfried wild-caught Alaskan salmon steak on a mashed
potato cake, topped with citrus sauce and roasted asparagus sprinkled
with black volcanic salt from Hawaii

set
double
space

é
Sautéed bone-in chicken breast with lemongrass and jasmine
rice, topped with its own pan juices and accompanied by ~~julian~~
julienned
carrots and ~~candied~~ walnuts   candied

Ham burger grodia: our chef's special take on this favorite.
Ground buffalo patty in a chia-seed bun, topped with tomatoes and an
anchovy & parsley salsa and served with a side of french fries.

Side Orders   add ornament
and space

French fries

coulis
Steamed seasonal vegetables drizzled with a tomato ~~coolie~~

tr
down
Trio of house-made ice creams, gelati, or sorbets; ask your
server for today's flavors—served with Grodia's special cellar-
aged biscotti.

]###[

DESSERTS

change
ok?
crème
~~Crenelated~~ brûlée delicately flavored with ginger

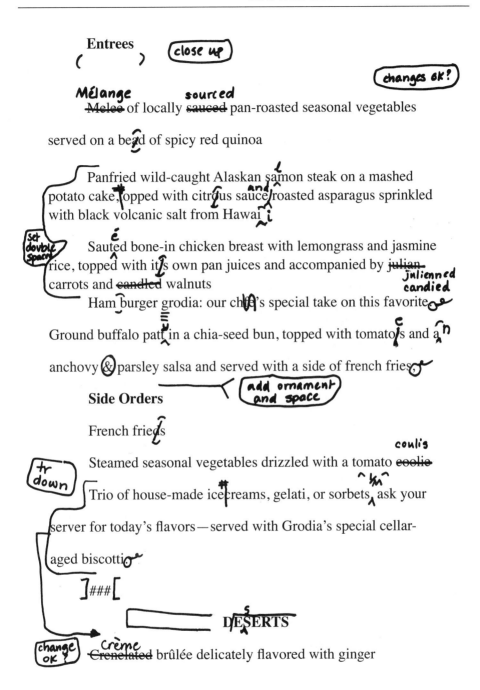

Pavlova: our chef's Down Under specialty of semicooked

meringue smothered with summer berry compote ~~compost~~   [change ok?]

Sinful, flourless chocolate cake flavored with Maker's Mark

(kentucky's finest bourbon), topped with whipped cream, floating

in a lake of raspberry coulis

[close up] (   )

Beverages

[rom]

Green, white, or black teas—ask your server for our

current selection Herbal tisanes—lemon balm or dandelion

flower

Espresso ~~coffee~~, single or double   [ok? Espresso is coffee.]

Macchiato

Latte

our ingredients are obtained from organic and fair ~~fare~~ trade

sources whenever possible.

We want you to have a happy dining experience; please

check with your server about special dietary requirements, and we'll

do our best to accommodate you!

EXERCISE 2-2: Key

Because this exercise allows for latitude in language editing, your version is unlikely to match the key exactly. Changes essential for correctness and internal consistency are highlighted.

A History of Sans-Serif ~~t~~Type

by Franklin Baskerville

In typography and lettering, a *sans-serif, gothic,* or simply *sans* letterform is one that does not have extending features called "serifs_~~"~~" at the end of strokes. The term comes from the French word *sans,* meaning "without_," and "serif_," of uncertain origin, possibly from the Dutch word *schreef_,* meaning "line" or "pen stroke." Sans-serif fonts are often used for headings rather than for body text. They are also used to convey simplicity and modernity or minimalism.

Letters without serifs have been common in writing ~~across~~ throughout history. Today~~,~~ sans-serif fonts have become ~~the most~~ prevalent for the display of text on computer screens.[1] On lower-resolution digital displays, fine details like ~~seraphs~~ serifs may disappear or appear too large.

The Origins of ~~Sans Serif~~ Sans-Serif ~~l~~Letterforms {AU: This looks like a subhead: OK to insert a break above it?}

~~Letters without serifs have been common in writing across history.~~ **{AU: Same sentence appears just above. OK to delete here?}** Printing in the Latin alphabet was originally "serif" in style, imitating the forms of manuscript lettering. The earliest printing typefaces ~~which~~ that omitted serifs were intended not to render contemporary texts~~,~~ but to represent inscriptions in Ancient Greek and Etruscan. Thus~~,~~ Thomas Dempster's ~~De Etruria regali libri VII~~ *De Etruria regali libri VII* (1723)~~,~~ used special typefaces intended for the representation of Etruscan epigraphy, and around 1745, the Caslon foundry made Etruscan typefaces for pamphlets written by the Etruscan scholar John Swinton.[31] **{AU: What does this number refer to?}** Another niche ~~used~~ of a printed sans-serif letterform from ~~in~~ 1786

---

1. Many typographers deplore the use of the term *font* to refer to a type design, such as Helvetica or Times Roman. In traditional usage, this is a *typeface*; a *font* is a subset of the typeface in a specific size, style, or weight, such as 14-point Helvetica Italic. In the digital age, however, with millions of users customizing the appearance of their phone and computer applications by way of the Font menu, this distinction has all but vanished.

onward was a rounded sans-serif script font developed by Valentin Haüy ~~for the use of the blind~~ to enable blind people to read with their fingers.

————Toward the end of the eighteenth century, neoclassical architects began to incorporate ~~ancient~~ Ancient Greek and Roman designs into their designs. The British architect John Soane, for example, commonly used sans-serif letters on his drawings and plans. The lettering style apparently became referred to as "old Roman" or "Egyptian" characters.

In London, "Egyptian" lettering became popular for advertising, apparently because of its mesmerizing effect on the public. The ~~H~~historian James Mosley~~,~~ has written that "in 1805 Egyptian letters were happening in the streets of London, being plastered over shops and on walls by signwriters, and they were astonishing the public, who had never seen letters like them and were not sure they wanted to."[2] A depiction of the style was shown in the *European Magazine* of 1805~~,~~; however, the style ~~did not become~~ was not used in printing ~~for some more years~~ until some years later. Around 1816, William Caslon IV produced the first sans-serif printing type in England for Latin characters.~~B,~~ but no examples of its use have been found. Its popularity ~~flaged~~ flagged until sans-serif typefaces ~~began~~ were again ~~to be~~ issued by London type foundries from around 1830 onward. These were quite different in design, arrestingly bold and similar in aesthetic to the ~~slab~~ slab-serif typefaces of the period.

Sans-serif lettering and fonts were popular ~~due to~~ for their clarity and legibility at a distance in advertising and display use, when printed very large or very small. (The same considerations drive their popularity in digital media today.) Because sans-serif type was often used for headings and commercial printing, many early sans-serif designs did not feature lowercase letters. Simple sans-serif capitals, without use of ~~lower-case~~ lowercase characters, graced Victorian tombstones. The term *grotesque* (from the Italian word for "cave") became commonly used to describe ~~sans-serifs~~ sans serifs. ~~The term grotesque comes from the Italan word for cave, it~~It was often used to describe Roman decorative styles found by excavation~~,~~ but had acquired the secondary sense of something malformed or ~~monsterous~~ monstrous.

The first use of sans serif ~~as a~~ in running text is believed to be in the short booklet *Feste des Lebens und der Kunst:* ~~**eine Betrachtung des Theaters als höchsten Kultursymbols**~~ *Eine Betrachtung des Theaters als höchsten Kultursymbols* (Celebration of Life and Art: A Consideration of the Theater as the Highest Symbol of a Culture), by Peter Behrens, in 1900.

2. James Mosley, "The Nymph and the Grot: An Update," Type Foundry blog, January 6, 2007, http://typefoundry.blogspot.com/2007/01/nymph-and-grot-update.html, accessed May 23, 2017.

Throughout the nineteenth and early ~~20th~~ twentieth centuries, sans-serif typefaces were viewed with suspicion by many printers, especially those of fine books, as being fit only for advertisements.~~,~~ Indeed, many of the common sans-serif types of the period now seem somewhat lumpy and ~~eccentricly~~ eccentrically shaped. In the 1920s, the master printer Daniel Berkeley Updike described sans-serif fonts as having "no place in any artistically respectable composing-room," **{AU: Add citation?}** and to this day most printed books use serif fonts for the body text.

Modern Sans-Serif Type

Through the early ~~T~~twentieth century, ~~an increase in popularity of sans serif fonts took place~~ the popularity of sans-serif fonts increased as more artistic and complex designs were created. Humanist and geometric sans-serif designs were shrewdly ~~were~~ marketed in Europe and America as embodying classic proportions while presenting a spare, modern image. While he disliked sans-serif fonts in general, the American printer J. L. Frazier wrote of Copperplate Gothic in 1925 that "a certain dignity of effect accompanies [it] . . . due to the absence of anything in the way of frills," **{AU: Add citation?}** making it a popular choice for the ~~stationary~~ stationery of professionals such as lawyers and doctors.

~~In the post-War period~~After World War II, ~~an increase of interest took place in~~interest in "grotesque" sans- serifs increased. ~~WL~~The leading type designer Adrian ~~Fruitiger~~ Frutiger wrote in 1961 ~~on~~ about the design of a new face, ~~Univers,~~ Univers, on the nineteenth-~~-~~century model: "Some of these old sans serifs have had a real reconnaissance **{AU: Should this read "renaissance"? Please check original.}** within the last twenty years, once the reaction of the 'New Objectivity' had been overcome. A purely geometrical form of type is unsustainable."[3]

By the ~~nineteen-sixties~~1960s, neo-grotesque typefaces such as Univers and Helvetica had become popular. These typefaces revived ~~through reviving~~ the nineteenth-century grotesques while offering a more unified range of styles~~than on previous designs~~, allowing ~~a wider range of~~text to be set artistically ~~through~~by setting headings and body text in a single ~~font~~typeface. For example, the Linotype version of the Frutiger type family, named for its designer, includes nineteen different weights and styles for various uses.

The relative merits of serif and sans-serif typefaces for various purposes are still hotly debated. Fans of the elegant serif faces used in many twentieth-century printed books lament the tyranny of screen-friendly fonts like Calibri and Arial. Numerous studies have asserted the superior legibility of ~~both~~each styles, though the most significant factor

3. Heidrun Osterer and Philip Stamm, *Adrian Frutiger: The Typefaces; The Complete Works*, ed. Swiss Foundation Type and Typographie (Basel: Birkhäuser, 2014), 88 (e-book).

affecting legibility may be the reader's familiarity with the typeface.[4] Wikipedia itself—in a reversal of the tradition of using serif type for body text and a sans-serif typeface for headings—compromised in its 2014 design makeover by using Hoefler Text, a sans-serif face, as the default for its articles but Linux Libertine, a public-domain serif font, for its own logo.

4. See Alex Poole, "Which Are More Legible: Serif or Sans Serif Typefaces?," Alex Poole blog, February 17, 2008, http://alexpoole.info/blog/which-are-more-legible-serif-or-sans-serif-typefaces/, Febuary 17, 2008, accessed May 23, 2017.

EXERCISE 2-3: Key

The two examples in this key illustrate different forms of markup. The first uses the built-in tools of Adobe Acrobat Reader, including text markup and commenting. Because this form of markup is optimized for on-screen use and doesn't reproduce well on paper, only a screenshot of a partial page is shown. The second is a complete version of the PDF file that uses custom markup stamps, drawing tools, and text boxes in an approach analogous to hand marking proofs. (This set of stamps was created by Diana Stirling in 2008 and is generously shared under the Resources tab of the Copyediting-L home page, http://www.copyediting-l.info.)

No matter which method you use to mark up a PDF file, it's important to remember that, unlike tracked changes in a word processor file, this type of markup does not alter the original text: someone must incorporate the marked changes into the source file from which the PDF file was generated. (PDF files can also be modified directly, but this is generally not a practical approach for copyediting, because the changes are not tracked, and often PDF is not the format in which the final version of the document will be disseminated.) Editors must take care to make PDF markup legible and unambiguous to other users: changes that are hard to see, such as alterations to formatting, spacing, and hyphenation, may require an explanatory comment.

EXAMPLE 1

Effectiveness and Safety of Popular Herbal Remedies

1. St. John's Wort

~~Historically,~~ St. John's wort has been used for centuries to treat mental disorders and nerve pain. ~~Saint John's wort~~ has also been used to ~~tread~~ malaria, as a sedative, and as a balm for wounds, burns, and insect bites. Today, St. John's Wort is used as a folk or traditional remedy for depression, anxiety, and/or sleep disorders.

Strength of Evidence

- St. John's wort has been studied extensively for depressive disorders in both the United States and Europe, and for its interactions with a number of drugs.

Study Results

- A 2009 systematic review of 29 international studies suggested that St. Johnste's wort may be better than a placebo and as effective as standard prescription antidepressants for major depressive of mild to moderate severity. St. John's wort also appeared to have fewer side effects than standard antidepressants. The studies conducted in German-speaking countries, where St. John's wort has a long history of use by medical professionals reported more positive results than those done in other countries, including the United States.

Delete extra sp.

Close up

	Reviewer 1 ▾
	Page 1 5/16/18, 7:37:40 PM
	It
	Reviewer 1 ▾
	Page 1 5/16/18, 8:23:47 PM
	treat
	Reviewer 1 ▾
	Page 1 5/16/18, 8:15:52 PM
	Delete extra sp.
	Reviewer 1 ▾
	Page 1 1/30/19, 12:03:50 PM
	Reviewer 1 ▾
	Page 1 1/30/19, 12:16:13 PM
	Lowercase.
	Reviewer 1 ▾
	Page 1 5/16/18, 7:37:40 PM
	Reviewer 1 ▾
	Page 1 5/17/18, 10:06:44 PM
	Reviewer 1 ▾
	Page 1 1/30/19, 12:30:07 PM
	Delete extra space.
	Reviewer 1 ▾
	Page 1 5/16/18, 8:02:06 PM
	Close up
	Reviewer 1 ▾
	Page 1 1/30/19, 12:22:33 PM
	episodes
	Reviewer 1 ▾
	Page 1 1/30/19, 12:29:31 PM
	Delete extra space.
	Reviewer 1 ▾
	Page 1 5/16/18, 7:50:20 PM
	side
	Reviewer 1 ▾
	Page 1 1/30/19, 12:04:07 PM
	,
	Reviewer 1 ▾
	Page 1 5/16/18, 7:49:57 PM
	,

A screenshot showing part of a page marked up with the built-in tools in Adobe Acrobat Reader.

EXAMPLE 2

> Add a note at the top or bottom crediting your source?

Effectiveness and Safety of Popular Herbal Remedies

1. St. John's Wort

[It] ~~Historically,~~ St. John's wort has been used for centuries to treat mental disorders and nerve pain. ~~Saint John's wort~~ has also been used to ~~tread~~ *[treat]* malaria, as a sedative, and as a balm for wounds, burns, and insect bites. Today St. John's Wort is used as a folk or traditional remedy for depression, anxiety, and~~/or~~ sleep disorders.

[Del extra sp.]

Strength of Evidence

- St. John's wort has been studied extensively for depressive disorders in both the United States and Europe, and for its interactions with a number of drugs.

Study Results

[Del extra sp.]

[insertion OK?] *[episodes / side]*

- A 2009 systematic review of 29 international studies suggested that St. John~~'s~~'s wort may be better than a placebo and as effective as standard prescription antidepressants for major depressive of mild to moderate severity. St. John's wort also appeared to have fewer ~~side~~ effects than standard antidepressants. The studies conducted in German-speaking countries, where St. John's wort has a long history of use by medical professionals reported more positive results than those done in other countries, including the United States.
- *[SP]* Two large studies sponsored by NCCAM and the National Institute of ~~Menial~~ Health *[Mental]* ~~did not~~ showed no benefit. Neither St. John's wort nor a standard antidepressant medication decreased symptoms of minor depression better than a placebo in a 2011 study. The herb was no more effective than placebo in treating major depression of *[a]* moderate severity in a 2002 study.
- Basic research studies suggest that St. John's wort may prevent nerve cells in the brain from reabsorbing certain chemical messengers, including dopamine and serotonin. These naturally occurring neurotransmitters are known to be involved in regulating mood, but much remains to be learned about exactly how they work.

[wrong font]

Side Effects and Cautions

- Research has shown that St. John's wort interacts with many medications in ways that can interfere with their intended effects. Examples of medications that can be affected include

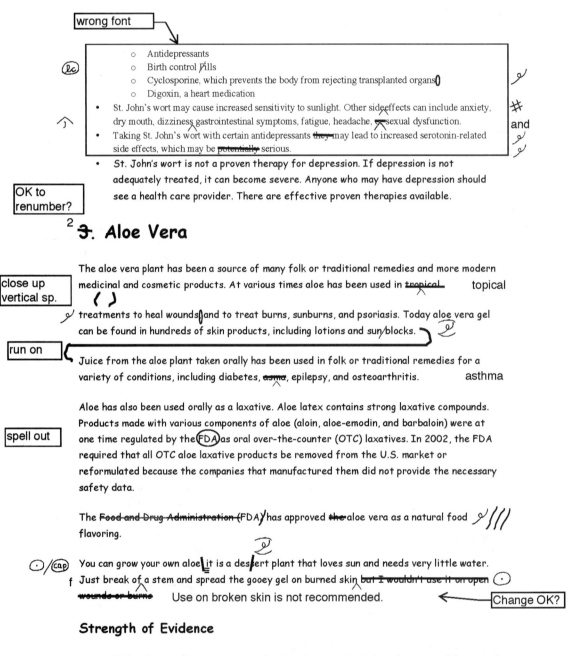

wrong font

lc

○ Antidepressants
○ Birth control Pills
○ Cyclosporine, which prevents the body from rejecting transplanted organs
○ Digoxin, a heart medication

• St. John's wort may cause increased sensitivity to sunlight. Other side effects can include anxiety, dry mouth, dizziness gastrointestinal symptoms, fatigue, headache, sexual dysfunction.

and

• Taking St. John's wort with certain antidepressants they may lead to increased serotonin-related side effects, which may be potentially serious.

• St. John's wort is not a proven therapy for depression. If depression is not adequately treated, it can become severe. Anyone who may have depression should see a health care provider. There are effective proven therapies available.

OK to renumber?

² 3. Aloe Vera

close up vertical sp.

The aloe vera plant has been a source of many folk or traditional remedies and more modern medicinal and cosmetic products. At various times aloe has been used in tropical   topical treatments to heal wounds and to treat burns, sunburns, and psoriasis. Today aloe vera gel can be found in hundreds of skin products, including lotions and sun/blocks.

run on

Juice from the aloe plant taken orally has been used in folk or traditional remedies for a variety of conditions, including diabetes, asma, epilepsy, and osteoarthritis.   asthma

spell out

Aloe has also been used orally as a laxative. Aloe latex contains strong laxative compounds. Products made with various components of aloe (aloin, aloe-emodin, and barbaloin) were at one time regulated by the FDA as oral over-the-counter (OTC) laxatives. In 2002, the FDA required that all OTC aloe laxative products be removed from the U.S. market or reformulated because the companies that manufactured them did not provide the necessary safety data.

The Food and Drug Administration (FDA) has approved the aloe vera as a natural food flavoring.

You can grow your own aloe it is a desert plant that loves sun and needs very little water. Just break of a stem and spread the gooey gel on burned skin but I wouldn't use it on open wounds or burns Use on broken skin is not recommended.

Change OK?

Strength of Evidence

• Only a few small exploratory studies have been conducted on aloe vera gel for wound healing and for treating burns or abrasions.

Study Results

- The results of these studies suggest that topical aloe gel may help heal burns and abrasions. One study, however, suggested that aloe gel inhibits healing of deep surgical wounds. Aloe gel has not been shown to prevent burns from radiation therapy.
- There is not enough scientific evidence to support ~~the use of~~ aloe vera for any of its many other ~~uses.~~ traditional applications. ← Change OK?

Side Effects and Cautions

Topical Aloe Vera

Topical use of
- ~~Use of topical~~ aloe vera is not associated with significant side effects.

Oral Aloe Vera

- A 2-year National Toxicology Program (NTP) study on oral consumption of an extract of aloe vera found clear evidence of carcinogenic activity (colon tumors) in male and female rats. Whether this finding is of relevance to humans has yet to be determined, but it raises concerns about use of oral products containing aloe vera.
- Abdominal cramps and diarrhea have been reported with oral use of aloe vera.
- Diarrhea, caused by the laxative effect of oral aloe ~~aloe~~ vera, can decrease the absorption of many drugs.
- People with diabetes who use glucose-lowering medications should be cautious if also taking aloe by mouth because preliminary studies suggest aloe may lower blood that glucose levels.
- There have been a few case reports of acute hepatitis following oral aloe vera use, causal but a ~~casual~~ relationship has not been established.

EXERCISE 2-4: Key

The tone of editorial queries will vary with the nature of the material, the relationship of the author and editor, and the editor's personal style, so your answers may differ substantially in wording from the sample responses here. Queries should always, however, be courteous and as concise as possible without being cryptic; they should clearly identify the problem; and they should specify what the author should do to resolve the matter.

1. By weight, cartilage has more water than bone (as much as 70 percent).

    {Does this mean that cartilage contains 70 percent more water than bone does, or that cartilage contains up to 70 percent water? Please reword to clarify.}

2. The bank had branches in New York, Boston, Charleston, and Washington.

    {To avoid ambiguity, please include the states (e.g., Charleston, West Virginia, or Charleston, South Carolina).}

3. The guru advocated a low-carbohydrate diet, sexual abstinence, and daily meditation, which was not popular with the community.

    {Please clarify: were all these regimens unpopular, or one in particular?}

4. The war in Iraq waged by President Bush has had far-reaching consequences.

    {"War in Iraq" could refer either to the war of 1991 (often called the Gulf War) or to the 2003 war, and "President Bush" could refer to either George H. W. Bush or George W. Bush. Please clarify.}

5. Yoga classes are offered on-site Wednesday–Friday.

    {Please spell out: does "Wednesday–Friday" mean Wednesday *through* Friday, or Wednesday *and* Friday?}

6. In 2014, according to the UN's FAOSTAT database, the world's top producer of whole dried milk was New Zealand (approximately 1.2 million), distantly followed by Brazil (612,000) and Argentina (230,000).

    {Please include the units of measure for these figures.}

7. It's been a long wait, but the Proofreaders' Society calendars and diaries for 2018 are nowhere!

    {Should this read "now here"?}

8. Stir the toffee mixture constantly over medium-high heat until it reaches a temperature of 300°C (the hard-crack stage).

    {"300°C" is dangerously hot. Revise to read "300°F" or the equivalent in degrees Celsius (approximately 150°C)?}

9. The designs of Augustus Pugin (1812–1852) for the interior of the Palace of Westminster adhered to the principles of the Arts and Crafts movement of the late 1800s and early 1900s.

   {Because Pugin died before the beginning of the Arts and Crafts movement, it's not clear how his designs could have "adhered" to its principles. Maybe reword to read "anticipated the principles"?}

10. After Sun Yat-sen's death, in June 1925, Wang Jingwei became the head of the Nationalist Party.

    {Did both Sun Yat-sen's death and Wang's succession occur in June? If not, revise to avoid misreading?}

11. Women are less successful than men in engineering and laboratory science because they cry when criticized.

    {~~Please tell me you're not serious.~~ This generalization about women's behavior may offend many readers (not only women) and seems hard to support. Consider explaining, rephrasing, or omitting?}

12. The high level of the hormones oxytocin and especially vasopressin in male prairie voles motivates them to care for their mate and offspring, since it is highly rewarding.

    {Which is rewarding: the high hormone levels or the caring behavior? Can you rephrase to clarify cause and effect?}

13. The New Zealand Romney is the country's largest sheep breed.

    {Please specify by what measure it's largest: number of sheep, physical size, or something else? }

14. The fractal patterns observed in deep time, and the imagery of descending scales they evoke, suggest that leaps are always built on other leaps in a nested hierarchy that unfolds deep into history's continuum.

    {~~Wait, what?~~ The multiple metaphors of scales, leaps, nested hierarchies, and folding make this sentence difficult to follow. Can you simplify?}

15. Bristol Student Accidentally Made Explosive [online news headline]

    {Did the student create an explosive or somehow become explosive?}

16. Mechanical keyboards are more expensive to make, so they are usually of higher quality than a standard keyboard.

    {Explain why higher cost implies higher quality?}

17. (Bonus) How many copyeditors does it take to screw in a lightbulb?

    {Does "screw in" refer to installing a lightbulb or to copulating in a lightbulb? Please clarify.}

EXERCISE 2-5: Key

This key lists examples of style and usage decisions you might record while copyediting. It takes a fairly lean approach: for a longer text, you might opt to include more proper names, your choices between equally acceptable variant spellings, decisions about hyphenation of compound terms, and the like. See, for example, the style sheets presented in the keys to exercises 4-4 and 15-3.

Author/Title: Baskerville/"A History of Sans-Serif Type"
Date: February 20, 2018
Dictionary: *Merriam-Webster's Collegiate Dictionary*, 11th ed.
Style Manual: *The Chicago Manual of Style*, 17th ed.

Alphabetical List of Names and Terms
(n. = noun, adj. = adjective)

Ancient Greek
e-book
Frutiger, Adrian
gothic (adj.)
lowercase (adj.)
Mosley, James
neo-grotesque
sans-serif (adj.)
sans serif (n.)
World War II

Special Symbols
Standard European diacritics

Dates and Numbers
In general, use Chicago style: one through one hundred, 101, 199, one thousand
Use numerals for type sizes: 14-point Helvetica
May 23, 2017
1920s
twentieth-century (adj.)
twentieth century (n.)

Miscellaneous Notes
Names of typefaces and fonts set c/lc: 14-point Helvetica Italic, Copperplate Gothic
Words used as words set italic: The term *grotesque*

Footnotes

Heidrun Osterer and Philip Stamm, *Adrian Frutiger: The Typefaces; The Complete Works,* ed. Swiss Foundation Type and Typographie (Basel: Birkhaüser, 2014), 88 (e-book).

James Mosley, "The Nymph and the Grot: An Update," Type Foundry blog, January 6, 2007, http://typefoundry.blogspot.com/2007/01/nymph-and-grot-update.html, accessed May 23, 2017.

Punctuation

Serial comma

No spaces around em dash

Double, not single, quotation marks (US style)

Wordspace between initials in personal names: J. L. Frazier

EXERCISE 2-6: Key

The following cover memo to an author, intended for email transmission, addresses the essential logistical points. Editorial correspondence may vary considerably from this example, of course, depending on the nature of the project, the level of editing involved, the editor's relationship with the author, the publisher's workflow, and other factors.

Dear Dr. Baskerville,

Attached please find the copyedited version of your informative and enjoyable article on the history of sans-serif typefaces for *The Editing Geek's Encyclopedia*. Please review the changes thoroughly, making any necessary corrections and additions and responding to all editorial queries. Please also bear in mind that this will be your only opportunity to make significant changes: at the proof stage, only essential corrections will be possible.

The text has been edited using the Track Changes feature of Microsoft Word, with changes struck through, insertions double-underlined, and editorial queries boldface and enclosed in braces, like this: **{AU: This is a query}**. To preserve a complete record of editing changes, the file has been "protected" so that any additions or other changes you make will also be tracked.

The copyediting is light: most of the changes are intended to bring the article and notes into conformity with the mechanical style of the encyclopedia, which is based on *The Chicago Manual of Style* and *Merriam-Webster's Collegiate Dictionary*. In a few places I've suggested minor wording changes for clarity or to avoid repetition, and I've also queried a few points that may be unclear to readers.

To help keep the encyclopedia project on track, please email the file, with your revisions and comments, to your managing editor, Perpetua Goudy (perpetua_goudy@editinggeek.com), by next Thursday, July 13. If you have any questions about the editing or the publication process, please contact me or Perpetua.

Sincerely,
Aldus Hoefler

EXERCISE 3-1: Key

1. *Mushfaker:* A mender of umbrellas or a peddler; sometimes, one who uses this job as a cover for more fraudulent pursuits. This esoteric word can be found in *Green's Dictionary of Slang.*

2. Masc.: *alumnus* (sing.), *alumni* (pl.). Fem.: *alumna* (sing.), *alumnae* (pl.). The clipped terms *alum* (sing.) and *alums* (pl.) are listed in *M-W Collegiate, M-W Unabridged, Web New World,* and *AHD. M-W Collegiate* traces these clippings back to 1877; *Web New World* and *AHD* label them "informal." That being the case, the use of *alums* in edited prose requires editorial judgment about the register, or level of formality, required by the social context: the clipping would blend into casual writing but might seem jarring in a professional or academic piece. In formal prose, writers often use the masculine *alumni* as a gender-neutral plural. Both *M-W Collegiate* and *AHD* recognize this use as legitimate while advising that many writers object to it. Duly cautioned, an editor might choose a work-around, such as rewording to avoid the problem or substituting a gender-neutral synonym (e.g., graduates).

3. *M-W Collegiate* (also *M-W Unabridged*): *log in* or *log on* (v.); *log-in* or *log-on* (n.). *Web New World:* no listings. The *AP Stylebook,* supplementing *Web New World's* somewhat sparse word list, has *log in* (v.); *login* or *logon* (n.).

   AHD: login (n.), with *logon* as a secondary variant; no verb form listed.

   Wiktionary: *log in, log-in, log on, log-on* (v.); *login, logon* (n.).

   With so many unranked choices, Wiktionary offers no help at all, but even authoritative dictionaries list several spellings for the noun and verb forms. So what's an editor to do? Consulting the dictionary specified by the publisher, if any, use the first-listed form for the relevant part of speech; check a reliable backup dictionary (or style manual) if the publisher's preferred dictionary fails to provide guidance. If the publisher does not select a dictionary, remember that most US book editors turn first to *M-W Collegiate* (or the online *M-W Unabridged*) and next to *AHD,* whereas most news editors consult *Web New World* (supplemented by the *AP Stylebook*), followed by *M-W Collegiate.* Or, as members of the Copyediting-L online forum (www.copyediting-l.info) have occasionally advised, "flip a coin and get on with your life" (FACAGOWYL). Just be consistent.

4. *M-W Collegiate* recognizes *rock 'n' roll* and *rock and roll,* in that order, as equally acceptable forms; *Web New World* lists *rock-and-roll; AHD* votes for either *rock-and-roll* or *rock 'n' roll.* An editor would normally choose the first form listed in the dictionary specified for the editing job—*rock 'n' roll* if *M-W Collegiate, rock-and-roll* if *Web New World* or *AHD*—but could be justified in electing a second-listed

equal variant if warranted by special considerations, such as the author's preference or readers' expectations.

5. The first-listed plurals *avocados* and *hooves* are the preferred forms in *M-W Collegiate*; *avocadoes* and *hoofs* are listed as secondary plural forms. *Web New World*
and *AHD* don't recognize the plural spelling *avocadoes* at all and disagree on the
preferred plural for *hoof*: *AHD* (like *M-W Collegiate*) lists *hooves* first, whereas
Web New World prefers *hoofs*.

6. *Skype* is not listed at all in either *M-W Collegiate* or *AHD*, but the crowdsourced
Wiktionary records *Skype* (usually capitalized, sometimes lowercased) as a verb
form derived from the trademarked name of a currently popular videoconferenc-
ing application. This suggests that if the so-named digital technology endures, the
word *Skype*, like *Google* (which does appear as a verb form, usually capitalized, in
both *M-W Collegiate* and *AHD*), may eventually be added to the general English
lexicon, and might lose its capitalization.

7. According to Wiktionary, *IoT* stands for "Internet of Things" (among other terms).
Dictionary.com, accessed through OneLook Dictionary Search, also defines this
trending term. The recent abbreviation dates to 2001, according to a new entry in
M-W Collegiate, but it is not yet listed in *M-W Unabridged* or *AHD*. If the abbreviation endures, it may eventually be recorded in the pages of these other standard
dictionaries, but the jury is still out.

8. *NIMBY* (not *nimby*)—alternatively, *Nimby* (*Web New World*)—is an acronym for
"not in my back yard." It means opposition to locating a socially beneficial project, such as a proposed recycling facility or a shelter for homeless people, in one's
own neighborhood; it can also refer to the person who opposes the placement of a
worthy project in the neighborhood (*Web New World*, *AHD*). The plural is formed
simply by adding an *s* to the root word, just as the plural is formed for proper
names ending in *y* (lots of *NIMBYs* at the neighborhood meeting; two *Marys* and
seven *Larrys* in my graduating class).

9. According to *M-W Collegiate*, *M-W Unabridged*, *Web New World*, and *AHD*, the
three plural forms of *octopus* are *octopuses*, *octopi*, and (listed only in *Web3* and
M-W Unabridged) *octopodes*. Preferred is the first-listed *octopuses*. Although these
dictionaries do not elaborate, the second-listed form, *octopi*, is based on a spurious analogy with Latin plurals such as *alumni*—an analogy so persistent that these
standard dictionaries now recognize this form as a variant plural. Unlike *alumnus*, however, *octopus* is not derived from Latin; it is Greek in origin. *Octopodes* is
a legitimate Greek plural form, but there is no need for it (except in scientific references to members of the biological order Octopoda), as the regular English plural
octopuses is well established.

10. *Gypsy* (capitalized, referring to a Romani person) or *gypsy* (lowercased, meaning any itinerant or unconventional individual) is the first-listed spelling in *M-W
Unabridged* and *AHD*; *M-W Collegiate* and *Web New World* record only this spell-

ing at the main entry but include a separate entry for *Gipsy* or *gipsy*, identified as a variant or "chiefly British" spelling and simply cross-referenced to the main entry. These authorities caution that the term is often considered offensive, especially as an ethnic designation; the word derives from a misconception that the Romani originated in Egypt.

EXERCISE 3-2: Key

The following table records the answers to the author's questions found in the nine style guides specified for exercise 3-2. (The editions used, with full publication details, are listed in the Selected Bibliography.) A *?* indicates that a manual does not offer advice on the question or that a provisional answer has been extrapolated from examples in the manual.

Question no.	1	2	3	4	5	6	7	8	9
Chicago	(a)	(b)	(b)	(c)	(c)	(a)	(c)	(b)	(a)
Gregg	(a)	(b)	(b)	(c)	?	(a)	(b)	(c)	(a)
Butcher's	?	(c)	(d)	?	?	(d) or (i)	(b)	(c)	(c)
Ed Can Engl	(a)?	(b) or (c)	(c)?	?	?	?	(b)	?	?
New Oxford	(a)?	(b) or (c)	(d)	?	?	(d)	(b)	(c)	(a) or (c)
AP Stylebook	(a)	(b)	(b)	(c)	(c)	(b)	(b)	(d)	(a)
GPO	(a)	(b)	(b)	(c)	(a)	(b)	(b)	(d)	(a)
APA	?	(b)	(c)	?	?	(a) or (j)	(c)	(c)?	?
CSE	?	(a)	(c)	?	?	(h)	(b)	(d)	(a)

COMMENTS

Style manuals are by no means unanimous in their recommendations, and some may not provide any advice on a given question or may offer many options. These differences reflect the conventions for different types of publications and readers and for different English-speaking regions of the world. Regardless of which manual you normally use, you should be able to spot different editorial styles and to consult alternative guides.

1. *Ed Can Engl* favors the capitalization of names of (Canadian) regions "even when used informally," noting that popular names for some locations "have become entrenched firmly enough to be uppercased, especially within the designated area" (5.6.1[c], 5.6.5). *New Oxford* advises editors to capitalize established vernacular names for regions and areas and cites "the Big Apple" among its examples.

2. British style (*Butcher's, New Oxford*) for quotation marks and accompanying punctuation differs substantially from the prevailing US style (*Chicago, Gregg, APA, AP Stylebook, GPO*). However, *New Oxford* notes, many British newspapers have adopted US conventions. And even though Canadian style observes many British conventions, it often employs US style for quotations (exception: a few major Canadian presses) and adopts other US conventions as well (*Ed Can Engl* 7.6.1, 7.6.3). *CSE* employs a hybrid form, combining the US use of double

quotation marks with the British practice of placing accompanying punctuation outside closing quotation marks.

3. For technical content, however, *Chicago, Gregg,* and *New Oxford* recommend (c).

4. Some style manuals do not fully cover the treatment of compound terms. For additional guidance an editor may need to use a current unabridged dictionary, compare forms in the Google Books Ngram Viewer, or consult one of the major language corpora (e.g., Corpus of Contemporary American English, Corpus of Historical American English) listed in the Selected Bibliography of *The Copyeditor's Handbook.*

5. Many style manuals do not provide guidance for the treatment of terms for regional historical events, although they may provide comparable examples (*GPO:* Dust Bowl). If such examples do not provide a model for the recommended style, the editor may need to consult authoritative publications in the specific subject matter to determine the convention.

6. As the ten possible answers to this question indicate, there are many styles for representing dates in notes, as well as in text, with variations in the order of day-month-year details and in the use of (arabic or roman) numerals or (spelled-out or abbreviated) names of months. *Ed Can Engl* surveys many styles for dates in citations rather than specifying one. *New Oxford* describes the various conventions for representing dates—British, US, continental, international—and cautions against possible misinterpretations of dates by readers unfamiliar with the style selected.

7. Should you add just an apostrophe or an apostrophe followed by an *s* to form the possessive of a singular proper noun that ends in *s* or a sibilant (an *x, sh,* or *ezz* sound)? Many style manuals recommend using pronunciation as a guide. Hence:

    • Hastings' proposal, *not* Hastings's proposal; *but* Morris's plane tickets (*Gregg*)
    • Bridges' car, *not* Bridges's car; *but* Thomas's apartment (*Butcher's*)
    • Ulysses' wanderings, *not* Ulysses's wanderings; *but* Keats's poetry (*Ed Can Engl*)
    • Williams' school, *not* Williams's school; *but* Marx's theory (*New Oxford*)
    • Jules' seat, *not* Jules's seat (*AP Stylebook*)

    CSE also advocates pronunciation as a guide in forming possessives of singular proper nouns, but it offers examples formed with *'s* that some English speakers would *not* pronounce with an added syllable (e.g., Charles's suggestion). Go figure. Because the aural guideline can result in the *appearance* of inconsistency among possessive forms in a manuscript—and, one might add, because it introduces an element of subjectivity—*Chicago* counsels the simple addition of *'s* to singular proper nouns in virtually all cases, regardless of pronunciation (exception: proper nouns that are plural in form but singular in meaning, e.g., United States').

8. The major style questions for the treatment of the names of newspapers are these:
   Should an editor use *The* as part of the formal name of the newspaper? Include the
   city of publication in the name? Italicize the name of the newspaper?

   • Regardless of whether *The* is part of the actual masthead, some style manuals
     (*Chicago, Butcher's, Ed Can Engl, CSE, GPO*) tolerate a relaxed treatment in text
     (e.g., either "*The New York Times*" or "the *New York Times*"), based on the syn-
     tax of the sentence in which the name is embedded; advice varies concerning
     the inclusion or omission of the definite article in source citations. Other man-
     uals (*Gregg, AP Stylebook*) mandate strict adherence to the wording of the mast-
     head. *Butcher's* and *New Oxford* stipulate the inclusion of *The* with all one-word
     periodical titles (e.g., *The Economist, The Times*). APA offers no explicit advice
     on this issue.
   • Several manuals (*Gregg, Ed Can Engl, AP Stylebook*) advise the provision of the
     city of publication only if the masthead includes it (e.g., "the *New York Times*"
     but "the *Daily News*"); the *AP Stylebook* and CSE recommend adding the city
     parenthetically if it is not in the masthead. *Butcher's, New Oxford, APA,* and
     GPO do not explicitly address this issue.
   • The *AP Stylebook,* CSE, and *GPO* do not italicize newspaper names.

   The stricter guidelines may require research to determine the actual wording in
   a newspaper's masthead, a task complicated by the fact that newspapers often
   change their names and redesign their mastheads over the years. Thus, for the sake
   of expediency, *Chicago* advises editors to avoid the time required to investigate the
   exact content of a newspaper masthead on a given date. Instead, editors may simply accord lowercase roman treatment of *the* and incorporate the city into newspaper titles, e.g., "the *New York Daily News*" for the New York paper called the *Daily
   News,* or "the *San Francisco Street Sheet*" for the San Francisco publication simply
   called *Street Sheet.*

9. British style (*Butcher's, New Oxford*) sometimes spells longer acronyms with an
   initial capital letter only (e.g., Unesco). To choose between the indefinite articles *a*
   and *an,* an editor must first determine whether a given abbreviation is pronounced
   as a word (an acronym) or as a series of letters (an initialism) and then choose the
   article based on the initial sound. Research may be needed to establish the pronunciation of an esoteric term. In fact, even some well-known abbreviations with
   several pronunciations may require investigation: Should *FAQ* be pronounced
   "eff-ay-cue" (*an* FAQ) or "fack" (*a* FAQ)? Should *URL* be pronounced "you-are-ell"
   (*a* URL) or "earl" (*an* URL)? The Google Books Ngram Viewer allows comparison
   of rival usages: with this tool, an editor can determine that *a FAQ* is declining in
   popularity while the frequency of *an FAQ* remains constant, and that *a URL* is far
   more widespread than *an URL.*

EXERCISE 3-3: Key

Answers are based on the specified print editions of the usage guides listed with this exercise; abbreviations for these references are identified in the front matter to the workbook. Publication details for supplementary sources mentioned in passing are provided in the comments. The abbreviations *s.v.* (*sub verbo,* "under the word") and *s.vv.* (*sub verbis*), its plural, identify the location of quoted usage advice.

1. A self-driving car will behave **differently** on the German autobahn **to** how it will in the Italian Alps.

Comment: Stet. This sentence is correct as written—assuming it is directed to a British or an international English readership. The expression *different(ly) to,* although unfamiliar to the American ear, is idiomatic in British English. Copperud, *DEU, Fowler's, Garner's, MAU,* and Partridge all recognize *different(ly) to* as unobjectionable in British English (s.v., respectively, "different from, than"; "different from, than, to"; "different"; "different"; "different[ly] than"; "than, different"). Bernstein, a longtime editor at the *New York Times,* makes no mention of it or of other Briticisms.

If revising the sentence for American readers, however, a copyeditor would have to choose between *different(ly) from* and *different(ly) than.* On this matter, authorities diverge. *Different(ly) from,* followed by a noun or noun phrase, is the impeccably correct choice—and the only choice acceptable to strict authorities (*MAU,* Partridge): "A self-driving car will behave *differently* on the German autobahn *from* how [*or* the way] it will in the Italian Alps." But supplying a noun or noun phrase after *from* sometimes results in a cumbersome, wordy construction, as this revision illustrates. Thus, other commentators (Bernstein, *DEU, Fowler's, Garner's*) accept the expression *different(ly) than* provided it is followed by a clause, even by an elliptical clause ("A self-driving car will behave *differently* on the German autobahn *than* [it will] in the Italian Alps").

2. The continuously variable automatic transmission (CVT) of the Subaru Forester doesn't seem as responsive and refined as a traditional automatic; **on the other hand**, the optional turbocharged engine provides spirited acceleration.

Comment: Stet. Most commentators would judge this sentence correct. Only *MAU* (s.v. "on the other hand") counsels against the expression unless it is paired with *on the one hand,* a precaution simply "to avoid the heckling" from persnickety readers who might object. On the other hand, *Garner's* (s.v. "on the other hand") considers it "pure pedantry" to insist on pairing hands, pointing out that *on the other hand* has been used for centuries without *on the one hand* and is a well-established idiom. The other manuals on the list for this exercise have nothing to say on this subject.

3. **All** cats are **not** alike.

Comment: Revise—unless the author is styling informal dialogue. The syntax of this statement, though imprecise, is common in speech, but the revision "Not all cats are alike" is more exact in writing. Bernstein, Copperud, *DEU, Fowler's, Garner's, MAU,* and Partridge (s.v., respectively, "not, placement of"; "not all, all . . . not"; "all"; "not"; "all"; "negatives, trouble with"; and "negation") agree that the syntax *all . . . not* is a well-established idiom—several cite Shakespeare's "All that glisters is not gold"—but advise scrupulous modern writers to revise in the interest of logic and precision. Instead of citing the Bard, the audaciously hip *DEU* quotes an advice columnist writing under the pseudonym Ann Landers ("Everyone in San Francisco is not gay") to demonstrate the point: even though "in conversations [such] constructions are not ambiguous," they can be misleading in print; "putting the *not* first will remove the ambiguity."

4. In an essay of **five hundred words or less**, explain why Santaclaws deserves a free lifetime supply of Fancy Feast cat food.

Comment: Stet. The phrase "five hundred words or less" is correct. To be sure, many of us have been taught that *fewer* should be used in expressions of number and *less* in expressions of quantity ("Fewer cows, less milk"). An oversimplified interpretation of this rule leads to hypercorrections such as the one sometimes seen in the express check-out line at the grocery store: "10 items or ~~less~~fewer." But all the usage authorities listed for this exercise (s.v. "less, fewer" or "fewer, less") acknowledge that the idiomatic use of *less* and *fewer* involves determining whether the context refers to quantity or number. *Less* is commonly used with plural nouns indicating a unit or composite amount, as in distances, periods of time, and sums of money. *Less* is the standard usage when followed by *than* plus a number and a plural noun, e.g., "less than ten years" or "less than five hundred words." (The proposed emendation of the grocery store sign in *Garner's,* from "10 items or less" to "10 or fewer items," cleverly avoids the usage problem altogether by circumventing the original phrasing—a sage solution for any writer who does not want to *appear* sloppy to hypercorrecting readers.) Both the announcement of the Fancy Feast essay contest and the sign in the grocery store use an elliptical construction with the same pattern as the idiom *"less than* plus a number and a plural noun"—"10 items or less [than 10 items]."

5. In 2011 we got two feet of floodwater in our basement **due to** unusually heavy rains.

Comment: Stet *or* revise. A decision to intervene depends on the required level of propriety and the readers' expectations. The use of "due to" as an adjective ("Her illness was *due to* stress") has never been questioned; the contested use is the adverbial one ("She became ill *due to* stress"). Opinions on "adverbial *due to*" (s.v. "due to") range from "false" (Partridge) to "impeccable" (*DEU*). In the 1926 edition of *A Dictionary of Modern English Usage,* H. W. Fowler condemned it as "illiterate," and the taint of his disapproval has continued into the twenty-first century. Even though adverbial *due to* is now well established in literate prose, many authorities still advise writers to shun this use lest they be suspected of negligence; *Garner's* counsels writers to avoid the "skunked term" altogether! Perhaps *Fowler's* offers the best advice by appealing to the judgment of the writer or editor concerning the preferences of a given readership: "Those wishing to avoid the tut-tutting of last-ditch pedants can, of course, replace *due to* with the straightforward *because of . . .* or the more formal *owing to* and *on account of.*" Thus, representations of dialogue and informal prose addressed to a contemporary audience of peers (unless they are nitpickers) can surely use adverbial *due to* without censure; formal prose pitched to conservative or doctrinaire readers should avoid this shibboleth of usage, which would risk annoying and distracting them.

6. **As far as our insurance coverage**, it's fortunate that our basement didn't flood again.

Comment: Revise. At minimum, the phrase "as far as" requires completion: "As far as our insurance coverage *is concerned . . .*" With the exception of Partridge, which has no comment on this construction, the usage guides (s.v. "as far as," "as," or "far") observe that the incomplete expression appears to be typical of speech but is "best avoided in formal writing" (*Fowler's*) unless a verb phrase such as *is concerned* or *goes* is added. Even so, authorities discourage the "as far as" construction as rambling and verbose and recommend a shorter formulation whenever possible, e.g., "Considering our insurance coverage, it's fortunate that our basement didn't flood again."

7. We had **over** four inches of rain yesterday!

Comment: Stet. The phrase "over four inches of rain" is perfectly acceptable. Some commentators have insisted that the adjective *over* be restricted to spatial expressions ("over the moon") and *more than* be reserved for expressions of quantity ("more than four inches of rain"). This strong opposition to "quantitative *over*" may have originated as a tradition in American journalism: the authoritative *AP Stylebook* tenaciously upheld the distinction until recently. But usage guides (s.v. "over") now recognize *over* and *more than* as interchangeable. *Garner's* explicitly dismisses the distinction between *over* and *more than* as "a baseless crotchet," and the current *AP Stylebook* accepts *over* "in all uses to indicate greater numerical value."

8. The last storm completely **decimated** our just-sprouted seedlings.

Comment: Revise. The sentence should be rephrased: "The last storm obliterated [*or* completely destroyed] our just-sprouted seedlings." According to its Latin origin, the word *decimate* originally meant "to reduce by one-tenth." Although purists try to restrict use to this definition, modern custom employs the word in the looser sense of "to destroy a considerable part of something." The usage guides (s.v. "decimate") accept this extended definition but caution writers that, to avoid a clash with the word's etymology, *decimate* should never be used to mean "utterly destroy, annihilate." *Garner's* in fact brands *decimate* a "skunked term," one that should perhaps be eschewed altogether because it is "infected with ambiguity." But many writers and editors will resist the diminution (not to say the decimation) of our rich English vocabulary because of petty quarrels between prescriptivists and descriptivists.

9. Profound political differences **among** the progressive, centrist, and conservative factions of the Democratic Party will be difficult to reconcile.

Comment: Revise. The correct preposition here is *between*. Many of us have learned a simple but misleading rule stating that *between* goes with two things or persons and *among* with more than two. Wrong! The usage guides (s.v. "between, among") all describe a more nuanced principle: "*Between* expresses one-to-one relations of many things, and *among* expresses collective and undefined relations. . . . Good writers commonly use *between* with more than two elements" (*Garner's*). Or "when three or more things are brought into a relationship severally and reciprocally, *between* is proper. . . . When the relationship is looser, *among* is the proper word" (Bernstein). Thus: "Policy arguments *among* constituents abound; profound political differences *between* the progressive, centrist, and conservative factions of the Democratic Party will be difficult to reconcile."

10. The television series *Okkupert* (*Occupied*)—a political thriller in which Russia, with support from the European Union, occupies Norway to "help" restore its oil production—**begs the question,** Would the peace-loving people of Norway cooperate with or violently oppose a velvet glove invasion?

Comment: Revise. Usage authorities (s.v. "beg the question") agree that the phrase "begs the question" is misused here and should be rewritten, e.g., as "raises the question." *Beg the question,* a translation of a Latin term in logic, originally referred to the fallacy of basing a conclusion on the very premise that must be proved (e.g., Fuji apples taste better than Granny Smith apples because Fujis have a superior flavor). The English phrase has come to signify, more broadly, "ignore the question" or "avoid giving a straightforward answer" but *not* "raise the question," despite this increasingly common misuse. Strict commentators (Bernstein, *MAU,* and Partridge) discourage using the phrase in *any* of the expanded senses. The liberal *DEU* allows its use in the sense of avoiding or sidestepping a question, but most other commentators strongly recommend revision. "In precise English, some punctilious writers will prefer to avoid [these newer meanings] in favour of the available alternatives" (*Fowler's*) or at least to eschew the ubiquitous misuse to mean "raise the question." "Though it is true that [this] new sense may be understood by most people, many will consider it slipshod" (*Garner's*).

11. When a couple are united in an arranged marriage, they have a lifetime to get to know **one another**.

Comment: Stet. "One another" is acceptable here. The finicky distinction between *each other* (for two) and *one another* (for more than two) is pure hokum. All the usage guides agree (s.v. "each or each other") that the terms are interchangeable. Although *Garner's* states that "careful writers and editors will doubtless continue to observe the distinction," even the advice in Fowler's original 1926 *Dictionary of Modern English Usage,* reprised in the contemporary *Fowler's,* dismissed the distinction as spurious and ahistorical.

12. The ASPCA is rounding up all cats *which* are not on leashes and placing them in animal shelters.

Comment: Stet *or* revise. The use of *which* instead of *that* in this restrictive relative clause is not incorrect, just a bit British. American English frequently—but not consistently—differentiates the relative pronouns *that* and *which: that* (without commas) restricts, or limits, the meaning of the term modified; *which* (with commas) simply adds nonessential information about the term. Hence: "The ASPCA is rounding up all cats *that* are not on leashes and placing them in animal shelters. But my free-range cats, *which* are impossible to herd, will indubitably evade capture." British English, on the other hand, uses both *that* and *which* restrictively. (Some British authors stoutly resist the Americanization—or, as they would put it, the "Americanisation"—of their prose when copyeditors change all their restrictive *which*es to *that*s.) *Fowler's* nevertheless advocates for observing the distinction between restrictive *that* and nonrestrictive *which,* as do most American usage commentators (Bernstein, *Garner's, MAU,* and Partridge, s.v. "that" or "which"). Copperud, however, recognizes restrictive *which,* and *DEU* concludes that "you can use either *which* or *that* to introduce a restrictive clause—the ground for your choice should be stylistic," e.g., to prevent a syntactic miscue or an undesirable word echo in a sentence also using the conjunction *that.* Thus the consistent use of *that* in restrictive clauses is a stylistic refinement in American English; it is not an Eleventh Commandment. Still, some house styles require copyeditors to enforce the distinction. (See *The Copyeditor's Handbook,* chapter 4, for further discussion.)

13. More than 11,900 male drivers died in US traffic accidents in 2009, *while* just under 4,900 women drivers perished that year.

Comment: Stet. *While* may legitimately be used to express a temporal relationship ("during the time that"), a contrast ("whereas"), or a concession ("although"). While some early commentators condemned the use of *while* in its nontemporal senses, most modern usage authorities (s.v. "while") accept the contrastive and concessive uses of the word but caution against possible ambiguity when the temporal sense of the word clashes with another meaning (e.g., "I exercise with free weights while [at the same time that? whereas?] my husband goes for long walks"). The strength of opposition to nontemporal *while* varies. *MAU* argues that "writers lose nothing by declining to use *while* in any other way" than the temporal sense and should "resist a general watering down of solid meanings." Bernstein recommends limiting the use of *while* to its temporal meaning to avoid even the risk of confusion: "It may be unduly restrictive to suggest that *while* be confined to its temporal meaning, but it is safe." Copperud "favors restricting the use of *while* to its temporal sense, particularly when there is danger of ambiguity." Some authors, however, stoutly resist the substitution of the upscale *whereas* for *while* in contrastive uses. And *DEU* firmly states that the contrastive and concessive meanings are "established and standard" and that "the specter of ambiguity is much exaggerated"; in the event that a writer composes an ambiguous sentence, it should of course be revised. *Garner's* and *Fowler's* agree.

14.   Lily, the caretaker's daughter, was ***literally*** run off her feet.

Comment: Stet—but only if your author is James Joyce! Otherwise, rewrite. This sentence, from Joyce's story "The Dead" (1914), is quoted in *DEU* as an example of the common error of using *literally* hyperbolically to mean "figuratively," "virtually," or "in effect." (In "The Dead," some critics argue, Joyce adopts Lily's point of view, deliberately describing the hard work of serving a dinner party in words the uneducated maid herself would use.) Even though contemporary dictionaries record these now-common definitions, authorities (s.v. "literally") unilaterally denounce the use of *literally* as an intensifier, calling it needless (Bernstein), "redundant" (*Fowler's*), "heedless" (Copperud), "meaningless" (*MAU*), "ludicrous" (*DEU*), "slovenly" (Partridge), and "paper-thin" (*Garner's*). Garner places the solecism at stage 3 of his five-stage Language-Change Index: "Commonplace even among many well-educated people but . . . still avoided in careful usage." *Fowler's* advises, "*Use your judgment.* Knowing that your readers may have the screaming abdabs (dated British English for 'have a fit') if they read *literally* prefacing a metaphor . . . , you might want to avoid using it altogether. Otherwise, I urge you to reread what you have written so as to avoid hilarity or ridiculousness you did not intend." Still, *Fowler's* thinks "all the fuss . . . [is] literally a storm in a teacup."

15.   A ***verbal*** contract isn't worth the paper it's written on.

Comment: Stet (assuming your author is joking) *or* revise if the context is ambiguous or your readership unfamiliar with the set phrase "verbal contract" to mean "unwritten contract" or "oral agreement," the kind sealed with a handshake. This quip, often misattributed to Samuel Goldwyn, illustrates the confusion that can arise between the two different but equally well-established senses of *verbal:* "in words" of whatever form; more specifically, "in spoken words." Most usage authorities (s.v. "oral, verbal" or "verbal, oral") argue for restricting the term *verbal* to its general meaning, "in words," and using *oral* and *written* to differentiate the forms of communication (Bernstein, Copperud, *Fowler's, MAU,* Partridge). Several commentators (Copperud, *DEU, Fowler's*) acknowledge the existence of the set expressions in law—*verbal contract, verbal agreement,* and *verbal evidence*—in which *verbal* is commonly understood to mean *oral,* but all caution writers to use the more precise words if there is any possibility of misunderstanding. *Garner's* explicitly criticizes Goldwyn's wordplay: "In fact, given the primary sense of *verbal,* the movie producer Samuel Goldwyn wasn't really very ironic when he remarked, 'A *verbal* contract isn't worth the paper it's written on.' After all, a written contract *is* verbal. The phrase requires *oral.*" But an industry insider accustomed to hearing the legal term *verbal contract* used to describe an unwritten agreement in Hollywood surely would discern Goldwyn's irony without the proposed revision in *Garner's.*

EXERCISE 3-4: Key

The following answers are based on data retrieved using the Google Books Ngram Viewer (https://books.google.com/ngrams) in April 2017, with a "smoothing" of 3. There are many ways of finding information with this tool to answer the questions in this exercise—and, as advertisements often say, actual results may vary.

1. In 2000, *Ping-Pong* slightly outnumbered *ping-pong,* at about 1.2 to 1; the form *Ping-pong* was a distant third. Use as a noun was more common than use as a verb by nearly 2 to 1, but the verb form is solidly established.

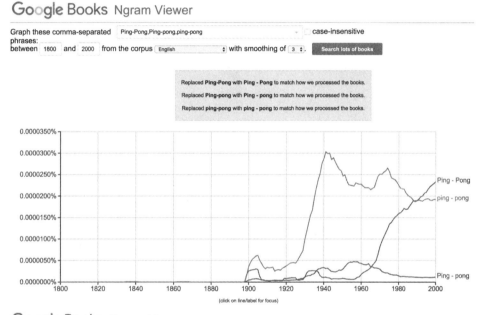

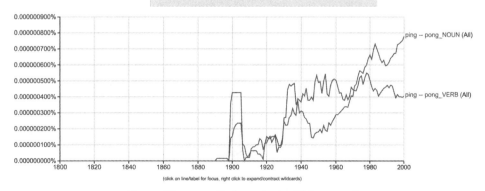

Ngram Viewer results for variants of "ping-pong."

2. Although *M-W Unabridged* and the online *AHD* list *chaise longue* and *chaise lounge* as equal variants, *Garner's* and several other standard usage guides brand the latter spelling an error. In British English, according to the Google Books Ngram Viewer, the unassailably proper *chaise longue* prevails over *chaise lounge* by more than 13 to 1; in American English the ratio is more like 1.8 to 1.

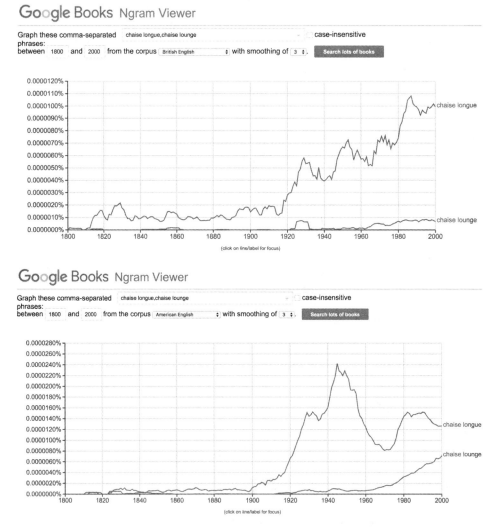

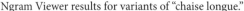

Ngram Viewer results for variants of "chaise longue."

3. A "case-insensitive" search of usage between 1991 and 2008—that is, from the year the World Wide Web went public to the most recent year covered by the Google Books Ngram Viewer—shows that the open form (*Web page* or *web page*) outweighed *webpage* by a ratio of about 13 to 1 at the end of this time period but that the solid form was slowly gaining ground.

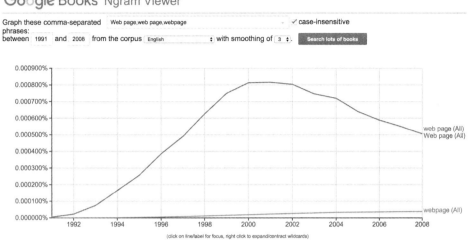

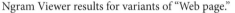

Ngram Viewer results for variants of "Web page."

4. The solid form *pantsuit* appears to have emerged in the mid- to late 1960s and to
    have exceeded *pant suit* and *pants suit* in usage by 1980. An interesting aside: The
    emergence of the solid spelling appears to parallel the second wave of US femi-
    nism (Betty Friedan's *The Feminine Mystique* was published in 1963) and Yves St.
    Laurent's 1966 creation of Le Smoking, the first tuxedo for women, as an alterna-
    tive to "the little black dress." Although the wearing of trousers in public remained
    controversial for US women for at least another decade, the pantsuit had become
    as well established as the solid form of the word by the end of that period. In 2016,
    supporters of a pantsuit-wearing woman candidate for the US presidency proudly
    described themselves as members of Pantsuit Nation.

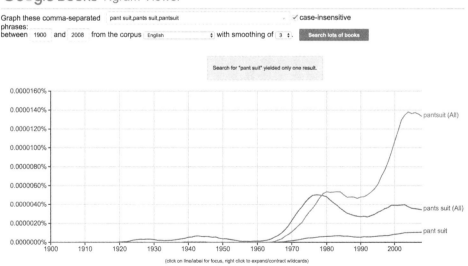

Ngram Viewer results for variants of "pant suit."

5. In the corpus of written prose searched by the Google Books Ngram Viewer, *people who are* appears far more common (by a ratio of over 19 to 1) than *people that are*. This result illustrates the challenges of formulating a valid search. To exclude constructions in which *that* is a conjunction (e.g., "I tell people *that* the best thing to do is to find something they enjoy doing") rather than a relative pronoun (e.g., "We need people *that* want to do things"; "I need people *that* I can depend on"), the search formula must include a verb following the relative pronoun ("people who are,people that are"); thus the result is limited to occurrences of these particular phrases. At best, the date ranges below the ngram, hot-linked in the Google Books Ngram Viewer, allow you to review extensive examples of usage in snippets from Google Books.

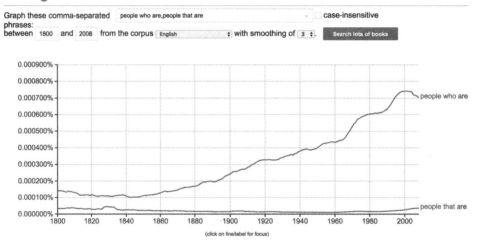

Ngram Viewer results for "people who are" and "people that are."

This key lists all possible correct examples, identified by number (grammatical element), letter (sentence), and the essential words or phrases.

1. Active voice verbs
   (a) [repertoire] excludes
   (b) [writers and type designers] have promoted
   (c) [who] were
   (d) [demand] has declined
   (e) [adman] campaigned
   (f) [mark] had
   (g) [American Type Founders] cast; [company] offered
   (h) [securing] proved
   (i) [decline . . . resistance] thwarted
   (j) [popularity] seems
   (k) [It] has [and] occupies; [fonts] include

2. Passive voice verbs
   (a) [symbols] were . . . proposed
   (b) [printing press] was invented
   (c) [*point d'ironie . . . SarcMark*] was intended

3. Independent clauses
   (a) Our repertoire . . . excludes . . . many quaint symbols
   (b) at least nine different writers . . . have promoted a distinctive character
   (c) this *point d'ironie* . . . was intended to aid readers
   (d) The demand . . . has declined
   (e) A twentieth-century Madison Avenue adman . . . campaigned for the *interrobang*
   (f) This mark had its day
   (g) American Type Founders . . . cast it . . . ; the Remington Rand typewriter company offered it
   (h) But securing a place . . . proved difficult
   (i) the decline of hot metal composition . . . thwarted advocates' efforts
   (j) the enduring popularity . . . seems surprising
   (k) It still has a cult following (and a T-shirt) and even occupies

4. Dependent clauses
   (a) [symbols] that were once proposed
   (b) Since the printing press was invented
   (c) [readers] who were unable to detect mockery
   (k) although few Unicode fonts include the character

5. Simple sentences
   (d), (e), (f), (h), (i), (j)

6. Compound sentences
    (g)

7. Compound predicates
    (k) [It still] has . . . and [even] occupies . . .

8. Appositive phrases
    (e) [the *interrobang*,] a fusion of the question mark and exclamation point
         conveying a mixture of doubt and surprise
    (g) [the newly designed typeface] Americana
    (k) [Unicode,] the standard computer character set

9. Prepositional phrases
    (a) of punctuation marks; for inclusion
    (c) without a typographic cue
    (d) for such a mark; with the invention; of emoticons and emoji
    (e) for the *interrobang*; of the question mark and exclamation point;
         of doubt and surprise
    (f) during the 1960s
    (g) for the newly designed typeface; as a replaceable key and typehead;
         on the Model 25 electric
    (h) for this mark; in the canon; of modern punctuation
    (i) of hot metal composition; of early photocomposition; to changing
         the modern writing system
    (j) of the interrobang
    (k) in Unicode

10. Participial phrases
    (c) Variously styled, [this *point d'ironie* . . .]
    (e) conveying a mixture of doubt and surprise

11. Absolute phrases
    (j) Considering this failure

12. Gerund phrases
    (h) securing a place for this mark

13. Infinitive phrases
    (b) to flag irony or sarcasm
    (c) to aid readers; [unable] to detect mockery

Bonus:
    Restrictive dependent clauses
    (a) [symbols] that were once proposed
    (c) [readers] who were unable to detect mockery
    Restrictive appositives
    (g) [the newly designed typeface] Americana

EXERCISE 3-6: Key

Answers are based on information accessed on the specified websites in June 2017. Your search methods (and possibly your results) may differ.

1. This quotation did not originate with Maya Angelou, although it calls to mind the title of her autobiographical work *I Know Why the Caged Bird Sings* (1969) and is attributed to her by many sources, including Pinterest and several inspirational posters. According to Quote Investigator, many sayings, some centuries old, concern the reasons that birds sing, but the earliest near match to this specific quotation appears in *A Cup of Sun: A Book of Poems* (1967) by the children's book author Joan Walsh Anglund. Anglund's verse is printed by itself on a dedicated page; the phrasing differs slightly from the words on the commemorative stamp because it uses the pronoun *he* instead of *it*.

2. Whatever you may want to believe about unidentified flying objects, this book about recent UFO sightings exists. It was released in 2017 through Amazon's CreateSpace Independent Publishing Platform and is sold on Amazon.com; listed publication information can be confirmed by viewing the actual copyright page using Amazon's "Look Inside" feature. In addition, this book is cataloged in WorldCat as available for circulation at Le Moyne College Library, Syracuse, New York. Several major media, including the *New York Times,* reviewed the book, as evidenced in the listings returned by some standard search engines.

3. The correct quotation is this: "But words do not live in dictionaries; they live in the mind." The source: "Craftsmanship," in *Virginia Woolf: Selected Essays,* ed. David Bradshaw (Oxford: Oxford University Press, 2008), p. 89. A search on the entire misquotation goes awry, but a search on the first sentence leads to the correct wording and complete source details in Google Books.

4. Yes, this is correct. According to an invaluable compendium of global information and statistics, the CIA's World Factbook, the US infant mortality rate in 2016 was 5.8 deaths per 1,000 live births, whereas the infant mortality rate in Iceland was 2.1 deaths per 1,000 live births, the third-lowest mortality rate (after Monaco and Japan) in the list of 225 countries surveyed. Among these countries, fifty-six have lower rates of infant mortality than the United States.

5. According to a reverse image search on TinEye, the National Gallery of Art in Washington, DC, which owns the original work of art, identifies this painting as Jean-Honoré Fragonard's *Young Girl Reading* (c. 1769); several other authorities simply title it *The Reader*. TinEye lists numerous sources for a digital copy, among them Wikimedia Commons (https://commons.wikimedia.org/wiki/File: Fragonard,_The_Reader.jpg), which declares that the image is in the public domain (permission is not needed to reproduce the image) but stipulates that correct identification and attribution are required for its use.

6. According to Wikipedia, the *S* in Truman's name doesn't stand for any *one* name, because Truman's parents chose the middle initial to honor both of his grandfathers, Anderson Shipp Truman and Solomon Young; the initial is usually written with a period. A Wikipedia entry on E. E. Cummings also discloses that

> Cummings's publishers and others have often echoed the unconventional orthography in his poetry by writing his name in lowercase and without periods . . . , but normal orthography (uppercase and periods) is supported by scholarship and preferred by publishers today. Cummings . . . most often signed his name with capitals.

But, as another Wikipedia entry explains, lowercase treatment is preserved in "bell hooks," the pen name of the activist-author Gloria Jean Watkins, out of respect for Watkins's strongly stated preference. A crowdsourced online encyclopedia such as Wikipedia cannot always be trusted, but the well-documented entries about these three individuals are probably reliable. The conventions for treating their names are confirmed by multiple citations of the individuals' publications in the Library of Congress Online Catalog, the online *Britannica,* and Amazon; *Chicago* also endorses the lowercase treatment of "bell hooks."

Popular artists and musicians often change their stage names and adopt pseudonyms for ancillary pursuits. Given sufficient cross-checking, internet searches of recent issues of news sources and industry publications are usually best for determining the most current stage name for a shape-shifting contemporary artist. Sean Combs, the wealthiest rapper in the world according to *Forbes* (May 10, 2017), has used all the names listed. He currently performs under the name Diddy, having simplified it in 2005 as an aid to cheering audiences. Prince (born Prince Rogers Nelson) reinvented his stage name and pseudonymous songwriting credits more than a dozen times. In a dispute with his then record label, Warner Bros., which had trademarked the name Prince, he adopted the unpronounceable "Love Symbol" as his moniker in 1993. Although the record label provided music journalists with a digital file of the symbol, most media used work-arounds in discussing the artist's new albums: "The Artist Formerly Known as Prince," "TAFKAP," "The Artist," "The Symbol," or even "O(+>." In 2000, when Prince was released from his contract with Warner Bros., he reclaimed his given name.

7. The following terms are listed as trademarked on INTA's Trademark Checklist: Loony Tunes, Photoshop, Levi's, Jeep, Popsicle, Frappuccino. *Spandex* is a generic term. Trademark owners rigorously observe certain protocols to protect their investment in brand identity and reputation: capitalization, adjectival use only (e.g., Kleenex tissues, not Kleenex), and consistent use of the symbol ™ (unregistered trademark) or ® (registered trademark) following the name. But writers and editors are *not* required to obey these rules—unless they are working for the company that owns the trademark—and can avoid using the fussy symbols that follow a trademarked name in business communications and advertisements. Editors normally just capitalize the trademark or substitute a generic equivalent unless an

authoritative dictionary sanctions a generic use of the name. *M-W Unabridged* recognizes *loony tunes* (adj., lowercased), *photoshop* (v., "often" capitalized), and *jeep* (n. or v., lowercased or capitalized) as generic terms. Thus a revision of this sentence might read: "In the loony tunes, heavily photoshopped [*or* retouched] version of Sarah's life on Facebook, Sarah, sheathed in skin-tight Levi's [*or* jeans] and a spandex top, is shown lounging in her jeep [*or, for a particular cachet,* Jeep] while eating a Popsicle and sipping a Frappuccino." In a work of fiction, an author might take further liberties (*levis, popsicle, frappuccino*) if aiming for a hip tone.

8. According to the United States Board on Geographic Names (BGN) website, all these quaint place names—courtesy of a list of unusual town names at the Internet Accuracy Project (https://www.accuracyproject.org)—are authentic. But Mosquitoville is in Vermont, not Florida, and Monkey's Eyebrow should be Monkeys Eyebrow. Most US place names omit the possessive apostrophe. The US Board on Geographic Names, *Principles, Policies, and Procedures: Domestic Geographic Names* (December 2016, Version 1.0), posted on the BGN website, states that

> apostrophes suggesting possession or association are discouraged within the body of a proper geographic name (Henrys Fork: not Henry's Fork). The word or words that form a geographic name change their connotative function and together become a single denotative unit. They change from words having specific dictionary meaning to fixed labels used to refer to geographic entities. The need to imply possession or association no longer exists.

9. Percy was driving more than 93 mph, about 28 mph over the speed limit. Standing slightly under 5 feet tall, Marcy weighs 182 pounds, overweight unless she's a Marine wearing all her combat gear at weigh-in. A tonne is a metric ton (1,000 kg, or 2,204.6 lb.), so 2 tonnes (2,000 kg, or 4,409.2 lb.) is more than 4,200 pounds. Numeric values can be converted to different units of measurement simply by typing, e.g., *150 km/h to mph* in the Google search box. (See https://support.google.com/websearch for this and other search tips.)

10. Google links the inquisitive editor not only to the Wikipedia article on the Hippocratic oath but also to a web page of oaths and codes posted by Johns Hopkins University, home of one of the top-ranked US medical schools. These sources concur that the famous phrase was never part of the Hippocratic oath, in either its traditional or its modern form.

11. According to the WHO website, in 2015 about 438,000 deaths occurred as a result of malaria, whereas an estimated 1.4 million HIV-negative and 0.39 million HIV-positive deaths were caused by tuberculosis, which remains one of the top ten causes of death by disease worldwide.

12. *Panthera uncia* (snow leopard) is listed on the IUCN's Red List of Threatened Species as Endangered C1: in a continuing decline of at least 20 percent within the past five years or two generations, whichever is longer. The current population is estimated at less than 2,500 mature individuals.

13. Sometimes all web browser paths lead to Wikipedia, according to which two contemporary novels feature this fascinating landscape garden near Dumfries, Scotland: Louise Penny's *The Long Way Home* and Cameron Jace's *Circus.* The article in Wikipedia and a short feature in Atlas Obscura state that the private garden is open to the public one day a year to raise money for charity; a website called Scotland's Gardens, found with any standard search engine (e.g., Google, Bing, Yahoo!, DuckDuckGo), provides ticket information. Numerous photographs of the garden can be viewed on Google Images, and many are reproduced elsewhere on the web as well. A 2005 book written by the garden's designer, the landscape architect Charles Jencks, is also extensively illustrated.

14. Google was founded on September 4, 1998; the first preserved image of Google's home page was captured for the Internet Archive and stored on the Wayback Machine on November 11, 1998.

Google's first home page. From the Internet Archive Wayback Machine, https://archive.org/web/, November 11, 1998.

EXERCISE 4-1: Key

1. The man wearing the long-sleeved red gingham shirt told amusing tall tales.

Comment: No commas are needed in "long-sleeved red gingham shirt," because the adjectives are not coordinate. (Test for coordination: One would not write "the long-sleeved and red shirt" or "the red and gingham shirt.") No commas are needed in "amusing tall tales" either, because these adjectives are not coordinate: "amusing" modifies the unit "tall tales." In contrast, a comma is required in "This is a tall, healthy tree" or "This is an amusing, sad tale."

2. The accountant asked whether the receipts were in order.

Comment: The sentence ends with a period, not a question mark, because the question is an indirect one.

3. The accountant asked, "Are the receipts in order?"

Comment: The comma after "asked" is mandatory to separate the speaker's tag from the direct quotation. The sentence ends with a question mark because the speaker's statement is a direct question. And since the question mark belongs to the dialogue being quoted, the question mark goes inside the closing quotation marks. In contrast, the question mark goes outside the closing quotation marks when the act of asking a question is not part of the quotation:

Who said "Beware of all enterprises that require new clothes"?

Do you have a copy of the poem "Sunday Morning"?

4. School curriculums have traditionally been the domain of politicians and educators, not judges.

Comment: The mandatory comma sets off the antithetical "not judges." Note that a midsentence antithetical phrase is both preceded and followed by commas:

Politicians and educators, not judges, have traditionally set school curriculums.

5. The promoter said that if no more ticket requests came in, the concert would be canceled.

Comment: There is a mandatory comma after a dependent clause that precedes an independent clause. In this sentence the comma also prevents the reader from construing "came in the concert" as a unit of thought. Notice that if we reverse the order of the clauses, the new sentence has no comma, because the restrictive dependent clause follows the independent clause.

The promoter said that the concert would be canceled if no more ticket requests came in.

No comma is needed before or after "that" in a phrase of the form "he said that *x*" or "she wrote that *y*."

6.   Harvard freshmen who have reading scores below the national average performed better than expected on the math aptitude test.

Comment: No commas are required here. The context signals that the *who* clause is restrictive (that is, the subject is *only* those Harvard freshmen who have below-average reading scores). If one inserts commas to set off this *who* clause, it becomes non-restrictive, which would mean that *all* Harvard freshmen have below-average reading scores. If you cannot determine from the context whether a clause is restrictive or non-restrictive, query the author (see the comment at sentence 10). Also, note that "better than expected" functions here as an adverb and therefore carries no hyphens; in "the better-than-expected results," in contrast, the attributive adjective is hyphenated.

7.   You can teach yourself basic computer skills using a how-to book, but a better choice is to ask a knowledgeable, sympathetic friend for tutoring.

Comment: A mandatory comma is supplied before "but" because this conjunction links two independent clauses. (To use a semicolon here would be unconventional; semicolons normally join two closely related independent clauses when there is no intervening conjunction.) A comma is also added between the coordinate adjectives "knowledgeable" and "sympathetic." (Tests for coordination: One could say "a sympathetic and knowledgeable friend" and "my friend is knowledgeable and sympathetic.")

8.   Each hospital has a service office whose staff members will answer your questions about hospital policies.

Comment: Initially, the *whose* clause appears nonrestrictive: it does not limit the meaning or extent of "service office." But the meaning of the sentence (that the service office's staff members will answer questions) requires us to treat the *whose* clause as restrictive. If you are under the misimpression that *whose* should not be used to refer to inanimate objects, see *DEU* (s.v. "whose"), which forcefully puts this bugaboo to rest.

9.   From June 1 through June 3, 1998, the Chamber of Commerce of Oakland, California, hosted its third annual conference for small businesses.

Comment: Mandatory commas are supplied before and after the year in a month-day-year construction. Mandatory commas are also added before and after the name of the state.

10. All part-time employees who are not covered by the new contract will be laid off.
    {Query}

    {Query}: Does the layoff affect *only* those part-time employees who are not covered by the contract *or* does it affect *all* the part-time employees (none of whom are covered by the contract)? If the former, the sentence could read

    > Those part-time employees who are not covered by the new contract will be laid off.

    If the latter, the sentence could read

    > None of the part-time employees are covered by the new contract, and all will be laid off.

Comment: Taken out of context, the *who* clause could be restrictive (the layoff affects *only those* part-time employees who are not covered by the contract) or nonrestrictive (the layoff affects *all* the part-time employees, none of whom are covered by the contract). You should query the author and perhaps propose a revision that will be clearer to readers.

11. The three-person Board of Appeals today dismissed the case arguing that employees' workplace email communications should constitute a "zone of privacy." **{Query}**

    {Query}: Which argues for the "zone of privacy"—the case or the Board of Appeals? If the former, the sentence could be revised thus:

    > . . . dismissed the case which argued that employees' workplace email communications should constitute a "zone of privacy."

    If the latter, the addition of a comma will clarify the meaning:

    > . . . dismissed the case, arguing that employees' workplace email communications should constitute a "zone of privacy."

Comment: Without context to clarify the meaning, this sentence too is ambiguous. Again, query the author and propose a revision that avoids the risk of misunderstanding.

12. ~~According to t~~The *New York Times*~~,~~ reported that Steve Bannon and Sean Spicer, the White House press secretary, began a campaign this weekend to blame congressional Democrats for the failure of the proposed bill.

Comment: The punctuation of this sentence is correct, but the combination of syntax and punctuation results in a miscue. The three names—"the *New York Times,* Steve Bannon and Sean Spicer"—can be misread as a series (AP style omits the series comma), so readers may temporarily misconstrue them as the compound object of "according to." As readers plunge onward, they may have to circle back to the beginning and reparse the sentence to identify the correct subject of the verb "began." A simple revision eliminates the difficulty.

13. Even if government officials cared about the poor~~,~~ and mostly black victims of Katrina enough to change their schedules, the administration would probably have bungled the relief effort, because FEMA is now run by political appointees with no experience in disaster relief.

Comment: This is another correctly but misleadingly punctuated sentence. Because of the comma between the coordinate adjectives "poor" and "mostly black," the first clause may be misread as ending at "poor," which will cause readers to interpret "mostly black victims" as the subject of the second clause. Here, the substitution of the conjunction "and" (for which the comma between coordinate adjectives stands in) eliminates the possibility of misreading.

14. What can individuals do to reduce traffic congestion? ~~Dont' drive,~~Don't drive: telecommute or take public transportation.

Comment: The comma once again invites the reader to interpret "drive, telecommute or take public transportation" as a set of actions to be avoided. Replacing the comma with a colon sets off the answer to the question and clarifies that telecommuting and taking public transportation are recommended alternatives to driving. When resolving this ambiguity, don't overlook the misplaced apostrophe in the contraction.

EXERCISE 4-2: Key

---

1. Beware of all enterprises *that require new clothes*.

Comment: Henry David Thoreau wrote this advisory in *Walden*. The phrase is *restrictive;* no comma is required. Thoreau was not warning readers about *all* enterprises but only about the subset of enterprises for which a new wardrobe would be necessary. Note his use of the relative pronoun *that*. In American English, careful stylists often distinguish between *that* (in restrictive relative clauses) and *which* (in nonrestrictive clauses). Despite the strong preference of some writers and editors to maintain this distinction, however, it is not a hard rule—British English rarely observes it—but rather a style choice. Arguably, in some contexts the observation of this distinction helps clarify meaning.

2. If my relative spent some of his money on a back-pain specialist, *who could teach him exercises that would prolong his working life by another decade*, shouldn't that be considered an investment?

Comment: As punctuated, the relative clause "who could teach . . . exercises" is *nonrestrictive*, and the clause "that would prolong . . . decade" is *restrictive*. That is, the first clause refers to *any* back-pain specialist (if the commas were omitted, the statement would refer only to that subset of back-pain specialists who teach specific therapeutic exercises). The second clause refers not to *all* therapeutic exercises but only to those capable of prolonging the relative's pain-free working life.

3. The Pentagon has decided that it will not award the Purple Heart to Desert Storm war veterans; *who suffer only from post-traumatic stress disorder*.{Query}

    {Query}: Has the Pentagon declined to award the Purple Heart to *all* Desert Storm veterans (who, incidentally, *all* suffer from PTSD)? Or is the Pentagon withholding the medal just from those veterans who have PTSD but no physical injuries?

Comment: It seems likely that the Pentagon excludes Desert Storm veterans suffering "only" from PTSD but awards the Purple Heart to veterans with physical injuries. If so, the phrase "who suffer . . . disorder" is *restrictive,* and the comma should be deleted as shown. The query to the author is intended to confirm this interpretation.

4. Repairs to windows *which are judged to be in the worst condition* will be prioritized.{Query}

    {Query}: Do you mean that (1) all windows, as opposed to other structures (e.g., doors or facades), are judged to be in the worst condition and will therefore be repaired first OR (2) those particular windows that are judged to be in the worst condition will be repaired before other windows?

Comment: If (1), then the phrase "which are judged . . . condition" is *nonrestrictive* and should be set off from the main clause with a pair of commas. If (2), then the phrase is *restrictive* and needs no commas; substituting *that* for *which* here, though not mandatory, would remove the possibility of misreading.

5. Ms. Chetwin said fresh chicken, **which is not cooked correctly,** is considered responsible for half of all campylobacter cases.

Comment: Not all fresh chicken is improperly cooked! Delete the commas to clarify that only improperly cooked fresh chicken (*restrictive*) is responsible for many campylobacter cases. Some editors would also propose replacing *which* with *that* here to emphasize the restrictive meaning of the relative clause, but some authors (speakers of British English, for example) would likely oppose this change.

6. When **my oldest brother Robert, who was a quiet, studious fellow**, went off to college, he turned into **Conan the Barbarian**.

Comment: The *nonrestrictive* "Robert" is in apposition to (a renaming of) "my oldest brother," since a person can have only one *oldest* brother, and his name happens to be Robert; hence, the name would normally be set off with a pair of commas. Note, however, that some commentators, including Bryan Garner, allow commas to be omitted in such short appositives of relationship, provided there is no ambiguity. See the discussion of "spousal commas" in *The Copyeditor's Handbook,* chapter 4, under "Function 3: Setting Off Phrases."

The relative clause "who was a quiet, studious fellow" is *nonrestrictive* and is correctly set off from the main clause with a pair of commas.

A capitalized epithet used *restrictively* as part of a name does not require internal commas: Mary Queen of Scots, Ivan the Terrible, Dennis the Menace, Conan the Barbarian. See the discussion of such personal nicknames in *The Copyeditor's Handbook,* chapter 6, under "Personal Names and Titles."

7. In Mao Zedong's writings, there is no distinction between Mao, **the theoretician,** and Mao, **the political strategist**.

Comment: The appositional phrases "the theoretician" and "the political strategist" are *restrictive:* they limit those aspects of Mao being referred to.

8. The greatest growth occurred in the northern half of Illinois, **where communities were newer and more progressive and where antislavery strength was concentrated**.

Comment: A comma should set off the compound adverbial clause, which is *nonrestrictive:* it merely adds information about "the northern half of Illinois."

9. But none of the Americans viewed the journey in quite the same light as did Baldwin Mollhausen, *whose drawings of the trip are a chronicle of German Romanticism.*

Comment: A comma should set off this *nonrestrictive* relative clause: it adds information about the one and only Baldwin Mollhausen; it does not restrict, or limit, a class of Baldwin Mollhausens.

10. The trail at the Oakland Zoo allows visitors to observe California wildlife species, *like mountain lions and ~~grisly~~ grizzly bears, which reside in the state today.*

Comment: Did you notice the misspelling of "grizzly"? Sometimes close attention to one type of problem causes an editor to overlook others! Always reread copyedited text for such oversights.

The *nonrestrictive* appositional phrase "like mountain lions and grisly [*sic*] bears" should be set off with a pair of commas: the species named here do not limit the class of California wildlife species but merely serve as examples of the class. Some editors would change *like* to the more formal *such as* here to introduce this list of examples, but most commentators do not insist on distinguishing the usage of these terms except to avoid ambiguity.

The relative clause "which reside in the state today" is *restrictive:* the reference is to the subset of species currently extant in California. The meaning would be more clear if *that* were substituted for *which* here.

EXERCISE 4-3: Key

When comparing your edited version with this key, read slowly to make sure you spot each correction. This answer key uses balloons alongside the redlined text to display revisions and queries; the latter, here called "Comments," are identified by bracketed numbers in balloons tethered to the queried word or phrase. Explanations of changes, flagged in the text with lettered superscripts, follow the redlined manuscript.

Some overly zealous copyeditors will pore over a manuscript,[A] and change every "till" to "until" or vice versa, depending on their training, their grammatical ear, and their ideas about prose style. Although editors must try to forestall the depreciation of English into colloquial swill, they should never adopt a self-styled purism that does not allow for some variety of expression. When a tyrannical editorial coordinator waves Fowler, Wilson Follett, and other venerable guardians,[B] the staff should wave back Theodore Bernstein's *Miss Thistlebottom's Hobgoblins*, a thoughtful debunking of sacred cows in usage, or William Morris and Mary Morris's *Harper Dictionary of Contemporary Usage*,[C][D] which explores the differences of opinion among the so-called experts.[E]

A second danger:[F] Some novice copyeditors misinterpret the recommendations in *The Elements of[G] Style* as a mandate to change such sentences as "The outcry was heard round the world" to "Everyone in the world heard the outcry."[H] True, the active voice is more forceful, and a procession of passive constructions is a sure cure for insomnia. But the passive voice is preferable when the writer's goal is variety or emphasis.[I]

Balloons:

Author
Deleted: pour

Author
Deleted: .

Author
Deleted: 'until'

Author 9/19/2018 5:38 PM
Comment [1]: OK or revise to avoid the sequence of negatives "they should never" and "that does not allow"?

Author
Deleted: vareity

Author 9/19/2018 5:38 PM
Comment [2]: Please supply Fowler's first name (for consistency with other authorities in this paragraph).

Author
Deleted: tyrranical

Author 9/19/2018 5:38 PM
Comment [3]: Word(s) missing? Guardians of what?

Author
Deleted: his

Author
Deleted: *Hobogoblins*

Author
Deleted: l

Author
Deleted: scared

Author
Deleted: Morrris's

Author
Deleted: "

Author
Deleted: "

Author
Deleted: *Of*

Author
Deleted: the

Author
Deleted: every-one

Author 9/19/2018 5:38 PM
Comment [4]: Rhyme ("sure cure") OK?

Author 9/19/2018 5:38 PM
Comment [5]: Revision for parallel structure OK?

Author
Deleted: emphasizing an impo▮▮▮

DID YOU CATCH MOST OF THE ERRORS?

There were ten typographical errors (typos) in this exercise:

- "pour" for "pore"
- double quotation marks on "till," single quote marks on "until"
- "deprecation" = disapproval; "depreciation" = decline in value
- "vareity" for "variety"
- "tyrranical" for "tyrannical"
- "Hobogoblins" for "Hobgoblins"
- "thoughtfull" for "thoughtful"
- "scared" for "sacred"
- "Morrris" for "Morris"
- "every-one" for "everyone"

If you missed more than two of these typos, you should try to read more slowly. Force yourself to read letter by letter, not word by word. Even if you rely on your word processor's spell-checker to back you up, you risk both overlooking the correctly spelled words that are wrong in the context ("pour," "deprecation," "scared," "every-one") and being misled by flags on correctly rendered names and terms not in your word processor's dictionary ("*Thistlebottom's*").

Many of the other errors in this passage are covered in chapters 5 through 8 of *The Copyeditor's Handbook,* so don't worry if you missed some of them here. This exercise offers a taste of the kind of reasoning and reliance on convention that copyeditors develop.

COMMENTS

A The comma after "manuscript" is incorrect because it interrupts the compound predicate "copyeditors will pore . . . and change."

B Change "his" to "the" to avoid the implication that all editorial coordinators are male. (See the discussion of generic *he* under "Bias-Free Language" in *The Copyeditor's Handbook*, chapter 15.)

C "William Morris and Mary Morris's" is correct. In cases of joint ownership, only the last owner's name takes the possessive *'s.* On the differing views about the possessive form for a proper name that ends in *s,* see "Possessives" in *The Copyeditor's Handbook*, chapter 5.

D A comma is needed to set off the nonrestrictive clause introduced by "which." (See *The Copyeditor's Handbook,* chapter 4, under "Function 2: Joining Clauses" and "Function 3: Setting Off Phrases.")

E By convention, no quotation marks are used around a word or phrase introduced by "so-called."

F   Some editors are uncomfortable about the colon here, believing that only an independent clause may precede a colon. But that isn't the case: "The colon is used after a word, phrase, or sentence to introduce something that follows, such as a formal question or quotation, an amplification, or an example" (*WIT*, p. 180). Here, "A second danger" functions as an introductory label; cf. "Warning: Do not leave the hot stove unattended" or "First order of business: Review last quarter's report." One could expand "A second danger" into an independent clause, such as "There is a second danger" or "Here is a second danger," but these additions are not required and do not significantly improve the text.

G   Lowercase a preposition in the title of a book. (See *The Copyeditor's Handbook*, chapter 6, under "Titles of Works.")

H   It is preferable to capitalize the first word of each quoted example here, because each is a complete sentence.

I   As a brief query to the author suggests (see Comment 5), parallel structure requires two nouns ("variety or emphasis"), two gerunds ("achieving variety or emphasizing an important word"), or two infinitives ("to achieve variety or to emphasize an important word").

DID YOU OVEREDIT?

If you made a number of other changes, they may have been for the better—in the sense of clarifying or tightening the prose—but they were probably unnecessary. And every time you make a change, you run two risks: that of introducing new errors and that of frustrating the author. Whenever you copyedit, consider the following:

- Almost any sentence can be improved, but a copyeditor has to be able to leave well enough alone.
- The text is the author's, not the copyeditor's.
- If the assignment is a light copyedit, copyeditors are not expected to spend their time working on a sentence that is already "good enough."
- If a copyeditor misses scattered mistakes in the text, he or she will be forgiven—after all, no one is perfect. But when a copyeditor introduces a mistake or changes something correct into something incorrect, those acts of commission are much harder to forgive.

EXERCISE 4-4: Key

Choices regarding editorial style, compound forms, and alternative spellings follow the guidelines in *Chicago* (other style manuals may recommend other conventions) and entries in *M-W Collegiate* and, as a supplement, *M-W Unabridged*. Explanations of changes, flagged in the text with lettered superscripts, follow the redlined manuscript and accompanying style sheet.

Your editing decisions may differ from the ones shown here. When comparing this key with your version, read slowly to make sure you spotted and corrected all the basic errors. Ask yourself whether you agree with the discretionary changes shown here. Would you propose different or additional improvements?

The style sheet is rather extensive. An experienced editor might omit many self-explanatory entries (e.g., preferred variant spellings in *M-W Collegiate*, style choices following *Chicago*), but new editors should keep scrupulous lists until they are secure in their knowledge. This list includes all proper names because frequent errors in the text suggest the advisability of checking and recording them.

The Liberation of American Humor

Among my ~~favourites~~ favorites in the galaxy of American humorists ~~are~~ is the icon-smashing, ~~potty mouth~~potty-mouthed, stand-up comic, who assaults cultural orthodoxies and speaks, —no, swears, —truth to power.**A** Lenny Bruce, ranked number three (after Richard Pryor and George Carlin) on *Rolling Stone* ~~*Magazine's*~~ magazine's 2017 list ~~of~~ in "50 ~~best standups of all time~~Best Stand-Up Comics of All Time,"**B** improvised comedy routines on politics, religion, and sex ~~were~~ so peppered with vulgarities that he, along with his ~~night club~~nightclub hosts, was repeatedly arrested for obscenity.**C** Bruce's transgressive humor caused ~~England~~Britain,**D** Australia, ~~as well as~~and several US cities to declare him ~~personal~~persona non grata,;**E** his unmuzzled performances prompted television executives to ban him. Undercover police began surveilling his comedy club act in New York in 1964,**F** and charged him with obscenity after a particularly blue monologue at the Cafe au Go Go.**G** The ~~widely~~widely publicized**H** 1964 trial that followed was regarded as a landmark case for freedom of speech in the United States. ~~Despite~~Bruce was convicted despite testimony and petitions on his behalf by artists, writers, and educators,**I** including Woody Allen, Bob Dylan, Jules Feiffer, Norman Mailer, ~~Alan~~Allen Ginsberg, William Styron, James Baldwin, and the sociologist Herbert Gans.,**J** ~~Bruce was convicted.~~

But so-called "dirty words" ~~was~~were not the real issue,: censorship of unpopular opinions, forcefully expressed, was.**K** Bruce prepared the way for an era of radical social and political opposition to "the Establishment"**L** in the form of black (and sometimes blue) humor. CBS's *Smothers Brothers Comedy Hour*—a typical comedy-variety television show launched in 1967,~~ —~~**M**pushed the boundaries of permissible network satire and hosted countercultural musical guests,**N** such as Buffalo Springfield, The Who, and the ~~folksinger/~~ folk singer–activist**O** Pete Seeger (blacklisted on commercial TV since 1950), ~~who's~~whose controversial sixth verse of ~~*Waist Deep in the Big Muddy*~~ "Waist Deep in the Big Muddy"**P** insinuated criticism of President Lyndon Johnson's ~~Viet Nam~~Vietnam war policy**Q** and resulted in a redaction of the entire performance from the ~~season two~~second-season premiere.**R** Due to**S** persistent conflicts with network censors over such political and social content, *The Smothers Brothers Comedy Hour* was abruptly ~~cancelled~~canceled**T**in 1969 despite its popularity with younger audiences. (~~f~~Older viewers preferred NBC's opposite show, the western saga *Bonanza*~~.]~~.)**U**

George Carlin, a disciple of Lenny Bruce, aired darkly comic remarks on the English language, psychology, religion, and various "taboo"**V** subjects. He often satirized contemporary US politics and the excesses of American culture. A riff on his famous "Seven Words You Can Never Say on Television" routine of the early 1970s~~,~~ later formed the basis of the 1978 ~~U.S.~~US Supreme Court case ~~*F.C.C.*~~*FCC* v. *Pacifica Foundation*, which affirmed the government's power to regulate indecent material on the public ~~airways~~airwaves.**W** (Obscene content is not protected under the ~~1st amendment~~First Amendment~~,~~;**X** ~~some~~content considered indecent or profane ~~content~~, which does not meet all three ~~criterions~~criteria**Y** for obscenity, may in some cases be protected but is regulated. This case resulted in the Federal Communications Commission ~~(F.C.C.)~~[FCC]**Z** guideline prohibiting such content on the public ~~airways~~airwaves between 6 a.m. and 10 p.m., when children are likely to be in the audience.)~~.~~ But Carlin's "dirty words" routine, ~~too~~like Bruce's nightclub act, was not actually ~~concerned not~~about ~~a list of~~proscribed words as such; it was~~ but~~ about the issue of censorship itself.**AA**

In the same tradition of transgressive humor,**BB** Bill Maher sparked controversy with his deliberately provocative remarks on *Politically Incorrect.* ABC canceled the show shortly after Maher's "politically incorrect" comments about the 9/11 attackers prompted outraged sponsors to ~~withdrew~~withdraw their support. The program was later revived as *Real Time with Bill Maher* on cable TV's HBO network, where its host can take jabs at conventional pieties with greater impunity. ~~John~~Jon Stewart's *Daily Show,* ~~Steven~~Stephen Colbert's *Colbert Report,***CC** and other edgy comedy acts testing the limits of political and social humor,~~ —~~**DD**all have likewise found audiences on cable ~~networks, which~~television. ~~as subscription~~As subscription-based**EE** broadcasters,**FF** cable networks answer primarily to their self-selected customers,**GG** not to the ~~Federal Communications Commission~~FCC, ~~that~~which regulates the public ~~airways~~airwaves more strictly.**HH** ~~Succeeding~~The successor to David Letterman as the host of CBS's *The ~~Tonight~~ Late Show,* Colbert now evinces (or perhaps feigns)**II** unease at broadcast TV's constraints on his free-range jokes. Is he poking the CBS censor in the eye or is he really on a five-second delay ?**JJ** Ultimately,**KK** the liberation of American humor may depend on the internet, that ~~wild west~~ Wild West**LL** of unfettered and sometimes horrifying ~~self~~ self-expression.**MM**

STYLE SHEET

Author/Title: Chuckles/"The Liberation of American Humor"
Date: February 21, 2018
Dictionary: *Merriam-Webster's Collegiate Dictionary,* 11th ed.; *Merriam-Webster Unabridged*
Style Manual: *The Chicago Manual of Style,* 17th ed.

Alphabetical List of Names and Terms
(n. = noun, adj. = adjective, sing. = singular, pl. = plural)

ABC (public network)
Allen, Woody
Baldwin, James
Bonanza (TV show)
Bruce, Lenny
Buffalo Springfield (musical group)
Cafe au Go Go (New York nightclub)
Carlin, George
CBS (public network)
Colbert, Stephen
The Colbert Report (TV show)
criterion (sing.), criteria (pl.)
The Daily Show (TV show)
Dylan, Bob
the Establishment
FCC (Federal Communications Commission)
FCC v. Pacifica Foundation (legal case)
Feiffer, Jules
First Amendment (of Constitution)
folk singer (n.)
Gans, Herbert
Ginsberg, Allen
HBO (cable network)
internet (n.; adj.)
Johnson, Lyndon

The Late Show (TV show)
Letterman, David
Maher, Bill
Mailer, Norman
NBC (public network)
nightclub (n.; adj.)
persona non grata (roman)
Politically Incorrect (TV show)
Pryor, Richard
Real Time with Bill Maher (TV show)
Rolling Stone (magazine)
Seeger, Pete
The Smothers Brothers Comedy Hour (TV show)
stand-up (n.; adj.)
Stewart, Jon
Styron, William
TV
US (adj.)
Vietnam
"Waist Deep in the Big Muddy" (song)
western (adj.)
The Who (musical group)
Wild West

Special Symbols
n/a

Dates and Numbers
Chicago style throughout
"Seven Words You Can Never Say on Television " (title of comedy routine)
But: "50 Best Stand-Up Comics of All Time" (title of article)
6 a.m., 10 p.m.
1970s
9/11
number three (ranking)

Miscellaneous Notes
US spellings throughout

Footnotes
n/a

Punctuation
Chicago style throughout
series comma
quotation marks for magazine articles, songs, and titles of comedy skits
scare quotes: "the Establishment," "dirty words," "politically incorrect"

COMMENTS

A Subject-verb agreement: Despite the possible miscue created by the inverted word order of this sentence, "stand-up comic" is the singular subject and requires a singular verb, "is."

Punctuation of noncoordinate adjectives: The adjectives "potty-mouthed" and "stand-up" are not coordinate, so there should be no comma between them.

Restrictive relative clause: The relative clause "who assaults . . . power" restricts, or limits, the class of stand-up comics referred to here, so the comma should be omitted.

Punctuation of interrupter: Because "no, swears" is an emphatic interruption, it is best set off with a pair of dashes.

B Name of magazine: The correct name, *Rolling Stone,* confirmed online.

Title of magazine article: The exact form of this magazine title verified online; quotation marks are conventionally used for article titles. Alternatively, the reference to the article can be styled as a description rather than an actual title: "*Rolling Stone* magazine's 2017 list of the fifty best stand-up comics of all time" (spell out the number, lowercase the words describing the subject of the article).

C Series comma: Following Chicago style, the series comma is supplied here and wherever it has been omitted.

Subject-verb agreement: In the subordinate clause "that he . . . was repeatedly arrested," the phrase "along with his nightclub hosts" is an interrupter that should be set off by a pair of commas; it does not affect the number of the singular subject or the singular verb that correctly agrees with the subject. But proximity to the plural "hosts" makes the singular verb sound wrong. A better solution: "that he *and* his nightclub hosts *were* repeatedly arrested for obscenity."

D   England, Great Britain, the United Kingdom: England is not a sovereign political entity, but part of the United Kingdom of Great Britain and Northern Ireland. It was actually the UK's Home Office that barred Bruce from entry into Great Britain (comprising the countries of the main island: England, Scotland, and Wales) by declaring him an "undesirable alien."

E   Semicolon: The comma between two independent clauses is incorrect. Here is an example of the legitimate use of a semicolon to connect two closely related statements absent a coordinate conjunction. A period would also be acceptable here, but the two statements would be less closely linked.

F   Comma in compound predicate: Delete this superfluous comma between the elements of the compound predicate. A discretionary comma may be supplied in a compound predicate to prevent misreading or to aid readers in navigating especially complicated syntax, but there's no need for such a prop here.

G   Name of nightclub: Cafe au Go Go (no acute accent over the *e* in *Cafe*) confirmed online.

H   Hyphenation of compound adjective: When the first member of a compound adjective is an adverb ending in *ly*, the compound is open.

I   Punctuation of appositive phrase: The following list of names should be set off from the main clause by a comma.

Names of Bruce's supporters: Names confirmed online; spelling of "Allen Ginsberg" has been corrected accordingly.

Definite article inserted before "sociologist Herbert Gans": A common practice in journalism is omission of the definite article with a restrictive appositive when it precedes a proper name (treating the descriptive term like a formal title, part of the name), but formal prose retains the defining article: the sociologist Herbert Gans, the comedian Lenny Bruce, the folk singer Bob Dylan, and, in the next paragraph, the folk singer–activist Pete Seeger.

Sentence structure: As a discretionary change, the subject and verb have been moved to the head of the sentence for easier reading.

K   Scare quotes: No need to use scare quotes after "so-called," which expression suffices to provide the desired ironic distance.

Subject-verb agreement: The subject "dirty words" requires the plural verb "were." Or, perhaps better: "But *the use of* so-called dirty words was not the real issue . . ."

Colon: The comma between two independent clauses not joined by a coordinate conjunction is just wrong. These two clauses can be connected with a full colon to suggest that the second clause is an elaboration or restatement of the first. A semicolon could also be used to suggest a close relation between the thoughts.

L   Scare quotes: Here, absent the phrase "so-called," the writer chooses to use scare quotes for distance from the possibly tendentious term "the Establishment," which implies the existence of a monolithic power structure.

M   Punctuation of interrupter: Use either a *pair* of dashes or a *pair* of commas, not one of each, to set off the phrase "a typical comedy-variety television show launched in 1967."

N   Punctuation of nonrestrictive modifier: The phrase beginning with "such as," which contains additional, nonessential information, is set off from the main clause with a comma.

O   Formation of compound term: Using a slash to combine related terms (e.g., comedy/variety) is discouraged; style books recommend a hyphen for such combinations (comedy-variety). Here, because one of the elements of this compound form is itself an open compound (folk singer), an en dash joins it to the second term (activist).

P   Punctuation of song title: Song titles are placed in quotation marks, not italicized.

Q   "Vietnam war policy": Why not "Vietnam War policy" if the names of wars should be capitalized? "Vietnam War" could be capitalized here if the meaning is Johnson's policy on the Vietnam War ("Vietnam War" treated as an attributive adjective modifying "policy"), or "war policy" could be lowercased if the meaning is Johnson's war policy pertaining to Vietnam ("Vietnam" treated as an attributive adjective modifying "war policy").

R   Discretionary change: "season two"? "Season Two"? "season 2"? "Season 2"? There doesn't appear to be a clearly established way to represent this reference; substituting the adjective "second-season" removes the momentary distraction for readers.

Spelling: The words "premier" (adjective: first in rank or importance) and "premiere" (noun: first performance) are commonly confused.

S   Adverbial "due to": The introduction of an adverbial modifier with this expression, long discouraged by language mavens, is now fully accepted. Bryan Garner and other conservative commentators still caution against adverbial "due to" in formal prose, lest readers judge the writer careless, but an editor should not revise the usage if a writer has chosen it.

T   Variant spellings: The single-consonant form "canceled" is the preferred variant in *M-W Unabridged*; the double-consonant form "cancelled" is chiefly British. English includes many such "canceled words," in which the final consonant may be doubled (BrE) or not (AmE) when a suffix is added. These should not be confused with words containing a stress on the final syllable (e.g., occur), in which the final consonant must be doubled when a suffix is added (occurred, occurring).

U   "western": It would also be acceptable to use "Western" here; *M-W Collegiate* lists the capitalized adjective referring to the American West as an equal variant. Cf. "Wild West" in the last sentence of the text.

Square brackets vs. parentheses: The brackets around this sentence have been corrected to parentheses—brackets are used only for parentheticals within parentheses and for editorial interpolations within direct quotations.

V   Scare quotes: When scare quotes are overused, the affectation can become annoying. Here there's no need to suggest that the term "taboo" is used ironically.

W   Abbreviation "FCC": Chicago style usually omits periods in initialisms.

Punctuation of nonrestrictive modifier: Comma before the nonrestrictive relative clause "which affirmed . . . airwaves."

X   Capitalization: By convention, amendments to the US Constitution are capitalized and amendment numbers spelled out.

Semicolon: Again, a semicolon can be used to connect two closely related independent clauses not joined by a coordinate conjunction.

Y   Plural formation: The first-listed plural form of "criterion" is "criteria"; "criterions" is a secondary variant.

Z   "[FCC]": This is the first time the abbreviation for the Federal Communications Commission has been used in the running text (the formal name of a Supreme Court case doesn't count), so it should be glossed here for the sake of readers unfamiliar with the US government's alphabet soup. The abbreviation can then be used instead of the full name in the following paragraph. Brackets replace parentheses around the abbreviation because this whole sentence is in parentheses.

AA   Discretionary revision: The rewording of this sentence is intended to express the idea more clearly and connect it to the material on Bruce, but it is not an essential correction. The semicolon inserted between the independent clauses of the revised sentence expresses the close relation of the two thoughts.

BB   Punctuation of introductory prepositional phrases: A short introductory prepositional phrase does not normally require a comma except to prevent misreading; a stack of prepositional phrases at the beginning of a sentence, as here, is often followed by a comma, at the writer's or editor's discretion, to aid the reader.

CC   Names of TV comedians and TV shows: Names and titles (here and in subsequent text) verified online.

DD   Em dash: A dash (or, in more formal writing, a colon) may follow an introductory appositional list that precedes the independent clause.

EE   Hyphenation of compound adjective: The adjective "subscription-based" is a unit modifier, hyphenated in accordance with Chicago style.

FF   Punctuation of introductory adjectival phrase: Use a comma to set off the phrase "As subscription-based broadcasters."

GG Punctuation of antithetical phrase: A comma precedes an antithetical phrase beginning with "not" or "but."

HH Punctuation of nonrestrictive relative clause: There is only one FCC, and it regulates the public airwaves (among other things); the clause "that regulates the public airwaves" should be nonrestrictive, introduced by a comma and beginning with the relative pronoun "which."

II Punctuation of interpolation: The phrase "or perhaps feigns" seems like an aside; parentheses set the interpolation apart.

JJ Punctuation of question: Obviously, a question calls for a question mark. The author's omission of a comma between the short independent clauses joined by *or* ("Is he poking . . . or is he . . .") is stetted at the editor's discretion (see *The Copyeditor's Handbook,* chapter 4, under "Function 2: Joining Clauses").

KK Punctuation of transitional expression: Comma after transitional adverb "ultimately."

LL Capitalization: According to *M-W Unabridged,* "wild west" is often capitalized, and capitalization seems appropriate for this context.

MM Treatment of compound terms with *self-:* Chicago style and standard dictionaries hyphenate compounds formed with the prefix *self-.*

EXERCISE 5-1: Key

The hyphenation choices shown here follow the guidelines in *Chicago* (other style manuals may recommend other conventions) and the permanent forms, where listed, in *M-W Collegiate* and *M-W Unabridged.* Copyeditors should enter their hyphenation decisions in the alphabetical list of names and terms on the style sheet.

One query addressed to the author is flagged in the text with the bracketed **{Query}**. Explanations of changes immediately follow each redlined sentence.

1. There was an ~~above~~ above-average turnout by ~~middle~~ middle-aged ~~working~~ working-class voters in the ~~south~~ southeastern states.

Comments:
- "above-average turnout": Attributive compound adjectives of the form "adverb (non -*ly*) + adjective" may be left open, or a hyphen may be added for clarity. They are open when they follow the noun: the turnout was above average.
- "middle-aged . . . [voters]": Hyphenate an attributive compound adjective whose first element is *high, low, upper,* or *middle* (for an exception, see sentence 3). Compounds of this form are open when they follow the noun: These voters are middle aged. Notice that there is no comma after "middle-aged," because "middle-aged" and "working-class" are not coordinate adjectives.
- "working-class voters": Hyphenate an attributive compound adjective of the form "adjective or participle + noun." Compounds of this form are open when they follow the noun: Most of the voters in this district are working class.
- "southeastern": Terms that denote points of the compass are solid.

2. He submitted a hastily written report that documented his ~~half~~ half-baked effort to revise his predecessor's ~~ill~~ ill-conceived ~~cost~~ cost-cutting plan.

Comments:
- "hastily written report": Compound adjectives of the form "-*ly* adverb + participle or adjective" are open in both the attributive and the predicate position.
- "half-baked effort": Compound attributive adjectives whose first element is *half* are hyphenated unless the word is shown closed in the dictionary—for example, *halfhearted, halfway.*
- "ill-conceived [plan]": Compound adjectives of the form "*well, ill, better, best, little, lesser,* or *least* + adjective or participle" are hyphenated in the attributive position. There is no comma after "ill-conceived" because "ill-conceived" and "cost-cutting" are not coordinate adjectives. (Test for coordination: One could not write "his ill-conceived and cost-cutting plan" or "his cost-cutting and ill-conceived plan," because "ill-conceived" modifies the unit "cost-cutting plan.")

- "cost-cutting plan": Compound adjectives of the form "noun + participle" are hyphenated in the attributive position.

3.   To replicate this ~~early nineteenth~~ early-nineteenth-century experiment, the high school students needed two gallon test bottles**{Query}**, a ~~four inch long~~ four-inch-long tube, a six-̲ or ~~seven~~ seven-foot plank, and two to three teaspoons of salt.

   {Query}: "two gallon test bottles": If the students need two test bottles, each of which is a one-gallon bottle, no hyphens are needed, but the text would be clearer if it read "two one-gallon test bottles." If the students need several two-gallon test bottles, the text should read "two-gallon test bottles."

Comments:
- When you cannot determine from the context which meaning is intended, you must query the author.
- "early-nineteenth-century experiment": Compound adjectives that include *century* are hyphenated. The modifier "early" may take a hyphen or be left open. The noun forms are open: in the early nineteenth century.
- "high school students": "High school" is a permanent open compound noun and adjective, as shown in *M-W Unabridged* and *M-W Collegiate*.
- "four-inch-long tube": Compound adjectives of the form "number + unit of measure" are hyphenated in the attributive position. Compare: The tube is four inches long.
- "six- or seven-foot plank": This expression is a shortened form of "six-foot or seven-foot plank." A hyphen and a wordspace follow the first element of a suspended compound.
- "two to three teaspoons of salt": No hyphens are needed, because "two to three teaspoons" is not a compound adjective. Compare: A two- to three-teaspoon dose is recommended.

4.   The ideal candidate will have strong skills in problem solving, ~~decision~~ decision-making, ~~film~~ filmmaking, ~~book~~ bookkeeping, and ~~proof~~ proofreading.

Comments:
- "problem solving," "decision-making": Compound nouns of the form "noun + gerund" are open unless they are shown in the dictionary as closed or hyphenated. But compound adjectives of the form "noun + gerund" are hyphenated when they precede the noun: problem-solving and decision-making skills. (*Achtung!* The hyphenated noun form *decision-making* was just added to *M-W Unabridged* in 2016, with the solid form *decisionmaking* listed as a secondary, or less common, variant; however, the print and online editions of *M-W Collegiate*, which many copyeditors rely on, do not yet register these changes. Whichever form you choose, record it on your style sheet and be consistent.)

- "filmmaking," "bookkeeping," "proofreading": The dictionary shows these words as closed.

5. He is ~~self~~ self-conscious about his 45 percent productivity decline and ~~five~~ fivefold increase in tardiness.

Comments:
- "self-conscious": Compound adjectives whose first element is *self-* are hyphenated in both the attributive and predicate positions.
- "45 percent . . . [decline]": Compound adjectives of the form "numeral + *percent*" are not hyphenated.
- "fivefold": Adjectives formed with the suffix *-fold* are solid unless the first element is a numeral—for example, *a 125-fold increase.*

6. As a comparison of the pre- and ~~post~~ posttest scores for the fourth-, fifth-, and ~~sixth~~ sixth-grade students showed, highly motivated young students can learn the most basic aspects of ~~socio~~ socioeconomic theory.

Comments:
- "pre- and posttest scores": This expression is a shortened form of "pretest and posttest scores." When a prefix stands as the first element in a suspended compound, the prefix is followed by a hyphen and a wordspace. Like most words that begin with a common prefix, "posttest" is solid; for exceptions to this rule, see *The Copyeditor's Handbook,* chapter 5, under "One Word or Two?"
- "fourth-, fifth-, and sixth-grade students": Compound adjectives of the form "ordinal number + noun" are hyphenated in the attributive position, as are all attributive adjectives of the form "adjective or participle + noun." When a comma follows an element in a suspended compound, there is no wordspace between the hyphen and the comma.
- "the most basic aspects": Compound adjectives of the form "adverb (non *-ly*) + adjective" may be left open unless the open form would be ambiguous. In this sentence, the only possible interpretation is that "most" modifies "basic" (i.e., students are learning those aspects of theory that are the most basic); an alternative reading—"students are learning the most [maximum number of] basic principles" makes no sense. In comparison, consider "much heralded music" and "much-heralded music." In the former, "much" denotes a quantity; in the latter, it modifies "heralded."
- "socioeconomic": Words that begin with the prefix *socio-* are solid.

7. He sat ~~cross~~ cross-legged at the ~~cross~~ crossroads ~~cross~~ cross-questioning the pollster about the ~~cross~~ crossover vote and the cross fire over the nomination.

Comments: "cross-legged," "crossroads," "cross-questioning," "crossover," "cross fire": There are no simple rules for compound adjectives, nouns, or verbs beginning with *cross*. You should always consult the dictionary to see which forms are conventional.

8.   The ~~state of the art~~ state-of-the-art amplifier is over there with the other ~~out of order~~ out-of-order equipment that the ~~under~~ underappreciated ~~copy~~ copyeditors and their ~~anti~~ anti-intellectual ~~co~~ co-workers left behind.

Comments:
- "state-of-the-art amplifier," "out-of-order equipment": Phrases that function as compound adjectives and precede the noun are hyphenated. Those phrases are usually not hyphenated in the predicate position: This equipment is out of order.
- "underappreciated": Words that begin with the prefix *under-* are solid.
- "copyeditors": See *The Copyeditor's Handbook,* chapter 1, n. 10.
- "anti-intellectual": Chicago style calls for closing up words beginning with the prefix *anti-* (anticlimax, antiauthoritarian, antitrust) unless the second element begins with *i* (anti-intellectual, anti-incumbent, anti-imperialism) or the closed form is misleading or hard to read (anti-union). Because strict adherence to *Chicago* yields *anticonsumerism, antifamily, antilabor,* and so on, some publishers prefer to hyphenate all *anti-* compounds that do not have specific, well-established meanings: antibiotic, antifreeze, antitrust *but* anti-consumerism, anti-family, anti-labor.
- "co-workers": "Coworkers" is an acceptable alternative. On the dispute over *co-* compounds, see the section on prefixes and suffixes under "One Word or Two?" in *The Copyeditor's Handbook,* chapter 5.

9.   Adult-sponsored and adult-supervised play, especially in middle- and upper-class suburbia, has taken the place of unorganized sport.

Comments:
- "adult-sponsored and adult-supervised play": Sentences 3 and 6 illustrate the convention for handling a suspended compound, one in which the second part of a term in a hyphenated or solid term is omitted. In this sentence the phrase "middle- and upper-class suburbia" applies the same convention. Suspended compounds in which the *first* part is omitted ("adult-sponsored and -supervised") are legitimate but awkward and potentially confusing. A better choice is to spell out both terms in full.

10.   This letter is addressed to all my Boston Red ~~Sox~~ Sox–fan friends.

Comments:
- "Boston Red Sox–fan friends": When one of the terms in a compound predicate adjective is an open compound, the connecting hyphen is rendered as an en dash

(see the discussion under "One Word or Two?" in *The Copyeditor's Handbook,* chapter 5). Some readers, however, may not discern the typographic distinction between a hyphen and the longer en dash, and some publishing environments don't support such refinements. A better solution would be revision to avoid such awkward compound constructions: This letter is addressed to all my fellow Boston Red Sox fans.

11.   The ~~cat loving~~ cat-loving but ~~severely asthmatic~~ severely asthmatic copyeditor wrote to the New Zealand ~~Siberian cat~~ Siberian-cat breeder about obtaining a pedigree ~~hypo-allergenic~~ hypoallergenic kitten to keep her company in her solitary ~~day job~~ day job.

Comments:
- "cat-loving . . . [copyeditor]": A compound adjective consisting of a noun and a present or past participle is hyphenated when it precedes the modified noun.
- "severely asthmatic": Again, adverbs ending in *ly* are not connected by a hyphen to adjectives they modify.
- "Siberian-cat": In a series of compound modifiers, judicious hyphenation avoids ambiguity and helps the reader parse the construction. Some readers may know that the Siberian breed of cats is reputed to cause fewer reactions among allergy sufferers, but for others it may not be clear on first reading that "Siberian" refers to the breed of cat rather than the ethnicity of the breeder.
- "hypoallergenic": The dictionary lists this term as closed.
- "day job": The dictionary lists this term as open.

12.   She concluded, however, that the ~~eyewatering~~ eye-watering ~~two thousand dollar~~ $2,000 ~~price tag~~ price tag for such a kitten was too high.

Comments:
- "eye-watering": This (now rather cliché) colloquial noun + gerund compound should be hyphenated (unlike the analogous *mouthwatering,* which has become closed with frequent use).
- "$2,000": In Chicago style, large monetary amounts are usually expressed in numerals, rendering the hyphenation question moot.
- "price tag": The dictionary lists this term as open.

13.   When ~~user defined~~ user-defined ~~application specific~~ application-specific keyboard shortcuts conflict with operating system commands, the application may freeze.

Comments:
- "user-defined," "application-specific": Both these terms should be hyphenated, in conformity with Chicago rules for noun compounds preceding a noun. In addition, hyphenation increases readability in a long string of compound modifiers preceding a noun—a common feature of technical and scientific

prose. (Publishers in these fields may, however, follow other guidelines for hyphenation.) Note that attempting to clarify the sentence by adding a comma between the two noun compounds would turn them into coordinate adjectives and change the meaning.

- "operating system commands": Although arguably "operating system" might be hyphenated according to the same principles, it is a well-established term (like *high school*) that is unlikely to create ambiguity.

14. Recent discussions of ~~longstanding~~ long-standing questions about funding ~~healthcare,~~ health care, child care, and ~~short~~ short- and ~~long term~~ long-term treatment for mental health disorders have been contentious.

Comments:
- "long-standing": This term is hyphenated according to *M-W Collegiate.*
- "health care," "child care": These are examples of similar compounds in different stages of evolution. *M-W Unabridged* and the online *M-W Collegiate* both list *health care* as open and *child care* and *childcare* as equal variants. All these forms are acceptable for general audiences; in this case, an editor might choose to leave both terms open for local consistency. But house style sometimes overrules these choices in specialized fields: for example, most health-related organizations prefer the solid compound *healthcare.* (See the discussion of compound forms in *The Copyeditor's Handbook,* chapter 5, under "One Word or Two?")
- "short- and long-term treatment": This is another example of a suspended compound.
- "mental health disorders": Again, this expression creates no ambiguity and may be left open.

15. This quick ~~on-line~~ online quiz will tell you whether your dress and demeanor qualify as ~~authentically hipster~~ authentically hipster, merely hipster adjacent, or hopelessly ~~main-stream~~ mainstream.

Comments:
- "online": Now a closed term, according to *M-W Collegiate.* (But note that the expression *on line*, meaning "in operation," is open; s.v. "line.")
- "authentically hipster": This *-ly* adverb + adjective compound is open.
- "hipster adjacent": This noun + adjective compound is not hyphenated in the predicate position.
- "mainstream": If you want to hyphenate this, you're not *even* mainstream.

EXERCISE 5-2: Key

Corrections are redlined. Queries to the author are signaled with numbers in curly brackets in the text and are reproduced after the selections. Explanatory comments are flagged in the text with superscript letters and are printed following the style sheet. Double hyphens have been replaced by em dashes throughout.

A FROLIC OF HIS OWN. William Gaddis. Poseidon. $25.00

A A ~~A~~ *Frolic of His Own,* **B** William ~~Gaddiss'~~ Gaddis's ~~long~~-long-anticipated **C** fourth novel, is a funny, accurate **D** tale of lives caught up in the toils of the law. Oscar Crease, middle-aged college instructor, savant, and playwright, **E** is suing a Hollywood producer for pirating his play *Once at Antietam,* **F** based on his grandfather's experiences in the Civil War, and turning it ~~in to~~ into a gory ~~block-~~blockbuster called *The Blood in the Red White and Blue.* **G** {Query1} Oscar's suit, **H** and a host of other lawsuits—which involve a dog trapped in an outdoor sculpture, wrongful death during a river baptism, a church versus a ~~soft-~~ soft-drink **I** company, and even Oscar himself after he is run over by his own car—engulf all who surround him, from his ~~free-~~freewheeling girlfriend to his draconian, nonagenarian **J** father, Federal Judge **K** Thomas Creese. {Query2} Down this tortuous path of depositions and decrees, suits and countersuits, the ~~most lofty~~loftiest **L** ideas of our culture are wrung dry in the often surreal logic and language of the law.

THE BIRD ARTIST. Howard Norman,—. FSG. $20.00 **M**

Howard Norman's spellbinding novel is set in Newfoundland in 1911. The novel shares not only ~~shares~~ its place, but also its tone and passion, **N** with *The Shipping News.* {Query3} Fabian Vas's story, told with simplicity and grace, takes place against a spare, beautiful **O** landscape. At age ~~20~~twenty, **P** Fabian is working at the boatyard, **Q** taking a correspondence course in bird painting, and sleeping with Maraget {Query4} Handle, a woman of great beauty, intelligence, and waywardness. When his father leaves on a long hunting expedition and his mother takes up with the lighthouse keeper, Fabian ~~looses~~loses his bearings. The author's intense observation of people and nature makes **R** for a remarkably good novel.

A PERSONAL MATTER. Kenzaburo Oë. $7.95 {Query5}

A Personal Matter, here translated by John Nathan, is probably Oë's ~~best-~~best-known **S** novel. It is the story of a man's relationship with his severely brain-damaged **T** child. As he plots the child's murder, he finally realizes that he must take responsibility for his son. The novel, written out of Oë's {Query6} profound despair after the birth of his own disabled child (now a ~~31~~thirty-one-year-old successful composer), **U** is original, different, tough in its candor, **V** and beautiful in its faithfulness to both intellectual precision and human tenderness.

QUERIES

{Query1}: No serial commas in title OK? Or *the Red, White, and Blue?*

{Query2}: Please reconcile: Creese here, but Crease above.

{Query3}: Supply name of author for *The Shipping News*. [Note: Readers unfamiliar with *The Shipping News* may assume that it is an earlier novel by Howard Norman. Not so: *The Shipping News* was written by E. Annie Proulx and was awarded the Pulitzer Prize for Fiction in 1994.]

{Query4}: Maraget OK? or Margaret?

{Query5}: Supply publisher's name, for consistency with the other entries.

{Query6}: Reconcile: Oé here, but Oë (twice) above.

STYLE SHEET

Author/Title: Daedalus Books/Winter Catalog
Date: February 21, 2018
Dictionary: *Merriam-Webster's Collegiate Dictionary*, 11th ed.
Style Manual: *The Chicago Manual of Style*, 17th ed.

Alphabetical List of Names and Terms
(n. = noun, adj. = adjective)

best-known (adj.)
blockbuster (n.)
boatyard
brain-damaged (adj.)
countersuits
freewheeling
girlfriend
long-anticipated (adj.)
middle-aged (adj.)
soft-drink company
spellbinding

Numbers
Spell out numbers under 101

Punctuation
Serial comma
Possessives of names ending in *s*: Gaddis's, Vas's

Miscellaneous
Listing line for each book is: **TITLE ALL CAPS.** Author's Name. Publisher. $xx.xx
Titles: In the body of the review, book titles are italic, upper- and lowercase

Note: Some copyeditors choose not to provide style sheet entries for words that have no recognized variants (e.g., blockbuster, countersuits). Entries for these items, however, may be helpful to the author, serve as an aide-mémoire for the copyeditor, and guide an indexer in setting up entries. Similarly, some copyeditors choose not to enter hyphenation choices that follow the house style manual. But an author who does not have a copy of the style manual will appreciate seeing the entries on the style sheet.

COMMENTS

When copyediting catalogs and similar types of documents, you should make a special pass to double-check that the entries are consistent in format. For example, in the headings for each of the three entries here, the writer has consistently used all-capital boldface for the book titles (followed by a period); the remaining elements (author's name, publisher's name, price) are in regular type, separated by periods—with the exception of an errant comma in the second heading. The three inconsistencies are discussed below.

A There is no need to indent the first paragraph in each of these short pieces. The decision about how to format the first paragraph following a line of display type (that is, large type, used for chapter titles and headings) is up to the publication's designer, although the editor is sometimes expected to insert type codes or apply a style template (see *The Copyeditor's Handbook*, chapter 13, under "Markup On-Screen"). Often the first paragraph after a line of display type is set flush left (that is, with no paragraph indent). In books and magazine articles, each subsequent paragraph is indented; in corporate documents, paragraphs may be indicated by the indentation of the first line or by extra linespacing between paragraphs.

B The writer has correctly used italics for the title of the book but failed to italicize the first word, "A."

C Hyphenate the two-word attributive adjective "long-anticipated."

D Keep the comma after "funny" because this pair of adjectives passes the test for coordination: one could write "a funny and accurate tale," "an accurate and funny tale," or "an accurate, funny tale."

E Add a comma at the end of the tucked-in "middle-aged college instructor, savant, and playwright" description that intervenes between "Oscar Crease" and the verb "is suing."

F By convention, italics are used for the titles of plays.

G   Italics are correct for the title of a film.

H   Delete the comma, since "Oscar's suit and a host of other lawsuits" is the compound subject of the verb "engulf."

I   Some copyeditors will view "soft drink" as a fixed open compound noun and will not add a hyphen to the adjective form here (cf. "post office hours"). Other copyeditors will insert a hyphen to prevent a momentary misreading.

J   No comma between the noncoordinate adjectives "draconian" and "nonagenarian." (This pair does not pass the test for coordination: one would not write "a draconian and nonagenarian father" nor "a nonagenarian and draconian father.")

K   "Federal Judge" capitalized because it is a civil title preceding a proper name.

L   For most two-syllable adjectives that end in *y*, the superlative form ends in *iest*, and, indeed, *loftiest* is the form shown in the dictionary; cf. *happy, happiest; funny, funniest.*

M   A period, not a comma, should precede the publisher's name, as in the other headings. Note, too, that in the other entries the price of the book is given in dollars and cents.

N   Revise for parallel structure: "shares not only its place but also its tone." Preferable not to have a comma interrupt a "not only . . . but also" chain.

O   Add a comma between the coordinate adjectives "spare" and "beautiful." (This pair passes the test for coordination: one could write "spare and beautiful landscape," "beautiful and spare landscape," or "beautiful, spare landscape.")

P   In nontechnical text, spell out numbers under 101; see "Words or Numerals?" in *The Copyeditor's Handbook*, chapter 7.

Q   The noun "boatyard" appears as a permanent closed compound in desktop dictionaries.

R   Subject-verb agreement requires either "observation . . . makes" or "observations . . . make."

S   Hyphenate the two-word adjective "best-known."

T   In the complex attributive adjective "severely brain-damaged," no hyphen is needed after "severely" (an adverb ending in *ly*); keep the hyphen in "brain-damaged" (a two-word attributive adjective).

U   Add a comma to indicate the end of the long interrupter that comes between the subject "The novel" and the verb "is."

V   Add a serial comma before "and."

EXERCISE 5-3: Key

Choices regarding editorial style, compound forms, and alternative spellings follow *Chicago* and the online *M-W Collegiate* and *M-W Unabridged*. Numbered queries to the author are flagged in the text within boldfaced curly brackets and are printed below the text. Explanations of changes, signaled in the text with lettered superscripts, follow the redlined manuscript, query list, and accompanying style sheet.

Your editing may differ from the changes shown here. Make sure you corrected all the basic errors in your version, and decide whether you agree with the proposed solutions and discretionary changes. Would you make different or additional improvements?

If you missed some errors and infelicities, read on. *The Copyeditor's Handbook,* chapter 6, covers capitalization; chapter 7, numbers and numerals; chapter 9, abbreviations. The last two chapters, 14 and 15, explore issues in grammar and usage and in literary expression.

The Bugs of Summer and Other Seasons

Mosquitoes^A

It's^B a ~~well~~-well-known^C fact that^D mosquitoes transmit ~~Malaria~~malaria, ~~Yellow Fever~~ yellow fever, West Nile ~~Virus~~virus, Zika virus (the most recent villain), ~~—Zika Virus~~and several other less well known ~~others~~diseases.^E Only female mosquitoes bite. When ~~she~~ ~~does~~they do, ~~she injects her~~they inject their^F saliva into your skin,^G which makes your blood flow. The saliva ~~is what caused~~causes ~~the~~swelling and ~~that itchy sensation~~ itching.^H

To avoid being bitten,^I eliminate any standing water in your yard.**{Query1}** Wear a ~~loose~~-loose-fitting ~~long~~-long-sleeved^J shirt and pants when you go outside. (The little ~~blood~~-bloodsuckers can bite through ~~tight fighting~~tight-fitting clothes.)^K Also apply DEET:**{Query2}** ~~(best to~~use a 20–~~30%~~ to 30 percent solution, not a higher ~~percentages~~concentration~~)~~.^L ~~For those who~~If you prefer a more natural approach,^M be aware that only the synthetic version of lemon eucalyptus (p-~~methanediol~~methanethiol) **{Query3}** is effective. ~~All~~The efficacy of other botanicals insect repellents ~~are~~is limited ~~in prevention~~.^N

If you get bitten, apply calamine lotion or a corticosteroid cream. Call your doctor if you develop aches, fever, headache, joint pain, or a rash—even weeks later, since the symptoms of ~~mosquito~~mosquito-borne diseases can take ~~awhile~~a while^O to ~~produce symptoms~~appear.^P

Ticks

Ticks bite and suck blood like tiny vampires. They transmit many serious diseases, including Lyme ~~Disease~~disease. This disease is mostly concentrated in states of the ~~northeast~~ Northeast and ~~midwest~~Midwest,**Q** but there are many cases in other states as well and on every continent except ~~Antartica~~Antarctica.

To avoid ticks, clear overgrown brush and piles of leaves from your property. When out in the woods or tall grass, wear a ~~light~~ light-colored**R** shirt with long sleeves and long pants tucked into socks or boots. Use an insect repellent containing DEET on your skin and permethrin**{Query4}** on your clothes.

After being outdoors, check your entire body for ticks with a magnifying glass (ticks are tiny). Check your children and pets too. If you discover a tick, don't use a lighted match, ~~vasoline~~Vaseline,**S** or gasoline to remove it. Instead, use tweezers to grasp its body as close to your skin as possible. Pull gently and steadily upward. Don't twist the tick, since that may break off the ~~mouth parts~~mouthparts and lead to an infection. Don't crush, puncture, or squeeze the tick's body. If the mouthparts break off in the skin, use tweezers as if removing a splinter. Thoroughly clean the area with rubbing alcohol or soap and water.

If a rash or fever or flu-like symptoms ~~develops~~develop**T** within a few weeks, ~~it~~ they could indicate Lyme disease. See a doctor if you have these symptoms. The disease is usually treated in early stages with ~~aural~~oral antibiotics. For later manifestations of Lyme disease, such as neurological, joint, or heart problems, you may need a longer course of antibiotics administered ~~intervenously~~intravenously.

Although some people eventually recover without treatment, antibiotics improve recovery time and help avoid complications of the disease. But taking antibiotics for more than ~~30~~thirty**U** days ~~offer~~offers**V** no added benefits and may be dangerous. A diagnosis of ~~so~~so-called "chronic Lyme disease"**W** and the efficacy of extended and alternative treatments advertised on the ~~Internet~~internet**X** are not supported by reputable scientific studies.

Chiggers

Chiggers are ~~miniscule~~minuscule,**Y** but their bites cause severe itching and redness. They attack tight areas, such as the groin, underarms, or waist.

To avoid getting bitten, use a repellent that contains DEET and spray permethrin on clothes. Wear long pants tucked inside socks, and long sleeves.**Z** To treat chigger bites, wash the area with soap and water immediately. Apply an ~~antiitch~~ anti-itch**AA** cream,**BB** such as calamine lotion or hydrocortisone. Wash clothes in hot water.

~~No See Ums~~No-See-Ums**CC**

The tiny insects called ~~no see ums~~no-see-ums, biting midges, or biting gnats appear in swarms with warm weather but are ~~only~~ active only**DD** for a few weeks in most places. Still, they can be very annoying. Their bite looks like a small red dot and sometimes develops into an itchy welt the size of a quarter.

To avoid ~~no see ums~~no-see-ums, apply an insect repellent containing DEET. Wear long sleeves and long pants to minimize exposed skin. Avoid swarms if you can. If you get bitten, apply a cold compress and ~~antiitch~~ anti-itch cream.

Wasps

Wasps often build their nests in trees or under the ~~eves~~eaves of houses. Don't mess with these nests if you can avoid them.

If you do get stung, wash the area with soap and water and remove the stinger by scraping a fingernail or the edge of a credit card over the area. Don't squeeze the sting or use tweezers. To reduce swelling, wrap ice in a cloth and apply to the ~~sight~~site. Swelling is usually mild and temporary, but if the ~~effected~~ affected area becomes large and red, you may have an infection and should see a doctor.

If you develop chest pain, shortness of breath, or intense sweating shortly after being stung, seek medical help immediately. These symptoms may indicate a severe allergic reaction.

QUERIES

{Query1}: Make the unstated connection between standing water and mosquito bites explicit?

{Query2}: For the city folks, would it be helpful to define DEET (abbreviation of diethyl toluamide?)? If house policy permits recommendations of specific products, can you mention a few brands that contain this ingredient in the recommended concentration?

{Query3}: Please verify the corrected spelling of methanethiol.

{Query4}: Briefly explain or define permethrin?

STYLE SHEET

Author/Title: Various/"The Bugs of Summer and Other Seasons"
Date: February 21, 2018
Dictionary: *Merriam-Webster's Collegiate Dictionary,* 11th ed.; *Merriam-Webster Unabridged*
Backup, as needed: *American Heritage Dictionary of the English Language,* 5th ed.
Style Manual: *The Chicago Manual of Style,* 17th ed.

Alphabetical List of Names and Terms
(n. = noun, adj. = adjective, pl. = plural)

anti-itch (adj.)
bloodsuckers (n., pl.)
DEET (n.)
internet (n.; adj.)
long-sleeved (adj.)
minuscule (adj.)
mosquitoes (n., pl.)
mouthparts (n.)
no-see-ums (n.)
Vaseline (n.)

Numbers
20 percent
thirty days

COMMENTS

A The preferred plural form is *mosquitoes; mosquitos* is a secondary variant.

B Contractions are used throughout these paragraphs. Assuming the author is striving for a casual tone, they can be allowed to stand; if the author wants a more formal register, these contractions should be spelled out.

C Compound adjectives with *well-* and *ill-* are usually hyphenated when they precede the noun they modify. (See an exception to this rule at **E** below.)

D "It's a . . . fact that" is a typically wordy construction. A discretionary improvement to this sentence would eliminate the phrase altogether: "Mosquitoes transmit . . . diseases."

E These diseases are lowercased except for words derived from proper place names (West Nile, Zika; *also, below,* Lyme). The series of diseases has been repunctuated and revised to clearly mark off the items in the list. Here, unlike the term glossed at note **C** above, the compound adjective "well known" does *not* require a hyphen, because the preceding adverb "less" clarifies the adjectival function of the unit modifier.

F   The sentence has been revised for plurals in accord with the previous sentence ("female mosquitoes").

G   A comma precedes the nonrestrictive relative clause.

H   These are discretionary changes: "The saliva is what caused" can be simplified to "The saliva causes"; "itching" more closely parallels "swelling" and is more succinct than "that itchy sensation."

I   The introductory adverbial phrase "To avoid being bitten" should be followed by a comma. Likewise, a comma should follow the introductory adverbial clause that begins the following paragraph ("If you get bitten").

J   The term "loose-fitting" is a unit modifier and should be hyphenated before the noun; likewise, "long-sleeved." There is debate over *long-sleeve* versus *long-sleeved*: *M-W Collegiate* provides no guidance, but *AHD* acknowledges *sleeved* as the past participle of the verb *to sleeve*; it can be used adjectivally (as can, e.g., *iced* in *iced tea*). The Google Books Ngram Viewer shows that the form *long-sleeved* is far more common than *long-sleeve*.

K   Likewise, the unit modifier "tight-fitting" is hyphenated. The term "bloodsuckers" is a solid compound according to *M-W Collegiate*. The entire sentence is placed in parentheses as an apparent aside, to judge from the tone ("The little bloodsuckers . . .").

L   Use Chicago style for percentages; rewording ("solution," "concentration") clarifies the intended meaning.

M   Continue the use of direct address ("If you prefer" rather than "For those who prefer"). A comma follows the introductory adverbial clause.

N   This is a discretionary revision to clarify meaning.

O   A point of usage: The word *awhile* is used as an adverb; *a while* is the correct noun form.

P   Note the distinction between *born* (existing as a result of birth) and *borne* (carried or transported by): Portland-born artist *but* waterborne parasite, airborne pathogen, mosquito-borne disease, etc. The remaining (discretionary) revisions in this sentence clarify the meaning.

Q   Terms that denote regions of the country (e.g., the Northeast, the Midwest, the South) are often capitalized.

R   This is another hyphenated unit modifier.

S   Vaseline (note the correct spelling) is a trademarked name, hence capitalized. Alternatively, substitute the generic term *petroleum jelly*.

T   When the elements of a compound subject are joined by *or* ("a rash or fever or flu-like symptoms"), the verb agrees with the nearest subject ("symptoms develop"). The hyphenated "flu-like" follows *Chicago*'s guidelines for *-like* compounds.

U Chicago style spells out whole numbers from zero through one hundred in such contexts.

V The subject of the verb is the singular "taking"; hence, "offers."

W There is no need to use scare quotes following the expression "so-called."

X Chicago style now lowercases "internet."

Y "Minuscule" is the preferred spelling in *M-W Collegiate;* "miniscule" is a secondary variant.

Z A discretionary comma is added after "socks" to prevent misreading "socks and long sleeves" as a unit, i.e., what "long pants" should be tucked into. Better still, reverse the terms in the compound direct object: "Wear long sleeves and long pants tucked inside socks."

AA Compounds formed with the prefix *anti-* are usually closed, but a hyphen is used to separate two *i*'s and other combinations that might be misread.

BB Use a comma to set off this nonrestrictive appositive phrase: calamine lotion and hydrocortisone are *examples* of anti-itch creams, not a limited subset of such creams.

CC The term is hyphenated according to *M-W Collegiate* and *AHD.*

DD This discretionary change places the adverb "only" closer to the phrase it modifies.

EXERCISE 6-1: Key

Editing of capitalization follows the guidelines for down style described in *The Copyeditor's Handbook*, chapter 6.

1. After serving for five years as President Eisenhower's ~~Staff Secretary~~staff secretary, General Andrew J. Goodpaster assumed many of the duties of ~~Chief~~chief of ~~Staff~~ staff in 1958. During Eisenhower's administration, General Goodpaster supervised the National Security Council ~~Staff~~staff, briefed the ~~President~~president on intelligence matters, and was White House ~~Liaison~~liaison for defense and national security.

Comments:
- Lowercase "staff secretary"; this title is not part of the general's name in this sentence but is in apposition to his name.
- Lowercase "chief of staff"; this title is not followed by a personal name.
- Author's lowercasing of "administration" follows the down style convention.
- Lowercase "staff"; this common noun is not part of the proper name of an organization.
- Lowercase "president"; this title is not followed by a personal name.
- Lowercase "liaison"; this common noun is not part of a proper name or title.

2. Before being appointed special assistant and counsel to President Johnson in 1965, Harry McPherson had served as counsel to the Democratic policy committee in the Senate, ~~Deputy Undersecretary~~deputy undersecretary of the ~~Army~~army, and assistant ~~Secretary~~secretary of ~~State~~state. He is now an attorney in Washington, DC, and vice-chair~~man~~ of and general counsel to the John F. Kennedy Center for the ~~performing arts~~Performing Arts.

Comments:
- The author's treatment of "Democratic policy committee" denotes that "policy committee" is a common noun (a generic term for a committee that debates policy) rather than a proper name. A copyeditor should either let this stand or query ("Should this be a proper name?") but should not independently make it uppercase (thereby creating an official committee, so named, out of thin air).
- Lowercase "deputy undersecretary" and "assistant secretary of state," since neither is followed by a proper name.
- In Chicago style *army*, *navy*, and similar words are lowercased when they stand alone and are not part of an official title.
- There is no uniformity in the treatment of *vice* compounds in dictionaries and editorial style manuals. For example, *M-W Collegiate* shows *vice admiral, vice-chancellor, vice-consul,* and *vice president* as the preferred forms. To maintain consistency throughout a document, always enter your choice about the hyphenation of *vice* compounds on your style sheet.
- Uppercase the full name of the Kennedy Center.

3. General Alexander Haig was deputy to ~~national security adviser~~ National Security Adviser Henry Kissinger during the early days of President Nixon's administration. He became Nixon's chief of staff in 1973. In 1974 he was named ~~Supreme Commander~~ supreme commander of NATO, a post he held until 1979, when he retired to enter private industry. He returned to ~~Government~~ government service as ~~Secretary~~ secretary of ~~State~~ state during the first eighteen months of President Reagan's first term.

Comments:

- Uppercase the title "National Security Adviser" preceding a proper name.
- Lowercase the title "supreme commander" because no proper name follows.
- A comma is needed after "1979" to set off the nonrestrictive *when* clause.
- Lowercase the common adjective "government" and the common noun "secretary of state."

4. Christine Lagarde became ~~Managing Director~~ managing director of the International Monetary ~~fund~~ Fund in July~~,~~ 2011. Born in Paris and raised in ~~le~~ Le Havre, as a teenager she was a member of the French ~~National Synchronized Swimming Team~~ national synchronized swimming team. She was educated at the ~~université~~ Université Paris Nanterre and the Institut d'études politiques d'Aix-en-~~provence~~ Provence (Sciences Po Aix). Specializing in labor and antitrust law, she went on to become the first woman to head the international ~~Law Firm~~ law firm Baker & McKenzie (now Baker McKenzie). From 2005, she held several French ministerial posts, including trade minister, ~~Minister of Agriculture~~ minister of agriculture, and ~~Minister for Economic Affaires, Finance, and Employment~~ minister for economic affairs, finance, and employment.

Comments:
- Lowercase "managing director" because no proper name follows.
- Uppercase "Fund" as part of the organization's formal name.
- Uppercase the definite article "Le" here because it is part of a geographic name.
- Lowercase the description of the team, which is not a formal name. Depending on the context, an editor might also query whether this information is relevant to a summary of Lagarde's professional career.
- In the names of French institutions, only the first word and any proper nouns are uppercased. Thus "Université" is uppercased as the first word in the name of a French institution. "Paris," "Nanterre," and "Aix-en-Provence" are uppercased because they are geographic names. In "Institut d'études politiques," only the first common noun is uppercased. Perversely, the institution's nickname is uppercased by convention (as are the names of its counterparts in other cities, such as Sciences Po Rennes).
- Lowercase "law firm" because it is not part of a formal name.
- Lowercase the names of the ministerial posts because they are not followed by a proper name. Delete the extraneous *e* in "affairs," which may be a stowaway from a translation into English.

5. At the international Meeting on Renewable Energy and Sustainable Technologies
    held in 2015, the ~~Keynote~~ keynote speech was given by Prof. Sunil Substrate of the
    Department of ~~applied~~ Applied Physics and ~~materials~~ Materials Science, ~~The~~ Ancient
    Ivy University, Bobonia. Members of the afternoon ~~Panel on Sustainable Computing~~
    panel on sustainable computing technologies included ~~Professor~~ Prof. Nina Nanochip,
    holder of the Ada Lovelace ~~chair in electrical engineering~~ Chair in Electrical
    Engineering at the Technical University of Bobonia, and Dr. Felix Fotovoltaio, ~~Research~~
    ~~and Development Director~~ research and development director of Bobonia Sunshine
    Industries SA.

Comments:

*   Query or search to determine whether "international" is part of the formal title
    of the meeting; if so, it should be uppercased.
*   Although designations like "keynote speech" and "plenary session" are often
    uppercased in conference programs and related materials, they should be lower-
    cased in running text. There is no need to capitalize such a generic term simply
    because it is capitalized in the display type of another document.
*   Uppercase the official name of an academic, business, or institutional department.
*   Although institutions may retain an uppercased definite article in their own
    publications and documents, others are not required to follow this practice.
*   Lowercase "panel on sustainable computing technologies," which functions as a
    descriptive rather than a formal name.
*   Abbreviate "Prof." for consistency with other academic titles in this passage
    (or spell out all of them).
*   Uppercase the name of an endowed (named) professorship or fellowship. If Prof.
    Nanochip were a garden-variety professor of electrical engineering, the title
    would be lowercased because no personal name follows—as for Dr. Fotovoltaio's
    title.

6. In early 2018, an article in *Nature Scientific Reports* ~~reported~~ revealed that the
    chameleon's beauty goes more than skin-deep: some chameleons (family
    Chamaeleonidae) found in Africa and on the ~~Island~~ island of Madagascar have
    bony formations in the skull and sometimes other parts of the skeleton that glow
    (~~flouresce~~ fluoresce) under ~~Uv~~ ultraviolet light. The study focused on the genus
    ~~Calumma~~*Calumma*, which includes the species *C. globifer, C.* tsaratananaense
    ~~*Tsaratananaense*~~, and *C. guibei*. A striking photograph of the fluorescence
    phenomenon was posted on the ~~Newsweek~~ *Newsweek* website.

Comments:

*   Verb changed to avoid the infelicitous word echo "*Reports* reported."
*   The family name is correct as shown: genus and species names are italicized, but
    names of higher classifications of organisms are capitalized and set roman.
*   Lowercase "island" because it is descriptive, not part of a geographic or political
    name.

- Watch out for common misspellings, particularly when other forms of a word are correctly spelled and you may be inclined to skip over them.
- Either spell out "ultraviolet" (without a hyphen) or, in contexts where readers are likely to be familiar with the term, correct it to "UV."
- In Latin binomials, names of genera are uppercased and italicized.
- But names of species are lowercased and italicized.
- In some styles, names of websites are set uppercase and roman. *Chicago* now recommends italicizing titles of websites that have well-known print analogues, such as major newspapers and reference works, but notes that because the definition of *well-known* is open to interpretation, editors should use their discretion.

EXERCISE 6-2: Key

Numbered queries are flagged in the text with boldface curly braces (e.g., {**Query1**}) and are printed directly below the text, followed by the style sheet. This key follows *M-W Collegiate, M-W Unabridged,* and *Chicago;* if you consulted other authorities, some of your style choices may differ from those shown here. Explanatory comments, keyed in the text with superscript letters, are printed at the end.

Finding Work

Back in the day[A], editors aspiring to break into ~~U.S.~~ US publishing were often advised to move to New York ~~city~~City. This advice sometimes rankled with professionals elsewhere; [B] so much so that one San Francisco Bay Area ~~area editor's~~ editors'[C] group produced a ~~t-shirt~~ T-shirt[D] printed with the slogan "We Don't Care How They Do It ~~In~~ in New York."[E] Today, beginning editors are far less likely to be gofer-ing[F] in a smoke-begrimed, book-lined office in Manhattan than sitting at home in front of a computer, working for employers and clients who may be thousands of miles away. Some may work night shifts to ~~liase~~ liaise with ~~Corporate~~ corporate offices in ~~EUrope~~ Europe or Asia.

These days, too, social media platforms like ~~Linkedin~~ LinkedIn[G] make it easy for editors to advertise their skills and services, network with professionals in related fields, and pursue opportunities advertised online. Organizations such as ACES and *Copyediting* ~~*Magazine*~~ magazine[H] (and Editors Canada for those north of the border) maintain job boards accessible to their members and subscribers. Remember, when using online platforms to find work, that prospective employers may search the ~~Internet~~ internet[I] for more information about you. Check the ~~Privacy Settings~~ privacy settings on your social media accounts, and keep your public presence dignified (and free of ~~missspellings~~ misspellings). If you don't want to use your real name as part of your ~~e-mail~~ email[J] address or login[K] name, choose an appropriately professional alternative moniker.

Despite advances in technology, some of the traditional advice for seeking publishing work still holds. Go to the ~~Public Library~~ public library[L] and look at the most recent edition of *Literary* ~~*Marketplace*~~ *Market Place* (*LMP,*[M] published by Information Today, Inc.[N])—or, when you have a block of time available to do some research, purchase a week's subscription to the online edition at ~~ww~~www.literarymarketplace.com. Turn to the subject index and notice how many different kinds of book publishers there are,[O] not just fiction and nonfiction but[P] el-hi[Q] (elementary and high school) and college textbook publishers, legal and medical publishers, science and math publishers, foreign language[R] publishers, and publishers of children's books, art books, scholarly books, wilderness books, computer books, gardening books, ~~cook books~~cookbooks, and every stripe[S] of how-to[T] ~~books~~ book.[U] Even as ~~brick-and-mortar~~ brick-and-mortar bookstores are reportedly vanishing from the landscape, book sales are thriving.

Turn to the full ~~entries~~ entry for each publisher that catches your eye and take note of how many titles the company publishes. A company that produces fewer than eight or ten titles a year is most likely[V] a ~~two-or~~ two- or three-person operation,[W] staffed by ~~it's~~ its owners.[X] But the names of any larger publishers should go on your ~~job~~ job-hunting[Y] list.

While you're at the library, you might also ~~also~~ look at the current edition of *Writer's Market* (Writers Digest Books). You'll be surprised to see how large the universe of magazine publishers is. There are hundreds of small trade magazines,[Z] and hundreds of local and regional magazines.[AA] ~~Aspirating~~ Aspiring scholarly editors might check out the annual *Association of ~~Univeristy~~ University Presses ~~directory~~ Directory*.**{Query1}**

As you're compiling your list, don't forget the corporate sector. The obvious employers in the corporate sector are retail companies that produce print and online catalogues[BB] and other promotional materials, but many firms whose primary business ~~lie~~ lies[CC] elsewhere[DD] do an enormous amount of publishing: banks, law firms, phone companies, hospitals, universities, museums, ~~manufactures~~ manufacturers of high-tech equipment, and consulting firms in all fields. Any business that provides client manuals, documents, or reports,[EE] or that produces a newsletter for employees or for clients, needs editors. Many companies do not advertise, but list their openings on their ~~Web~~ websites.[FF]

Finally, there's the government sector. Hordes of editors**{Query2}** are employed in almost every department of municipal, county, state, and federal ~~goverments~~ governments. Some of these positions require subject-matter expertise, but others do not. Check with nearby government offices to find out whether you need to take a ~~Civil Service Exam~~ civil service exam[GG] and how openings are posted.

In all four sectors, there is stiff competition for entry-level[HH] jobs. To improve your chances of landing a job, whether ~~shortterm~~ short-term[II] or permanent:[JJ]

1. Follow the employer's directions for submitting an application. Candidates who fail to do so are often ~~wedded~~ weeded out immediately; ~~Don't~~ don't be one of them! If the application process requires a résumé and cover letter, make sure these are easy to read, error free,[KK] and ~~have a~~ consistent in editorial style[LL] (punctuation, treatment of dates, use of abbreviations, etc.[MM]). Tailor these documents to the job at hand, incorporating key terms from the job description and stated requirements. Don't just list your previ-

ous job titles—take a sentence or two to describe what you did in those positions.**NN** Be sure to include any relevant subject-matter expertise and auxiliary skills (such as graphic design~~,~~ or ~~ebook~~ e-book**OO** production).

    2.   Don't dwell**{Query3}** on your writing skills (unless the job ~~calls~~ calls for writing)—**PP**~~most managing editors believe there is little or no correlation between writing skills and editing skills.~~ And don't dwell on your academic credentials**QQ** unless you're applying to a scholarly press or journal.

    3.   If you have work samples, prepare a portfolio, which may include published books or articles and screenshots of online material. (Be sure that none of these samples violate**RR** ~~Non-Disclosure Agreements~~ nondisclosure agreements signed with previous employers or clients.) Include a description of the work you did on each project.

    4.   Be prepared to take ~~proofeading~~proofreading,**SS** copyediting, and other proficiency tests. If you are invited for an interview, present yourself professionally. If it's a ~~skype~~ Skype**TT** interview, remove any distracting items, including kittens, from the background.

QUERIES

{Query1}: For consistency, include the publisher for the AUP directory, or omit for the other published works mentioned?

{Query2}: Horde = swarm, teeming crowd, throng. Tone OK or revise?

{Query3}: Both sentences in this item contain "don't dwell." OK or reword?

STYLE SHEET

Author/Title: Edna Editrix/"Finding Work"
Date: February 21, 2018
Dictionary: *Merriam-Webster's Collegiate Dictionary*, 11th ed.; *Merriam-Webster Unabridged*
Style Manual: *The Chicago Manual of Style*, 17th ed.

Alphabetical List of Names and Terms
(adj. = adjective)

brick-and-mortar (adj.)
catalogue
civil service exam
cookbook
copyediting

e-book
el-hi (adj.)
email
entry-level (adj.)
error free (predicate adj.)
high-tech (adj.)
how-to book
human resources department
internet
job-hunting (adj.)
public library
résumé
short-term (adj.; predicate adj.)
subject-matter expertise
T-shirt
two-person (adj.)
US (adj.)
web (internet)
website

Numbers and Dates
Spell out numbers under 101

Punctuation
Serial comma
Contractions OK
Suspended compound: two- or three-person (adj.)

Abbreviations
LMP (italic)
etc. is OK in parenthetical expressions only

Miscellaneous
Author to decide whether to include publishers for printed works.

COMMENTS

A   This colloquial expression would be out of place in a formal document but is acceptable for the conversational tone of this piece.

B   The semicolon creates a sentence fragment; use a comma or an em dash.

C   By convention, "San Francisco Bay Area" is capitalized. Use the plural possessive, "editors'," or the plural attributive form, "editors," to refer to a group for editors. See *The Copyeditor's Handbook,* chapter 5, under "Possessives."

D Use an uppercase *T,* because this expression is based on the shape of the letter.

E Slogans are often capitalized, but the short preposition "in" should be lowercased.

F The meaning of the coinage "gofer-ing" can be readily inferred from the noun form in *M-W Unabridged*; think carefully before rewording.

G The name of the site uses the intercap: LinkedIn, *not* Linkedin.

H "Magazine" is roman and lowercased because it is not part of the periodical's title. (Note: Sadly, *Copyediting* has ceased publication.)

I Originally capitalized, "internet" is now usually lowercased.

J The closed form "email" has superseded "e-mail," according to *Chicago* and other style guides.

K "Login" *or* "log-in"? *M-W Unabridged* lists the latter (as a variant of "log-on"), but this dictionary's own website asks for a "subscriber login." It's possible that the web programmers are ahead of the lexicographers in acknowledging evolving usage. (See also the discussion of this term in the key to exercise 3-1.)

L Do not add a comma after "library." Although this sentence contains two verbs joined by "and," no comma is needed since both imperatives are short, there is no change of subject (implied *you*), and there is no danger of ambiguity or misreading.

M Notice that "*LMP*" is (correctly) in italics. Both the full title and the shortened title of a book are italicized. Also, although the common noun "marketplace" is one word, the name of this publication is *Literary Market Place*. (The author recommends going to the library because a copy of *LMP* costs several hundred dollars; as of early 2018, a weeklong online subscription costs $24.95.)

N According to *Chicago* 6.44, "Commas are not required with *Inc., Ltd.,* and such as part of a company's name." In fact, *Chicago* 10.24 advises that the abbreviations may be omitted entirely. In this case, however, "Inc." signals that the common words "Information Today" constitute a corporate name.

O The author's comma after "there are" is correct. A colon would be incorrect here because "not just fiction" is not the first item in a list but rather an antithetical phrase. Compare: There are many kinds, not just two or three. In the following example, in contrast, a colon is required because "there are" introduces a list:

> Notice how many different kinds of book publishers there are: fiction and nonfiction, legal and medical . . .

P No commas are needed between coordinate clauses such as "not just . . . but." Some people insist that the pairs must be "not just . . . but also" and "not only . . . but also"; however, this is a personal preference, not a requirement (see *DEU,* s.v. "not only . . . but also").

Q *M-W Collegiate* shows "elhi," but most people in publishing use "el-hi." If you have a question about a piece of jargon, query the author.

R No hyphen is needed in "foreign language publishers" because "foreign language" is a permanent open compound noun being used as an attributive adjective and there is no possibility of misreading. For other compounds in the *foreign* family, a hyphen is needed if the hyphenless compound is ambiguous: foreign-currency restrictions *and* foreign-service officers *but* foreign aid bill *and* foreign policy staff.

S The word "stripe" is unobjectionable; see *M-W Collegiate*, s.v. "stripe," definition 3: "a distinct variety or sort: TYPE <persons of the same political stripe>." When "stripe of" precedes a noun, the noun is singular (every stripe of person). Or you could change this to read "and how-to books of every stripe."

T Dictionaries show a hyphen in the adjective "how-to," but there's no hyphen between the adjective "how-to" and the noun "book."

U This is a long sentence. Nonetheless, it is clear and coherent, the punctuation is correct, and the very length of the sentence seems designed to convey the breadth and diversity of the industry. Thus a copyeditor need not intervene. If you are tempted to intervene, it would be better to query ("Consider splitting this long sentence in two?") than to take up arms and rewrite. Resist the urge to delete some of the instances of "publishers"; they serve a useful function in signaling the end of the individual items in this long list.

V The author's "most likely" is correct. There are two common functions for *most:* (1) it is used to form the superlative of an adjective or an adverb (likely, more likely, most likely), and (2) it is used before an adjective or an adverb as an intensifier (she is a most effective speaker). Here "most" serves the second function.

W This is a suspended compound: "two- or three-person operation." Make sure the hyphens and wordspaces are indicated correctly. Similarly:

> The fourteen- and fifteen-year-old students attended.

X Here, "staffed by its owners" could be deemed restrictive or nonrestrictive; follow the author's lead.

Y Hyphenate a compound adjective of the form "noun + participle" when it precedes a noun: "job-hunting list." In contrast, the noun *job hunting* is not hyphenated: I detest job hunting.

Z The term "small trade magazines" is correct. *Trade magazine* is a standard term in publishing, used to describe a magazine written for readers in a particular industry (as opposed to general interest magazines like *Time, Newsweek,* or *Reader's Digest*). To write "small, trade magazines" is to convert "small" and "trade" into coordinate adjectives, which they are not. (Test: It is nonsense to say "The magazines are small and trade.") To write "small-trade" is to create an entity known as a "small trade" (as opposed to a "big trade" or a "large trade"). Although we do have "small business," there is no set phrase "small trade."

> The comma after "magazines" isn't needed, but it isn't incorrect.

AA   A copyeditor should resist the temptation to save a word or two by changing this to "There are hundreds of small trade, local, and regional magazines." That revision is inaccurate: the author uses "small" to modify only "trade magazines," not the local and regional magazines.

BB   The entry in *M-W Collegiate* reads "catalog *or* catalogue," which means that the two spellings are equal variants. Some copyeditors always respect the author's choice among equal variants; other copyeditors tend to impose the first spelling, even when the variants are equal. Whichever form you choose, be sure to enter it on your style sheet.

CC   The verb "lies" agrees with the singular "primary business," not with "many firms."

DD   The author has correctly punctuated the *whose* clause as restrictive; the sentence is not about "many firms" but about "many firms whose primary business lies elsewhere."

EE   Keep the comma after "reports," even though the syntactical skeleton ("that provides x . . . or that produces y") does not require one. The comma alerts the reader that "or that produces" is not an add-on to the series "client manuals, documents, or reports."

FF   The comma after "advertise" is not needed, because one usually does not have a comma between the parts of a compound predicate. But the comma is not incorrect either; it emphasizes the contrast between the two methods of publicizing openings.

GG   Lowercase "civil service exam" because it is a generic term, not a specific test. That's why the author used the indefinite article "a." Compare:

   Applicants must take the Calculus Achievement Test.

   Applicants must take a calculus achievement test.

   Do not add a hyphen to "civil service exam"; "civil service" is a permanent open compound, and the hyphenless term poses no danger of misreading.

HH   Keep the hyphen in the attributive adjective "entry-level."

II   "Short-term" functions as a predicate adjective. The style here follows *M-W Unabridged,* which shows it as a hyphenated compound. But you might also choose to omit the hyphen for consistency with "error free" just below (not listed in *M-W Unabridged*).

JJ   The author has chosen to treat the following items as a series of numbered paragraphs, with the numerals serving to emphasize the items on the list. This technique is fine. One could also convert the numbered paragraphs into a set-off list, as shown below. Publishers' typecoding systems vary; the items in the numbered list here are differentiated as <NL-f> (first numbered list item), NL-m (middle numbered list item[s]), and <NL-l> (last numbered list item). (The formatting and typecoding of numbered lists are discussed in *The Copyeditor's Handbook,* chapter 13, under "Lists.")

In all four sectors, there is stiff competition for entry-level jobs. To improve your chances of landing a job, whether short-term or permanent:

<NL-f>1. Follow the employer's directions for submitting an application. . . .

<NL-m>2. Don't dwell on your writing skills (unless the job calls for writing). . . .

<NL-m>3. If you have work samples, prepare a portfolio. . . .

<NL-l>4. Be prepared to take proofreading, copyediting, and other proficiency tests. . . .

KK   No hyphens are required in the predicate adjectives "easy to read" and "error free." In the attributive position, these adjectives are hyphenated: She has an easy-to-read résumé. She has an error-free résumé.

LL   The author's construction is not parallel. Fix it by changing the last item into an adjective ("consistent in editorial style") or break the sentence in two and reword slightly: ". . . make sure your résumé and cover letter are easy to read and error free. They should also have a consistent editorial style . . ." The least appealing way to mend a faulty parallel is to insert a *with* ("easy to read and error free, with a consistent editorial style"). *Garner's* labels *with* as a "quasi-conjunction" in this context and discourages its use (s.v. "with").

MM   Some publishers consider the abbreviations *e.g., i.e.,* and *etc.* too informal to appear in print. Other publishers allow these abbreviations only in parenthetical comments and in notes. Always follow house policy. Here, "etc." could be changed to "and the like."

NN   Some readers might find this dash overly informal, although dashes are common in contemporary writing and consistent with the overall register of this piece (e.g., the use of contractions). A light edit would likely stet the dashes here and in the following paragraph. If the author wanted a more formal, professional register, the choices would be these:

Don't just list your previous job titles. Take a sentence . . .

Don't just list your previous job titles; take a sentence . . .

Don't just list your previous job titles: take a sentence . . .

OO   The term "email" is closed, but "e-book" is hyphenated, according to *Chicago.* With technical terms whose usage is evolving, it's wise to check the publisher's house style or preferred dictionary.

PP   Parentheses are fine here to deemphasize the comment "unless the job calls for writing." As in the previous paragraph, the dash is not incorrect, but it is informal.

QQ   There should be no comma before "unless" because the clause is restrictive.

RR   "Violate" or "violates"? See the discussion of notional agreement of "none of" in *The Copyeditor's Handbook,* chapter 14, under "Subject-Verb Agreement." Here, because the noun following "none of" is plural ("samples") and the sentence refers to multiple agreements, the plural verb seems preferable.

SS   It's alarmingly easy to overlook errors in words directly related to one's professional competence.

TT   Uppercase "Skype" as the name of a specific online platform. Like "Google," this is a proprietary name that may soon evolve into a generic term. (See also the discussion of this term in the key to exercise 3-1.)

EXERCISE 7-1: Key

Queries addressed to the author are flagged in the text within curly brackets and are placed directly below the emended sentences, followed by explanatory comments.

1. The mortgage loans in default range from $35,000{**Query**} to $500,000.

    {Query}: Corrected amount OK?

Comment: The context suggests that "$35 to $500,000" is shorthand for "$35,000 to $500,000"—no mortgage loan is for a mere $35! The query asks the writer to confirm the change.

2. For more information, see Degas's article in volume ~~xlii~~ 42 of the *Journal of Higher Studies*.

Comment: In regular text, arabic numerals are used for volume numbers, even if the publication uses roman numerals on its cover and title page. If you are hand marking hard copy, supply the arabic numeral; do not circle the roman numeral and expect the typesetter to "translate" it. The last clause could also read: "see Degas's article in the *Journal of Higher Studies*, volume 42."

3. From 1991~~-1994~~ to 1994, the town's population increased by ~~ten~~ 10 percent.

Comment: By convention, an en dash is not allowed in a "from [number] to [number]" or "between [number] and [number]" construction. Percentages are always expressed in numerals; in nontechnical text, *percent*—not %—is correct.

4. The new fighter planes cost ~~$.25 billion~~ $250 million each.

Comment: It is awkward to have a decimal less than 1.0 in this construction, unless this sentence appears in a paragraph in which other sums of money are expressed in billions. One billion = 1,000,000,000 = 1,000 million; therefore, 0.25 billion = 250 million.

5. The insurance surcharge is $.75 for ~~twenty-five-dollars' coverage,~~ coverage up to $25; $1.40 for ~~$25-50,~~ coverage up to $50; and $1.80 for ~~$50-100~~ coverage up to $100.{**Query**}

    {Query}: Does a package to be insured for exactly $25 cost $.75 or $1.40? And is the cost $1.40 or $1.80 for a package to be insured for exactly $50?

Comment: If you feel that 75¢ is clearer than $.75, change it. Or keep $.75 for consistency with the $1.40 and $1.80 later in the sentence. Either choice is acceptable. Revise to avoid the awkward possessive "dollars'" and to clarify the indecipherable cluster of numbers. Query the overlapping inclusive ranges. Using commas between the items in this series would be more conventional, but semicolons are not incorrect and here arguably serve to separate the clusters of numbers more clearly than commas would. In matters of discretionary punctuation, assuming no ambiguity exists, the author's choices should normally be respected.

6.   The atmosphere weighs 5,700,~~000,000,000,000~~ trillion tons.

Comment: A sixteen-digit number is hard to comprehend and can produce awkward line breaks in typeset copy. (When a line break comes midnumeral, a hyphen is inserted after one of the commas in the numeral.) One could also change this to read "5.7 quadrillion tons."

7.   The sales data for the ~~3d~~ third quarter of ~~'94~~ 1994 are presented on pages 113–15, 300–308, and 201–~~09~~.**{Query}**

{Query}: Should these page numbers be placed in ascending numerical order?

Comment: In running text, one would spell out "3d," and one would not abbreviate "1994"; use these shortcuts only in tables or when space is at a premium. You should also regularize the treatment of the inclusive numbers using one of the three systems discussed under "Inclusive Numerals" in *The Copyeditor's Handbook,* chapter 7. The other choices are these:

pages 113–115, 300–308, 201–209

pages 113–5, 300–8, 201–9

8.   ~~Amendments 1 through 10 of~~ The first ten amendments to the Constitution are known as the Bill of Rights.

Comment: By convention, amendments to the US Constitution are referred to by spelled-out ordinal numbers and are capitalized. Here, "The first ten amendments" seems less clumsy than "The First through Tenth Amendments."

9.   ~~The~~ In 1876 the vote in the Electoral College was 185 to 184.~~in 1876.~~

Comment: The sentence reads better when the year is moved. The use of "to" in the tally is fine; only sports scores take an en dash (The Giants beat the Dodgers, 8–2). *GPO* shows "electoral college," but *Chicago* and the *AP Stylebook* uppercase the term.

10.   The year 2008 is ~~a year~~ one most investors would like to forget.

Comment: A sentence should not begin with a numeral. There are other ways to revise this sentence, including spelling out the year (Two thousand eight is . . .).

11. Using ~~Carbon~~ carbon-14 dating, scientists have determined that the Hopewell earthworks first appeared in ~~Southern~~ southern Ohio in about 100 ~~B.C~~ BC, and that the last elaborate valley earthwork was constructed in about AD 550. ~~A.D.~~

Comment: Traditionally, BC follows the year and AD precedes the year. Some publishers use periods with these abbreviations (in the original sentence one period was dropped from "B.C."); other publishers omit the periods. House style may also call for setting these abbreviations in small capitals: BC, AD. Note too that some publishers prefer the nonsectarian BCE (before the Common Era) and CE (Common Era), both of which follow the year.

12. The burial mounds on the Hopewell farm range from 160 to 470 feet (48 to 141 ~~km.~~ m){**Query**} in length and from 20 to 32 feet (6 to 10 m) in height.

    {**Query**}: Change OK?

Comment: SI abbreviations do not take periods. Even if you're not a metric expert, you should have noticed the discrepancy between the two sets of equivalences: If 160 feet = 48 kilometers, then 20 feet ≠ 6 meters. Use a conversion table or a rule of thumb (a meter is roughly a yard) to detect the error and ask the author to verify the change.

13. Alexander ~~the Third~~ III of Macedon (Alexander the Great) was born in 356 ~~B.C.E.~~ BCE and ruled 336–324 ~~BP~~ BCE.

Comment: By convention, roman numerals are used to differentiate monarchs and other rulers with the same name within a dynasty or line of succession. To avoid confusion, numbers are never elided in descending date spans designated by BC, BCE, BP, or mya (million years ago). Cf. "Valentinian I was born 321 CE and ruled 364–75 CE." The abbreviation *BP* (before the present) is used in astronomy and archaeology; it cannot be used in conjunction with precise historical dates (see *The Copyeditor's Handbook*, chapter 9, under "Abbreviations"). The retention or deletion of periods in these abbreviations is a matter of house style.

15. With a number of camera phones now boasting resolutions in the range of 16–20 ~~megapixies~~ megapixels (MP), it's hard to recall the days, only ~~10~~ ten years ago, when the technology writer for the *New York Times* assured readers that a resolution of 5 or 6 MP was more than enough. But he had a point: larger images require more storage space, and many phone users find that 64 ~~Gb~~ GB ~~SSD's~~ storage drives soon fill up with selfies.

Comment: In keeping with nontechnical style, all the numbers in this passage could certainly be spelled out. However, because consumers are used to seeing specifications for electronic devices expressed as numerals, there's an argument for leaving them that way. Note the replacement of the hyphen with an en dash in the number range

"16–20." "Ten" should be spelled out, as it is not a specification. The abbreviation "GB" could be expanded to "gigabyte," since the writer spells out "megapixels" (or attempts to do so), but, again, the former is now common in writing about electronics. (No hyphen is required in "64 GB," but one should be added if the expression is spelled out: 64-gigabyte.) "SSD," a less common abbreviation (standing for "solid-state drive"), is replaced here with a less technical term; if retained, the plural should be rendered SSDs, with no apostrophe (see *The Copyeditor's Handbook,* chapter 9, under "Abbreviations").

16. Between 25%~ and 30% ~~percent~~ of students complained that the 2ⁿᵈsecond-year chemistry course was too hard.

Comment: "Between" requires an "and," which cannot be represented by an en dash in a number span. "Percent" is spelled out in nontechnical style. Although signs are generally repeated for number ranges in technical writing, "percent" may be omitted after the first number in this nontechnical copy because no ambiguity exists in the expression "between 25 and 30 percent." Spell out the ordinal "second." When ordinal numbers are expressed as numerals, they should not appear as superscripts (2nd, *not* 2nd).

17. Google's name is reportedly derived from mistyping *googol,* which is the number 10^{100} (the numeral 1 followed by ~~100 0s~~ one hundred zeros).

Comment: Leave "1" as a numeral, because the text explicitly refers to it as such. Spell out "one hundred" and "zeros" (or "zeroes," but not "zero's") in nontechnical style.

18. The small New Zealand town of Kaitangata, located at 46°16′~~:~~ S 169°51′~~:~~ ~~East~~, became famous in July ~~of~~ 2016 when international media outlets incorrectly reported that it was offering free housing worth up to ~~NZD230K~~ NZ$230,000 (then worth approximately ~~U.S.~~ US$~~160K~~ 160,000 or ~~GB£130~~**{Query}**) to new immigrants.

     {Query}: Should this read "GB£130,000"?

Comment: Many authors use single and double quotation marks rather than prime (′) and double prime (″) symbols to indicate minutes and seconds. Using the correct Unicode symbols prevents autocorrect routines from replacing these marks with curly quotation marks. In latitude and longitude readings, compass directions are conventionally abbreviated: E, *not* East. "Of" between month and year is common in colloquial speech but not necessary in writing. Specify the currencies referred to by adding the initials of the respective countries. Although "K" is a common abbreviation for "thousand" in real estate listings and similar contexts, numerals are clearer. As in example 1, editorial judgment should prompt a query to the author about the discrepancy between "£130" and the other sums mentioned.

19. To calculate the shrinkage rate of your fabric, measure before and after washing, subtract the finished dimensions from the original dimensions, and divide the results by the original dimensions. If your sample measured 10 × 10 inches before washing and 9 × 8 inches afterward, the shrinkage in width is 10 percent (10 – 9 = 1, and 1 ÷ 10 = 0.1, or 10 percent), and the shrinkage in length is 8 percent.**{Query}**

{Query}: Please recheck calculation for shrinkage in length.

Comment: All the numbers and mathematical operators here are styled correctly (note the use of a true multiplication sign rather than an *x*), but don't let that blind you to the error in the second calculation: (10 – 8) ÷ 10 = 0.2, or 20 percent. Editors are typically not responsible for verifying calculations, but if the numbers look odd, query.

20. In a questionnaire on the probability of a bioterrorist attack, ~~29~~ twenty-nine respondents suggested at least a 75~~%~~ percent likelihood~~, on a scale from 0 to 100 percent,~~ that there would be an attack causing at least ~~one hundred~~ one hundred people to fall ill.

Comment: Both the number of respondents and the number of potential victims may be spelled out or rendered as numerals, depending on house style (some style guides recommend spelling out only numbers smaller than ten). Omit "on a scale from 0 to 100 percent": it's implicit when probabilities are expressed as percentages (though a scholarly author might be more explicit about the number and range of possible responses offered in the questionnaire).

A final note: Did you notice that number 14 is missing in this exercise and answer key? We didn't either! This oversight reinforces the standard advice to authors, copyeditors, and proofreaders to double-check all numerical and alphabetical sequences. Make it a habit.

EXERCISE 7-2: Key

Numbered queries addressed to the author are flagged in the text within curly brackets and printed below the text. Explanatory comments follow the query list.

Bobonia's economy contracted sharply in the 2nd quarter.**A** Exports declined by 14.5%, the worst monthly performance in ~~12 and a half years~~12½ years.**{Query1}** Electronics manufacturers**B** were particularly ~~hard hit~~hard-hit.**C** Imports, however, continued to rise, which ~~plunged~~caused the trade deficit to soar to $1.25 billion.**D** This deficit is likely to worsen before it improves, **E** and the revised government forecast ~~calls for it to~~predicts that the deficit will reach**F** $1.75 billion by late ~~Fall~~fall.**G**

     H~~Domestically, inflation~~Inflation remains almost ~~nonexistent~~invisible,**I** at an annual rate of only 1%. ~~Unemployment rates~~The unemployment rate fell to 6.5% in June, ~~compared to~~from 6.8% in March ~~also continued to move lower.~~**J** ~~On~~In the good news, consumer confidence, as measured by the ~~Univeristy~~University of Bobonia National Feelgood Scale, rose from 105.5 in March to 109 in June.**K{Query2}**

     Short-term interest rates were unchanged: the overnight rate is 5.25%, and the average yield on 30-year government notes is 5.35%.**{Query3}**

     The currency has strengthened since mid-March,**L** when the Bobonian ~~Bobble~~bobble**M** traded at 5.4550 to the ~~U.S.~~US**N** dollar. On June 30,**O** the ~~Bobble~~bobble closed at 5.580 to the dollar**P{Query4}** on the London Worthless Currency ~~exchange~~Exchange.

QUERIES

{Query1}: Supply name of month (previous sentence places us in the second quarter but not in any particular month), or should this read "worst quarterly performance"?

{Query2}: Reconcile treatment of confidence survey scores; both to one decimal place?

{Query3}: Can't have the rate for 30-year notes in a sentence that's about short-term rates. Do you mean 30-day rate? Or else start a new sentence for 30-year rate.

{Query4}: Give both rates to the same number of decimal places. Also, the move from 5.4550 to 5.580 is a weakening, not a strengthening. Please recheck numbers.

COMMENTS

If you were working for a company, you would, of course, have a copy of the in-house style guide, which would detail preferences for the treatment of numbers. Absent such guidelines, editorial judgment suggests that the density of numerical data in this summary calls for using the percentage sign, rather than spelling out *percent,* and using numerals for all sums of money and other quantities. Decimal expressions are appropriate for technical measurements (a 14.5% decline in exports) but would imply a false degree of precision in nontechnical numerical values: hence "12½ years," not "12.5 years."

A In corporate publishing, there are four common conventions for treating the quarters of the year:

> first quarter, second quarter, third quarter, fourth quarter
>
> 1st quarter, 2d (*or, in Chicago style,* 2nd) quarter, 3d (*or, in Chicago style,* 3rd) quarter, 4th quarter
>
> Q1, Q2, Q3, Q4
>
> 1Q98, 2Q98, 3Q98, 4Q98 (where the last two digits represent the year)

B The industry is "the electronics industry"; thus, "Electronics manufacturers" (compare: "an electronic device").

C A new addition to *M-W Unabridged* notes that the adjective "hard-hit" is now hyphenated in both the attributive and predicative uses.

D The context makes it clear that the trade deficit is increasing. (Exports fell and imports continued to rise.) An increasing deficit does not plunge—it soars, balloons, or swells.

E A comma before a coordinating conjunction that joins two independent clauses is mandatory.

F The wording "calls for it to reach" suggests that a higher deficit is a sought-after goal.

G In running text, names of seasons are capitalized only when an author is employing personification. (Seasons are also capitalized in journal dates cited in reference notes and bibliographies.)

H "Domestically" is awkward (not every adverb can be called into service as a sentence adverb) and contributes nothing to the meaning. (By definition, inflation is a domestic economic indicator.)

I Whether anything can "remain nonexistent," much less "remain almost nonexistent," is a question best left for philosophers.

J There are many ways to revise this awkwardly constructed sentence. In the revision shown here, the comma marks "from 6.8% in March" as a nonrestrictive phrase. Note that "also continued to move lower" is illogical, since nothing else in this paragraph has moved lower.

K It is clearer to treat "consumer confidence" as the subject, add "as," and insert a pair of commas to set off the long nonrestrictive descriptor ("as measured . . . Scale").

L A comma is needed to set off the nonrestrictive clause; here "when" is in apposition to "mid-March."

M Lowercase the name of the currency.

N Chicago style now accepts "US" (without the periods) in both noun and adjective uses.

O No comma is required after this short introductory adverbial phrase.

P Do not simply lop off a digit or add a zero to regularize the decimals in this paragraph. As for the exchange rate, the more bobbles per dollar—5.580 compared to 5.4550—the less each bobble is worth, and so these numbers show a weakening bobble.

EXERCISE 7-3: Key

As noted, recipes can vary in details of style and format even when they adhere to a consistent overall structure. Here's one workable version of this recipe. Note that units of measure and metric conversions are styled and placed consistently, that the ingredients for the two elements of the recipe (cookie dough and frosting) are listed separately, and that the instructions have been revised into complete, clear sentences. Depending on the intended audience, a recipe author might also provide more detailed instructions on how to cream butter with sugar and other ingredients, the types of flour and sugar to use, how to melt chocolate, how to tell when the cookies are baked through, and how to store them. Comments on specific elements are keyed to superscripts in the recipe.

Frosted Chocolate Logs

(This recipe comes from my mother's older sister, my aAunt May), who was a great cook.)

CreamCookies:

1 cup. margarine (about 220 grams)**A**, or you can use butter or margarine

3/44 cup. (150 grams gm) sugar**B**

2 squares (2 ozounces;, or 55 grams) melted unsweetened baking chocolate or extra-dark bittersweet chocolate, melted**C**

3/4 c. (150 gm) sugar

1 egg

1 Tbsp tablespoon vanilla

1 egg

Sift together & add:

3 cups. (350 grams) flour (350 grams)

1 teaspoon salt

1 tsp teaspoon baking soda

FrostingTopping:

1 cup (110 grams) powdered sugar

1 tablespoon milk, or more as needed

1 cup finely chopped or grated nuts or flaked coconut

Preheat the oven to 350°F (180°C). **D** In a large mixing bowl, cream the butter, sugar, melted chocolate, and vanilla. Beat in the egg. In a separate bowl, sift together the flour, salt, and baking soda. Add the dry ingredients to the butter mixture and mix until thoroughly combined.

~~Try to h~~Handle the dough as little as possible~~,~~. ~~if~~If it feels too sticky to roll out, ~~chill~~refrigerate for ~~1/2~~½ hour; if it feels too dry, add ~~1/2T to 1T~~½ to 1 tablespoon more vanilla. Form the dough into rolls ½ inch (12 millimeters) thick and cut into 2-inch (5-centimeter) logs. ~~Roll into 1/2" (1 1/4 cm) thick rolls and cut into 2" (5 cm) lengths to form logs.~~

Bake on greased cookie sheets ~~at 350°F (180C)~~ for 10 minutes. Allow to ~~C~~cool ~~and frost~~.

Frosting:

~~To 1 cup (110g)~~ Place the powdered sugar in a small bowl and very slowly ~~add~~ stir in enough milk~~, stirring until the mixture is~~ to make a thick but spreadable frosting. Cover the top of each log with frosting. Dip the frosted surface into ~~1 c. finely chopped or grated~~ the nuts or coconut.

COMMENTS

A In this revision, units of measure for ingredients are all spelled out. Abbreviations are also acceptable, as long as they are consistent and unambiguous: teaspoons and tablespoons, in particular, need to be clearly distinguished. Butter is specified in preference to margarine, as it is now considered a healthier choice.

B The order in which the ingredients are listed has been changed to match the order in which they are used.

C When an ingredient has to be prepared in some way (e.g., chopped or melted) before measuring, this instruction is often placed immediately after the quantity (e.g., 1 cup ground walnuts). If it is measured before preparation (like chocolate or butter, which are much easier to weigh or measure in solid form), the instruction is placed after the ingredient.

D Because cookie dough is quick to make, recipes typically instruct users to turn on the oven to preheat before mixing the dough.

EXERCISE 8-1: Key

One query addressed to the author is flagged in the text with the bracketed {Query}. Explanatory comments appear under certain sentences.

1. Einstein said, "God doesn't play dice with the world."

2. Einstein also said ~~to,~~ "Never wear a ~~plait~~ plaid shirt with striped pants."{Query}

   {Query}: OK to correct "plait" to "plaid"? But can we be sure that Einstein said this? Can you identify a source?

3. In her entertaining account of working as an editor at the New Yorker, Mary Norris describes learning to exercise restraint when reviewing the prose of some of the magazine's most famous contributors: "When Pauline Kael typed 'prevert' instead of 'pervert,' she meant 'prevert' (unless she was reviewing something by Jacques Prévert)" ("Holy Writ: Learning to Love the House Style," New Yorker, February 23 and March 2, 2015).

Comments:
   - The use of single quotation marks around *prevert* is correct according to US usage, but the closing quotation mark following the first instance is turned the wrong way, probably as a result of a word processor's autocorrect routine.
   - Although the back-to-back parentheses and quotation marks may look puzzling, the punctuation is correct for a parenthetical source citation within a sentence.
   - When you're focusing on small punctuation marks, it's easy to overlook other typos, such as the missing wordspace before *New Yorker*.

4. In another New Yorker piece, an unflattering review of Lynne Truss's Eats, Shoots and Leaves, Louis Menand comments on the common punctuation errors that Truss finds maddening: "When deli owners put up signs that read "'Iced' Tea," the ~~single~~ quotation marks around "Iced" are "intended to add extraliterary significance to the message, as if they were the grammatical equivalent of red ink" ("Bad Comma," New Yorker, June 28, 2004).

Comment: This quotation poses a conundrum. In US style, of the three sets of nested quotation marks, the outermost and innermost sets should be double quotation marks, but to change them would make the marks inconsistent with Menand's observation about single quotation marks. One solution is to break the quotation at the troublesome point (after the word *Tea*) and paraphrase Menand. Note that the comma following *Tea* goes inside both sets of quotation marks. Note also that when single and double quotation marks are juxtaposed, it can be difficult to identify which is which; some publishers insert thin spaces or hair spaces between the marks for clarity.

An alternative solution, if house style allows it, would be to treat the quotation as a block quotation and reproduce the quotation marks exactly as they appear in the original text.

5. Will the Middle French motto "Honi soit qui mal y pense" (roughly translated as~ "Shame on anyone who thinks evil of it") be removed from British passports after ~~'Brexit'~~Brexit?

Comment: No commas are needed before the motto or the translation: in grammatical terms, the motto is a restrictive appositive, and the English version is the object of "translated as." Although some styles use single quotation marks to denote unfamiliar, colloquial, or ironic terms, *Brexit* is now familiar enough not to warrant such identification.

6. As Michael Ignatieff has observed, "Samuel Beckett's 'Fail again. Fail better' captures the inner obstinacy necessary to the political art" ("Getting Iraq Wrong," *New York Times,* August 5, 2007).

Comment: All the punctuation is correct here. Although the advice from Beckett consists of two (short) sentences, the quotation does not require terminal punctuation if it appears within a sentence.

EXERCISE 8-2: Key

Numbered queries are flagged in the text with boldface curly braces (e.g., **{Query1}**) and are printed below the text, followed by the style sheet. Explanatory comments, keyed in the text with superscript letters, are printed at the end.

Every month the It's Our Money Institute in New York ~~city~~ City publishes a list of particularly outrageous, ironic, or ridiculous wastes of ~~tax~~ taxpayers' ~~taxes~~money. Here are some of last year's winners:[A]

The Economic ~~Developement~~ Development**{Query1}** gave Bedord,**{Query2}** Indiana, ~~$.7 million dollars~~ $700,000[C] to build a model of the pyramid[D] of Cheops and an[E] 800-~~feet~~foot replica of ~~The~~ the Great Wall of China to "attract[F] tourists and "demonstrate the value of limestone in the building industry."

The National Science Foundation ~~spends~~ spent[G] $14,4012**{Query3}** to test the ~~affects~~effects of inflation on the behavior of rats and pigeons. The studies'**{Query4}** ~~conclusions~~conclusion:[H] ~~when~~When given a choice, animal "consumers" opt for cheaper goods, just as people do.

The Federal Highway Administration broke the record for cost ~~over-runs~~overruns on a civilian project. Due to inflation, delay, and mismanagement,[I] ~~The~~the Interstate Highway System has now cost ~~$100,300 million~~$100.3 billion,[J] or 267~~%~~ percent of what ~~congress~~ Congress originally approved. ~~due to inflation, delay, and mismanagment.~~

The Department of Agriculture spent ~~fourty thousand dollars~~ $40,000 on a ~~year~~yearlong study of food preferences and popular stereotypes. Results ~~?~~[K] The public sees fast-food ~~addicts~~ addicts as patriotic, conservative, and ~~hard workers~~hardworking.[L] Vegetarians are viewed as intellectual and creative, and gourmets are thought to[M] like small families, mixed doubles in tennis, and "~~live~~life in the fast lane."**{Query5}**

{Query6}The National Endowment ~~For~~for the Arts[N] granted $7,000 for a ~~sound and light~~ sound-and-light show to make ~~Wisconsins'~~Wisconsin's state ~~capital building~~capitol[O] in Milwaukee**{Query7}** "send forth human and planetary energies in a ~~massage~~message of world peace."**{Query8}** The one performance was marred when half the lights failed to work and the recorded broadcast from the dome was ~~illegible~~unintelligible.

The ~~U. S.~~ US Army's Materiel Development and ~~Readyness~~ Readiness Command (DARCON)**{Query9}** spent $38 million and ~~13~~ thirteen years to develop a new gas mask, the XM30, ~~that~~ which**P** usually malfunctions within ~~48~~ forty-eight hours. The ~~A~~army's ~~training~~ Training and Doctrine Command found the XM-30s**Q{Query10}** generally inferior to the ~~17~~ seventeen-year-old ~~old~~ M17AL mask it was designed to replace.

The Defense Department paid ~~#~~$13,000 to test the possible ~~side-effects~~ side effects of ~~extremely-low-frequency~~ extremely low frequency**R** radio waves on a ~~hereford~~ Hereford bull named Sylvester. After ~~6~~ six years, Sylvestre**{Query11}** was autopsied and judged "essentially a normal bull though somewhat obese." A ~~Navy Vice Admiral~~ navy vice admiral**S** admitted that the experiment has no value due "~~to~~**T** the limited size of the data sample ~~data base~~."**U**

QUERIES

{Query1}: Supply full name of agency (e.g., Office of Economic Development?).
{Query2}: Bedord or Bedford?
{Query3}: Please fix $14,4012. Is it $144,012 or $14,xxx?
{Query4}: "Studies'" or "study's"?
{Query5}: Correction of "live" to "life" in quote (an error in transcription?) OK?
{Query6}: New paragraph here (to mark new list item) OK?
{Query7}: Milwaukee or Madison (the current capital)?
{Query8}: Correction of "massage" to "message" in quote (an error in transcription?) OK?
{Query9}: DARCON or DARCOM (for Command)?
{Query10}: XM30 or XM-30? See previous reference.
{Query11}: Sylvester or Sylvestre?

STYLE SHEET

Author/Title: It's Our Money Institute/"It's Our Money Awards"
Date: February 21, 2018
Dictionary: *Merriam-Webster's Collegiate Dictionary*, 11th ed.; *Merriam-Webster Unabridged*
Style Manual: *The Chicago Manual of Style*, 17th ed.

Alphabetical List of Names and Terms
(n. = noun, adj. = adjective)

Congress
data sample
extremely low frequency radio waves

fast-food addict
the Great Wall
hardworking
Hereford bull
Interstate Highway System
National Endowment for the Arts
overruns (n.)
pyramid of Cheops
side effects
sound-and-light show
taxpayers
vice admiral
yearlong

Punctuation
Serial comma
Commas before and after geographical units

Numbers and Dates
Spell out numbers under 101, except percentages
seventeen-year-old (adj.)
267 percent

Abbreviations
DARCON (or DARCOM?)
U.S. (no internal space)

Miscellaneous
XM30 or XM-30?

COMMENTS

A Either a colon or a period may be used to introduce a multiparagraph list.

B Commas are needed both before and after the state's name.

C Avoid the decimal numeral. The symbol "$" cannot be used with "dollars"; use the dollar sign with numerals.

D Lowercase or uppercase for "pyramid" is OK, since the word may be construed as either a generic descriptor or part of a proper name; indicate your choice on your style sheet.

E Use "an," not "a," before "800-foot" (read aloud to hear the numeral).

F There are two sets of opening quote marks but only one closing set. Since this is not a formal research paper with citations from published articles, you can simply delete the extra set of opening quote marks rather than ask the author to supply a second set of closing quote marks.

G Use past tense—"spent"—to match other paragraphs.

H Use "conclusion," since only one is given here. The first word following a colon may be capitalized or lowercased, depending on house style: see the discussion of colons in *The Copyeditor's Handbook,* chapter 4, under "Mark-by-Mark Pitfalls."

I Move the "due to" clause to prevent the misreading that it modifies "what Congress originally approved." (For a discussion of this use of "due to" as a sentence modifier, see *The Copyeditor's Handbook,* chapter 14, under "Prepositions.")

J A comma is needed to set off appositive introduced by "or."

K A nitpicky point: An analysis of survey data yields "findings," not "results." In either case, there should be no space between the word and the question mark.

L Use "hardworking" (one word) for parallel structure.

M Revise to clarify that these descriptions of vegetarians and gourmets are the stereotypes people hold.

N Capitalization of the names of organizations follows the rules for titles (see "Titles of Works" in *The Copyeditor's Handbook,* chapter 6).

O The building in a state capital (= a city) is a "capitol." (Mnemonic: A capit*o*l building usually has a d*o*me.)

P The restrictive "that usually malfunctions" makes it sound as though the goal was to develop a mask that would malfunction. Change "that" to "which" to make the clause nonrestrictive.

Q The plural "XM-30s" cannot be the antecedent of "it."

R Compound adjectives of the form "adverb ending in *ly* + adjective" are not hyphenated: extremely low scores. Additionally, here the noun form "extremely low frequency" is a set phrase (see *M-W Collegiate,* s.v. "extremely low frequency"), and such phrases are not hyphenated when they serve as attributive adjectives unless some ambiguity would result. See "Compound Adjectives: Attributive and Predicate" in *The Copyeditor's Handbook,* chapter 5, under "One Word or Two?"

S Lowercase the title since no proper name follows. *M-W Collegiate* shows "vice admiral" as preferred, but see the discussion of *vice* compounds in the answer key for exercise 6-1.

T It's awkward to have the opening quotation mark interrupt the phrase "due to."

U In quantitative research methodology, a "data sample" is a set of data collected or selected from a statistical population. Computer programs create databases, but in social science research the number of subjects is often called the "data sample."

EXERCISE 9-1: Key

Numbered queries are flagged in the text with boldface curly braces (e.g., {**Query1**}) and are printed below the text, followed by the style sheet. Explanatory comments, keyed in the text with superscript letters, are printed at the end.

Until recent times, doctors spoke a magic language, usually Latin, and mystery was part of your cure. But ~~modren~~ modern doctors are rather in the situation of modern priests; having lost their magic language, they run the risk of losing their magic powers too.

For us, this means that ~~the~~ doctors[A] may lose ~~his~~ their ability to heal us by our faith; and doctors, sensing powerlessness, have been casting about for new languages in which to conceal the nature of our afflictions and the ingredients of their cures.{**Query1**} They have devised two dialects,{**Query2**} but neither seems ~~quiet~~ quite to serve for every purpose. For this is a time of ~~transtion~~ transition and trial for them, marked by various strategies, of which the ~~well known~~ well-known illegible handwriting on your prescription is but one. For doctors themselves seem to have lost faith too, in ~~themsevles~~ themselves and in the old mysteries and arts. They have been taught to think of themselves{**Query3**} as scientists, and so it is first of all to the language of science ~~they~~ that they turn, to control, [B] and confuse us.

Most of the time scientific language can do this perfectly. We are terrified, of course, to learn that we have "prolapse of the mitral valve"—we promise to take our medicine and stay on our diet, even though these words describe a usually ~~innocous~~ innocuous finding in the investigation of an innocent heart murmur. Or we can be lulled into a false sense of security when the doctor avoids a scientific term: "You have a little spot on your lung"—even when what he[C] puts on the chart is "probable bronchogenic carcinoma."

With patients, doctors can use either scientific or vernacular speech, but with each other they speak Science,[D] a strange argot of Latin terms, new words, and acronyms,[E] that yearly becomes farther[F] removed from everyday speech and is sometimes ~~comprised~~ composed[G] almost entirely of numbers and letters: "His pO_2 is 45; pCO_2, 40; and pH,[H] 7.4." Sometimes it is made up of peculiar verbs originating from the apparatus[I] with which ~~they~~ doctors[J] treat people: "~~well~~ Well, we've bronched him, tubed him, bagged him, cathed him, and PEEPed[K] him," the intern tells the attending physician. ("We've explored his airways with a bronchoscope, inserted an ~~endotrachial~~ endotracheal tube, ~~positioned a cathater in his bladder to monitor his urinary output,~~ provided assisted ventilation with a resuscitation bag, positioned a catheter in his bladder to monitor his urinary output,^L and used positive end-expiratory pressure^M to improve oxygenation.") Even when discussing things that can be expressed in ordinary words, doctors will prefer ~~to~~ saying "he had a pneumonectomy," to saying^N "he had a lung removed."

One physician remembers being systematically instructed, during the fifties, in scientific-sounding^O euphemisms to be used in the presence of patients. If a party of interns were^P examining an alcoholic patient, the wondering victim might hear them say he was "suffering from ~~hyperingestation~~ hyperingestion of ethanol." In front of a cancer patient they would discuss his "mitosis." But in recent years such discussions are not conducted in front of the patient at all, because, since ~~Sputnik~~ _Sputnik_,^Q ~~laymen's~~^R understanding of scientific language has increased so greatly,^S that widespread ignorance cannot be assumed.

Space exploration has <u>also</u> had its influence ~~, especially~~ on the _sound_ of medical language.**{Query4}** A ~~CAT scanner~~ CAT (computerized ~~automated~~ axial tomography) scanner,^T ~~de rigueur~~ de rigueur^U in an up-to-date diagnostic unit, might be something <u>used</u> to look at the surface of Mars. ~~with.~~**{Query5}** The resonance of physical, rather than biological,^V science has doubtless been fostered by doctors themselves, who,^W mindful of the extent to which their science is really luck and art, would like to sound microscopically precise, calculable and exact,^X even if they cannot <u>be so</u>.^Y

{Query6}Acronyms and abbreviations play the same part in ~~medical language~~ medicine that they do in other walks of modern life.^Z We might be irritated to read on our chart ~~"that~~ "this SOB patient complained of DOE five days PTA." (It means ~~:~~ "this ~~Short Of Breath~~ short-of-breath patient complained of ~~Dyspnea~~ dyspnea on ~~Exertion~~ exertion five days ~~Prior To Admisssion~~ prior to admission.")^{AA} To translate certain syllables, the doctor must have yet more esoteric information. Doctor A, reading Doctor ~~B.~~'s note that a patient has TTP, must know whether ~~Dr.~~ Doctor B is a hematologist or a chest specialist in order to know whether the patient has thrombotic ~~thrombocytopoenic~~ thrombocytopenic purpura ~~,~~ or traumatic tension ~~pnuemothorax~~ pneumothorax.^{BB} That pert little ~~ID~~ _ID_^{CC} means "identification" to us, but ~~Intradermal~~ "intradermal" to the dermatologist, ~~Inside Diameter~~ "inside diameter" to the physiologist, and ~~Infective Dose~~ "infective dose" to the bacteriologist.

~~But sometimes~~ Sometimes doctors must speak vernacular English, but this is apparently difficult for them.^{DD} People are always being told to discuss their problems with their doctors, which, considering the general inability of doctors to reply except in a given number of reliable phrases, must be some of the ~~worse~~ worst advice ever given.**{Query7}** Most people,^{EE} trying to talk to the doctor ~~-~~—trying to pry or to wrest meaning from ~~his~~ evasive remarks ("I'd say you're coming along just fine ~~.~~")—have been maddened by the vague and slightly inconsequential nature of statements ~~which~~that, meaning everything to you, ought in themselves to have meaning but do not, are noncommittal~~,~~; or unengaged, or have a slightly rote or rehearsed quality, sometimes a slight inappropriateness in the context ("~~it's~~ It's nothing to worry about really").**{Query8}** This is the doctor's alternative dialect, phrases so general and bland as to communicate virtually nothing.

This dialect originates from**FF** the emotional situation of the doctor.**{Query9}** In the way ~~passers-by~~ passersby avert their eyes from the drunk in the gutter or from**GG** the village idiot, so ~~the~~ doctors must avoid any involvement with**HH** the personality, the individuality, ~~any involvement with~~ the destiny~~,~~ of ~~his~~ patients. ~~He~~ Doctors must not let ~~himself~~ themselves think and feel with ~~them~~ patients. In order to retain objective professional judgment, ~~the~~ doctors ~~has~~ have long since learned to withdraw ~~his~~ their emotions from the plight of the patient.**II**

QUERIES

{Query1}: Three of the first four sentences in this paragraph begin with "For." OK or revise?

{Query2}: Name the two dialects here?

{Query3}: Three "themselves" here. OK or revise?

{Query4}: Revision OK to clarify transition here?

{Query5}: Unclear how this example relates to the "sound of medical language." Revise?

{Query6}: New paragraph here OK?

{Query7}: Two "givens" in one sentence OK?

{Query8}: Repetition of "slight" in "slightly inconsequential," "slightly rote," and "slight inappropriateness." OK or revise?

{Query9}: "emotional situation of the doctor"—too clinical, abstract?

STYLE SHEET

Author/Title: Johnson/"Doctor Talk"
Date: February 21, 2018
Dictionary: *Merriam-Webster's Collegiate Dictionary,* 11th ed.; *Merriam-Webster Unabridged*
Style Manual: *The Chicago Manual of Style,* 17th ed.

Alphabetical List of Names and Terms
(adj. = adjective)

CAT scanner
computerized axial tomography
de rigueur (roman)

hyperingestion
passersby
PEEPed
positive end-expiratory pressure
Science (as language)
Sputnik (italics)
up-to-date (adj.)
well-known (adj.)

Numbers and Dates
Spell out numbers under 101 except for medical test values
the fifties (decade)

Punctuation
Serial comma

Abbreviations
DOE (no internal periods)
pCO_2
pH
pO_2
PTA
SOB
Doctor A, Doctor B

Miscellaneous
Italics for words used as words

COMMENTS

The instructions called for a light copyedit that preserved the author's distinctive style. If your version was much more heavily marked than this key, go back and review your editing: Did you make revisions that weren't necessary? Did you change sentences that were not incorrect simply because they were not the sentences you would have written? If so, you are running the risk of straining the author's patience and wasting both your and the author's time. Remember, the author must read every syllable of your editing, deciding whether to accept or reject each of your suggestions and whether to reword a queried passage. And then, either you or a cleanup editor will have to read through the author's responses and revisions.

A Plural "doctors" avoids the generic *he* and matches the second half of the sentence.

B Stet the comma after "turn" (to avoid misreading of "turn to" and to set off the qualifying "to control and confuse"). Delete the comma after "control"—syntactical framework is simply an *a* or *b* choice.

C   It's OK to have a male pronoun here and there, as long as not every doctor and patient in the piece is male, but a circumspect query about the pervasive male pronouns might prompt a conscientious stylist to revise.

D   Stet "Science"—uppercase indicates that it is being treated as a language, just like English, French, Italian, or Spanish.

E   Delete the comma after "acronyms"—to avoid breaking the phrase "a strange argot . . . that yearly becomes." Remember, no comma is used after the last item in a series: *A, b,* and *c* are my goals. If *x, y,* or *z* cannot be calculated, we must revise our procedure.

F   Although the usage of *farther* and *further* was once differentiated, the words are now wholly interchangeable; see *DEU* s.v. "farther, further."

G   The verb "is comprised" is frowned on. As *Garner's* puts it (s.v. "compose, comprise"): "The parts *compose* the whole; the whole *comprises* the parts. The whole *is composed* of the parts; the parts *are comprised* in the whole."

H   The commas after pCO_2 and "pH" indicate an elliptical expression. If "pO_2," "pCO_2," or "pH" looks odd to you, ask the author to confirm; never change technical notations on your own. Here, all the notations are correct: pO_2 and pCO_2 are measures of oxygen and carbon dioxide in the blood, and pH is a measure of acidity or alkalinity.

I   The choice of "apparatus" is fine. Do not change to "apparatuses": *apparatus* is both a collective singular noun and one of the equal variants for the plural noun.

J   In this sentence "they" lacks an adequate referent.

K   "PEEPed" is an acronym for "positive end-expiratory pressure" transmuted into a verb, and the unusual capitalization distinguishes it from "peeped." If you think there's a problem, query the author. Don't just charge ahead and change the capitalization of a technical term.

L   Reorder the "translation" to match the order of the clipped expressions: "positioned a catheter" ("cathed") should follow "provided assisted ventilation" ("bagged").

M   The term refers to positive pressure (= pressure that exceeds atmospheric pressure) applied at the end of the patient's exhalation. It is styled with a hyphen: positive end-expiratory pressure.

N   The construction "to say . . . to saying" is not parallel. No commas after either "saying" because the quotations function as direct objects of the verb.

O   Stet the hyphen in "scientific-sounding," an attributive compound adjective of the form "noun + participle."

P   One could argue that "a party of interns were" is OK if "a party of" stands in for "a number of," which can take a plural verb ("a number of interns were"). (See *The Copyeditor's Handbook,* chapter 14, for a discussion of "a number of" and "the number of" under "Subject-Verb Agreement.") Still, it would be better to avoid notional agreement in this construction: either "a party of interns was" or "a number of interns were."

Q   *M-W Collegiate* shows "Sputnik" uppercase, as the generic term for the satellites the USSR launched in the 1950s. The wording here, however—"since Sputnik"—indicates that the author is referring to the launch of the first satellite (named *Sputnik I*) in 1957. *Chicago* calls for names of spacecraft to be set in italic.

R   To avoid gender bias, use *lay, laypersons',* or *laypeople's.*

S   Delete the comma after "greatly" (to avoid breaking the "so + adverb + that" phrase).

T   The hyphenation and correct spelled-out form of "CAT scanner" are in the dictionary.

U   Italics are unnecessary for "de rigueur" because the expression has been naturalized into English. (Test: If a foreign-sounding term appears in the main section of your dictionary, it is a bona fide English word and should not be italicized.)

V   Use commas to set off the antithetical "rather than biological."

W   Stet the commas before and after "who." The first comma marks the *who* clause as nonrestrictive; the second sets off "mindful . . . luck and art."

X   No serial comma is needed in "precise, calculable and exact," because this phrase is not a list of three. Here, "calculable and exact" is meant as a pair in apposition to "precise."

Y   The sentence stops midphrase with "even if they cannot." Fix, or query the author.

Z   A "medical language" is not a "walk of life" and thus cannot be compared to "other walks."

AA   Lowercase spelled-out expressions; caps are used only for initialisms and acronyms.

BB   All these terms are in a desktop dictionary.

CC   There are two choices here for treating "ID" (a word used as a word): italicize it or place quotation marks around it. All the spelled-out versions should be lowercased.

DD   Fix (or query the author on) two "buts" in one sentence.

EE   Delete the comma after "people"; the subject of the sentence is "Most people trying to talk to the doctor" (not just "Most people" in general).

FF   *WIT* provides three examples of prepositions with *originate*: "Baseball originated *from* the old game of rounders. The idea originated *in* his own mind. This plan originated *with* the board" (p. 442).

GG   Add a "from" to prevent misreading.

HH   Move "any involvement with" for clarity and cadence.

II   Avoid the generic *he*: "Doctors must not let themselves think and feel with patients. In order to retain objective professional judgment, doctors have long since learned to withdraw their emotions from the plight of the patient." Other changes you could suggest: (1) for "think and feel," substitute "empathize"; (2) change "have long since learned" (since when?) to "learn" or "are taught to."

EXERCISE 9-2: Key

Numbered queries to the author are flagged in the text with boldface curly braces (e.g., {Query1}) and are printed below the text, followed by the style sheet. Explanatory comments, signaled in the text with superscript letters, are printed at the end.

Outdoor Activities in Bobonia

Although tiny, remote, and seemingly preoccupied with financial affairs, Bobonia offers surprisingly rich outdoor opportunities ~~in Bobonia are surprisingly rich.~~**A** Bobonians are ~~a happy, outgoing people,~~ often{Query1} happy to share their knowledge of mountain trails, fishing spots, and safe swimming beaches. Many of these lie only a short drive or bus ride from the center of Bobonia City. Here are a few things to know before you head out.

Weather

Because of its temperate latitude (42–44 ~~deg~~ ° N) and maritime climate, Bobonia enjoys mild weather most of the year. Summer high temperatures rarely exceed 30°C (~~86~~ 86°F)**B**, and winter temperatures rarely drop below freezing, except in the highest peaks of the Caringian Mountains. Even so, conditions can change rapidly: hikers and ~~boatmen~~ boaters{Query2} should be prepared for high winds (gales exceeding 80 kph/50 mph{Query3} are not unusual) and heavy rain, especially above altitudes of 1,000 m (3,300 ft.). Weather forecasts are provided hourly on Radio Bobonia FM (99.5 ~~Mhz~~MHz) and online at www.bobweather.bo.

Transportation

Car rental agencies like Hertz~~,~~ and Avis~~, etc.,~~ have branches at Casimir Bobon Airport;~~ ;~~however, taking the bus may be a safer and more relaxing option for visitors unfamiliar with Bobonian road conditions. Drivers should keep in mind that Bobonia City imposes heavy congestion charges at peak traffic times (7:30–9:30 a.m. and 4:00–6:00 ~~P.M.~~p.m.), collected by means of an electronic transponder ~~(ETP)~~.**C** Within the city, a single-ride bus ticket costs

10 bobbles (BB); children under five ride free. A 10-ride pass is available for BB80. For destinations outside the city, fares range ~~15–65 BB~~from BB15 to BB65**D**, depending on distance. Bus schedules are available on the Bobonian Transportation ~~Dept~~Department website (~~www.bobtrans.bo//bus~~www.bobtrans .bo/bus).**E**

Ride services, ~~e.g.,~~such as ~~Uber~~Uber**F** and Lyft, are banned in Bobonia, but hitchhiking is common. Riders are expected to contribute a couple of ~~BB~~bobbles toward the cost of a long trip. (~~N.B.~~NB**G**: Hitch at your own risk. This guide does not recommend hitchhiking.)~~.~~

Cycling is a popular way of getting around in Bobonia. You can rent a mountain bike at City Sports (34 Casimir Ave., ph. 32345) for BB150/ day.

Visiting Caringia National Park

Only 45 ~~min~~minutes' drive from central Bobonia City, this jewel of a park is well worth a visit. Trek up the steep slopes of ~~2100-m Mt~~Mount**H** Casimir (2,100 m/6,900 ft.) and view the turquoise waters of Caldera Lake, or follow the forested Casimir Circle ~~trail~~Trail around the lower slopes of the volcano and catch a glimpse of the brilliantly colored ~~Vermilion-Winged~~vermilion-winged Caringian ~~Parrot~~parrot.**I** A full circuit takes 10 to 14 hours (most hikers spend a night at the hut on the ~~NE~~northeast side of the mountain) and requires crossing the sometimes-turbulent Caringia ~~river~~River, but many shorter hikes are possible. See the excellent park map issued by the Bobonian Department of Conservation (BobDoc). A ~~wheelchair~~wheelchair- and stroller-accessible trail starts from the ~~visitor's~~visitors'**J** center at the main park entrance and winds along the creek for about ~~a~~1.6 km (1 mi.), and a Bobdoc**{Query4}** ranger leads interpretive walks along this trail at 11:30 and 2:30 daily.**K**

To get to the park from Central Square, follow the red signs for ~~highway~~Highway 2 north or take bus #3, which runs every hour from the stop outside the Bobonia Global Bank.

QUERIES

{Query1}: This phrasing could come across as patronizing or overgeneralizing; OK to revise for tone and to eliminate repetition of "happy"?

{Query2}: Change OK, to avoid gendered language? But also, are boaters in Bobonia likely to encounter altitudes above 1,000 m, as this sentence seems to suggest? Maybe recast simply as "visitors" or revise another way?

{Query3}: Change OK, for consistency with number style elsewhere in text?

{Query4}: Which abbreviation form is preferable: BobDoc or Bobdoc? See just above.

STYLE SHEET

Author/Title: Bobonia Tours/"Outdoor Activities in Bobonia"
Date: February 22, 2018
Dictionary: *Merriam-Webster's Collegiate Dictionary,* 11th ed.; *Merriam-Webster Unabridged*
Style Manual: *The Chicago Manual of Style,* 17th ed.

Alphabetical List of Names and Terms
Bobdoc or BobDoc?
Caringia, Caringian
Casimir Bobon Airport
Casimir Circle Trail
Mount Casimir

Numbers and Dates
Spell out numbers under 10
Give metric units first, followed by US equivalent in parentheses
If number is already enclosed in parentheses, separate metric and US measures with a slash: (2,100 m/6,900 ft.)
44° N (space between degree or minute symbol and direction for latitude and longitude)
30°C, 86°F (no space between number and symbol)
4:00 p.m.
Highway 2
bus #3

Punctuation
Serial comma

Abbreviations
a.m., p.m.
Ave.
BB (Bobonian bobble): BB80
ft.

km

kph

m (meter)

MHz

mi.

mph

NB

ph. (phone)

Miscellaneous

spell out and lowercase compass directions (unless part of a proper name):
    north, western

COMMENTS

A Change needed to fix grammatical dangler.

B Why is there a space after the degree symbol for latitude but not for degrees Celsius or Fahrenheit? Degrees Celsius and degrees Fahrenheit are different units (degrees Celsius are larger increments of temperature change), and the letter is part of the symbol for the unit. By contrast, a degree of latitude or longitude represents the same increment regardless of which hemisphere it's in. (Note that Chicago style for units of temperature differs from SI style, which includes a space between the number and the degree symbol.)

C Unless the transponder is mentioned frequently in the subsequent text, providing this abbreviation is unnecessary. Look out for the missing wordspace after the period.

D Constructions such as "from X to Y" or "between X and Y" cannot be abbreviated with an en dash. An alternative, more concise phrasing would be "fares are BB15–65."

E Note the incorrect double slash in the URL.

F Although the company name may be derived from the German *über,* the name does not include an umlaut.

G *Chicago* now omits periods when this abbreviation is capitalized, but "N.B." (i.e., adding a period after the *B*) is also an acceptable choice.

H *Chicago* spells out the names of geographic features, but "Mt. Casimir" is also acceptable.

I Although common names of biological species are frequently capitalized in specialized reference books, they are lowercased in general text.

J Or "visitor center" (attributive), but not the singular possessive "visitor's": the center presumably caters to more than one visitor.

K It's fine to add "a.m." and "p.m." here for consistency with times shown above, but the time of day can readily be inferred from the context.

EXERCISE 10-1: Key

Numbered queries are flagged in the table with boldface curly braces (in stenographic style, e.g., {Q1}, to preserve table formatting) and are printed directly below the table, followed by comments.

Many tables are still marked by hand because of the difficulty of reading tracked changes in tabular material. A hand-marked version of this table is also shown below.

TABLE 20. Present Value of One Dollar{Q1}

Year	5%	6%	8%{Q4}	9%
1	0.952	0.943	.00.926{Q5}	0.917
2	0.907	0.890	0.857	0.842
3	0.864	0.840	0.794	0.772
34{Q2}	0.823	0.592{Q3}	0.735	0.708
5	0.784	0.747	0.681	0.65{Q6}

TABLE 20. Present Value of One Dollar

Year	5%	6%	8%	9%
1	0.952	0.943	.0926	0.917
2	0.907	0.890	0.857	0.842
3	0.864	0.840	0.794	0.772
34	0.823	0.592	0.735	0.708
5	0.784	0.747	0.681	0.65

(hand-marked annotations: "add squib or note explaining percentages?"; "7% is missing — pls fix."; "ok?"; "ok?"; "supply final digit"; "pls recheck value")

QUERIES

{Q1}: Add a table squib or note explaining what percentages represent?

{Q2}: OK?

{Q3}: Please recheck value.

{Q4}: Is 7% missing? Please fix the omission or explain it in a note to the table.

{Q5}: OK?

{Q6}: Supply final digit.

COMMENTS

Reading column by column from top to bottom, the trouble spots are these:

- The stub contains two lines labeled 3. Logic strongly suggests that the second 3 should be a 4; change it and ask the author to confirm.
- The numbers decrease by a small fraction in each row as one reads across from left to right and the numbers also decrease as one reads down each column. According to this pattern, the entry 0.592 for year 4 at 6% looks incorrect; query the author.
- The column heads jump from 6% to 8%. Query the author about the missing column for 7%.
- When you look at the numbers as a set, you should suspect that the first entry under 8% has its decimal point in the wrong place: 0.926 is far more likely than .0926 in this context. Correct it and ask the author to confirm. (If .0926 is correct, you need to add a zero before the decimal point and round off to three decimal places: 0.093.)
- The rightmost column head lacks a percentage sign. Add it.
- The last entry in the last column is missing its final digit.

When checking tables, you should also make sure that the entries in a given column are shown to the same number of decimal places, that commas (not periods) are used in large numbers, and that periods (not commas) appear in decimals, in conformity with US conventions.

EXERCISE 10-2: Key

Table A demonstrates how the data in tables 21, 22, and 23 can be consolidated. You may have thought of an alternative way to arrange this table; for example, your solution might look like table B. The advantage of table B is that it takes up fewer lines than table A, but the drawbacks are several: (1) table B is harder to use, because the reader cannot easily pick out trends by department; (2) table B looks crowded and unappealing; (3) the ten-column layout may present problems in page design. Thus, unless vertical space is at an absolute premium, table B is not a good solution.

Note also that a copyeditor who proposes table B must query the author about whether the column for master's degrees should read "MA" or "MA/MS" because students in the psychology department (although not those in English or history) may have earned a master of science rather than a master of arts degree.

TABLE A. Degree Recipients, Departments of History, English, and Psychology, 1993–1995

Department	1993	1994	1995
History			
Bachelor's	456	778	892
Master's	87	95	106
Doctoral	5	8	12
English			
Bachelor's*	745	798	695
Master's	47	52	65
Doctoral	9	11	9
Psychology			
Bachelor's	275	298	302
Master's	32	29	30
Doctoral	4	7	9

Source: Office of the President, *Utopia University Data Profile,* 1995, pp. 13, 15, and 18.
*Does not include students in the dual-major program.

TABLE B. Degree Recipients, Departments of History, English, and Psychology, 1993–1995

	1993			1994			1995		
	BA	MA/MS	PhD	BA	MA/MS	PhD	BA	MA/MS	PhD
History	456	87	5	778	95	8	892	106	12
English*	745	47	9	798	52	11	695	65	9
Psychology	275	32	4	298	29	7	302	30	9

Source: Office of the President, Utopia University Data Profile, 1995, pp. 13, 15, and 18.
*Does not include students in the dual-major BA program.

EXERCISE 10-3: Key

The edited table appears on the facing page. Both author queries and comments on the editing are keyed to row and column numbers, which appear outside the borders of the table.

QUERIES

Title: Include time span for these data (source note suggests 2015).
Row 1, head 3: Should this head span the three rightmost columns, including "% of Cell Phone Drivers"?
Row 4, column 1 (stub): Should this age group read "20–29"?
Row 5, column 9: 2% looks too low; please check.
Row 6: Is omission of 40–49 age group intentional? Do all data from this point refer to correct age groups?
Row 9: Please check totals; it looks as if they may include data (from the missing age group?) that are not shown in the table.

COMMENTS

- Title: Specifying a date or time span is essential.
- Column and spanner heads: All heads of the same level should be consistently treated: in this case, boldface and uppercased for the first-level heads (spanner heads) and roman and uppercased for the second level (individual column heads).
- Table stub: Age groups should not overlap. Use an en dash for number ranges.
- Columns 2 and 4: Numbers should be consistently treated: right- or decimal-aligned, with a comma (and no space) separating thousands. The tracked changes in rows 5–7 of column 4 reflect only this format change: numbers are right-justified rather than centered.
- Columns 3, 5, 6, 8, and 9: The repeating percent signs are arguably redundant because the column heads clearly identify these numbers as percentages. In a table like this, however, where percentages alternate with other kinds of numbers, they can be helpful reminders.
- Table footnote: Because the note applies to the entire bottom (total) row, the note signal should appear in the stub for that row, not at the end of the row.

TABLE 2.

Drivers Involved in Fatal Crashes by Age, Distraction, and Cell Phone Use

Age Group	Total Drivers		Distracted Drivers			Drivers Using Cell Phones		
	Number	% of Total Drivers	Number	% of Total Drivers	% of distracted Drivers	Number	% of distracted Drivers	% of Cell Phone Drivers
15-19	3,181	7%	290	9%	9%	64	22%	14%
20-30	11,428	24%	891	8%	27%	151	17%	33%
30-39	8,479	17%	612	7%	19%	101	17%	2%
50-59	7,785	16%	376	5%	12%	50	13%	11%
60-69	5,012	10%	275	5%	8%	15	5%	3%
70+	4,255	9%	287	7%	9%	12	4%	3%
Total[a]	48,613	100%	3,263	7%	100%	456	14%	100%[a]

Source: National Center for Statistics and Analysis, *Distracted Driving 2015*, Traffic Safety Facts Research Note, Report No. DOT HS 812 381 (Washington, DC: National Highway Traffic Safety Administration, March 2017), available online at http://www.nhtsa.gov /sites/nhtsa.dot.gov/files/documents/812_381_distracteddriving2015.pdf.

[a]The total includes 60 drivers 14 and younger, 6 of whom were noted as distracted. The total also includes 973 drivers of unknown age, 44 of whom were noted as distracted.

EXERCISE 10-4: Key

Figure 1. Percentage ~~Distribution Of Drivers Involved In Fatal Crashes~~ distribution of drivers involved in fatal crashes by age, distraction, and ~~cell phone~~cell phone use, 2015~~.~~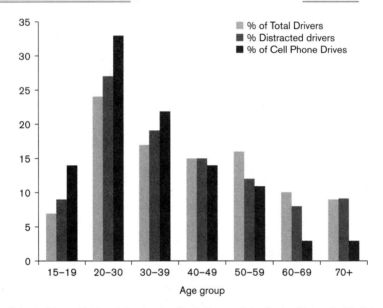

Age group

Source: Adapted from National Center for Statistics and Analysis, *Distracted Driving 2015,* Traffic Safety Facts Research Note, Report No. DOT HS 812 381 (Washington, DC: National Highway Traffic Safety Administration, ~~3/17~~March 2017), available online at http://www .nhtsa.gov/sites/nhtsa.dot.gov/files/documents/812_381_distracteddriving2015.pdf.

QUERIES

Note: In the queries that ask for revisions or additions to labels, punctuation appears outside quotation marks (in contrast to standard US punctuation style) to prevent an overly literal author (or typesetter) from including the terminal punctuation in revisions to the graph.

Y axis: Add label: "Percentage".

Legend: Set all elements lowercase. Add "of" before "distracted drivers". Change "Cell Phone Drives" to "cell phone drivers".

X axis: Change "20–30" to "20–29"?

COMMENTS

A Capitalization of a title can be either sentence style or headline style, depending on house style, but not a little of each. Omit hyphen in "cell phone," for consistency with graph legend. No terminal punctuation is needed unless additional information follows the title.

Although many spreadsheet and graphing applications enable authors to include titles within the body of the graph, treating titles as part of the manuscript text may be preferable for ease of editing, ensuring stylistic and typographic consistency with titles of other figures in the document, creating front-matter lists of figures, and other editorial and production tasks.

B Y axis labels are often rotated so that the type runs parallel to the axis.

C The same error appears in the table in exercise 10-3. When related material is presented in different places in a document, it's wise to check whether errors have also been replicated.

EXERCISE 11-1: Key

Numbered queries are flagged in the text with boldface curly braces and, as in exercise 10-1, exemplify a terser style for embedded query flags (e.g., **{Q1}**) than usually shown in the answer keys. Queries are printed directly below the text; a few pointers about reference lists are provided at the end.

Abben, Pilar. 1985. "A Modern Approach to Algebra~~,~~." *Mathematical Monthly* ~~17:~~17:55–68.

Adder, William, and Mary. 1980. *Statistics in the Social Sciences.* Evanston, ~~Illinois~~Ill.: Schoolbooks Press~~, 1980~~.**{Q1}**

Adder, William, and Mary. ~~1982.~~1982. *How ~~To~~to Write Social Science Papers.* New York: Wise Owl.**{Q2}**

Aiken, Lydia, ed.~~,~~ ~~Probelms~~Problems *in English Grammar.* Boston~~,~~: Tiara Books.**{Q3}**

Akmore, G. 1983~~,~~. "A Study of the ~~Affects~~Effects of Peer Teaching in College Remedial Mathematics Courses." *American Mathematical Monthly* ~~18:~~18:149–67.**{Q4}{Q5}**

~~Aiken, Lydia, ed., Probelms in English Grammar. Boston, Tiara Books.~~

Allen, Pattrick. 1993. *Composition for Beginnñing ESL Students.* New York: Language Laboratory.**{Q6}**

Allen, P., and Anita Zamorra~~,~~. 1994. "Error Analysis in Quasi-Experimental Designs." *Analytic Quarterly* 9:63–53.**{Q7}{Q8}**

Ammonds, Carolyn. 1794. *A Short Course in Speedwriting.* Santa Barbara, Calif.: Santa Luisa Community College.**{Q9}**

Anderson, Vito. 1991. "A Response to President Clinton's Proposal for Head Start." *Preschool Reporter* 15:1.**{Q10}**

QUERIES

{Q1}: Supply Mary's last name.

{Q2}: Supply Mary's last name.

{Q3}: Please supply year of publication.

{Q4}: Supply Akmore's full first name.

{Q5}: If Akmore article is from the same journal as Abben article, reconcile the title (*Mathematical Monthly* or *American Mathematical Monthly*) and the volume numbers (we have Akmore's 1983 article in vol. 18 and Abben's 1985 article in vol. 17).

{Q6}: Double *t* in Pattrick OK?

{Q7}: For Allen, P., supply full first name.

{Q8}: Recheck page range; can't be 63–53.

{Q9}: Recheck year: 1974 or 1994?

{Q10}: Recheck 1991 as date of publication (Clinton was inaugurated in January 1993). Is this article only one page long, as the page number indicates?

A FEW POINTERS ABOUT REFERENCE LISTS

Take extra care in hunting for typographical errors in reference lists. Few authors are diligent enough to proofread this section, and many do not bother spell-checking the reference list because it is so time consuming (the spell-checker stops and questions almost every proper name).

Remember the rules for capitalizing titles (see "Titles of Works" in chapter 6 of *The Copyeditor's Handbook*). Thus the "to" in the second Adder entry should be lowercased.

Don't make assumptions about names: for example, don't assume that the Mary in both the Adder entries is "Mary Adder." Always ask the author to supply the facts. If her surname is Adder, it is preferable for the entry to read "Adder, William, and Mary Adder." (One surname is sufficient on a social invitation to a married couple, but a reference list is not a casual document, and William and Mary may well be father and daughter, brother and sister, son and mother, or first cousins.)

When two or more works are written by the same author or authors, some publishers use a 3-em dash in the author slot for the second and subsequent listings:

Frank, F. 1990. *Short History of Uruguay.* New York: International Press.

———. 1993. *Short History of Argentina.* New York: Overseas Press.

———. 1996. *Short History of Chile.* Los Angeles: Small World Press.

If you are observing this convention, you would want to make a note to yourself to use a 3-em dash in the second Adder entry if indeed both books are written by the same pair of authors:

Adder, William, and Mary Adder. 1980. *Statistics in the Social Sciences.* Evanston, Ill.: Schoolbooks Press.

———. 1982. *How to Write Social Science Papers.* New York: Wise Owl.

Note, however, that *Chicago* now recommends repeating an author's name rather than using a 3-em dash if a reference list or bibliography will be published in digital form. In some electronic formats, linked-to items in a bibliography or reference list are viewed separately rather than in the context of the list as a whole. Note, too, that even if "Allen, P." turns out to be "Allen, Pattrick [*sic*]," one would repeat his name (and not use a 3-em dash) because a second author appears in the second entry.

Always query illogical numbers (e.g., 63–53 in the Allen and Zamorra entry; 1794 as the date for the Ammonds entry); don't guess.

Try to catch possible inconsistencies in the titles of journals (e.g., in the Abben and Akmore entries) and in the context of each entry (e.g., the date in the Anderson entry, which predates Clinton's election).

If you know the name of the state (e.g., in the Ammonds entry), add it; otherwise, query the author.

EXERCISE 11-2: Key

1. APA STYLE

Basu, N., Kaplan, C.M., Ichesco, E., Larkin, T., Harris, R.E., Murray, A., . . . Clauw, D.J.
(n.d.). Neurobiological features of fibromyalgia are also present among rheumatoid
arthritis patients. *Arthritis & Rheumatology, n/a-n/a.***{Query1}**[A]
https://doi.org/10.1002/art.40451

Blood simple? (2016, September 1). *The Economist.* Retrieved from https://www
.economist.com/news/science-and-technology/21706241-new-test-may-
diagnose-mysterious-illness-and-also-help-explain-it-blood**{Query2}**[B]

~~Blood simple? - Chronic fatigue syndrome. (n.d.). Retrieved February 14, 2018, from
https://www.economist.com/news/science-and-technology/21706241-new-test-
may-diagnose-mysterious-illness-and-also-help-explain-it-blood~~

~~Basu, N., Kaplan, C.M., Ichesco, E., Larkin, T., Harris, R.E., Murray, A., . . . Clauw,
D.J. (n.d.). Neurobiological features of fibromyalgia are also present among
rheumatoid arthritis patients. *Arthritis & Rheumatology, n/a-n/a.* https://doi.
org/10.1002/art.40451~~

[C]~~In~~ Engdahl, S. (2012). *Chronic fatigue syndrome.* Detroit: Greenhaven Press.

Janse, A., Worm-Smeitink, M., Bleijenberg, G., Donders, R., & Knoop, H. (2018).
Efficacy of web-based cognitive—[D]behavioural therapy for chronic fatigue
syndrome: ~~r~~Randomised[E] controlled trial. ~~The~~ British Journal of Psychiatry,
~~212~~*212*(2), 112–118. https://doi.org/10.1192/bjp.2017.22

Ostrom, ~~Neenyah~~N. (1993). ~~50 things you should know about the chronic fatigue
syndrome epidemic~~ *50 things you should know about the chronic fatigue
syndrome epidemic.* ~~/ Neenyah Ostrom. TNM ed.~~ New York, ~~N.Y.~~NY: St. ~~Martin's~~
Martin's Press~~, c1993~~.

~~Janse, A., Worm-Smeitink, M., Bleijenberg, G., Donders, R., & Knoop, H. (2018).
Efficacy of web-based cognitive—behavioural therapy for chronic fatigue
syndrome: randomised controlled trial. *The British Journal of Psychiatry, 212*(2),
112–118. https://doi.org/10.1192/bjp.2017.22~~

Wang, Y.-Y., Li, X.-X., Liu, J.-P., Luo, H., Ma, L.-X., & Alraek, T. (2014). Traditional
Chinese medicine for chronic fatigue syndrome: A systematic review of
randomized clinical trials. *Complementary Therapies in Medicine,* ~~22~~*22*(4), 826–
833. https://doi.org/10.1016/j.ctim.2014.06.004

QUERIES

{Query1}: Please supply year of publication and volume, issue, and page numbers for article.

{Query2}: OK to delete duplicate citation below?

2. BASIC CHICAGO STYLE

Cole, Teju. ~~2015.~~ ~~Every day is for the thief.~~ Day Is for the Thief. CITY: PUBLISHER, 2015.

Cole, Teju. ~~2012.~~ ~~Open city: a novel.~~ City: A Novel. CITY: PUBLISHER, 2012.**{Query1}ᶠ**

~~Cole, Teju. 2015. Every day is for the thief.~~

ᴳCole, Teju. "Teju Cole on A House for Mr Biswas by VS Naipaul~~—~~ ~~a~~A

Novel of Full-Bore Trinidadian Savvy ~~| Books | The Guardian~~."

Guardian, February 12, 2016.**{Query2}** Accessed February

14, 2018. https://www.theguardian.com/books/2016/feb/12

/teju-cole-vs-naipaul-a-house-for-mr-biswas-trinidad-novel.

Kakutani, Michiko. "'Open City' by Teju Cole ~~—~~ Review." ~~The~~ New York Times,

May 18, 2011~~, see. Books~~. https://www.nytimes.com/2011/05/19/books/

open-city-by-teju-cole-book-review.html.**{Query3}**

QUERIES

{Query1}: For both novels by Cole, please provide city and publisher and confirm date of publication.

{Query2}: Author, source, and date correct as edited?

{Query3}: Add access date?

COMMENTS

A Every modern scientific journal identifies issues of its print edition by date and volume number (and most by issue number). It's not clear why these facts of publication were not included in the exported citation, but editors need to be vigilant for such omissions.

B Citations may be duplicated when a citation manager misconstrues the title of an article and creates two separate listings. The *Economist* favors punning article titles that are not always descriptive; the subject matter is often described in a reading line above the title, which has been parsed as a subtitle in the second citation here. A visit to the website confirms that the article title is just "Blood simple?" In APA style, no retrieval date is required for online sources, and no period follows a URL.

C This APA-style citation copied from WorldCat mysteriously begins with the word "In," which could lead to erroneous sorting. This is a book by Sylvia Engdahl.

D This en dash, an example of erratic formatting in imported citations, should be changed to a hyphen.

E When moving a citation up or down to its correct place in an alphabetized list, don't forget to check its innards. Here the first letter of the subtitle has been capitalized.

F Although WorldCat purportedly offers citations in Chicago style, it provides them only in author-date format, uses sentence-style capitalization, and omits the full facts of publication. An editor can easily supply facts of publication from the full WorldCat listing, but it's wise to confirm that they refer to the edition the author has consulted: *Open City*, for example, first appeared in 2011, not 2012. Also, in Chicago style, multiple works by the same author are usually listed alphabetically rather than by date, so the entries for the two novels should be transposed.

G The *Guardian*'s headline and byline style is not easy for software to parse. This article is part of a series in which well-known contemporary authors (here Teju Cole) review older novels by other well-known authors (here, V. S. Naipaul's *A House for Mr Biswas*). The section and periodical names ("Books | The Guardian") are not part of the title of the article. The exported citation omits the date; this can be inferred from the URL and verified online. Note that the *New York Times* and the *Guardian* use different styles for a book title within a headline; the differences should be allowed to stand. Note also that the absence of a period after "Mr" is correct in British style.

EXERCISE 11-3: Key

In this answer key, notes and bibliography are edited with revision tracking on, applying the conventions preferred in many humanistic disciplines and described in *Chicago,* chapter 14, "Notes and Bibliography." Queries (flagged in curly brackets in the text) and comments follow the bibliography. The text has not been edited except to correct stacked note signals.

Founded in 1853, when the state of California was only three years old, the Riggers and Stevedores Union Association was the first major representative body for waterfront employees in the San Francisco Bay Area. In the era of sailing vessels this union consisted of skilled ship riggers and seasoned cargo handlers. Stevedore foremen often hired less experienced "men along the shore," or *longshoremen,* to physically work cargo. Between 1890 and 1910, as bigger steel ships replaced wooden vessels, cargo handling became casual work. Eventually, the label *stevedore* came to refer to a cargo-moving contractor or company; the label *longshoreman* (or *docker*) came to refer to a hold worker or a dockworker. In those years of change, the Riggers and Stevedores opened its membership, expelled contracting stevedores, and became a more broadly based union.[1]

In 1901 the San Francisco longshoremen joined a major strike by the City Front Federation, a coalition of wagon drivers, sailors, ship fitters, and other waterfront workers. The strike began with a lockout of city teamsters who were demanding union recognition and improved working conditions. The strike had only limited success. But the violence against strikers that erupted during the confrontation led directly to the creation of a Union Labor Party in San Francisco. This independent third party successfully elected its candidate to the office of mayor in late 1901 and reelected him in 1903 and 1905. The Union Labor Party played a dominant role in San Francisco politics over the next decade.[2]

Elsewhere along the Pacific Coast, local groups of longshore workers forged a regional alliance during the early years of the twentieth century. By 1916 the dockworkers in all the major West Coast ports were affiliated nationally with the American Federation of Labor's International Longshoremen's Association (ILA) as an autonomous unit called the Pacific Coast District No. 38, ILA.[3] San Francisco's Riggers and Stevedore's Union had joined the ILA around 1900; it later left that organization but rejoined shortly before 1916. At the time, San Francisco was the biggest port along the West Coast, so San Francisco's membership was crucial to the unity of ILA District 38. The necessity of coastwide

1. Robert W. Cherny, "Longshoremen of San Francisco Bay, 1849–1960," in *Dock Workers: International Exploration in Comparative Labour History, 1790–1970,* ~~edited by~~ ed. Sam Davies et~~.~~ al., ~~Vol.~~ vol. 1 (Aldershot, Eng~~land~~.: Ashgate Publishers, 2000), 102–~~103~~, 120.**{Query1}**

2. Robert Edward Lee Knight, *Industrial Relations in the San Francisco Bay Area, 1900–1918* (Berkeley ~~and Los Angeles~~: University of California Press, 1960), ~~pp.~~ 72–93; Cherny, "Longshoremen," 120–~~1~~21. See also Walton Bean, *Boss Ruef's San Francisco: The Story of the Union Labor Party, Big Business, and the Graft Prosecution* (Berkeley: University of California Press, 1968).

3. <u>International Longshore and Warehouse Union (ILWU),</u> *The ILWU Story: Six Decades of Militant Unionism,* 2nd ed., <u>ed. Steve Stallone and Marcy Rein, with</u> text and research by Eugene Dennis Vrana~~, additional research by~~ and Harvey Schwartz~~, edited by Steve Stallone and Marcy Rein~~ (San Francisco: ILWU, 2004), 3; Cherny, "Longshoremen," 122; Ronald Magden, *The Working Waterfront: The Story of Tacoma's Ships and Men* (Tacoma, ~~Wash.~~WA: ILWU Local 23, 1982), 31.**{Query2}**

unity became clear in 1916, when, in the first major coastwide strike of Pacific Coast dockworkers, the 10,000 to 12,500 members of District 38 shut down all the West Coast's key ports from Bellingham, Washington, to San Diego, California. The district's main demands were for standard coastwide wages and working conditions and a closed shop, which would have required all employees to be ILA members.[4]

The 1916 strike was bitter and violent. On June 16, when the strike was just over two weeks old, Lewis A. Morey, an ILA member from Oakland, California, was shot and killed by an armed guard who was protecting strikebreakers. Two days later, Thomas Olsen, another ILA man, was shot in the back on a San Francisco dock. He died immediately. Nearly a month later, a strike committee member from Tacoma, Washington, was knifed when he confronted two strikebreakers. Another Tacoma striker was killed when a company guard fired his weapon into a crowd of longshoremen.[5]

In response to the strike, the San Francisco Chamber of Commerce organized a Law and Order Committee to inflame anti-union sentiment among business leaders and the general public. On July 17, San Francisco's more than 4,000 members negotiated a separate peace with employers because they were worried about the possibility of an open shop campaign. (This campaign materialized during the 1920s despite the San Francisco longshoremen's efforts to prevent it.) They retained their union conditions, but they did not win a closed shop or standard coastwide wages and conditions. With the San Francisco longshoremen under contract, the shipowners were able to bleed the rest of the coast workers into submission. The employers started by hiring nonunion men. Soon it was obvious that the strike was lost. The ill feeling aroused between groups of longshoremen following the experience of 1916 led to a split in the Pacific Coast longshoremen's ranks. After the strike, the San Francisco longshoremen seceded from the ILA and assumed independent status. Coastwide, all the ILA locals lost control of jobs on the docks except for the longshoremen of the Port of Tacoma, who soon regained the union hiring hall they had initially lost and who maintained it into the "nonunion" 1920s and early 1930s.[6]

The independent San Francisco Riggers and Stevedores Union did not last long. Reacting to heavier sling loads and a speeded-up work pace, the union struck in 1919. This strike was doomed from the start. It coincided with the emergence of a decade-long conservative open shop drive across the entire United States. Anti-union organization and sentiment among employers was intense. A minor faction of the San Francisco union's membership, which was influenced by the radical Industrial Workers of the World (the IWW, or "Wobblies"), persuaded the union to pass a resolution instructing R and S negotiators to demand stock ownership in steamship companies and seats on the shipowners' boards of directors. The R and S negotiators did not push these radical demands, but the employers used them against the union. Instead of gaining their goals, the San Francisco longshoremen, alone and without coastwide waterfront

4. Cherny, "Longshoremen," 120–123; Magden, *The Working Waterfront*, 31–33; Knight, *Industrial Relations*, 302.

5. Magden, *The Working Waterfront*, 33–35; Knight, *Industrial Relations*, 303.

6. Magden, *The Working Waterfront*, 35–37; Knight, *Industrial Relations*, 304–305; Cherny, "Longshoremen," 123, 133; Harvey Schwartz, *Solidarity Stories: An Oral History of the ILWU* (Seattle, WA: University of Washington Press, 2009), 127–128.

allies, were utterly defeated. One union man was killed during this showdown. The union was destroyed when the employers replaced it with another, ostensibly independent, organization that in reality functioned like a "company union."[7]

This new employer-backed group was officially called the Longshoremen's Association of San Francisco and the Bay District. Its chief officer, Jack Bryan, had longshoring experience, but his organization existed to thwart worker controlled unionism. The new Association issued a membership book with a blue cover to distinguish it from the red membership book of the old Riggers and Stevedores Union. During the company union's heyday, 1919 through 1933, the organization was known on the waterfront simply as "the Blue Book." Workers had to pay dues and maintain Blue Book membership just to qualify for waterfront jobs. But membership conferred no real benefits, such as union representation.[8]

Corrupt hiring practices and inhumane working conditions prevailed in the Blue Book era. In San Francisco, workers were forced to stand in a "shape-up" on the waterfront early each morning in order to get employment, even if they belonged to a regular work gang. Harry Renton Bridges, the future union leader, stood among them. The San Francisco longshoreman vividly recalled this shape-up: "We were hired off the street like a bunch of sheep standing there from six o'clock in the morning in all kinds of weather."[9] To get a job, workers often had to bribe the hiring bosses with money, alcohol, or other favors. Henry Gaitan, a longshoreman in the equally corrupt hiring system at the Port of Los Angeles, later attested that "if you had a nice-looking sister, and liquor, and a wife that would put out, you'd have a job. I seen it here on these docks before we had the [real] union."[~~10~~,11]

Those fortunate enough to be hired found that the work was fast-paced and dangerous. The Port of San Francisco was known for its high productivity—but also for an extremely high rate of injury.[12]**{Query4}** Bosses raced gangs of longshoremen against each other in an effort to increase the speed of work, at times using ethnic rivalries to provoke such competitions: a predominantly German work gang, for example, would be set against a gang of longshoremen of Portuguese or Italian background. Harry Bridges himself was injured on the job in 1929. In those days, he remembered, injured longshoremen rarely applied for workmen's compensation because they feared being blacklisted by the employers, who were charged by the state for accident claims. Fatigue from long hours of heavy labor with few or no work breaks also contributed to the high injury rate during the

7. Cherny, "Longshoremen," 124–~~1~~27. See also Mary Joy Renfro, "The Decline and Fall of the San Francisco Riggers and Stevedores Union: A History of the Years 1916 to 1919~~;~~" (senior thesis, San Francisco State University, 1995), ~~in~~ Labor Archives and Research Center, San Francisco State University.

8. David Selvin, *A Terrible Anger: The 1934 Waterfront and General Strikes in San Francisco* (Detroit: Wayne State University Press, 1996), 44–45; Bruce Nelson, *Workers on the Waterfront: Seamen, Longshoremen, and Unionism in the 1930s* (Urbana: University of Illinois Press, 1988), 53; Schwartz, *Solidarity Stories*, 11; Cherny, "Longshoremen," 126–~~1~~27.

9. <u>Harry Bridges, quoted in</u> Charles P. Larrowe, *Harry Bridges: The Rise and Fall of Radical Labor in the United States,* 2nd ed. rev. (Westport, CT: Lawrence Hill, 1977), 8. See also Cherny, "Longshoremen," 103–4, 133.**{Query3}**

~~10. Bridges quoted in Charles P. Larrowe, *Harry Bridges: The Rise and Fall of Radical Labor in the United States,* 2nd ed. rev. (Westport, CT: Lawrence Hill, 1977), 8. See also Cherny, "Longshoremen," 103–104, 133.~~

11. ~~Unpublished~~ <u>Henry</u> Gaitan<u>,</u> interview ~~with~~ <u>by</u> Daniel S. Beagle and David Wellman, ~~14~~ May <u>14</u>, 1983,~~in the~~ ILWU Oral History Collection, Anne Rand Research Library, International Longshore and Warehouse Union, San Francisco.

12. Harvey Schwartz, *Building the Golden Gate Bridge: A Workers' Oral History* (Seattle: University of Washington Press, 2015).

nonunion years. Work shifts of twelve, sixteen, and more hours were well known on the San Francisco waterfront.[13]

13. Schwartz, *Solidarity Stories*, 12–13; Cherny, "Longshoremen," 106, 111, 133; International Longshore and Warehouse Union (ILWU), *The ILWU Story*, 3.

BIBLIOGRAPHY

Afrasiabi, Peter. *Burning Bridges: America's 20-Year Crusade to Deport Labor Leader Harry Bridges.* Brooklyn, NY: Thirlmere Books, 2016.

Bean, Walton. *Boss Ruef's San Francisco: The Story of the Union Labor Party, Big Business, and the Graft Prosecution.* Berkeley: University of California Press, 1968.

Cherny, Robert W. "Longshoremen of San Francisco Bay, 1849–1960." In *Dock Workers: International Exploration in Comparative Labour History, 1790–1970,* vol. 1, ~~edited by~~ ed. Sam Davies et al., 102–~~1~~40. Aldershot, Eng~~land~~.: Ashgate Publishing, 2000.

Cole, Peter. *Dockworker Power: Race, Technology, and Unionism in Durban and the San Francisco Bay Area.* Champaign: University of Illinois Press, forthcoming ~~in 2018~~.

~~Davies, Sam, et al., ed. Dock Workers: International Exploration in Comparative Labour History, 1790–1970. Vol. 1. Aldershot, England: Ashgate Publishing, 2000.~~

Gaitan, Henry. Interview by Daniel S. Beagle and David Wellman. May 14, 1983. ILWU Oral History Collection, Anne Rand Research Library, International Longshore and Warehouse Union, San Francisco.

~~Kimeldorf, Howard. Reds or Rackets? The Making of Radical and Conservative Unions on the Waterfront. Berkeley: University of California Press, 1988.~~

International Longshore and Warehouse Union (ILWU). *The ILWU Story: Six Decades of Militant Unionism.* 2nd ed. Edited by Steve Stallone and Marcy Rein. ~~Text~~ With text and research by Eugene Dennis Vrana~~. Additional research by~~ and Harvey Schwartz. ~~Edited by Steve Stallone and Marcy Rein.~~ San Francisco: ILWU, 2004.

Kimeldorf, Howard. *Reds or Rackets? The Making of Radical and Conservative Unions on the Waterfront.* Berkeley: University of California Press, 1988.

Knight, Robert Edward Lee. *Industrial Relations in the San Francisco Bay Area, 1900–1918.* Berkeley: University of California Press, 1960.

Larrowe, Charles P. *Harry Bridges: The Rise and Fall of Radical Labor in the United States.* 2nd ed. rev. Westport, CT: Lawrence Hill, 1977.

Levinson, Marc. *The Box: How the Shipping Container Made the World Smaller and the World Economy Bigger.* Princeton, NJ: Princeton University Press, 2006.

Magden, Ronald. *The Working Waterfront: The Story of Tacoma's Ships and Men.* Tacoma, WA: ILWU Local 23, 1982.

Nelson, Bruce. *Workers on the Waterfront: Seamen, Longshoremen, and Unionism in the 1930s.* Urbana: University of Illinois Press, 1988.

Quin, Mike. *The Big Strike.* Olema, CA: Olema Publishing, 1949.

Renfro, Mary Joy. "The Decline and Fall of the San Francisco Riggers and Stevedores Union: A History of the Years 1916 to 1919." Senior thesis, San Francisco State University, 1995. Labor Archives and Research Center, San Francisco State University.

Schwartz, Harvey. "Harry Bridges and the Scholars: Looking at History's Verdict." *California History: The Magazine of the California Historical Society* 59, no. 1 (Spring 1980): 66–79.

————.Schwartz, Harvey. *The March Inland: Origins of the ILWU Warehouse Division, 1934–1938.* Los Angeles: Institute of Industrial Relations, University of California, 1978. Reprint, San Francisco: ILWU, 2000.

————.Schwartz, Harvey. *Solidarity Stories: An Oral History of the ILWU.* Seattle, WA: University of Washington Press, 2009.

Selvin, David. *A Terrible Anger: The 1934 Waterfront and General Strikes in San Francisco.* Detroit: Wayne State University Press, 1996.

Wellman, David. *The Union Makes Us Strong: Radical Unionism on the San Francisco Waterfront.* Cambridge: Cambridge University Press, 1995.

QUERIES

{Query1}: Please reconcile n. 1 and biblio entry: (a) Are Davies et al. the eds of the multi-volume work (in which case ed info precedes the volume number) or the eds of vol. 1 only (ed info follows the volume number)? (b) Ashgate Publishers (n. 1) or Ashgate Publishing (biblio)?

Please confirm or correct: Place of publication listed as "England," not "UK," on copyright page?

{Query2}: Should *The ILWU Story* be cited here and also alphabetized in the bibliography under the research-writers, Vrana and Schwartz? under the editors, Stallone and Rein? Or is the "author" in fact the institution (ILWU), as currently indicated in n. 3 and the emended biblio entry?—and if so, should the abbreviation be spelled out as "International Longshoremen's and Warehousemen's Union" (WorldCat and the Library of Congress Online Catalog)? or "International Longshore and Warehouse Union" (ILWU's website)? (Note to self: Answer may require updating the shortened citation in n. 13 as well.)

{Query3}: Is this a revised version of the *second* edition of *Harry Bridges?* Please confirm or correct.

{Query4}: Book about the construction of the Golden Gate Bridge sounds interesting, but does this source have any bearing on injuries in a different industry on the waterfront in this earlier Blue Book era? Please revise the text and note to clarify the connection and add this source to the bibliography—or, if this is an orphaned note (e.g., from a previous version of this paper), delete.

GENERAL COMMENTS

Grouped citations. As exemplified in the text, citations in a paragraph of heavily documented scholarly content are sometimes consolidated in a single note and separated with semicolons. The order of the citations follows the order of the sources used in the paragraph. (But see also the specific comment below regarding notes 9 and 10.)

En dashes. In traditional typesetting, en dashes, not hyphens, are typically used within ranges of numerals (e.g., ranges of page numbers and inclusive dates). In this answer key a cleanup script has swapped en dashes for hyphens in such ranges throughout. These changes are not redlined here: to avoid the distraction of redlined nondiscretionary changes, basic file cleanup scripts are often run with revision tracking off.

Number ranges. Throughout the notes and bibliography, number ranges are emended to follow Chicago style for inclusive numbers. See a description of this style in *The Copyeditor's Handbook,* chapter 7, under "Inclusive Numerals."

Use of p. and pp. (for "page" and "pages"). Chicago omits these abbreviations before page numbers unless ambiguity might result. Accordingly, they are deleted throughout.

Country and state names in publication details. When the country or state of publication must be specified along with the city to avoid ambiguity in publication details (e.g., for Cherny, "Longshoremen of San Francisco Bay," cited in note 1 and the corresponding bibliographic entry, where in the world is Aldershot?), *Chicago*'s style abbreviates the name of the country or state. (*Chicago* prefers US postal codes for the latter.) The country or state need not be specified when it is self-evident: in the citation for Schwartz, *Solidarity Stories* (note 6 and the corresponding bibliographic entry), for example, Seattle, the location of the University of Washington Press, needs no disambiguation.

SPECIFIC COMMENTS: NOTES

Note 1. (1) Avoid the all-too-common error of using a period with "et" (Latin for "and," not an abbreviation) in the expression "et al." (2) *Chicago* lowercases the abbreviation "vol." and uses arabic numerals for volume numbers, regardless of how these volume numbers are represented in the source. (3) It also abbreviates "edited by" as "ed." when citing articles and chapters in edited works. (4) "England" should be abbreviated in the imprint—assuming that the author responds to query 1 by confirming that the imprint actually specifies "England," not "UK."

Note 2. When a publisher's imprint lists several offices located in different cities, use the first-listed city only.

Note 3. The editing of this citation (and the corresponding bibliographic entry) follows *Chicago*'s model (14.84) for a publication that has an organization as both "author" and publisher, along with a large cast of editors and contributors. This format assumes that the author's reply to query 2 confirms that the ILWU is, in fact, the author of record.

Notes 4–6. These notes exemplify the use of short forms for works previously cited in full.

Note 7. The Renfro source has been styled to follow *Chicago*'s model for unpublished theses and dissertations (14.215). The location of the thesis, not normally specified in such citations because it can be inferred from the name of the degree-granting institution, has been retained at the copyeditor's discretion to aid researchers who might have difficulty finding it in the specialized collection.

Note 9. (1) Scrupulous citation of a direct quotation derived from an intermediate source takes this form: "Harry Bridges, quoted in [citation details for intermediate source]" (*Chicago* 14.260). It is considered a breach of scholarly ethics to cite a primary source as though one had consulted it directly rather than deriving the information through an intermediate work of scholarship. See the discussion of plagiarism in *The Copyeditor's Handbook,* chapter 15, under "Publishing Law." (2) Assuming that, in reply to query 3, the author confirms that this work is a *revision* of the second edition, retain the formulation "2nd ed. rev." The redlining here obscures the correction of "2d" to "2nd," the abbreviation preferred in Chicago-style citations.

Notes 9 and 10 (note signals in original text). Stacked note superscripts like this ([9,10]) are common in the citation-sequence system of reference appearing in some natural science, social science, and medical literature (see *The Copyeditor's Handbook,* chapter 11, under "Citation-Sequence System"), but they are never used in a reference note (humanities) system. Note 9 clearly identifies the source of the first quotation in the paragraph, and its signal should immediately follow that quotation. Redlining this correction causes the auto-numbering of note signals and footnotes to change: the number 10 disappears and the number 13 is added. The transmittal memo should reassure the author that when the tracked changes are accepted, this automatic numbering self-corrects.

Note 11 in edited text (note 10 in original). (1) The edited note follows *Chicago*'s models for unpublished recordings and transcripts of interviews (14.211). (2) A Google search confirms the name of the repository, which might seem implausible for a labor union's research library. But Anne Rand is not to be confused with Ayn Rand: Anne established the ILWU library and created its cataloging system.

Note 12 (11 in original). Watch out for any notes that seem unrelated to the main text—e.g., an obviously incorrect duplication, a cut-and-paste error, or an incomplete deletion of some text. At least one copyediting pass should compare the text and notes to identify any such errors: see step 1 in the description of copyediting procedures in *The Copyeditor's Handbook,* chapter 11, under "Reference Note System."

SPECIFIC COMMENTS: BIBLIOGRAPHY

The bibliography includes several works not cited in the notes. Academic authors sometimes consult works for background without explicitly citing them. They acknowledge their indebtedness by listing these works in a full bibliography, which may also serve to guide further research in the field.

A cross-check between notes and bibliography discloses that four cited works (Bean, Gaitan, Knight, and Renfro) were missing from the bibliography. They have been added. *Chicago* advises that "unpublished interviews are best cited in text or in notes, . . . [but] they occasionally appear in bibliographies" (14.211); in this scholarly work, partly based on published and unpublished oral history sources, the inclusion of the Gaitan interview is advisable.

The separate, redundant entry for Davies can be deleted. It serves only to identify the source of Cherny's chapter and is fully cited in the Cherny entry. (If the author cited other chapters from the Davies book as well or consulted the book as background, the separate Davies entry should be retained.)

The entry for *The ILWU Story,* like note 3, lists the ILWU as the institutional "author" as well as the publisher of this work. Publications issued by organizations that are not traditional publishers often present bibliographic challenges for scholars, copyeditors, and library catalogers, especially if many contributors are credited in sometimes unconventional front matter. In this instance, WorldCat (http://www.worldcat.org/) names the International Longshoremen's and Warehousemen's Union, Vrana, and Schwartz as equal authors of *The ILWU Story;* the Library of Congress Online Catalog (https://catalog.loc.gov) favors Vrana as the author but lists "Schwartz, Harvey" and "International Longshoremen's and Warehousemen's Union" as "related names." The attribution of authorship is thus a matter of scholarly judgment, and the correct name of the ILWU must be confirmed if it is used. Query 2 can resolve these matters. If the author explains that Vrana, Schwartz, Stallone, and Rein, all either members of the union's staff or affiliates, prepared the union's publication in the scope of their employment, then the ILWU is arguably the official author of this work, in the same way that the University of Chicago Press is the author of *The Chicago Manual of Style,* despite the numerous staff members and consultants who contributed to its pages (see *Chicago* 14.84).

The Kimeldorf entry has been moved into correct alphabetical order.

The 3-em dashes for the second and third Schwartz entries should be replaced by the author's full name. *Chicago* now counsels against the use of 3-em dashes for repeated names in bibliographies and reference lists because dashes don't work in computerized sorts, may obscure significant publication details (such as the addition of "ed." or "trans."), and don't function well in some electronic publishing formats. Note that the three Schwartz entries are ordered alphabetically by title rather than chronologically by publication date: either ordering principle is acceptable in a general bibliography as long as the system is consistently applied.

EXERCISE 11-4: Key

Editorial changes are shown in-line; queries directed to the author follow the reference list. Explanatory comments are placed at the end of the answer key.

Founded in 1853, when the state of California was only three years old, the Riggers and Stevedores Union Association was the first major representative body for waterfront employees in the San Francisco Bay Area. In the era of sailing vessels this union consisted of skilled ship riggers and seasoned cargo handlers. Stevedore foremen often hired less experienced "men along the shore," or *longshoremen,* to physically work cargo. Between 1890 and 1910, as bigger steel ships replaced wooden vessels, cargo handling became casual work. Eventually, the label *stevedore* came to refer to a cargo-moving contractor or company; the label *longshoreman* (or *docker*) came to refer to a hold worker or a dockworker. In those years of change, the Riggers and Stevedores opened its membership, expelled contracting stevedores, and became a more broadly based union (Cherny 2000, 102–3, 120).[1]

In 1901 the San Francisco longshoremen joined a major strike by the City Front Federation, a coalition of wagon drivers, sailors, ship fitters, and other waterfront workers. The strike began with a lockout of city teamsters who were demanding union recognition and improved working conditions. The strike had only limited success. But the violence against strikers that erupted during the confrontation led directly to the creation of a Union Labor Party in San Francisco. This independent third party successfully elected its candidate to the office of mayor in late 1901 and reelected him in 1903 and 1905. The Union Labor Party played a dominant role in San Francisco politics over the next decade (Knight 1960, 72–93; Cherny 2000, 120–21; see also Bean 1968).[2]

Elsewhere along the Pacific Coast, local groups of longshore workers forged a regional alliance during the early years of the twentieth century. By 1916 the dockworkers in all the major West Coast ports were affiliated nationally with the American Federation of Labor's International Longshoremen's Association (ILA) as an autonomous unit called the Pacific Coast District No. 38, ILA (ILWU 2004, 3; Cherny 2000, 122; Magden 1982, 31).[3] San Francisco's Riggers and Stevedore's Union had joined the ILA around 1900; it later left that organization but rejoined shortly before 1916. At the time, San Francisco was the biggest port along the West Coast, so San Francisco's membership was crucial to the unity of ILA District 38. The necessity of coastwide unity became clear in 1916, when, in the first

---

1. Robert W. Cherny, "Longshoremen of San Francisco Bay, 1849-1960," in *Dock Workers: International Exploration in Comparative Labour History, 1790-1970,* edited by Sam Davies et. al., Vol. I (Aldershot, England: Ashgate Publishers, 2000), 102-103, 120.

2. Robert Edward Lee Knight, *Industrial Relations in the San Francisco Bay Area, 1900-1918* (Berkeley and Los Angeles: University of California Press, 1960), pp. 72-93; Cherny, "Longshoremen," 120-121. See also Walton Bean, *Boss Ruef's San Francisco: The Story of the Union Labor Party, Big Business, and the Graft Prosecution* (Berkeley: University of California Press, 1968).

3. *The ILWU Story: Six Decades of Militant Unionism,* text and research by Eugene Dennis Vrana, additional research by Harvey Schwartz, edited by Steve Stallone and Marcy Rein (San Francisco: ILWU, 1997), 3; Cherny, "Longshoremen," 122; Ronald Magden, *The Working Waterfront: The Story of Tacoma's Ships and Men* (Tacoma, Wash.: ILWU Local 23, 1982), 31.

major coastwide strike of Pacific Coast dockworkers, the 10,000 to 12,500 members of District 38 shut down all the West Coast's key ports from Bellingham, Washington, to San Diego, California. The district's main demands were for standard coastwide wages and working conditions and a closed shop, which would have required all employees to be ILA members (Cherny 2000, 120–23; Magden 1982, 31–33; Knight 1960, 302).[4]

The 1916 strike was bitter and violent. On June 16, when the strike was just over two weeks old, Lewis A. Morey, an ILA member from Oakland, California, was shot and killed by an armed guard who was protecting strikebreakers. Two days later, Thomas Olsen, another ILA man, was shot in the back on a San Francisco dock. He died immediately. Nearly a month later, a strike committee member from Tacoma, Washington, was knifed when he confronted two strikebreakers. Another Tacoma striker was killed when a company guard fired his weapon into a crowd of longshoremen (Magden 1982, 33–35; Knight 1960, 303).[5]

In response to the strike, the San Francisco Chamber of Commerce organized a Law and Order Committee to inflame anti-union sentiment among business leaders and the general public. On July 17, San Francisco's more than 4,000 members negotiated a separate peace with employers because they were worried about the possibility of an open shop campaign. (This campaign materialized during the 1920s despite the San Francisco longshoremen's efforts to prevent it.) They retained their union conditions, but they did not win a closed shop or standard coastwide wages and conditions. With the San Francisco longshoremen under contract, the shipowners were able to bleed the rest of the coast workers into submission. The employers started by hiring nonunion men. Soon it was obvious that the strike was lost. The ill feeling aroused between groups of longshoremen following the experience of 1916 led to a split in the Pacific Coast longshoremen's ranks. After the strike, the San Francisco longshoremen seceded from the ILA and assumed independent status. Coastwide, all the ILA locals lost control of jobs on the docks except for the longshoremen of the Port of Tacoma, who soon regained the union hiring hall they had initially lost and who maintained it into the "nonunion" 1920s and early 1930s (Magden 1982, 35–37; Knight 1960, 304–5; Cherny 2000, 123, 133; Schwartz 2009, 127–28).[6]

The independent San Francisco Riggers and Stevedores Union did not last long. Reacting to heavier sling loads and a speeded-up work pace, the union struck in 1919. This strike was doomed from the start. It coincided with the emergence of a decade-long conservative open shop drive across the entire United States. Anti-union organization and sentiment among employers was intense. A minor faction of the San Francisco union's membership, which was influenced by the radical Industrial Workers of the World (the IWW, or "Wobblies"), persuaded the union to pass a resolution instructing R and S negotiators to demand stock ownership in steamship companies and seats on the shipowners' boards of directors. The R and S negotiators did not push these radical demands, but the employers used them against the union. Instead of gaining

---

4. Cherny, "Longshoremen," 120-123; Magden, *The Working Waterfront*, 31-33; Knight, *Industrial Relations*, 302.

5. Magden, *The Working Waterfront*, 33-35; Knight, *Industrial Relations*, 303.

6. Magden, *The Working Waterfront*, 35-37; Knight, *Industrial Relations*, 304-305; Cherny, "Longshoremen," 123, 133; Harvey Schwartz, *Solidarity Stories: An Oral History of the ILWU* (Seattle, WA: University of Washington Press, 2009), 127-128.

their goals, the San Francisco longshoremen, alone and without coastwide waterfront allies, were utterly defeated. One union man was killed during this showdown. The union was destroyed when the employers replaced it with another, ostensibly independent, organization that in reality functioned like a "company union." (Cherry 2000, 124–27; see also Renfro 1995).[7]

This new employer-backed group was officially called the Longshoremen's Association of San Francisco and the Bay District. Its chief officer, Jack Bryan, had longshoring experience, but his organization existed to thwart worker-controlled unionism. The new Association issued a membership book with a blue cover to distinguish it from the red membership book of the old Riggers and Stevedores Union. During the company union's heyday, 1919 through 1933, the organization was known on the waterfront simply as "the Blue Book." Workers had to pay dues and maintain Blue Book membership just to qualify for waterfront jobs. But membership conferred no real benefits, such as union representation (Selvin 1996, 44–45; Nelson 1988, 53; Schwartz 2009, 11; Cherry 2000, 126–27).[8]

Corrupt hiring practices and inhumane working conditions prevailed in the Blue Book era. In San Francisco, workers were forced to stand in a "shape-up" on the waterfront early each morning in order to get employment, even if they belonged to a regular work gang. Harry Renton Bridges, the future union leader, stood among them. The San Francisco longshoreman vividly recalled this shape-up: "We were hired off the street like a bunch of sheep standing there from six o'clock in the morning in all kinds of weather." (Larrowe 1977, 8; see also Cherry 2000, 103–4, 133). To get a job, workers often had to bribe the hiring bosses with money, alcohol, or other favors. Henry Gaitan, a longshoreman in the equally corrupt hiring system at the Port of Los Angeles, later attested that "if you had a nice-looking sister, and liquor, and a wife that would put out, you'd have a job. I seen it here on these docks before we had the [real] union." (Gaitan 1983).[9,10]

Those fortunate enough to be hired found that the work was fast-paced and dangerous. The Port of San Francisco was known for its high productivity—but also for an extremely high rate of injury (Schwartz 2015).[11]{Query1} Bosses raced gangs of longshoremen against each other in an effort to increase the speed of work, at times using ethnic rivalries to provoke such competitions: a predominantly German work gang, for example, would be set against a gang of longshoremen of Portuguese or Italian background. Harry Bridges himself was injured on the job in 1929. In those days, he remembered, injured longshoremen rarely applied for workmen's compensation because they feared being

7. Cherry, "Longshoremen," 124-127. See also Mary Joy Renfro, "The Decline and Fall of the San Francisco Riggers and Stevedores Union: A History of the Years 1916 to 1919," senior thesis, San Francisco State University, 1995, in Labor Archives and Research Center, San Francisco State University.

8. David Selvin, *A Terrible Anger: The 1934 Waterfront and General Strikes in San Francisco* (Detroit: Wayne State University Press, 1996), 44-45; Bruce Nelson, *Workers on the Waterfront: Seamen, Longshoremen, and Unionism in the 1930s* (Urbana: University of Illinois Press, 1988), 53; Schwartz, *Solidarity Stories*, 11; Cherry, "Longshoremen," 126-127.

9. Bridges quoted in Charles P. Larrowe, *Harry Bridges: The Rise and Fall of Radical Labor in the United States*, 2d ed. rev. (Westport, CT: Lawrence Hill, 1977), 8. See also Cherry, "Longshoremen," 103-104, 133.

10. Unpublished Gaitan interview with Daniel S. Beagle and David Wellman, 14 May, 1983, in the ILWU Oral History Collection, Anne Rand Research Library, International Longshore and Warehouse Union, San Francisco.

11. Harvey Schwartz, *Building the Golden Gate Bridge: A Workers' Oral History* (Seattle: University of Washington Press, 2015).

blacklisted by the employers, who were charged by the state for accident claims. Fatigue from long hours of heavy labor with few or no work breaks also contributed to the high injury rate during the nonunion years. Work shifts of twelve, sixteen, and more hours were well known on the San Francisco waterfront (Schwartz 2009, 12–13; Cherny 2000, 106, 111, 133; ILWU 2004, 3). ~~12~~

~~12. Schwartz, *Solidarity Stories*, 12-13; Cherny, "Longshoremen," 106, 111, 133; *The ILWU Story*, 3.~~

~~BIBLIOGRAPHY~~WORKS CITED

~~Afrasiabi, Peter. *Burning Bridges: America's 20-Year Crusade to Deport Labor Leader Harry Bridges*. Brooklyn, NY: Thirlmere Books, 2016.~~

Bean, Walton. 1968. *Boss Ruef's San Francisco: The Story of the Union Labor Party, Big Business, and the Graft Prosecution*. Berkeley: University of California Press.

Cherny, Robert W. 2000. "Longshoremen of San Francisco Bay, 1849–1960." In *Dock Workers: International Exploration in Comparative Labour History, 1790–1970*, vol. 1, ~~edited by~~ ed. Sam Davies et al., 102–~~1~~40. Aldershot, Eng.~~land~~: Ashgate Publishing~~, 2000~~.**{Query2}**

~~Cole, Peter. *Dockworker Power: Race, Technology, and Unionism in Durban and the San Francisco Bay Area*. Champaign: University of Illinois Press, forthcoming in 2018.~~

~~Davies, Sam, et al., ed. *Dock Workers: International Exploration in Comparative Labour History, 1790-1970*. Vol. 1. Aldershot, England: Ashgate Publishing, 2000.~~

Gaitan, Henry. 1983. Interview by Daniel S. Beagle and David Wellman. May 14, 1983. ILWU Oral History Collection, Anne Rand Research Library, International Longshore and Warehouse Union, San Francisco.

International Longshore and Warehouse Union (ILWU). 2004. *The ILWU Story: Six Decades of Militant Unionism*. 2nd ed. Edited by Steve Stallone and Marcy Rein. With text ~~Text~~ and research by Eugene Dennis Vrana. ~~Additional research by~~ and Harvey Schwartz. ~~Edited by Steve Stallone and Marcy Rein.~~ San Francisco: ILWU~~,~~ ~~2004~~.**{Query3}**

~~Kimeldorf, Howard. *Reds or Rackets? The Making of Radical and Conservative Unions on the Waterfront*. Berkeley: University of California Press, 1988.~~

Knight, Robert Edward Lee. 1960. *Industrial Relations in the San Francisco Bay Area, 1900–1918*. Berkeley: University of California Press.

Larrowe, Charles P. 1977. *Harry Bridges: The Rise and Fall of Radical Labor in the United States*. 2nd ed. rev. Westport, CT: Lawrence Hill~~, 1977~~.**{Query4}**

~~Levinson, Marc. *The Box: How the Shipping Container Made the World Smaller and the World Economy Bigger*. Princeton, NJ: Princeton University Press, 2006.~~

Magden, Ronald. 1982. *The Working Waterfront: The Story of Tacoma's Ships and Men*. Tacoma, WA: ILWU Local 23~~, 1982~~.

Nelson, Bruce. 1988. *Workers on the Waterfront: Seamen, Longshoremen, and Unionism in the 1930s*. Urbana: University of Illinois Press~~, 1988~~.

~~Quin, Mike. *The Big Strike*. Olema, CA: Olema Publishing, 1949.~~

Renfro, Mary Joy. 1995. "The Decline and Fall of the San Francisco Riggers and Stevedores Union: A History of the Years 1916 to 1919." Senior thesis, San Francisco State University, Labor Archives and Research Center.

~~Schwartz, Harvey. "Harry Bridges and the Scholars: Looking at History's Verdict." *California History: The Magazine of the California Historical Society* 59, no. 1 (Spring 1980): 66-79.~~

~~———. *The March Inland: Origins of the ILWU Warehouse Division, 1934-1938*. Los Angeles: Institute of Industrial Relations, University of California, 1978. Reprint, San Francisco: ILWU, 2000.~~

Schwartz, Harvey. 2015. *Building the Golden Gate Bridge: A Workers' Oral History*. Seattle: University of Washington Press.

~~———.~~ Schwartz, Harvey. 2009. *Solidarity Stories: An Oral History of the ILWU*. Seattle~~,~~ ~~WA~~: University of Washington Press~~, 2000~~.

Selvin, David. 1996. *A Terrible Anger: The 1934 Waterfront and General Strikes in San Francisco*. Detroit: Wayne State University Press~~, 1996~~.

~~Wellman, David. *The Union Makes Us Strong: Radical Unionism on the San Francisco Waterfront*. Cambridge: Cambridge University Press, 1995.~~

QUERIES

{Query1}: Schwartz book about the construction of the Golden Gate Bridge sounds interesting, but does this source have any bearing on injuries in a different industry on the waterfront in this earlier Blue Book era? Please revise the text to clarify the connection—or, if this source has been cited in error (e.g., as a leftover from a previous version of this paper), delete the reference here, along with the corresponding (provisionally added) entry in Works Cited.

{Query2}: Please reconcile n. 1 and biblio entry: (a) Are Davies et al. the eds of the multivolume work (in which case ed info precedes the volume number) or the eds of vol. 1 only (ed info follows the volume number)? (b) Ashgate Publishers (n. 1) or Ashgate Publishing (biblio)?

Please confirm or correct: Place of publication listed as "England," not "UK," on copyright page?

{Query3}: Should this work be cited here or alphabetized in the reference list under the research-writers, Vrana and Schwartz? or under the editors, Stallone and Rein? Or, if the author of record is in fact the institution (ILWU), as indicated in the original n. 3 and in the biblio entry here, should the abbreviation be spelled out as "International Longshoremen's and Warehousemen's Union" to match records in WorldCat and the Library of Congress Online Catalog? or "International Longshore and Warehouse Union" to match the ILWU's own website?

{Query4}: Is this a revised version of the *second* edition? Please confirm or correct.

COMMENTS

Parenthetical author-date citations have been optimally positioned at the ends of sentences to avoid distracting readers in midsentence.

Hyphens in ranges of numerals (page numbers, inclusive dates) have been replaced by en dashes throughout.

Number ranges have been emended to follow Chicago style for inclusive numbers, as described in *The Copyeditor's Handbook,* chapter 7, under "Inclusive Numerals."

Sources that are not explicitly cited in the text (Afrasiabi, Cole, Davies, Kimeldorf, Levinson, Quin, two works by Schwartz, and Wellman) have all been deleted from Works Cited.

Sources cited in the text but not included in the original bibliography (Bean, Gaitan, Knight, Renfro, and Schwartz 2015) have been added to Works Cited. If the author's reply to query 1 results in the deletion of the in-text citation of Schwartz 2015, the corresponding entry in Works Cited should also be deleted.

In the author-date format, publication dates immediately follow authors' names in Works Cited listings. However, the year appears twice in the Gaitan entry, in keeping with *Chicago*'s recommendation at 15.14 that "when the date of publication includes month and day, the year may be repeated to avoid any confusion."

Watch out for any in-text citations that seem entirely unrelated to the main text. At least one copyediting pass should compare these parenthetical citations against the entries in Works Cited to identify possible mismatches. See step 5 in the description of copyediting procedures in *The Copyeditor's Handbook,* chapter 11, under "Author-Date System."

The in-text citation and the Works Cited entry for *The ILWU Story* list the International Longshore and Warehouse Union as the institutional "author" of the work. Publications issued by organizations that are not traditional publishers often present bibliographic challenges for scholars, copyeditors, and library catalogers, especially if many contributors are credited in sometimes unconventional front matter. In this instance, WorldCat (http://www.worldcat.org) names the International Longshoremen's and Warehousemen's Union, Vrana, and Schwartz as equal authors of *The ILWU Story;* the Library of Congress Online Catalog (https://catalog.loc.gov) favors Vrana as the author but lists "Schwartz, Harvey" and "International Longshoremen's and Warehousemen's Union" as "related names." The attribution of authorship is thus a matter of scholarly judgment, and the correct name of the ILWU must be confirmed. Query 3 can resolve these matters. If the author explains that Vrana, Schwartz, Stallone, and Rein, all either members of the union's staff or affiliates, prepared the union's publication in the scope of their employment, then the ILWU is arguably the official author of this work, in the same way that the University of Chicago Press is the author of *The Chicago Manual of Style,* despite the numerous staff members and consultants who contributed to its pages (see *Chicago* 14.84).

EXERCISE 12-1: Key

~~Table of~~ Contents**A**: ~~A history of Western Cartooning~~

~~Dedication   000~~**B**

List of ~~iIIustrations~~Illustrations   000

~~Contributors   000~~**C**

~~Forward~~Foreword,**D** *by Dorothy Dessin*   000

Preface   000

~~Acknowledgements~~Acknowledgments**E**   000

Introduction**{Query1}**   000

Part ~~1~~**F** • The Early History of Cartoons———— ~~000~~

Chapter 1. The ~~drawings~~Drawings of Lascaux: ~~sacred representations~~Sacred
    Representations or ~~man-cave comics~~Man-Cave Comics?, *by Charlene Chauvet*   000

Chapter 2. The Art of Iconic Caricature in European Incunabula, *by Sir Nicholas
    Nozalot***{Query2}**   000

Part 2 • Cartoons and Mass Culture— ~~000~~

Chapter 3. Political Cartoons in England in the Eighteenth Century, *by Barry Boswell* 000

Chapter 4. Monikers of Midcentury Superheroes, *by Diana Kent*   000

Part 3 • Animation~~000~~**{Query3}**

Chapter 6.: Mickey through the Decades: From Ratlike Rodent to Mellow Mouse, *by
    Donald D. Mintz*   000

Chapter 5.: Fred, Barney, and Bam-Bam: Representations of Masculinity in Prehistoric
    Bedrock, ~~by Wilma Wilkinson~~*by Wilma Wilkinson***G**   000

Part 4 • :—Serials— ~~000~~

Chapter 7.: *Dilbert* and Late ~~20th-century~~Twentieth-Century Workplace Culture, *by Adam
    Scott*   000

Chapter 8.: Mouseover Messages: Tooltips and Subversion in ~~Xkcd~~xkcd**H**, *by Jane Curzon*
    000

Color plates follow pages 000 and 000 **K**

QUERIES

{Query1}: Any byline for the introduction?
{Query2}: Is inclusion of the honorific desirable or necessary here? **L**
{Query3}: Please check chapter order and numbering: should the two chapters in this part be renumbered, or should the listings be transposed?

COMMENTS

A "Contents" suffices.

B A dedication is considered part of the prelims and not included on the contents page.

C A list of contributors usually appears in the back matter. If the contributors are especially significant from a marketing or editorial perspective, their names may also be listed on the title page or elsewhere in the prelims.

D The erroneous use of "forward" for "foreword" is surprisingly common.

E In US English, "Acknowledgments" has only two *e*'s.

F Use arabic numeral for consistency with the other part numbers (or change the others to roman numerals). Although the styling of numbers in display type (e.g., spelled out, roman, or arabic) is often the designer's decision rather than the editor's and may be changed during page layout, ensuring stylistic consistency in the manuscript helps prevent errors in proofs.

Part-opening pages typically do not bear page numbers (although they are included in the total page count) unless text appears on the page (see *Chicago* 1.8).

G Set the byline italic for consistency with prevailing style.

H *Xkcd, xkcd,* or *XKCD*? *Chicago* is firm about capitalizing titles of works according to the style of the current document, not that of the original source, but on the website for this comic, its creator, Randall Munroe, states explicitly that he prefers the all-lowercase form and adds: "In formal contexts where a lowercase word shouldn't start a sentence, 'XKCD' is an okay alternative. 'Xkcd' is frowned upon" (https://xkcd.com/about/, accessed February 20, 2018). If the author of the chapter, the editor of the volume, or the publisher has a strong preference in the matter, the copyeditor should respect it; if not, the copyeditor has the choice here of offending against *Chicago* or against Munroe.

I A single appendix needs no identifying letter or number. Multiple appendixes may be designated by letters or numbers according to publisher or author preference.

J Footnotes, by definition, appear at the foot of the text page and therefore are not included in a table of contents. Endnotes (or backnotes) are most often identified in the table of contents simply as "Notes." When notes appear at the end of each chapter of a book, they are not listed separately on the contents page.

K This is a common way of noting the location of galleries of color or grayscale images that are printed on different paper and "tipped in" between signatures of the text when the book is bound.

L Scholarly works typically do not include honorific titles for authors or contributors, but since their use is sometimes a sensitive matter, it's best to query.

EXERCISE 12-2: Key

Queries and explanatory comments follow the text.

alphanumeric sorting. ~~Sorting~~ A sorting that treats numbers like letters so that words with numbers and numbers of equal length can be sorted.**{Query1}**

ASCII. An acronym for ~~American Standard Code for Information Interchange~~American Standard Code for Information Interchange, one of the standard forms for representing characters so that files can be shared between programs. A DOS Text File is in ASCII format.**{Query2}**

backspace. A key on ~~your~~ the keyboard ~~which~~ that deletes the character to the left of the cursor.

backup. To copy files for ~~safe keeping~~safekeeping.**{Query3}**

~~bandwith~~bandwidth. ~~How fast~~ The capacity of a computer network or connection ~~can~~ to transfer data, usually measured in bits per second, or bps.

bit. A ~~binary digit~~binary digit; the smallest storage unit for data in a computer.

boot. To start a computer by loading the operating system into the computer's memory.

buffer. A temporary internal data storage area used by computers and some printers.
     {Query4}

byte. The amount of space needed to store a single character (number, letter, or code)~~.~~; 1,024 bytes equals ~~one~~1 kilobyte (~~Kb~~KB or K).**{Query5}**

~~buffer. A temporary data storage area used by computers and some printers.~~

QUERIES

{Query1}: Please revise to avoid defining "alphanumeric sorting" as "A sorting . . . that can be sorted."

{Query2}: DOS Text File—caps OK?

{Query3}: *Merriam-Webster Unabridged* shows "back up" (verb) and "backup" (noun, adjective), as does *Wired Style*; change here? Also, add where or how files are copied? (Since this glossary is for beginners, you wouldn't want naive readers to look for a file-copying machine.)

{Query4}: Addition of "internal" OK? (Again, to prevent novice readers from looking for a piece of equipment called a buffer.)

{Query5}: Okay? *Merriam-Webster Unabridged* and *Wired Style* both capitalize "KB" for kilobyte; lowercase "b" is used for bit ("Kb" for kilobit).

COMMENTS

Yes, even today some novice computer users might think there's a special machine for copying files or a separate piece of equipment called a buffer! When editing definitions in a glossary, try to imagine the level of understanding of (and possible misunderstanding by) the intended readers.

If you know something about computer jargon and if your schedule and editing budget allow, you could help this author by rewriting the weaker definitions. Otherwise, you should draw the author's attention to the definitions that need work and supply a quick comment about the problems.

When copyediting glossaries, always be on the lookout for

circular definitions. It is circular to define "alphanumeric sorting" as a type of "sorting" that allows words and numbers to be "sorted."

inconsistency in point of view. The definition of "backspace" uses the second person ("your keyboard"), while the definition of "boot" is impersonal ("To start a computer").

inconsistent treatment of the spelled-out versions of abbreviations. The author uses bold for the initials in the spelling out of "ASCII," italics in the spelling out of "bit" (and the italics are misplaced: "binary digit" yields "bid"), and regular roman type for the spelling out of "KB."

mysteries lurking in the corners of the definitions. Here both "backup" and "buffer" are likely to remain rather baffling to the novice user. Adding "internal" to the definition of the latter will at least prevent readers from wondering where their buffer is.

faulty classification. A definition must indicate whether the term is a verb, a noun, or an adjective. Thus the definition of a verb always contains an infinitive, the definition of a noun is headed by an article (a, an, the) or by a noun, and the definition of an adjective starts with an adjective or a phrase such as "used to describe." Here the author usually begins the definitions of common nouns with an article; the exceptions—"alphanumeric sorting" and "ASCII"—have been corrected. Alternatively, one could delete the original articles, yielding

> backspace. Key on the keyboard . . .
> bandwidth. Capacity of a computer network . . .
> bit. Binary digit; smallest storage unit . . .
> buffer. Temporary internal data storage area . . .
> byte. Amount of space . . .

EXERCISE 13-1: Hand-Marked Key

3   Quick Guide to Typecoding: It's All Greek to Me

Lorem ipsum dolor sit amet, con sectetuer adipiscing elit, sed dis nonummy nibh euismod tincidunt ut laoreet dolore magna aliquam:

⌐.   Lorem ipsum dolor sit amet.

(BL) .   Con sectetuer adipiscing elit.

└˙   Sed dis nonummy nibh euismod.

Aliquam erat voluptat. Ut wisi enim ad minim veniam, quis nostrud exerci tation ullamcorper suscipit lobortis nisl ut aliquip ea commodo consequat:

Lorem ipsum dolor	Dolore magna ut
sit amet, con sect	aliquam erat ut
etuer adipiscing	voluptat ut wisi
elit, sed dis	enim ad minim ad
nonummy nibh.	veniam.

(MCL)

Lorem ipsum dolor sit amet, con sectetuer adipiscing elit.

Sed dis nonummy nibh euismod tincidunt ut laoreet dolore magna aliquam erat voluptat. Ut wisi enim ad minim veniam, quis nostrud:

 $\sum fx$ ffl $4y \geq 6$

Lorem ipsum dolor sit amet, con sectetuer adipiscing elit.

Sed dis nonummy nibh euismod tincidunt ut laoreet dolore magna aliquam

erat voluptat:

Lorem ipsum "dolor sit amet," con sectetuer adipiscing elil, sed dis

nonummy nibh euismod tincidunt ut laoreet dolore magna aliquam erat

voluptat.

Lorem ipsum dolor sit amet, con sectetuer adipiscing elit, sed dis nonummy

nibh euismod:

1. Voluptat suscipit lobortis nisl.

2. Wisi enim dolore magna aliquam erat.

3. Ad minim veniam dis nonummy nibh.

A Quis Nostrud Exerci

Tation ullamcorper suscipit lobortis nisi ut aliquip ea commodo consequat.

Lorem ipsum dolor sit amet, con sectetuer adipiscing.

EXERCISE 13-1: Typecoded Key

`<CN>`3`</CN>`   `<CT>`Quick Guide to Typecoding:`</CT>`
`<CST>`It's All Greek to Me`</CST>`

Lorem ipsum dolor sit amet, con sectetuer adipiscing elit, sed dis nonummy nibh euismod tincidunt ut laoreet dolore magna aliquam:

`<BL>`•   Lorem ipsum dolor sit amet.
•   Con sectetuer adipiscing elit.
•   Sed dis nonummy nibh euismod.`</BL>`

Aliquam erat voluptat. Ut wisi enim ad minim veniam, quis nostrud exerci tation ullamcorper suscipit lobortis nisl ut aliquip ea commodo consequat:

`<MCL>`Lorem ipsum dolor   Dolore magna ut
sit amet, con sect   aliquam erat ut
etuer adipiscing   voluptat ut wisi
elit, sed dis   enim ad minim ad
nonummy nibh.   veniam.`</MCL>`

Lorem ipsum dolor sit amet, con sectetuer adipiscing elit.

Sed dis nonummy nibh euismod tincidunt ut laoreet dolore magna aliquam erat voluptat. Ut wisi enim ad minim veniam, quis nostrud:

`<EQ>`$\sum fx$ ffl $4y \geq 6$`</EQ>`

Lorem ipsum dolor sit amet, con sectetuer adipiscing elit.

Sed dis nonummy nibh euismod tincidunt ut laoreet dolore magna aliquam erat voluptat:

`<EX>`Lorem ipsum "dolor sit amet," con sectetuer adipiscing elit, sed dis nonummy nibh euismod tincidunt ut laoreet dolore magna aliquam erat voluptat.`</EX>`

Lorem ipsum dolor sit amet, con sectetuer adipiscing elit, sed dis nonummy nibh euismod:

<NL>1. Voluptat suscipit lobortis nisl.

2. Wisi enim dolore magna aliquam erat.

3. Ad minim veniam dis nonummy nibh.**</NL>**

<A>Quis Nostrud Exerci**</A>**

Tation ullamcorper suscipit lobortis nisi ut aliquip ea commodo consequat. Lorem ipsum dolor sit amet, con sectetuer adipiscing.

EXERCISE 13-2: Key

Even for a relatively straightforward procedure, it can be surprisingly difficult to create instructions that are clear, error free, and consistently formatted and phrased. This is perhaps partly because such instructions are often created not by skilled technical writers but by committees, after extensive wrangling, and updated piecemeal by different people; a copyeditor is often in a position to spot problems that weary contributors can simply no longer see. Most of the errors and inconsistencies in this exercise are drawn from real first-aid instructions.

This exercise uses a fairly simple set of typecodes. Specifications for a full-length first-aid manual or a textbook might include codes for several styles of subheads and lists, block quotations, figure and table captions and legends, text boxes and sidebars, checklists, mnemonics, quizzes, and other elements. Although in theory the copyeditor may simply have the mechanical task of assigning the appropriate codes to all the elements, in practice this task may require careful attention to the structure and content of a document and the logical relationships between its parts.

Numbered queries are flagged in the text with boldface curly braces (e.g., {**Query1**}) and are printed below the text. Explanatory comments, signaled in the text with superscript letters, are printed at the end.

<TI>How to ~~do~~ Do CPR

<TXT>If you witness a cardiac arrest, ~~it's crucial to~~ [A]call 999{**Query1**} and start CPR immediately. Read ~~this page~~ these instructions[B] to learn how to do CPR, and watch our CPR training video for a step-by-step demonstration. It is easy to learn and saves lives.

To ~~learn how to~~ [C]perform CPR, follow these simple ~~six~~ seven{**Query2**} steps:

[D]<NL>1. Assess dangers.

<NL>2. Check responsiveness.

<NL>~~2.~~3. Send for help.

<NL>~~3.~~4. Check for normal breathing.

<NL>~~4.~~5. Give 30 chest compressions.

<NL>~~5.~~6. Give two rescue breaths.

<NL>~~6.~~7. ~~Repeat~~ Continue cycles of 30 chest compressions and two rescue breaths until an ambulance arrives.{**Query3**}

<TXT>Remember—even if you haven't been trained in CPR with rescue breathing, you can still use compression-only CPR.{**Query4**}

<H1>CPR ~~steps~~ Steps

~~To learn more about performing CPR in an emergency, read the rest of this page and watch our CPR training video.~~{Query5}

<H2>Step 1. Assess Dangers{Query6}

<TXT>—If you come across someone who is unconscious, always check for danger and look for risks before you start helping. ~~Especially~~ —especially traffic, fire, or electrical hazards.

<H2>Step ~~1.~~2. Check Responsiveness

<TXT>Check for a response. Gently shake the person's shoulders and ask loudly, ~~'are~~ "Are you ~~alright~~ all right?"~~:~~ or "~~can~~ Can you hear me?" Someone who is responsive but cannot speak might be able to open their**E** eyes or squeeze your hand.

<H2>Step ~~2.~~3. Send for Help

<TXT>If the person is unresponsive:

<BL>•   ~~stay~~ Stay with the person.

<BL>•   ~~ask~~ Ask a bystander to call 911 immediately.

<BL>•   ~~ask~~ Ask a bystander to fetch an automatic ~~electrical~~ external defibrillator (AED).

<BL>•   If you can't find anyone to help, call 911 before you start CPR.

<H2>Step ~~3.~~4. Check for Normal Breathing

<TXT>In an unconscious person, the muscles of the tongue relax, so ~~that~~ the tongue can block the airway, obstructing breathing. Open the person's airway by gently tilting the head back and lifting the chin ~~—when you do this you open their airway~~.

If there seems to be something in the person's mouth, remove it by sweeping it away with two fingers.

A person in cardiac arrest won't be breathing, or won't be breathing normally. ~~They also won't be conscious.~~**F**

Check for normal breathing by ~~looking for:~~**G**

<BL>•   looking for regular chest movements

<BL>•   listening for breathing

<BL>•   feeling for breath on your cheek.

<TXT>Look, listen, and feel for no more than 10 seconds. Occasional gasps don't count as normal breathing. If you're not sure ~~if their~~ breathing is normal, act as if it's not normal.

If you're sure the person is breathing normally, ~~then~~ put them in the recovery position,~~,~~**{Query7}** and call 911. Keep monitoring the person's breathing.

———————— ~~If breathing isn't normal, open their airway. Place one hand on the person's forehead, gently tilt their head back, then lift their chin using two fingers of your other hand under their chin.~~**{Query8}**

<H2>Step ~~4~~5. Give 30 Chest Compressions

<BL>• Place the person on their back.**H**

<BL>• ~~Kneeling~~ Kneel next to the person's chest.

<BL>• Place the heel of one hand in the center of the chest. Place your other hand on top of the first. Interlock your fingers.

<BL>• With straight arms, use the heel of your hand to push the chest down firmly and smoothly, so that the chest is pressed down about 2 inches (5–6 centimeters), and release. Use your body weight to help you push.

<BL>• Push hard and fast, at a rate of 100 to 120 chest compressions per minute— that's around 2 per second,**ı** or similar to the beat of the song "Stayin' Alive." Don't worry about pushing too hard.

<BL>• Give 30 chest compressions. Count them out loud.

<H2>Step ~~5~~6. Give Two Rescue Breaths

<TXT>Open the airway again by tilting the head back and lifting the chin.

~~You need to p~~Pinch the soft part of the person's nose closed.

Take a normal breath, place your mouth around the other person's mouth to make a seal, and breathe out steadily.

The chest should rise and fall. Keeping the person's head back and the chin lifted, take your mouth away, take another normal breath, and give a second rescue breath.

<H2>Step ~~6~~7. Continue ~~CPR~~Chest Compressions and Rescue Breaths

<TXT>Keep performing cycles of 30 compressions and two rescue breaths.

If you can't or would rather not give rescue breaths, then call 911 and deliver compression-only CPR (perform compressions constantly at a rate of 100–120 per minute, with no breaths).**{Query9}**

Keep going until trained emergency responders arrive and take over, an AED becomes available, or the ~~victim~~ person**{Query10}** starts to show signs of regaining consciousness, such as opening their eyes, breathing normally, coughing, vomiting, or speaking.

If an AED becomes available, turn it on immediately and follow the voice prompts.

Discontinue CPR if the situation becomes unsafe or you become too exhausted to continue.

QUERIES

{Query1}: 999 or 911? See text in steps 3 and 4 below.

{Query2}: Change OK? See also renumbering of list and subheads below.

{Query3}: Changed wording here and in the subhead below to clarify which steps are repeated, OK? Also, compare "until an ambulance arrives" to wording under step 7 below, which gives arrival of AED and person's recovery as other valid reasons to stop CPR. Reconcile?

{Query4}: Will readers know what "compression-only CPR" is? Add brief explanation, or a cross-reference to the description below? (See also query 9.)

{Query5}: This sentence repeats information given just above. While there may be good reasons to include multiple references to this resource, the repetition seems out of place in step-by-step instructions for a life-or-death procedure; OK to omit here?

{Query6}: OK to add, for consistency with numbered list above?

{Query7}: Define "recovery position," or rephrase?

{Query8}: OK to delete, since airway was opened at the beginning of this step?

{Query9}: Consider moving this comment up to the previous step, where rescue breaths are described?

{Query10}: OK to change, for consistency with more current usage elsewhere in document?

COMMENTS

A This wording can be deleted in the interests of conciseness and for consistency with the imperative voice in the rest of the instructions.

B "This page" is appropriate for a website, but not for printed information.

C The stated purpose here is doing, not learning.

D Many word processors offer automated formatting of numbered and bulleted sub-heads and lists; the drawback is that such formatting can be inadvertently changed, removed, or applied where it's not wanted by a single misdirected mouse click.

Because each of these items is a complete sentence, all can be styled with terminal punctuation. Alternatively, an editor might choose to omit terminal punctuation to match the subheads, which use the same wording.

E In this context, the contentious "singular *they*" (or *their*) is more idiomatic and less cumbersome than formal alternatives like "his or her." Sometimes it's possible to avoid this problem by referring to parts of the body without a personal pronoun: the head, the neck (see examples below).

F This observation is irrelevant here, because determining the person's responsiveness is covered in step 2.

G The first bulleted list item should be edited to begin with a participle, for consistency with the other two. Note that making these items parallel also makes the steps easier to memorize: look, listen, and feel. Because the list items are sentence fragments, the colon should be omitted. Adding semicolons to the first two list items for consistency with the period following the last item would be correct here, but the streamlined omission of all terminal punctuation seems more appropriate to the context.

H These brief sentence-style instructions can be formatted as a bulleted list, like those in step 3.

I Why "2" and not "two" here? In the style for technical numbers described in *The Copyeditor's Handbook*, chapter 7, single-digit numbers are spelled out, but exceptions are made for "regional consistency." In this sentence, other numbers in the same category (rate of chest compressions) are rendered as numerals, so "2" is preferable.

An editor might equally well choose to treat chest compressions and rescue breaths as "numerical values of the same class or type" and use numerals for both where they appear close together in the text: "Give 30 chest compressions and 2 rescue breaths."

EXERCISE 14-1: Key

1. Jessica took to Instagram to share a hilarious and absolutely adorable photo of her ~~toe-headed~~ <u>towheaded</u> daughter with a rose petal on her tongue.

Comment: "Toe-headed" (for "towheaded," a solid compound) is a dismayingly common homophone error. See *The Copyeditor's Handbook,* chapter 5, under "Homophones."

2. Jennifer Molleda looks at the blood-specked face of her husband, Alan Wakim, who <u>was on the way to work</u> ~~had~~ <u>when</u> two bullets whizz<u>ed</u> ~~by~~ <u>through his windshield and</u> <u>past</u> his head. ~~after going through his windshield on the way to work.~~

Comment: The phrases "after going through his windshield" and "on the way to work" are misplaced modifiers. See *The Copyeditor's Handbook,* chapter 14, under "Dangling and Misplaced Modifiers."

3. As a technical writer, <u>I reach first for</u> the *Microsoft Manual of Style* ~~is the first style~~ ~~guide I reach for~~ when I am a working on <u>a</u> documentation project ~~when the~~ <u>for an</u> organization <u>that</u> doesn't have a corporate style guide.

Comment: "As a technical writer" is a dangling modifier: it attaches to the subject of the main clause, "the *Microsoft Manual of Style,*" but modifies "I." See *The Copyeditor's Handbook,* chapter 14, under "Dangling and Misplaced Modifiers."

4. Enid takes an interest in playing pranks on other people, purely for her own benefit, especially a classmate named Josh<u>,</u> ~~who~~ <u>whom</u> she attempts to seduce. OR: <u>". . .</u> <u>especially Josh, a classmate that she attempts to seduce."</u>

Comment: The case of the relative pronoun "who" is incorrect: "whom" is required by its function in the relative clause. An alternative solution simply avoids *whom,* which some readers consider stilted. See *The Copyeditor's Handbook,* chapter 14, under "Case of Nouns and Pronouns." In the first revised version, the nonrestrictive relative clause must be set off by a comma, as explained in *The Copyeditor's Handbook,* chapter 4, under "Function 2: Joining Clauses."

5. Over the past five years, hundreds of millions of dollars of debt attached to Trump's properties ~~has~~ <u>have</u> been securitized and sold to mutual funds and other investment institutions.

Comment: The verb doesn't agree with the subject: amounts of money take a singular verb when a specific sum is named but a plural verb when the sum is vague. See *The Copyeditor's Handbook,* chapter 14, under "Subject-Verb Agreement."

6. In some cases, United will now reimburse providers ~~more than 40 percent~~ less than 60 percent of what it paid out previously.

Comment: The phrase "more than 40 percent less" is a head-scratcher; it should be reworded for clarity. See *The Copyeditor's Handbook,* chapter 7, under "Ambiguous Numerical Statements."

7. Margarine, however, contains trans fatty acid, which is as harmful <u>as,</u> if not ~~more, than~~ more harmful than, saturated fat.

Comment: This construction is an example of faulty ellipsis, the omission of essential words from the construction. See *The Copyeditor's Handbook,* chapter 14, under "More Muddled Syntax."

8. But when the team analyzed the skull fragments, they realized that the skulls ~~neither~~ fit the bill <u>neither</u> for *Homo sapiens* nor <u>for</u> Neanderthals, but that they shared characteristics of both human species.
   OR: "... that the skulls did not fit the bill for either *Homo sapiens* or Neanderthals ..."

Comment: This is an example of faulty parallelism with the correlative conjunctions *neither . . . nor.* The minimally intrusive alternative version sounds a bit more natural. See *The Copyeditor's Handbook,* chapter 14, under "Parallel Form." The addition of a discretionary comma after "Neanderthals" helps readers keep the syntax of the sentence sorted.

9. His hypothesis was based on studies of London taxi drivers, who must memorize thousands of streets and landmarks for a notoriously difficult test called "The Knowledge." Their brains were previously found to have larger hippocampi.

Comment: There's nothing wrong with these sentences: quotations and capitalization with "The Knowledge" are conventional, and *hippocampi* is the correct plural form of *hippocampus.*

10. Still ~~fewer~~ less than five days old, the House Republican bill to repeal Obamacare has an uncertain legislative path ahead.

Comment: The use of "less than" (not "fewer than," as in the original) preceding amounts with plural nouns and numbers (e.g., distances, sums of money, units of time, and statistical enumerations) is completely idiomatic. The criterion for differentiating *fewer* and *less* is not the presence or absence of numbers and count nouns but rather the meaning: does the sentence refer to a countable number or to a unitary quantity? See the discussion of *fewer* and *less* in *The Copyeditor's Handbook,* chapter 14, under "Adjectives and Adverbs."

11. Criminality aside, the fact that so many scientists turn to these informal networks [for distributing scientific literature] ~~begs~~ raises the question of why barriers to access exist in the first place.

Comment: The first meaning of "to beg the question" is "to engage in circular reasoning: to assume the conclusion of an argument in its premise." A secondary meaning, "to raise the question," is now recorded in authoritative dictionaries and is widespread in everyday speech and writing. But this meaning is still spurned by most usage manuals, and it may be misunderstood by those readers familiar with the term from philosophy or logic. See *The Copyeditor's Handbook,* chapter 3, under "Four Essential Books," for a discussion of consulting dictionaries and usage guides to investigate such matters.

12. Geographic disclosure [of profits instead of profitability by product line] was adequate when pretty much all Apple sold ~~were~~ was computers.

Comment: When a noun phrase with *all* is the subject of the verb *to be* and is followed by a plural complement, the linking verb is singular. See *The Copyeditor's Handbook,* chapter 14, under "Subject-Verb Agreement." Better: ". . . when computers were pretty much all Apple sold."

13. ~~Helicobacter pylori~~ *Helicobacter pylori* bacteria, not spicy foods or stress, cause ulcers.~~, not spicy foods or stress.~~

Comment: In most style guides, the scientific (Latin) names of plants and animals are italicized; the genus is capitalized, and the species and subspecies are lowercased. See *The Copyeditor's Handbook,* chapter 6, under "Names of Plants and Animals." Moving the phrase "not spicy foods or stress" avoids a possible misreading as "*H. pylori* bacteria cause ulcers but do not cause spicy foods or stress." See *The Copyeditor's Handbook,* chapter 14, under "Dangling and Misplaced Modifiers."

14. You don't have to read very much about Spermophilus beecheyi . . . to realize that California ground squirrels are nearly human in their adaptability. And humans consider them pests, like all creatures that are nearly human in their adaptability.~~, humans consider them pests.~~

Comment: The phrase "like all creatures that are nearly human in their adaptability" is a misplaced modifier (again, see *The Copyeditor's Handbook,* chapter 14, under "Dangling and Misplaced Modifiers"). And if you were wondering why the species name appears in roman type, *The New York Times Manual of Style and Usage* explicitly says, "Do not use italics for genus and species names." The prohibition or limited use of italics in the *New York Times* (the source of this sentence) and in other newspapers and magazines that follow Associated Press style is "a convention rooted in the era of metal type, when [italics] were usually inaccessible" (*New York Times Style Manual,* s.v. "italics"). (The roman treatment of the scientific name in the previous sentence would also be stetted if the publication in which it appeared followed AP style.)

15. About 20 percent of women who reach menopause ~~naturally~~ by natural means use hormone replacement at least temporarily.

Comment: The adverb "naturally" is a squinting modifier: does it modify "reach" ("who reach menopause *by natural means*") or "use" ("*of course* they use hormone replacement temporarily")? The edited version assumes the former, more likely interpretation. For more examples of squinting modifiers, see *The Copyeditor's Handbook,* chapter 14, under "Dangling and Misplaced Modifiers."

16. Sometimes, to get to the next object the ~~participant~~ participants simply walked across the room. Other times, they had to walk the same distance, but through a door into a new room. From time to time, the researchers gave them a pop quiz, asking which object was currently in their backpack. The quiz was timed so that when they walked through a doorway, they were tested right afterwards. As the title ~~said~~says, walking through doorways caused forgetting: Their responses were both slower and less accurate when they'd walked through a doorway into a new room than when they'd walked the same distance within the same room.

Comment: The problem is one of pronoun-antecedent agreement: the passage switches from the singular noun ("participant") in the first sentence to the plural pronoun ("they") in the following sentences. The simplest solution is to make "participant" plural. Note that the use of the singular "their backpack" rather than the plural "their backpacks" is idiomatic: an example of distributive possession. See *The Copyeditor's Handbook,* chapter 14, under "Pronoun-Antecedent Agreement." "Afterwards" and "afterward" are equal variants—that is, equally acceptable spellings—in American English, although some house styles may specify "afterward" for consistency with the preferred AmE forms "toward," "upward," "downward," "forward," and "backward." Present tense is conventionally used to narrate events described in written texts ("Hamlet says . . ."), hence "As the title says." Although you might be tempted to make other changes to improve this awkwardly worded passage, further revision is unnecessary unless you have been instructed not only to correct errors but also to undertake medium-level editing.

17. For non-Australian readers, it cannot be ~~understated~~ overstated how politically damaging the refugee and detention situation has become for Turnbull and his government, with shocking stories of injury, sickness and scandal coming to light seemingly every week.

Comment: Several common errors of usage involve tangled negatives, which even native English speakers find especially difficult to sort out. When authors write "it cannot be understated" or "it is impossible to underestimate," they usually mean the exact opposite. Tangled negatives are discussed in *The Copyeditor's Handbook,* chapter 15, under "Expository Style," and they are described in *Garner's* (s.v. "underestimate"). Also, note the absence here of the series comma in "injury, sickness and scandal": the *Huffington Post* (now rebranded as *HuffPost*) follows AP style, which omits the series comma unless it is required to prevent misreading.

18. Increase raw and slightly cooked fruits and vegetables, low-fat dairy~~diary fat~~, whole
     grains, fish, poultry, beans, seeds and nuts.

Comment: Your spell-checker won't detect the sneaky typo ("diary" for "dairy"), nor the
inadvertent transposition of words ("low-dairy fat" instead of "low-fat dairy"). The limitations of spell-checkers are described in *The Copyeditor's Handbook,* chapter 5, under
"Spell-Checkers." Once again, the series comma is omitted ("raw and slightly cooked
fruit and vegetables, . . . poultry, beans, seeds and nuts"), possibly following AP style.

19. Algorithms have the capability to shape individuals' decisions without ~~them~~ their
     even knowing it, giving those who have control of the algorithms an unfair position of
     power.

Comment: Is the phrase "without *them* even *knowing* it" a grammatical error of the type
once excoriated as a "fused participle" by H. W. Fowler in *A Dictionary of Modern English
Usage* (1926)? Fowler insisted that the genitive (possessive) form of a noun or pronoun
should always precede any participle used as a noun (i.e., a gerund). But linguists and
subsequent usage commentators from the easygoing Theodore Bernstein (*The Careful
Writer, Miss Thistlebottom's Hobgoblins*) to the decorous Bryan Garner (*Garner's Modern English Usage*) have moderated Fowler's intractable opposition to *all* such constructions. Some of these constructions take the objective case before the gerund as a matter
of idiom: "The chance of that [*not* that's] ever happening is slight"; "Imagine children
as young as twelve years old [*not* old's] being hauled into court." Barring such exceptions, in which the genitive form would sound unnatural to the native English speaker,
the genitive is preferable in the context of a professional report ("their even knowing
it"), although the objective case is common in speech and informal writing ("them even
knowing it"). See the discussion of disputed usages in *The Copyeditor's Handbook,* chapter 14, under "Case of Nouns and Pronouns."

20. ~~Trump~~Trump's demands dog 'Dreamers' deal

Comment: In a quest for concise headlines, journalists sometimes produce amusing
ambiguities. The linguist Ben Zimmer and others have dubbed these gaffes "crash blossoms" after an infamous headline, "Violinist Linked to JAL Crash Blossoms," that once
appeared in the newspaper *Japan Today* (see exercise 15-3). Here, readers may initially
assume that "dog" is a noun, the direct object of the verb "demands." A simple revision
prevents this misreading. Following British style, the headline (from a British publication) uses single quotation marks to flag "Dreamers" as a newly coined term. Note,
too, that the headline uses the plural attributive noun "Dreamers" instead of the plural
possessive form "Dreamers'" to modify "deal." This attributive construction is discouraged by some traditional usage guides but widely accepted in journalism: the *AP Stylebook* explicitly endorses attributive use for plural nouns ending in *s* when the meaning
is *for* or *by* rather than *of* (citizens band radio, teachers college, a Teamsters request).
The sentence-style capitalization of the headline reflects the style of the *Financial Times.*

EXERCISE 14-2: Key

Queries to the author are shown in the Comments panel. Explanations of editorial decisions are provided in endnotes keyed to the text with superscript letters.

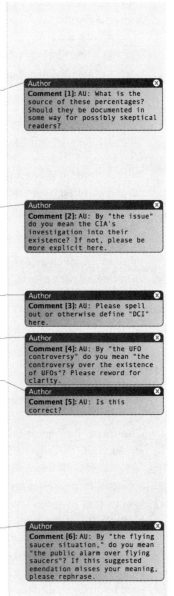

The CIA's Role in the Study of ~~UFO's~~ UFOs, 1947-90 **A**

Some 95 ~~%~~ percent of all Americans ~~at least~~ have at least heard or read something about ~~Unidentified Flying Objects~~ unidentified flying objects (UFOs), and 57 ~~%~~ percent believe they are real. **B** ~~Former U.S. Presidents~~ The former US presidents Jimmy Carter and Ronald Reagan claim~~ed~~ to have seen one. **C** Many ~~UFOlogists~~ ufologists (as UFO buffs are called) and private UFO organizations ~~are found~~ throughout the United States. ~~Many~~ are convinced that the ~~U.S. Government~~ US government—and particularly ~~the Central Intelligence Agency~~CIA ~~are~~ is engaged in a massive conspiracy ~~and coverup of~~ to cover up ~~the issue~~its investigation into their existence. **D** The ~~idea~~ suspicion that the CIA has ~~secretly~~ concealed its research into ~~UFO's~~ UFOs has been a major theme of UFO buffs since the modern UFO ~~phenomena~~ phenomenon emerged in the late ~~1940's~~1940s. **E**

In late 1993, after being ~~pressurized~~ pressured **F** by ~~UFOlogists~~ ufologists for the release of CIA information on ~~UFO's~~UFOs, DCI R. James Woolsey ordered a review of all Agency files on ~~UFO's~~UFOs. Using CIA records compiled from that review, this study traces CIA interest and involvement in the UFO controversy from the late 1940s to 1990. It ~~chronologically examines~~ chronicles the Agency's efforts to solve the mystery of UFO~~'~~s, its programs ~~that had an impact on~~ to investigate UFO sightings, and its attempts to conceal CIA involvement in the entire UFO issue. **G** What emerges from this examination is that, while Agency concern over ~~UFO's~~UFOs was substantial until the early 1950s, the CIA has since ~~only~~ paid only limited and peripheral attention to the ~~phenomena~~phenomenon. **H**

~~Due to~~ Because of the tense Cold War situation and increased Soviet military capabilities, a CIA ~~Study Group~~ study group in the early 1950s saw serious national security concerns in the ~~flying saucer situation~~public alarm over flying saucers. **I** The group believed that the Soviets could use UFO reports to touch off mass hysteria and panic in the United States. The group also believed that the Soviets might use UFO sightings to overload the ~~U.S.~~ US air warning system so that it could not distinguish real targets from phantom ~~UFO's~~UFOs. H. Marshal Chadwell,

Author
Comment [1]: AU: What is the source of these percentages? Should they be documented in some way for possibly skeptical readers?

Author
Comment [2]: AU: By "the issue" do you mean the CIA's investigation into their existence? If not, please be more explicit here.

Author
Comment [3]: AU: Please spell out or otherwise define "DCI" here.

Author
Comment [4]: AU: By "the UFO controversy" do you mean "the controversy over the existence of UFOs"? Please reword for clarity.

Author
Comment [5]: AU: Is this correct?

Author
Comment [6]: AU: By "the flying saucer situation," do you mean "the public alarm over flying saucers"? If this suggested emendation misses your meaning, please rephrase.

Assistant Director of ~~OSI~~, ~~added that he~~ considered the problem of such importance "that it should be brought to the attention of the National Security Council, in order that a communitywide coordinated effort towards ~~it~~ solution ~~may~~ [might] be initiated." **J**

Chadwell briefed DCI ~~Smith~~ on the subject of ~~UFO's~~ UFOs in December~~,~~ 1952. **K** He urged action because he was convinced that "something was going on that must have immediate attention~~.~~," ~~and~~ ~~adding,~~ **L** that ~~"sightings~~ "Sightings of unexplained objects at great altitudes and traveling at high speeds in the vicinity of major U.S. defense installations are of such nature that they are not attributable to natural phenomena or known types of aerial vehicles." He drafted a ~~memoranda~~ memorandum from the DCI to the National Security Council ~~(NSC)~~ and a proposed NSC ~~Directive~~ directive establishing the investigation of ~~UFO's~~ UFOs as a priority project throughout the intelligence and the defense research and development ~~community~~communities. **M** Chadwell also urged Smith to establish an external research project of ~~top level~~ top-level scientists to study the problem of ~~UFO's~~UFOs. **N**

In January~~,~~ 1953, Chadwell and H._P. Robertson, **O** a noted physicist from the California Institute of Technology, put together a distinguished panel of nonmilitary scientists to study the UFO issue. The panel concluded unanimously that there was no evidence of a direct threat to national security in the UFO sightings. Nor could the panel find any evidence that the objects sighted might be ~~extraterrestrials~~extraterrestrial in origin. It did find that continued emphasis on UFO reporting might threaten "the orderly functioning" of the government by clogging the channels of communication with irrelevant reports and by inducing "hysterical mass behavior" harmful to constituted authority. The panel also worried that potential enemies contemplating an attack on the United States might exploit the UFO ~~phenomena~~ phenomenon and use ~~them~~ it to disrupt ~~U.S.~~ US air defenses.

To meet these problems, the panel recommended that the National Security Council debunk UFO reports and institute a policy of public education to reassure the public of the lack of evidence behind ~~UFO's~~UFOs. It suggested using the mass media, advertising, business clubs, schools, and even the Disney corporation to get the message across. Reporting at the height of ~~McCarthyism,~~ the campaign against alleged Communists in the US government and other institutions carried out under Senator Joseph McCarthy, the panel also recommended that such private UFO groups as the Civilian Flying Saucer Investigators in Los Angeles and the Aerial Phenomena Research Organization in Wisconsin be monitored for subversive activities.

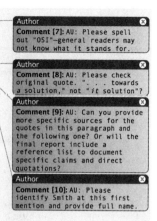

Author ⊗
Comment [7]: AU: Please spell out "OSI"—general readers may not know what it stands for.

Author ⊗
Comment [8]: AU: Please check original quote. ". . . towards *a* solution," not "*it* solution"?

Author ⊗
Comment [9]: AU: Can you provide more specific sources for the quotes in this paragraph and the following one? Or will the final report include a reference list to document specific claims and direct quotations?

Author ⊗
Comment [10]: AU: Please identify Smith at this first mention and provide full name.

Author ⊗
Comment [11]: AU: Rewording OK?

Author ⊗
Comment [12]: AU: OK to explain McCarthyism briefly here? Sorry to say, some readers have never heard the term.

STYLE SHEET

Author/Title: Haines/"The CIA's Role in the Study of UFOs, 1947–90"
Date: February 22, 2018
Dictionary: *Merriam-Webster's Collegiate Dictionary,* 11th ed.; *Merriam-Webster Unabridged*
Style Manual: *The Chicago Manual of Style,* 17th ed.

Alphabetical List of Names and Terms
(n. = noun, adj. = adjective)

Agency (*Chicago* 8.62, 8.63: capitalized as short form of "Central Intelligence Agency")
Assistant Director (*Chicago* 8.20: capitalized in "ceremonial contexts" or "for reasons of courtesy or diplomacy")
Cold War
percent
top-level (adj.)
ufologist
UFOs
unidentified flying objects
US (n., adj.)

Numbers
1947–90 (inclusive years in title)
arabic numerals with percentages (95 percent)
decades: 1940s

COMMENTS

A   "CIA" or "the CIA"? *Chicago* advises that "whether to include the article" before an initialism "may depend on established usage. . . . If no established usage can be determined, use the definite article if it would be used with the spelled-out form" (10.9). To be sure, the CIA's own usage (https://www.cia.gov/) omits the definite article before the initialism. But general interest publications such as Wikipedia typically use the definite article with "CIA," and the editing of this passage for a general interest readership observes this convention.

The plural form "UFOs" (*not* "UFO's") applies the guideline in *Chicago* at 7.15.

Following convention, a comma separates inclusive dates from the preceding elements of the title. According to *Chicago* (9.64), "it is customary but not obligatory to repeat all digits" for inclusive years when they are specified in titles; here the author's styling is preserved.

B   Virtually all general style manuals advise against beginning a sentence with a numeral. (*Chicago* suggests several workarounds at 9.5.) One way to avoid doing so is to insert "some" before the opening number. "Percent" is normally spelled out in nontechnical text.

The repositioning of the adverbial phrase "at least" between the auxiliary and main verbs is discretionary, but the revised syntax sounds more idiomatic than the original.

The initialism "UFO" should be introduced parenthetically at the first mention of unidentified flying objects; the full term is lowercased (*M-W Collegiate*), even though the initialism is capitalized (*Chicago* 10.6).

C   "Former US Presidents" is not a formal title accompanying the personal names. Rather, the names with "presidents" are here used in apposition; hence the term is lowercased and "the" is grammatically mandated. The provision of the presidents' first names is discretionary but consistent with the moderately formal style of this piece.

Chicago (10.32) no longer requires periods with the abbreviation "US" in either the noun or the adjectival form.

The verb "claim" is put in the past tense because that is less jarring: the claims were made in the past, and Reagan died in 2004.

D   A discretionary change: The third and fourth sentences of the original text have been consolidated.

The all-lowercase term "ufologists" is listed in *M-W Collegiate*. A brief parenthetical definition of the term seems desirable for the sake of readers who are *not* "UFO buffs."

"Government" is used descriptively here, hence lowercased.

Although many US readers are likely to know what "CIA" stands for, spell out the name at first occurrence. A parenthetical identification seems unnecessary here, in contrast to the treatment of "UFO," because of readers' likely familiarity with the initials; the initialism can simply be insinuated into the subsequent text (see *Chicago* 10.3).

The verb should agree with the grammatical subject, "the US government"; the term that is set off with a pair of dashes does not affect the number of the verb.

"The issue" is imprecise (as are subsequent references to "the situation"); more direct language can be suggested, subject to the author's approval.

E   Another discretionary change: "suspicion" seems more precise than "idea."

"Secretly concealed" is redundant.

The correct singular form is "phenomenon."

Chicago's recommended plural form for decades has no apostrophe before the *s*.

F   Although many verbs are formed by the addition of the suffix *-ize* to a noun or adjective, usage guides generally caution against unnecessary neologisms, such as "pressurize" for "pressure."

G   Some discretionary improvements in this sentence: "chronologically examines" can be simplified to "chronicles"; parallel structure in the series of items can be improved.

H The roving adverb "only" is here moved closer to the word it modifies; "phenom-ena" is corrected to the singular form, "phenomenon."

I Although the adverbial use of "due to" is fully acceptable, it remains a "skunked" usage; "because of" works well here and is less likely to irritate finicky readers.

By "Soviet capabilities" the author is presumably referring to *military* capabili-ties, but some readers, especially those who weren't alive during the Cold War, may not share this assumption. It seems preferable to make it explicit.

The descriptive "study group" doesn't require capitalization.

J In the direct quotation, the modal verb "may" is replaced by "[might]," in brackets to denote an editorial interpolation or substitution, so that the quotation better fits with the past tense of the sentence in which it is embedded.

K No comma is needed in a date consisting only of a month and year. See also the correction in "January 1953" at the beginning of the following paragraph.

L The following part of the quotation is now formally introduced (". . . adding, 'Blah blah blah'") so that the present tense verb "are" works in the context.

M The singular form, "memorandum," is required here.

"Directive" in "a proposed NSC directive" is descriptive; capitalization is not required.

N The compound adjective "top-level" should be hyphenated.

O *Chicago* calls for a space (or fixed space) between personal initials preceding a sur-name: H. P. Robertson.

EXERCISE 15-1: Key

Queries demonstrate possible ways to address issues and to explain proposed revisions to an author. Adjudication of deep issues, ones that cannot be solved by sentence-level revisions alone, may need to be referred to the publisher.

As usual, the queries in this key are directed to an imaginary author; stricken-through text suggests the sort of restraint sometimes required to address biased language or offensive content in a professional manner. Queries are followed by explanatory comments.

1. [From a health pamphlet addressed to first-time parents:]

    ~~A new mother~~ New parents can begin bonding by cradling ~~her baby~~ and gently stroking ~~him or her~~ their baby in different patterns. ~~She~~ They can also take the opportunity to be "skin-to-skin," holding ~~her~~ their newborn against ~~her~~ their own skin while feeding or cradling.

    Query: Rewording OK to include both parents? Suggested changes also allow you to avoid the clunky "him or her" wording.

Comment: A document advising first-time parents should not unnecessarily exclude spouses and partners. The author deserves credit for trying to avoid "generic *he*" when referring to a newborn of unspecified sex, but the "him or her" construction is cumbersome and can often be avoided by using other strategies.

2. [From a Wikipedia article about a medical breakthrough:]

    Surgery to separate ~~Siamese~~ conjoined twins may be easy or difficult. The surgery can result in the death of one or both twins, especially if they are joined at the head or share vital organs. In 1955 the neurosurgeon Harold Voris and his team at Mercy Hospital in Chicago performed the first successful operation to separate ~~Siamese~~ twins joined at the head.

    Query: Changed to the medical term now in use: "conjoined twins."

Comment: The fame of the conjoined twins from Thailand, Chang and Eng Bunker, who traveled with P. T. Barnum's circus for many years, gave rise in the nineteenth century to the misnomer "Siamese twins." It is now considered an offensive and misleading label for a rare condition that occurs throughout the world.

3. [From a review of a television program:]

    Carrie Mathison (Claire Danes), the protagonist of the series *Homeland*, ~~suffers from manic depression~~ has bipolar disorder, which makes her volatile and unpredictable.

Query: The *Diagnostic and Statistical Manual of Mental Disorders (DSM)* now uses "bipolar disorder" for this mood disorder. Does the condition cause Carrie to be totally unreliable, as the wording implies? If her volatility manifests only when the disorder is not being medically managed, please reword ~~so she doesn't get fired~~.

Comment: Careful writers and editors avoid outmoded and often prejudicial terms referring to mental illnesses. They choose neutral verbs, such as *to have* or *to experience,* instead of phrases such as *suffer from* and *afflicted with,* which imply passivity or victimization. And, to deflect the stigmatization of words such as *crazy, nuts, unpredictable,* and the like, they describe some mental disorders, including bipolarity, as chronic conditions similar to medically managed organic diseases. (Bipolar disorder affects about 2.6 percent of the US adult population.)

4. [From a history of the US moonwalk in 1969:]

    Mission commander Neil Armstrong was the first man to set foot on the lunar surface. His description of the event—"one small step for man, one giant leap for mankind"— was broadcast on live television worldwide.

    Query: Armstrong was also the first *human* to set foot on the lunar surface ~~unless some nameless woman got there first~~. Change or stet? Your choice.

Comment: Although NASA later parenthetically emended Armstrong's words ("for [a] man") on his say-so, an editor would never change Armstrong's actual words. And probably the next astronaut, man or woman, who walks on a celestial body other than Earth will choose gender-neutral language to announce *humanity's* achievement.

5. [From a financial adviser's letter to clients:]

    In the stock market crash of September 29, 2008, the Dow Jones Industrial Average fell 777.68 points in intraday trading. The largest point drop in history until 2018, it was a ~~literal holocaust~~ calamity for individual retirement accounts, which lost 40 percent of their value overnight.

    Query: "Holocaust" is so freighted with historical significance (the Nazi Holocaust) that even when the word is lowercased, it is usually understood to refer only to actual genocide. Readers may find this use of the word offensively trivializing, even when modified by "literal" (in the popular but proscribed sense of "figurative" or "virtual").

Comment: Don't let the author solve the problem by putting *holocaust* in scare quotes, those distancing quotation marks that mean "so-called." This is not a word to be used lightly or ironically.

6. [From the website for an art gallery expanding its US-based business to Canada:]

We source the best objects of ~~Eskimo~~ Inuit and Indian art for serious collectors, offer a fine selection of ethnic jewelry for our discriminating customers, and restore Oriental rugs.

Query: Canadians consider "Eskimo" offensive and prefer "Inuit." Also, please revise to clarify whether "Indian" art means art from India, American Indian art, or the art of First Nations peoples of Canada.

Comment: If the term "ethnic" seems condescending here (i.e., to mean "not of the dominant culture"), the author could consider using "folk," "traditional," or "tribal." Note that the word "Oriental" is highly offensive when used as a noun or adjective referring to people, but it is accepted when used to describe rugs.

7. [From an academic study of Christianity:]

According to the belief system of the followers of this Christian sect, God does not need to be reconciled to man, for ~~His~~ his divine love is unchanging. Rather, it is man who must be reconciled with his Maker.

Query: Scholarly studies generally lowercase God-related pronouns ("his" rather than "His") but capitalize synonyms for God as a supreme being ("Maker").

Comment: The gendered language of these sentences presumably reflects this religious sect's belief system and should be stetted as an accurate description.

8. [From parking instructions for a public building:]

Handicapped parking spots are reserved for ~~the disabled~~people with disabilities. Be considerate! ~~People confined to wheelchairs~~ Individuals with impaired mobility need ramp access to the entrance.

Query: "People with disabilities" and "disabled persons" are the currently preferred terms. "People confined to wheelchairs" is revised here because handicapped parking is used by individuals with many different kinds of disabilities who require easy access to a building.

Comment: "The disabled" reduces whole persons to a single attribute (a disability); "confined to wheelchairs" describes people solely in terms of a limitation. Note, too, that the term "handicap" is in disfavor but persists in some official signage: many signs marking such parking spots really do say "Handicapped parking" (or "Handicap parking"), so this term must stand.

9. [From a sociological analysis of gender relations in the workplace:]

Why do ~~we~~ some colleagues resent a woman who interrupts a male speaker? The answer may be that ~~we~~ they fear female ~~aggression~~ assertiveness and expect deference to male authority. Why do ~~we~~ they fail to take women's opinions seriously when ~~their~~ women end sentences ~~end~~ with ~~that characteristic~~ a rising intonation? Because ~~we~~ they hear "uptalk" in women's speech as diffidence.

Query: ~~Dude, speak for yourself!~~ Revised because the use of "we" (meaning colleagues? supervisors?) may seem presumptuous here: some readers will not share these reactions to female assertiveness or perceive diffidence in certain speech patterns. Also, many linguists hold that a rising intonation at the end of a statement ("uptalk") is not characteristically female but occurs with equal frequency in men's speech.

Comment: Watch out for the presumptuous "we"! But note that this passage may require the publisher's adjudication: what the writer perceives as "aggression," the editor characterizes as "assertiveness"; the editor also directly challenges the author's description of uptalk as a "characteristic" female speech pattern. Justified or not, these emendations trespass on the author's domain: interpretation and content.

10. [From the introduction to a book on the "exceptionalism" of US art:]

The element of frontiering individualism that is so historically distinctive in the ~~American~~ US condition has endowed ~~our~~ the country's artists and thinkers with an appetite for risk and exploration that sets them off from the European backdrop of ~~our~~ its settlement and ancestry.

Query: I assume you mean "US" here. (In this context, "American" could be misunderstood to refer to North and South America.) Also, in a publication intended for a world audience, "our" and "the European backdrop of . . . settlement and ancestry" may sound parochial. I suggest you avoid any such misperception by qualifying the terms ("*early* settlement and ancestry") so the reference to the formation of the original colonies is explicit.

Comment: Watch out for the presumptuous "our" too. Once again, the publisher may have to weigh in. Wait and see whether this author proves intransigent.

11. [From the preface to a lower division college textbook:]

The composition of the undergraduate student body at American colleges and universities has significantly changed in recent decades. It now includes a far more diverse group of people in terms of backgrounds and ages. While encouraging the enrollment of these new students, colleges and their faculties have not always adapted their curriculum, learning-skills programs, and teaching styles to fit these new students' needs and concerns. The result is that today students and faculty often come into classrooms not sharing important understandings regarding what needs to be learned and how to learn it. What students often require is a short guide to the "secrets" of learning —how-to lessons of ways to navigate a challenging book, for example, without getting lost in a sea of details. Someone should have shown you this in high school. Unless you went to an elite private or public school, however, it is likely that they did not. Do not fear, it is easy to learn.

Comment: This passage drips with condescension. Call the publisher for guidance.

EXERCISE 15-2: Key

The balloons alongside the redlined text show insertions, deletions, and author queries; the queries, here called "Comments," are identified by bracketed numbers tethered to the queried word or phrase. An author would peruse the changes and queries, along with the provisional style sheet (here placed at the end of the document), when reviewing the editing.

Substantive and discretionary changes are explained in the comments addressed to the author. Explanations of minor and mechanical changes, which are flagged in the text with lettered superscripts and printed after the redlined manuscript and style sheet, are provided here only for purposes of this answer key. An author would, of course, never see these remarks.

Make sure you have provided the appropriate markup, corrected all the basic errors and inconsistencies, and recorded your style decisions on your style sheet. Then review the language editing. The discretionary language editing in your corrected version will doubtless differ from that of this answer key: no two editors are likely to make exactly the same discretionary changes in a manuscript. Ask yourself whether you would have made or refrained from making the changes shown on the following pages. If you made other changes, can you explain them?

<GT-ni>The Plain Language Action ~~And~~ and Information Network (PLAIN) is a community of Federal employees dedicated to the idea that citizens deserve clear communications from the Government. **A** We first developed this document in the mid-1990s. **B** ~~. We continue to revise~~ and we update it every few years ~~to provide updated advice on clear communication~~. We hope ~~you find this document useful, and~~ that it helps you improve ~~your writing – and~~ your agency's writing —so ~~your users~~ citizens can: **C**

- <BL-f>find what they need,
- <BL-m>understand what they find; , and
- <BL-l>use what they find to meet their needs.

<GT>We've divided the document into five major topics, ~~although many of the subtopics fit within more than one topic~~. We ~~start~~ begin **D** with a discussion of your ~~audience~~ readers because you should think about them before you start to write ~~your document or your web content. In fact, you should start to think about them~~ and even **E** before you start to plan. From there we move to organization, because developing a good organization is important during your planning stage. Next, we discuss writing principles, starting at the word level and moving up through paragraphs and sections. ~~This is the most extensive topic~~. We ~~follow~~ describe both principles of writing ~~documents with~~ for print and principles of writing for the web. **F** We conclude with a short discussion of testing techniques. **G**

When we first wrote this document, we were primarily interested in regulations. We've broadened our coverage, but the document still bears the stamp of its origin. If you have a suggestion ~~about something we should add to address other types of writing,~~ or ~~have~~ **H** a comment on this edition, contact us at www.plainlanguage.gov/contactus.cfm.

[• • •]

<H1>I. Think about your audience

<GT-ni>One of the most popular plain language **I** myths is that you have to "dumb down" **J** your content so that everyone everywhere can read it. That's not true. The first rule of plain language is: **K** to write for your audience. Use

---

Author ⊗
Comment [1]: AU: OK to prune and consolidate the three sentences beginning "We first developed . . ."? In keeping with the spirit of the plain language guidelines, some nips and tucks of this sort are suggested throughout—all subject to your approval, of course.

Author ⊗
Comment [2]: AU: To avoid eliciting a defensive response here, better to suggest that the agency's writing—but not necessarily that of the individual reader of this document—may need help to improve? Also use "citizens," consistent with previous term, rather than "users," a term not yet introduced or defined?

Author ⊗
Comment [3]: AU: To "find what they need . . . [to] meet their needs" (this formulation is repeated below) sounds somewhat tautological. Consider shortening the last point (in both instances) to read, simply, "use what they find"? Or is this a set-in-stone formulation among plain language advocates?

Author ⊗
Comment [4]: AU: OK to delete this potentially distracting explanation?

Author ⊗
Comment [5]: AU: Substituting "readers" here solves the agreement problem with the subsequent plural pronoun "them." Change OK?

Author ⊗
Comment [6]: AU: OK to delete this aside?

language your audience knows and feels comfortable with. Take your audience's ~~current~~ level of knowledge into account. Don't write for an ~~8th~~ eighth-grade class if your audience is composed of PhD candidates, small business owners, working parents, or immigrants. ~~Only w~~Write for ~~8ᵗʰ~~ eighth graders _only_ if your audience is, in fact, an ~~8ᵗʰ~~ eighth-grade class. **L**

        <GT>Make sure you know who your audience ~~us~~is— don't guess or assume.

[• • •]

<H1>IV~~.~~—.—Write for the web

<GT-ni>This section refers to ~~the audience~~ readers as _users,_ since that is a more common term in the web community. To <u>write web content that</u> effectively communicate_s_ with your ~~web~~ users, you must use ~~plain-language~~ <u>plain language</u> techniques ~~to write web content~~. This section ~~will~~ explain_s_ the differences between print and web writing and ~~how to create~~ <u>the methods for creating a web</u>sites**M** that work_s_ for your users.

<H2>a. ~~How do people use the web?~~<u>Learn how people use the web</u>

<GT-ni>People use the internet to easily find, understand, and ~~use~~ <u>apply</u> information <u>needed</u> to complete a task. Unlike <u>readers of</u> print media, ~~people~~ <u>web users</u>**N** do not read entire ~~web~~ pages. They scan instead. Nielsen and Morkes, in a famous 1997 study, found that 79 percent of their test users always scanned ~~any~~ new web page_s_ ~~they came across~~; only 16 percent read ~~word by word~~<u>word for word</u>.

    <GT>Even with more people using the web, the percentage**O** of content that is read on a website has not increased by much. ~~—~~Here are some facts to consider when writing web content:

- <BL-f>In a 2008 study, based on analysis of 45,237 page views, Nielsen found that web users ~~only~~ read <u>only</u>**P** about 18% <u>percent</u> of ~~what's one~~ <u>the text on a web</u> page.

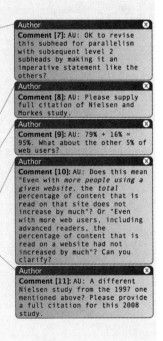

- <BL-m>As the number of words on a ~~web~~ page goes up, the percentage read goes down.
- <BL-l>To get people to read half ~~of~~ your words, you must limit your page to 110 words or ~~fewer~~ less. **Q**

<H3>What do web users look |at|?

Comment [12]: AU: This is the only level 3 subhead, an asymmetry that may seem illogical to readers. Integrate this lonely heading with subsequent running text?

<GT-ni>Since we know web users scan web pages, we need to learn what they look at. Users often scan ~~web~~ pages in an F pattern‸ focusing on the top left side of the page, headings, and the first few words of ~~a~~ sentence~~s~~ ~~or~~ and bulleted list~~s~~. On average, users ~~only~~ read only **R** the first two words on each line. Also, ~~users can~~ they may decide in as little as five seconds whether your site is useful to them.

<H2>b. Write for your users

<GT-ni>Think about how well your website allows ~~customers~~ users to get something done.

Comment [13]: AU: Switch from "users" to "customers" (here and in the bulleted list that follows) might momentarily confuse readers. Better to stick with "users," defined at the beginning of this section as the preferred term?

- <BL-f>~~Customers~~ Users come to your site to perform a task.
- <BL-l>They ~~come because they~~ expect ~~to get~~ self-service.

<GT>~~People come to your website with a specific task in mind.~~ If your website doesn't help them complete that task, they'll leave.

Comment [14]: AU: Sentence is a nearly verbatim repetition of the first bullet point above. OK to delete here?

You need to identify ~~the mission — the purpose — of your website, to help you clarify~~ the top task~~s~~ your website should help people accomplish.

<H2>c. Identify your users and their |needs ~~top tasks~~|

Comment [15]: AU: Revised subhead wording to avoid nearly verbatim repetition of the previous sentence. OK?

<GT-ni>In order to write for your users, you need to know who they are! Here are some general tips to help you identify ~~your users~~ them:

- <BL-f>Listen to user~~s~~' questions‸ ~~—~~ ~~w~~What do your visitors ask when they send you an email or call your office?

- <BL-m>Talk to users and ask them what they want.
- <BL-l>Analyze your web metrics to figure out what people are looking for on your website:

<UL1-f>What are your most-visited pages and where do people spend the most time?

<UL1-l>What top search phrases do people use?

<GT>There are many techniques to help you learn about your users. For details and best practices, visit www.usability.gov.

<H2>d. Write web content

<GT-ni>After identifying your users and their top tasks, ~~it is time to actually~~ begin to write your web content. ~~If you think it would be easy to just duplicate information you've~~ You can't simply reuse what you've written for print documents~~, you are wrong~~. While the information is helpful, it's not in the right format for the web. Remember, people scan web pages and ~~only~~ read only**s** about 18 percent of what's on the page~~!~~. This means you need to cut whatever you have in print form by 50 percent! Good web content uses÷

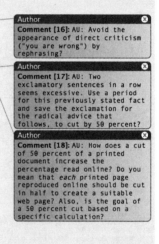

- <BL-f>~~T~~the inverted pyramid style. Begin with the shortest and clearest statement you can make about your topic. Put the most important information at the top and the background at the bottom.
- <BL-m>~~C~~chunked content. Don't try to pack everything into long paragraphs. Split topics up into logical sections separated by informative headings.
- <BL-l>~~O~~only necessary information÷. ~~Use~~ Provide only the information your users need to achieve their top~~s~~ tasks. Omit unnecessary information.

<GT>Remember: your content is NOT clear unless your users can

~~Your content is NOT clear unless your users can:~~

- <BL-f>~~Find~~ _find_ what they need~~.~~
- <BL-m>~~Understand~~ _understand_ what they find_, and_
- <BL-l>~~Use~~ _use_ what they find to meet their needs_._

<H2>e. Repurpose print material for the web

<GT-ni>Don't _just_ cut and paste the text of print documents to create web content. _Print writing is different from web writing. It is linear and narrative driven. In print you can include details and interesting stories. But interesting stories don't work on the web. Instead they slow down users who are trying to accomplish a task._ People are more likely to leave your web_page, potentially costing you time and money_, because they will not take the time to find what they are looking for.

~~Print writing is different from web writing. Print is very linear and narrative driven. In print, you can go into great detail about mundane things like eating breakfast. If you are a great writer, that can be an interesting story. But, those interesting stories don't work on the web. Instead they slow down web users who are trying to accomplish a task.~~

<GT>Jakob Nielsen (useit.com) explains that "web users want _actionable_ content; they don't want to fritter away their time on (otherwise enjoyable) stories that are tangential to their current goals." _Because the web is "action-oriented," you need to repurpose your print document._ Pick out ~~necessary~~ _only the essential, helpful_ information in your print version ~~document that will help your web users~~ _and create a new web page._

~~Because the web is "action-oriented," you need to repurpose your print document. Pick out necessary information in your print document that will help your web users and create a new web page.~~

- <BL-f>Keep the _clearest,_ most important ~~and clear~~ message at the top of the web page~~.~~
- <BL-m>Chunk your content into logical sections~~.~~
- <BL-m>Use headings to help users navigate the content~~.~~
- <BL-m>Highlight key facts in ~~a~~ bulleted list_s._
- <BL-l>Explain complex instructions in a visually appealing If/Then table.

Author ⊗
Comment [19]: AU: Repeated goals are reformatted (initial lowercasing, punctuation at the end of items) to match the first iteration above. See my query there about the apparent redundancy in the third item. OK to revise this item?

Author ⊗
Comment [20]: AU: The following paragraph seems to belong here, but the asides about "mundane things like eating breakfast" and "if you are a great writer . . . ." are potentially distracting. OK to consolidate here?

Author ⊗
Comment [21]: AU: Loss of "time and money" seems irrelevant here. Government institutions that provide services to citizens just want website visitors to find and use needed information without leaving in frustration, right? Consider deleting "potentially costing you time and money" as a misdirection?

Author ⊗
Comment [22]: AU: This partial URL leads to a website of the Nielsen Norman Group, of which Jakob N. is presumably a partner. But where is this quotation to be found? Can you provide a more complete citation?

Author ⊗
Comment [23]: AU: OK to add these two sentences to the previous one to create a single paragraph?

STYLE SHEET

Author/Title: US Government Publishing Office/From *Federal Plain Language Guidelines*
Date: February 22, 2018
Dictionary: *Merriam-Webster's Collegiate Dictionary*, 11th ed.; *Merriam-Webster Unabridged*
Style Manual: *GPO Style Manual*, 31st ed. (*GPO*); *The Chicago Manual of Style*, 17th ed.

Alphabetical List of Names and Terms
(n. = noun, adj. = adjective)

action-oriented (adj.)
eighth graders
eighth-grade class
Federal (adj.)
Government (referring to US; n., adj.)
internet (n., adj.)
percent (with numerals)
PhD
Plain Language Action and Information Network (PLAIN)
plain language (adj.)
web (n., adj.)
web page (n.)
website (n.)

Capitalization and Numbers Treatment
follow *GPO*
1990s

Punctuation
Use series comma

Styles for Vertical Lists
Lowercase first words of items completing an introductory sentence (unless proper nouns); separate items by the punctuation that would separate them in a run-in list; conclude with a period
Capitalize first words of list items that are full sentences; use terminal periods

COMMENTS ON EDITING

You may appreciate the irony of correcting deficiencies in a text intended as a model of the very principles of clear writing that it advocates. Some of the features of plain language style in this excerpt, annoying though they may seem to advanced writers, should be preserved: short paragraphs; frequent bulleted lists; simple sentences; basic, sometimes repetitive, diction; informal (but not incorrect) register, characterized by direct address ("you"), contractions, occasional split infinitives, and prepositional endings to sentences. Still, these excerpts could benefit from applying plain language guidelines more rigorously, particularly the timeless advice to "omit needless words" and to eliminate digressions, distracting details, and unnecessary exceptions. The result is more direct, but it's hardly elegant. Editing, like politics, is the art of the possible.

A   Capitalization of "Federal" and "Government" in this sentence follows GPO style.

B   Treatment of decades follows GPO style.

C   The colon has been deleted because the words that precede the list do not form an independent clause.

D   In this and the next sentence, the verb "start" is deployed four times to refer to different "starting" actions. Substituting "begin" for the one action with a different actor (i.e., the writers of this document) helps keep things sorted.

E   The changes here and below ("This is the most extensive topic") consolidate and excise more needless verbiage, as a polite query to the author explains.

F   The word "follow" could be misread here as meaning "to heed or obey." The suggested "describe" clarifies the meaning, and the parallelism created with the addition of "both . . . and" enforces the intended contrast between print and web writing.

G   This paragraph provides a road map of the document. Such signposting is considered inelegant in literary writing (see the discussion of signposting in *The Copyeditor's Handbook,* chapter 15, under "Organization") but is commonplace in instructions and in business and technical writing. Just keep it brief.

H   These changes omit more needless words.

I   Why no hyphen in "plain language" when it is used as an attributive adjective? *Chicago* hyphenates the form in an interview with the plain language (plain-language) advocate Iva Cheung at *CMOS Shop Talk* (http://cmosshoptalk.com/2018/01/16/ iva-cheung-talks-about-plain-language-accessibility-and-cartooning/); however, *GPO,* the manual specified for this exercise, advises that "when meaning is clear and readability is not aided, it is not necessary to use a hyphen to form a temporary or made compound. Restraint should be exercised in forming unnecessary combinations of words used in normal sequence" (6.16). In other words, *Chicago* uses hyphens more liberally than *GPO* in forming temporary compounds; *GPO* concedes more editorial discretion in the matter.

J   There is no need to use scare quotes to set off this informal but standard expression (according to *M-W Unabridged*); if it seems too informal to stand without the distancing quote marks, better to substitute another word, such as *simplify*.

K   Again, no colon is used directly after a verb: the preceding words of the sentence must form an independent clause.

L   The treatment of ordinal numbers (eighth-grade, eighth graders) follows GPO style. The adverb "only" is moved closer to the words it modifies here and in several subsequent sentences—not a correction but an improvement in precision (see the discussion of "roving *only*" in *The Copyeditor's Handbook,* chapter 14, under "Dangling and Misplaced Modifiers").

M   This change corrects faulty parallelism between "differences between" and "how to create."

N   Here is a classic dangling modifier: the phrase beginning with "unlike" must modify the subject of the following main clause. See *The Copyeditor's Handbook,* chapter 14, under "Dangling and Misplaced Modifiers."

O   *Percent,* used with numerals in nontechnical writing, is not interchangeable with the noun *percentage:* "Only 16 percent of web users read text word for word; that's a very small percentage of users." See *The Copyeditor's Handbook,* chapter 7, under "Percentages, Percentage Points, Basis Points, Percentiles, and Portions."

P   Once again, moving "only" closer to the word it modifies clarifies the meaning.

Q   The expression "*x* words or less" (not *fewer*) is idiomatic. See the discussion of *fewer* and *less* in *The Copyeditor's Handbook,* chapter 14, under "Adjectives and Adverbs."

R   Again, moving "only" closer to the word it modifies provides greater clarity.

S   Yep, moving "only" again.

EXERCISE 15-3: Key

A transmittal letter or, sometimes, a less formal message typically accompanies an edited manuscript when the editor returns it to the editorial coordinator or sends it directly to the author for review. Transmittals usually include the features described in the headnote to exercise 2-6 and discussed in *The Copyeditor's Handbook*, chapter 2, under "Informal Communications and Transmittal Letters."

This letter goes a bit beyond the standard boilerplate in engaging with the author on issues of content and writing style. It also suggests how such heavy editing might be presented to an author. (To be sure, there's no guarantee that every author will tolerate this level of intrusion.) A printout of the "final," or clean, view can be sent to the author along with the redlined version. Although the embedded query flags are retained, the final view (here following the transmittal letter) allows the author to read the edited text without the distraction of the underlying tracked changes; the printout of the "final showing markup" (redlined) view allows the author to peruse the proposed changes behind the polished version.

Corrections to grammar and editorial style follow *M-W Unabridged* and *Chicago*. A style sheet accompanies the redlined version. Discretionary changes are flagged in curly brackets, using a stenographic style for embedded query flags (e.g., {**Q1**}); the proposed changes are explained in the query list below the style sheet.

February 15, 2018

Dear Mr. Newsman:

What an entertaining piece! I enjoyed learning about the old skill of "counting heads" and the transformation of headline writing in our era of computerized production and newsfeeds. The readers of [newsletter title] will doubtless share my interest in this history.

In the file-sharing folder that my separate email communication invites you to access, you will find the following documents to download and review:

a clean edited version of your newsletter article (with my queries)
an edited version (also with my queries) showing all proposed changes
a style sheet for reference

I have followed the publisher's stipulated style manual (*The Chicago Manual of Style*, 17th edition) and dictionary (the online *Merriam-Webster Unabridged*). The accompanying style sheet itemizes style decisions.

My editing uses the Track Changes feature of Microsoft Word, showing deletions struck through and insertions underlined. Queries are flagged in-line with boldface braces ({**Q1**}) and placed below the document. The edited files are "protected," so your on-screen changes and comments in response to the editing will also be tracked. If you are unfamiliar with the process of on screen review, don't hesitate to ask me for help!

Please review the proposed changes carefully, make any desired corrections and additions, and answer the editorial queries. This will be your last chance to make substantive changes. In the proof stage the publisher allows only essential corrections.

I encourage you to read through the "clean" edited draft first in order to form a clear impression of the revised version. Then peruse the "redlined" draft to view the proposed changes in detail and respond to the editing queries on this version. Bear in mind that where I have suggested moving a word, phrase, or sentence from one position to another, the manuscript will show two changes: the deleted copy in its original position and the (same) added copy in the new position. (In other words, the editing is not as radical as it might first appear! This is just the way Track Changes represents such alterations.)

As you requested, I cut nearly 100 words by trimming and consolidating where possible. In addition, I suggested reformatting the instructions for counting heads to help readers grasp this complex system, breaking up several extra-long paragraphs in view of the [newsletter title's] two-column format, and adding a needed transitional sentence. These discretionary changes are, of course, subject to your approval.

The production schedule for [newsletter title] calls for you to email the edited manuscript back to me by [date]. Meanwhile, if you have any questions or concerns, please phone or email me.

Edna E. Editor
[phone number]
[email address]

CLEAN COPY

Headlines, Counting Heads, Crash Blossoms, Eisenhower, and Clickbait{Q1}

{Q2}"If you had to reduce all the rules and recommendations of headline writing to two, they would be: the head must fit and it must tell the story." That's what the veteran newsman John B. Bremner used to tell his journalism students at the University of Kentucky. In the era of print news, language and aesthetics intersected in the creation of newspaper headlines. They consisted of words but also broke up text-heavy pages of news, directed the eye's attention, and sometimes startled readers with unusual typography and shapes. Reporters{Q3} called them *heads*, but when news editors wrote instructions on the layout for a news page, they would deliberately misspell the word *hed* to make sure it was not accidentally typeset and printed along with the news copy that Linotype operators retyped from the layout sheet, or dummy.{Q4}

In a printed newspaper, headlines can run a single line or two or three lines deep, depending on the number of columns given to a story. A single line may suffice for the head of a story that occupies half the width of the news page, but the head for a single-column story may require several lines and cannot exceed the width of the column. That's where "counting heads" came in before computer technology supplanted traditional printing skills. Al JaCoby{Q5}, who reported for the *San Diego Union* from the 1950s through the 1970s, could remember when an experienced news editor exactly fit headlines to the width of a newspaper column by counting heads.

{Q6}Typically, the editor would calculate this way:

0.5 points: lowercase f's, l's, i's, t's, and j's; punctuation; wordspaces
1.0 points: other lowercase letters (except m's and w's); capital I; number 1
1.5 points: lowercase m's and w's; all capital letters and numerals except capital I and number 1 (above) and capital M and W (below)
2.0 points: capital M's and W's

Thus "Ike" counted as 3 points, "JFK" and "LBJ" were each allotted 4.5, and "Nixon," the subject of many headlines, counted as 5. "I knew guys who used their knuckles to count out heads. Others would tap out the count with their fingers," JaCoby recalled. One editor of his acquaintance could write a headline in his mind and compare it to a model line and simply know if it would fit.{Q7}

If a head was too long, an editor would eliminate or substitute words until it fit the allotted measure. But attempts to abridge headlines sometimes went awry. Fitting headlines into the procrustean bed of column width drove some news editors to extremes. JaCoby recalled the practice of the now-defunct *San Antonio Light* of using "ack-ack" (6.5) for "machine gun" (10.5) and "hijack" (5) for "holdup" (5.5), possibly misleading readers into thinking that an anti-aircraft gun had been used in a gang dustup or that a bodega had been not merely robbed but hauled away on a flatbed truck. The annals of print journalism (and now the internet) are full of examples of miscues that owe to the overly telegraphic wording of headlines:

Eye Drops off Shelf
Kids Make Nutritious Snacks
Stolen Painting Found by Tree
Violinist Linked to JAL Crash Blossoms

This last example—about a violinist whose career blossomed after his father was killed in the crash of a Japan Airlines flight—has given these misleading headlines a name: crash blossoms.

In the days of hot metal typesetting, even the skillful pruning and swapping of words in heads didn't always work. JaCoby recounted the story of the *New York Times*'s "Eisenhower Skinny S." The tradition-bound *Times* would never stoop to using "IKE" in an all-caps headline. But "EISENHOWER SAYS" was a half-count too long for a single-column article in the *Times,* so in 1952 the *Times*'s editors sent off to Linotype's foundry to have a custom brass matrix made for the president's name, half a count shorter, to use whenever "EISENHOWER SAYS" was needed. According to a 1952 account, the typecasters redrew the letters of Eisenhower's name (not just the *S*) and reduced the spaces between them, creating a logotype—a single piece of type that prints a cluster of letters—so "EISENHOWER SAYS" would fit over a single-column news report.

{Q8}Although the skill of counting heads declined with the advent of computers in newspaper production, the clever headline remains. Wordplay is often encouraged, particularly in features and humorous pieces, although some newspapers explicitly prohibit humor and punning, at least in serious news pieces. Attention-grabbing headlines often play opposites against each other, use a word with a double meaning, invert an idiomatic expression, alter the spelling or pronunciation of a common expression, build a series, surprise with an unusual combination, or use alliteration or rhyme. One of the most memorable headlines of the twentieth century (along with "Dewey Defeats Truman") is

Headless Body in Topless Bar

It was printed in the *New York Post* in 1983 and made its creator, Vincent A. Musetto, so famous that it was mentioned in his 2015 obituary.

{Q9}Today, if you encountered such a headline in your social media newsfeed, you might dismiss it as clickbait. True, the internet didn't create sensational headlines. Wordplay and provocative content have always characterized journalists' efforts to attract readers. The difference is this: traditional news aims to capture the essence of a news report in a pithy, attention-grabbing headline; clickbait overpromises and often misrepresents content to lure readers to another website and thus to generate advertising income that is based on page views. Copyfitting skill and linguistic ingenuity are rarely required to create these nearly irresistible headlines, which depend on manipulative formulas, such as so-called listicles ("7 Reasons You Can't Resist This Headline"), and appeals to the emotions of curiosity and outrage ("You Won't Believe" or "What Happened Next Will Shock You").

{Q10}Sources: Jane T. Harrigan and Karen Brown Dunlap, *The Editorial Eye*, 2nd ed. (Boston: Bedford/St. Martin's, 2004). "John B. Bremner," Wikipedia, https://en.wikipedia .org/, accessed February 15, 2018. Adrienne LaFrance, "The Legend of Eisenhower's Skinny 'S,'" *The Atlantic*, June 14, 2016, https://www.theatlantic.com/. Blanca Gonzalez, "Obituary: Alfred JaCoby," *San Diego Union-Tribune*, June 4, 2008, http://legacy .sandiegouniontribune.com/. Ben Zimmer, "Crash Blossoms," *New York Times Magazine*, January 27, 2010, http://www.nytimes.com/. Margalit Fox, "Vincent Musetto, 74, Dies; Wrote 'Headless' Headline of Ageless Fame," *New York Times*, June 9, 2015, https://www .nytimes.com/. Jeffrey Dvorkin, "Why Click-Bait Will Be the Death of Journalism," PBS NewsHour (website), April 27, 2016, https://www.pbs.org/. Bryan Gardiner, "You'll Be Outraged at How Easy It Was to Get You to Click on This Headline," *Wired*, December 18, 2015, https://wired.com/.

REDLINED COPY WITH STYLE SHEET AND QUERIES

Headlines, Counting Heads, Crash Blossoms, Eisenhower, and ~~Click-Bait~~Clickbait{Q1}

~~Australian-American~~ newsman ~~and Professor of Journalism at the University of Kentucky John B. Bremner, who was born in 1920 and died of cancer in 1987, taught his students that~~ {Q2}"If you had to reduce all the rules and recommendations of headline writing to two, they would be: the head must fit and it must tell the story." That's what the veteran newsman John B. Bremner used to tell his journalism students at the University of Kentucky. In the era of print news, language and ~~esthetics~~ aesthetics intersected in the creation of ~~a~~ newspaper headlines. They consisted of words but also broke up ~~text~~ text-heavy pages of news, directed the eye's attention, and sometimes startled readers with unusual typography and shapes. ~~Copy boys~~ Reporters{Q3} ~~used to~~ called ~~it a~~ them _heads_, but when ~~they~~ news editors wrote ~~an~~ instructions on the layout for a news page, they would ~~spell~~ deliberately misspell the word _hed_ to make sure it was not accidentally typeset and printed along with the news copy. ~~This misspelling was deliberate. Before the introduction of computers into newspaper production,~~ that Linotype operators ~~had to~~ retyped from the layout sheet, or dummy.{Q4} ~~every story and headline on the layout sheet or dummy, and copy editors wanted to make sure their instructions were not accidentally typeset and printed along with the news copy. Sometimes they used the abbreviation HTK for "hed to kum," which became the title of Bremner's brief book on headline-writing.~~

In a printed newspaper, headlines ~~may~~ can run a single line or two or three lines deep, depending on the number of columns given to a story. A single line may suffice for the head of a story that occupies half the width of the news page, but the head for a ~~single~~ single-column story may require several lines and cannot exceed the width of the column. That's where "counting heads" came in before computer technology supplanted traditional printing skills. Al JaCoby{Q5}, ~~a long-time reporter~~ who reported for ~~The~~ the _San Diego Union,_ ~~plied his trade back in the 'fifties~~ from the 1950s, ~~'sixties, and 'seventies. JaCoby, who died in 2008~~ through the 1970s, could remember when an experienced ~~copy boy~~ news editor ~~could~~ exactly fit headlines to the width of a newspaper column by 'counting heads'.

{Q6}Typically, ~~he~~ the editor would calculate this way:

0.5 points: lowercase f's, l's, i's, t's, and j's; punctuation; wordspaces
1.0 points: other lowercase letters (except m's and w's); capital I; number 1
1.5 points: lowercase m's and w's; all capital letters and numerals except capital I and number 1 (above) and capital M and W (below)
2.0 points: capital M's and W's

~~a half point for lower-case Fs, Ls, Is, Ts, and Js and for punctuation and wordspaces, a full count for other lower-cased letters except Ms and Ws, which got 1½, as did all capitols and numerals but cap I and number 1 (1), and Ms and Ws (2). All numerals counted as 1½ except 1, which counted 1.~~ Thus "Ike" counted as ~~three~~ 3 points, "JFK" and "LBJ" ~~each was~~ were each allotted 4.5, and "Nixon," the subject of many headlines, counted ~~5~~ five. "I knew guys who used their knuckles to count out heads. Others would tap out the count with their fingers," JaCoby recalled. ~~The late Tom Keevil, who was one of the best and most competitive smaller-city editor around in the 50s and 60s . . . had a set set of headlines in his mind as models. Thus, the 142 Erbar condensed model line was something like "Mayor Says." Keevil~~ One editor of his acquaintance could write a headline in his mind and compare it to ~~the~~ a model line and simply know if it would fit." {Q7}

If a head was too long, an editor would eliminate or substitute words until it fit the allotted measure. But attempts to abridge headlines sometimes went awry. Fitting headlines into the ~~Procrustrean~~ procrustean bed of column width drove some ~~callow copy boys~~ news editors to extremes. JaCoby recalled the practice of the now-defunct *San Antonio Light* of using "ack-ack" (6.5) for "machine gun" (10.5) and "hijack" (5) for "holdup" (5.5), possibly misleading readers into thinking that an anti-aircraft gun had been used in a gang dustup or that a bodega had been not ~~just~~ merely ~~been~~ robbed but hauled away on a ~~flat-bed~~ flatbed truck. The annals of print journalism (and now the internet) are full of examples of ~~misreadings~~ miscues that owe to the overly telegraphic wording of headlines:

Eye Drops off Shelf
Kids Make Nutritious Snacks
Stolen Painting Found by Tree
Violinist Linked to JAL Crash Blossoms

This last example—about a violinist whose career blossomed after his father was killed in the crash of a Japan Airlines flight—has given these misleading headlines a name: crash blossoms.

In the days of hot metal typesetting, even the skillful pruning and swapping of words in heads didn't always work. JaCoby recounted the story of the *New York Times*'s "Eisenhower Skinny *S*.": The tradition-bound *Times* would never stoop to using "IKE" ~~Ike~~ in an all-caps headline. But "EISENHOWER SAYS": was a half-count too long for a ~~single~~ single-column article in the *Times*, so in 1952 the *Times*'s editors sent off to Linotype's foundry to have a custom brass matrix made for the ~~President's~~ president's name, half a count shorter, to use whenever "EISENHOWER SAYS": was needed. According to a 1952 account, the typecasters redrew the letters of Eisenhower's name (not just the *S*) and reduced the spaces between them, creating a logotype~~,~~—a single piece of type that prints a cluster of letters—so "EISENHOWER SAYS" would fit over a ~~single~~ single-column news report.

{Q8} Although the skill of counting heads declined with the advent of computers in newspaper production, the clever headline remains. Wordplay ~~may be~~ is often ~~acceptable~~ encouraged ~~in headlines~~, particularly in features and humorous pieces, although some newspapers explicitly prohibit humor and punning, at least in serious news pieces. Attention-grabbing headlines often play opposites against each other, use a word with a double meaning, invert an idiomatic expression, alter the spelling or pronunciation of a common expression, build a series, surprise with an unusual combination, or use alliteration or rhyme. One of the most ~~famous~~ memorable headlines of the twentieth century (~~if you discount~~ along with "Dewey Defeats Truman") is:

Headless Body in Topless Bar

It was printed in the *New York Post* in 1983 and made its creator, Vincent A. Musetto, so famous that it was ~~featured~~ mentioned in his 2015 obituary.

___{Q9}Today, if you encountered such a headline in your social media newsfeed, you might dismiss it as ~~click-bait~~clickbait. True, the internet didn't create sensational headlines~~:~~. Wordplay and provocative content have always characterized journalists' efforts to attract readers. The difference is ~~that, whereas~~ this: traditional news aims to capture the essence of a news report in a pithy, attention-grabbing headline~~,~~; ~~click-bait~~ clickbait overpromises and often misrepresents content to lure readers to another ~~Web-site~~ website and thus to generate advertising income that is based on page views. ~~No~~ eCopyfitting skill and ~~scant~~ linguistic ingenuity ~~is~~ are rarely required to create these nearly irresistible headlines, which depend on manipulative formulas, such as so-called "listicles~~"~~ ("7 Reasons You Can't Resist This Headline"), and ~~emotional~~ appeals to the emotions of curiosity and outrage ("You Won't Believe" or "What Happened Next Will Shock You").

{Q10}Sources: Jane T. Harrigan and Karen Brown Dunlap, *The Editorial Eye*, 2nd ed. (Boston: Bedford/St. Martin's, 2004). "John B. Bremner," ~~*Wikipedia,*~~ Wikipedia, https://en.wikipedia.org/, accessed February 15, 2018. Adrienne LaFrance, "The Legend of Eisenhower's Skinny 'S,'" *The Atlantic*, June 14, 2016, https://www.theatlantic.com/. Blanca Gonzalez, "Obituary: Alfred JaCoby," *San Diego Union-Tribune*, June 4, 2008, http://legacy.sandiegouniontribune.com/. Ben Zimmer, "Crash Blossoms," *New York Times Magazine*, January 27, 2010, http://www.nytimes.com/. Margalit Fox, "Vincent Musetto, 74, Dies; Wrote 'Headless' Headline of Ageless Fame," *New York Times*, June 9, 2015, https://www.nytimes.com/. Jeffrey Dvorkin, "Why Click-Bait Will Be the Death of Journalism," PBS NewsHour (website), April 27, 2016, https://www.pbs.org/. Bryan Gardiner, "You'll Be Outraged at How Easy It Was to Get You to Click on This Headline," *Wired*, December 18, 2015, https://wired.com/.

STYLE SHEET

Author/Title: Newsman/"Headlines"
Date: February 23, 2018
Dictionary: *Merriam-Webster Unabridged*
Style Manual: *The Chicago Manual of Style*, 17th ed.

Alphabetical List of Names and Terms
(n. = noun, adj. = adjective)

aesthetics (n.)
anti-aircraft (adj.)
clickbait (n.)
copyfitting (adj.)
flatbed (adj.)

hed (n., newspaper lingo for *head*, or *headline*)
internet (n.)
JaCoby, Al (capitalization to be confirmed)
listicle (n.)
newsfeed (n.)
procrustean (adj.)
website (n.)
wordplay (n.)

Numbers
1950s
0.5 points, 1.0 points, 1.5 points, etc.

Letters (contra *Chicago* because of mix of lowercase and caps)
Lowercase f's, l's, i's, t's, j's
Capitalized M's and W's

QUERIES

{Q1}: Speaking of headlines, this list of topics covered seems excessively long. Can you suggest a short, snappy title for this article (e.g., "Watch Your Hed!")?

{Q2}: This deletion isn't as extreme as it might appear at first glance. I thought the Bremner quote would make a great opening for this piece and accordingly moved the details about Bremner himself to follow the quote. In the interest of reducing the word count, as you asked, I consolidated the Bremner info and omitted some superfluous details about him, such as the cause of his death and (at the end of the paragraph) the title of his book. OK?

{Q3}: I thought the copy boys of old just ran errands at newspapers and in publishing houses; later discussion suggests that the reporters and news editors wrote the heads, so I've emended the language here and below. Please review and revise as necessary.

{Q4}: I consolidated the sentences about heads, heds, and Linotype operators into a single sentence here, again to help reduce the word count. OK? (As Q2 explains, the details about Bremner's book seem like an aside, hence deleted.)

{Q5}: Please verify the unusual capitalization of "JaCoby."

{Q6}: Start a new paragraph here to avoid an overlong paragraph in newsletter format? Also, I had a lot of trouble following the point-counting instructions (and I noted some repetition), so I recast them as a list. OK thus?

{Q7}: Again, in the interest of reducing the total word count and cutting out distracting details, I consolidated this information about Tom Keevil. OK?

{Q8}: Some sort of transitional sentence seems needed here to get from the era of counting heads to today's clever headlines. Something like what I've suggested here? Please revise if this suggestion doesn't suit you.

{Q9}: I suggest starting a new paragraph here: it's a natural break, and the newsletter format you're writing for typically favors shorter paragraphs than, say, a book format. OK?

{Q10}: Are these sources listed in the order they were used in this piece? Should the listings be reordered alphabetically by author? Are sources to be included in the final word count?—the edited piece weighs in at 7 words more than your goal if so. (Also note that "Wikipedia" is not italicized, according to the current edition of *The Chicago Manual of Style.*)

¶ Manual Copyediting Symbols

Mark	Name or Meaning	Example
∧	caret	Use a caret to add letters or words.
ϙ	delete	Use a delete sign to delete letters or a few or words.
◡ or ⌢	close up	An easy way to remove extra spaces.
⌒ or ⌒	delete and close up	Don't ask the typesetter to guess about whether to close up the space.
# or ⊞	space	So the words don't run together. Also used to add linespacing. Some copyeditors prefer to use a backslash—or a backslash and a space sign—to indicate a wordspace. So the words don't run together.
∼	transpose	Transpose a letter or misplaced a word.
•••	stet	Reinstates deleted material. Also used to mean *as is*, to annotate an unusual spelling: Gorge Johnson cain't spell.
∼	run in	An easy way to correct typing errors or to delete a paragraph break.
¶ or ⑨	para	¶ Adds a new paragraph. No marking is needed when the text shows a paragraph indent.
◯	spell out	When an editor circles 1 or 2 numerals or an abbrev, the compositor will spell out the circled items.

Mark	Name or Meaning	Example
		When an abbreviation is unusual or could be spelled in several ways, the copyeditor should write out the desired term.
		Nineteen ninety ~~1990~~ was a good year for the ~~NHL~~ *National Hockey League*⊙
⊙	period	Dr⊙Kim L⊙Jones delivered the report.
		Copyeditors circle an inserted period to make it more visible; only handwritten inserted periods should be circled. Circling is also used to convert a typed comma into a period.
		Dr⊙ Kim L⊙ Jones delivered the report.
⌄	comma	Similarly⌄ for visibility editors place a roof over handwritten commas.
		The roof makes the comma more visible. Do not mark a correctly typed comma; mark only handwritten commas and periods that are to be converted into commas.
		She left⌄ But he did not.
⌄	apostrophe	It⌄s just a matter of practice.
⌄ ⌄	quote marks	You're doing well⌄ she said.
⟨ ⟩	parens	⟨Parentheses always come in pairs.⟩
		The crosshatches clarify that the character is not a *C* or an *l*.
⸗	hyphen	Copyeditors need to handmark hard end-of⸗ line hyphens.
		Use the hyphen mark only to insert a hyphen or to indicate that a hyphen appearing at the end of a line is to be retained. Other hyphens need not be marked.
N̲	en dash	Used in numerical ranges: pp. 45ᴺ47.
		Most word processing programs can print an en dash (–) instead of a hyphen, but not all users take advantage of this feature.
M̲	em dash	Your everyday dashᴹsee?
		Most word processing programs can print an em dash (—), but some users type two hyphens instead.

Mark	Name or Meaning	Example
/	lowercase	To loWercase a letter or a WORD.
≡	capitalize	turns a lowercase letter into a capital.
=	small cap	So that B.C., a.m., P.M. will be set as
		B.C., A.M., P.M.
V	superscript	Mark mc2 so that it will be typeset as mc².
∧	subscript	Mark O2 so that it will be set as O₂.
—	italic	Use italics sparingly!
		Typists used to underline words that were to be set in italics, but now word processing programs can print *italic letters*.
⬭	delete italic or bold	Instructs the typesetter to ignore underlining, printed italics, or boldface type.
∿	bold	The typesetter will set boldface type.
Ⴤ	flush left	Moves text to align at the left margin.
Ⴧ	flush right	Moves text to align at the right margin:
		Jane L. Jones
⅃Ⴤ	center	This line will be centered.
│	align	Combine
		2 cups fresh basil, chopped
		1 cup olive oil
		2 teaspoons chopped garlic

Selected Bibliography

Only those references mentioned in the exercises and keys to this workbook are included here. For a comprehensive bibliography with annotations, see the Selected Bibliography in *The Copyeditor's Handbook*.

1. STYLE MANUALS

AMA Manual of Style: A Guide for Authors and Editors. 10th ed. Edited by Cheryl Iverson. New York: Oxford University Press, 2007.

The Associated Press Stylebook and Briefing on Media Law 2018. New York: Basic Books, 2018. Also available by subscription at https://www.apstylebook.com/.

Butcher, Judith, Caroline Drake, and Maureen Leach. *Butcher's Copy-editing: The Cambridge Handbook for Editors, Copy-editors and Proofreaders.* 4th ed. Cambridge: Cambridge University Press, 2006.

The Chicago Manual of Style. 17th ed. Chicago: University of Chicago Press, 2017. Also available by subscription at https://www.chicagomanualofstyle.org/.

Editing Canadian English: A Guide for Editors, Writers, and Everyone Who Works with Words. 3rd ed. Toronto: Editors' Association of Canada, 2015. Also available by subscription at https://editingcanadianenglish.ca/.

GPO Style Manual: An Official Guide to the Form and Style of Federal Government Publishing. 31st ed. Washington, D.C.: US Government Publishing Office, 2016. Available as a free PDF at https://www.govinfo.gov/content/pkg/GPO-STYLEMANUAL-2016/pdf/GPO-STYLEMANUAL-2016.pdf.

The Gregg Reference Manual. 11th ed. Edited by William A. Sabin. New York: McGraw-Hill, 2011.

MLA Handbook. 8th ed. New York: Modern Language Association, 2016.

New Oxford Style Manual. 3rd ed. Oxford: Oxford University Press, 2016.

The New York Public Library Writer's Guide to Style and Usage. Edited by Andrea Sutcliffe. New York: HarperCollins, 1994.

The New York Times Manual of Style and Usage. 5th ed. Edited by Allan M. Siegal and William G. Connolly. Revised and updated by Philip B. Corbett, Jill Taylor, Patrick LaForge, and Susan Wessling. New York: Three Rivers Press, 2015.

Publication Manual of the American Psychological Association. 6th ed. Washington, D.C.: American Psychological Association, 2009.

Scientific Style and Format: The CSE Manual for Authors, Editors, and Publishers. 8th ed. Chicago: University of Chicago Press, 2014. Also available by subscription at https://www.scientificstyleandformat.org/.

Turabian, Kate L. *A Manual for Writers of Research Papers, Theses, and Dissertations.* 9th ed. Revised by Wayne C. Booth et al. Chicago: University of Chicago Press, 2018.

Words into Type. 3rd ed. Englewood Cliffs, N.J.: Prentice-Hall, 1974.

2. DICTIONARIES AND CORPORA

American Heritage Dictionary of the English Language. 5th ed. Boston: Houghton Mifflin, 2016. Also available at https://www.ahdictionary.com/.

Dorland's Pocket Medical Dictionary. 29th ed. Philadelphia: Elsevier Saunders, 2013.

Google Books Ngram Viewer. https://books.google.com/ngrams.

Green's Dictionary of Slang. https://greensdictofslang.com/.

Merriam-Webster's Collegiate Dictionary. 11th ed. Springfield, Mass.: Merriam-Webster, 2003. Also available at https://www.merriam-webster.com/ or with a subscription to the online *Merriam-Webster Unabridged* (q.v.).

Merriam-Webster Unabridged. http://unabridged.merriam-webster.com/.

OneLook Dictionary Search. https://www.onelook.com/.

Urban Dictionary. https://www.urbandictionary.com/.

Webster's New World College Dictionary. 5th ed. New York: Macmillan, 2016.

Webster's Third New International Dictionary of the English Language, Unabridged. Springfield, Mass.: Merriam-Webster, 1993.

Wiktionary. https://www.wiktionary.org/.

Your Dictionary. http://www.yourdictionary.com/.

3. LANGUAGE, GRAMMAR, AND USAGE GUIDES

Bernstein, Theodore. *The Careful Writer: A Modern Guide to English Usage.* 1965. Reprint, New York: Free Press, 1995.

Bernstein, Theodore. *Miss Thistlebottom's Hobgoblins: The Careful Writer's Guide to the Taboos, Bugbears, and Outmoded Rules of English Usage.* New York: Farrar, Straus & Giroux, 1971.

Copperud, Roy H. *American Usage and Style: The Consensus.* New York: Van Nostrand Reinhold, 1980.

Follett, Wilson. *Modern American Usage: A Guide.* Rev. ed. Edited by Erik Wensberg. New York: Hill & Wang, 1998.

Fowler's Dictionary of Modern English Usage. 4th ed. Edited by Jeremy Butterfield. Oxford: Oxford University Press, 2015.

Garner, Bryan A. *The Chicago Guide to Grammar, Usage, and Punctuation.* Chicago: University of Chicago Press, 2016.

Garner, Bryan A. *Garner's Modern English Usage.* 4th ed. New York: Oxford University Press, 2016.

Jacob, Dianne. *Will Write for Food: The Complete Guide to Writing Cookbooks, Blogs, Reviews, Memoir, and More.* 3rd ed. Cambridge, Mass.: Da Capo Lifelong, 2015.

Lester, Mark, and Larry Beason. *The McGraw-Hill Handbook of English Grammar and Usage.* 2nd ed. New York: McGraw-Hill Education, 2012.

Loberger, Gordon, and Kate Shoup. *Webster's New World English Grammar Handbook.* 2nd ed. Hoboken, N.J.: Wiley, 2009.

Merriam-Webster's Dictionary of English Usage. Reprint. Springfield, Mass.: Merriam-Webster, 1994.

Ostmann, Barbara Gibbs, and Jane L. Baker. *The Recipe Writer's Handbook.* New York: Wiley, 2002.

Partridge, Eric. *Usage and Abusage: A Guide to Good English.* New ed. Edited by Janet Whitcut. New York: W. W. Norton, 1995.

Strunk, William, Jr., and E. B. White. *The Elements of Style.* 4th ed. Boston: Allyn and Bacon, 2000.

4. WRITING AND EDITING GUIDES

Hacker, Diane, and Nancy Sommers. *A Writer's Reference.* 8th ed. Boston: Bedford-St. Martin's, 2015.

Plain Language Action and Information Network (PLAIN). *Federal Plain Language Guidelines.* https://www.plainlanguage.gov/.

5. ASSORTED ONLINE RESEARCH TOOLS

Amazon. https://www.amazon.com/.

Atlas Obscura. https://www.atlasobscura.com/.

Encyclopaedia Britannica. https://www.britannica.com/.

Google Books. https://books.google.com/.

International Union for Conservation of Nature. https://www.iucn.org/.

Internet Archive. https://archive.org/.

Library of Congress Online Catalog. https://catalog.loc.gov/.

Quote Investigator. http://quoteinvestigator.com/.

TinEye Reverse Image Search. https://www.tineye.com/.

Trademark Checklist, International Trademark Association. https://www.inta.org/Media/Lists/Trademark%20Checklist/AllItems.aspx.

United States Board on Geographic Names. https://geonames.usgs.gov/.

US Geological Survey: Gazetteer. https://geonames.usgs.gov/domestic/.

Wikipedia. https://www.wikipedia.org/.

The World Factbook. https://www.cia.gov/library/publications/resources/the-world-factbook/index.html.

World Health Organization. http://www.who.int/.

WorldCat. https://www.worldcat.org/.

Copyeditor: Juliana Froggatt

Proofreaders: Anne Canright and Sue Heinemann

Designer: Barbara Haines

Compositors: Barbara Haines and BookMatters, Berkeley

Text: Minion Pro and Benton Gothic

Display: Minion Pro

Printer and Binder: Sheridan Books, Inc.